MW01027601

Pagans and Christians in the City

EMORY UNIVERSITY STUDIES IN LAW AND RELIGION

John Witte Jr., General Editor

This series fosters exploration of the religious dimensions of law, the legal dimensions of religion, and the interaction of legal and religious ideas, institutions, and methods. Written by leading scholars of law, political science, and related fields, these volumes will help meet the growing demand for literature in the burgeoning interdisciplinary study of law and religion.

RECENTLY PUBLISHED

For a complete list of published volumes in this series, see the back of the book.

Pagans and Christians in the City

Culture Wars from the Tiber to the Potomac

Steven D. Smith

WILLIAM B. EERDMANS PUBLISHING COMPANY

GRAND RAPIDS, MICHIGAN

Wm. B. Eerdmans Publishing Co.
4035 Park East Court SE, Grand Rapids, Michigan 49546
www.eerdmans.com

Published 2018
Printed in the United States of America

24 23 22 21 20 19   3 4 5 6 7

ISBN 978-0-8028-7631-7

Library of Congress Cataloging-in-Publication Data

A catalog record for this book is available from the Library of Congress.

To our children—
Nathanael, Rachel, Maria, Jesse, Christian

Contents

They cried with one voice. A city is what they pray for.

VIRGIL, *The Aeneid*

The universe is, so to say, the shared dwelling of gods and men, or a city which houses both.

CICERO, *The Nature of the Gods*

Most glorious is the City of God: whether in this passing age, where she dwells by faith, as a pilgrim among the ungodly, or in the security of that eternal home which she now patiently awaits. . . . We must not pass over in silence the earthly city also.

AUGUSTINE, *The City of God*

Foreword

It was the distinctive claim of the most influential late twentieth-century liberal political philosophers, including most notably John Rawls and Ronald Dworkin, to be proposing theories of political morality that identified principles of justice (and suggested institutional structures and practices to implement those principles) that were neutral as between controversial conceptions of what makes for or detracts from a valuable and morally worthy way of life. This was liberal orthodoxy for something approaching forty years. Of course, it had its critics, including conservatives, natural law theorists and other neo-Aristotelians, certain sorts of utilitarians and libertarians, and even a few unorthodox ("perfectionist") liberals; but it was far and away the dominant view.

Like a number of other critics, I argued (first in my 1993 book *Making Men Moral: Civil Liberties and Public Morality* and then in many other writings) that the "antiperfectionism" (or "neutrality") to which the orthodox liberalism of the period aspired (or at least purported to aspire) was neither desirable nor possible. What Rawls would eventually dub and defend as (merely) *political* liberalism was—unavoidably—built on premises into which had been smuggled controversial substantive ideas about human nature, the human good, human dignity, and, indeed, human destiny—ideas that competed with those proposed by alternative religious and secular "comprehensive views."

Today little effort is made by liberals (or what are these days more often called "progressives") to maintain the pretense of neutrality. Having gained the advantage and in many cases having prevailed (at least for now) on battlefront after battlefront in the modern culture war, and having achieved hegemony in elite sectors of the culture (for example, in education at every level, in the news and entertainment media, in the professions and in corporate America, and even in much of religion), they no longer feel any need to pretend.

Take, for example, the issue of marriage. When, in the 1990s, the effort began in earnest to redefine marriage to include same-sex partnerships, advocates of that position frequently claimed that they merely sought to establish a regime of matrimonial law that was neutral as between competing conceptions of what marriage is or ought to be, and similarly neutral as between competing ideas of good and bad, right and wrong, in the domain of human sexual conduct and relationships. This reflected the orthodox liberal political theory of the day—or, in any event, its rhetoric. But twenty-five years or so later, with marriage having been redefined by the Supreme Court of the United States (and by referenda or legislative action in a number of other nations), virtually no one on either side doubts that marriage as redefined embodies substantive ideas about morality and the human good— ideas that differ significantly (indeed, in key respects profoundly) from those embodied previously in marriage law, ideas that, according to partisans of the redefinition of marriage, are to be preferred precisely because they are superior to the ideas they supplanted.

So now that the pretense of neutrality has been more or less abandoned, and is on its way to being forgotten, what is the substance of the perspective (or ideology or, perhaps, religion) that is now fully exposed to view—and not merely to the view of its critics? And what shall we call it? In the book you are now reading, Steven Smith sets for himself the task of describing and analyzing it, and he gives it a name: paganism. The label is provocative. Professor Smith's reasons for choosing it, however, go well beyond a mere desire to provoke. What he perceives (rightly in my view) is that contemporary social liberalism ("progressivism") reflects certain core (and constitutive) ideas and beliefs—ideas and beliefs that partially defined the traditions of paganism that were dominant in the ancient Mediterranean world and in certain other places up until the point at which they were defeated, though never quite destroyed, by the Jewish sect that came to be known as Christianity.

Of course, some progressives will suppose that Smith is deploying the term "pagan" epithetically, that he is resorting to disparagement or a kind of rhetorical abuse of his religious or political opponents. The term "pagan" (despite being claimed—or reclaimed—by followers of certain New Age movements) continues to have largely negative connotations in our culture, so few people (outside New Age circles) formally identify themselves as pagan. But the first and most important thing for a reader to understand in approaching this volume is that Smith means something very particular in using the word—he uses it to characterize ideas and beliefs that a great many people today, especially those in the ideological vanguard, have in common with people of, for example, pre-Christian Rome. This does not mean that the modern people Smith has in mind share *all* the ideas and beliefs of ancient Romans (such as belief in gods like Jupiter, Neptune, and Venus), but rather that *some* of the central ideas and beliefs that distinguish them from orthodox Christians and Jews—and, one could add, Muslims—in our day are ideas and beliefs they have in common with the people whose ideas and beliefs Christianity challenged in the ancient world.

Secular progressives, no less than other people, or people of other faiths, have cherished, deeply held, even identity-forming beliefs about what is meaningful, valuable, important, good and bad, right and wrong. They may not believe in God, or a transcendent and personal deity, but certain things (as Professor Dworkin expressly acknowledged—indeed, asserted—in work published near the end of his life) are *sacred* to them—things they live for and would be willing to fight and even die for (racial justice, LGBT rights, environmental responsibility, etc.). They have faith—and a faith. They generally regard it as a reasoned and reasonable faith, but that doesn't mean it's not a faith. (Many Christians and Jews regard their faith as reasoned and reasonable. Indeed, it is a doctrine of Catholicism that true faith is reasoned and reasonable.) So what is it about the secular progressive faith that warrants Smith's labeling it "pagan"? After all, though not theistic, it is certainly not (in any literal sense) polytheistic. Smith explains:

> Pagan religion locates the sacred *within* this world. In that way, paganism can consecrate the world from within: it is religiosity relative to an *immanent* sacred. Judaism and Christianity, by contrast, reflect *transcendent* religiosity; they place the sacred, ultimately, *outside* the world.

Now, Smith concedes that this characterization oversimplifies things a bit. But the oversimplification is mainly in the description or characterization of Judaism and Christianity, not secular progressivism. The biblical faiths conceive God as transcendent, to be sure, but not in a way that excludes elements of divine immanence. In Jewish and Christian doctrine, a transcendent God sanctifies the world of human affairs by entering into it, while still transcending it. And God's transcendence means that for the believer this world is not one's true or ultimate home—we are "resident aliens." Smith contrasts Jews and Christians with pagans on precisely this point: "The pagan orientation . . . accepts this world as our home, and does so joyously, exuberantly, and worshipfully."

Now, Christianity, had it been a religion of pure and exclusive transcendence, might have simply rejected this world and not concerned itself with its affairs. The authorities of pagan Rome might then have left it alone, treating it as one more odd or exotic religion. But it's not that kind of faith. So it took an interest in the world's affairs and developed ideas about such things as authority; obligation; law, including natural law; justice; and the common good—ideas that challenged pagan ideas in practices in a variety of areas, some of them profoundly important. A central area was sex.

Smith argues that within the pagan "matrix of assumptions, the Christian view of sexuality was not only radically alien, it was close to incomprehensible." About this he is certainly right historically. But consider that the Christian view of sexuality is today, within the "matrix of assumptions" of secular progressivism, perfectly aptly described as "not only radically alien, but close to incomprehensible." Consider again the debate over marriage, as just one of many possible examples. The biblical and natural law conception of marriage as the one-flesh union of sexually complementary spouses is not only "alien" to secular progressives, who understand "marriage" as a form of sexual-romantic companionship or domestic partnership, but nearly incomprehensible—except as a form of bigotry against people who are attracted to and wish to marry (as progressives understand the term) people of their same sex. Or consider the view that nonmarital sexual conduct and relationships, including homosexual ones, are inherently immoral. That, too, is regarded by a great many secular progressives as not only unsound, but unreasonable, outrageous, scandalous, even hateful. They can account for it, if at all, only as religious irrationalism, bigotry, or, as many today now claim, a psychopathology.

As the historian Kyle Harper notes in a passage of his recent book on the transformation of beliefs about sexuality and morality in the ancient world (quoted by Smith), sexuality "came to mark the great divide between Christians and the world." Christian ideas about sexual norms (rejecting fornication, adultery even by men, homosexual acts, pornographic displays, and so forth) were revolutionary; and the pagan establishment was no more welcoming of revolutionaries—even nonviolent ones—than any other establishment is. So paganism could not, and did not, tolerate the Christians—even when Christianity was far too weak to pose any real challenge to political authority. It was not that Roman authorities refused to allow minority religions of any kind in the empire; those that could coexist with the dominant paganism were allowed to do just that. But the Romans perceived Christianity as a threat—and Christian ideas about sex (and, in consequence, about Roman sexual practices) figured significantly in that perception. They feared that Christianity would, in Smith's evocative phrase, "turn out the lights on that 'merry dance.'" And that, of course, is what Christianity eventually did.

But in our own time the lights have been turned back on and the party is going again. In the 1940s, Alfred Kinsey, the Saint Paul of the modern sexual revolution, convinced a lot of people that sex is a human need—that psychological health and wholeness generally require it, and that Judeo-Christian norms of sexual morality, when embraced, result in stilted, even twisted, personalities. In the 1950s, Hugh Hefner, neopaganism's very own Saint Augustine, persuaded people that pornography was, or could be, innocent fun and that the "Playboy philosophy" of sexual indulgence was the way for up-to-date, sophisticated people to lead their lives. The "gay rights" or "LGBT" movement has made the affirmation of homosexual conduct and relationships the "civil rights cause" of our day. Disagree? "Bake the cake, bigot!"

Christians and other traditional religious believers have been knocked back on their heels. Reversing the sexual revolution (despite the growing evidence of its doleful social consequences, especially for children) in any of its major dimensions seems inconceivable. Few believe that its forward march can be paused or even meaningfully slowed down. The vast majority of Christians think that the most they can hope for in this new epoch of pagan ascendancy are some protections for their own liberty to lead their lives as *they* see fit, in conformity with their faith, and not to be forced to facilitate or participate in activities that they cannot in good conscience condone. Progressives say, after all, that they are all for individual autonomy and liberty. Of course, that claim will likely prove to be, to borrow a phrase from Hillary Clinton, "no longer operative." Many Christians and other believers despair even of the possibility of protecting their children from being indoctrinated into the beliefs of the governing elite, the new ruling class (or what perhaps might better be described as the old, but repaganized, ruling class). They believe we have entered a new Diocletian age. They not unreasonably suppose that it is precisely this reality that is being signaled when progressive intellectuals, such as Mark Tushnet of Harvard Law School, say things like this:

> The culture war is over; they lost, we won. . . . Taking a hard line ("You lost, live with it") is better than trying to accommodate the losers, who—remember—defended, and are defending, positions that

liberals regard as having no normative pull at all. Trying to be nice to the losers didn't work well after the Civil War, nor after *Brown*. (And taking a hard line seemed to work reasonably well in Germany and Japan after 1945.) I should note that LGBT activists in particular seem to have settled on the hard-line approach, while some liberal academics defend more accommodating approaches. When specific battles in the culture wars were being fought, it might have made sense to try to be accommodating after a local victory, because other related fights were going on, and a hard line might have stiffened the opposition in those fights. But the war's over, and we won.

So there you are. The neopagans are in no mood to be "accommodating." Christians and others who dissent from progressive orthodoxy can expect "the hard-line approach." They are to be treated like the defeated Germans and Japanese after World War II.

For Christians and other dissenters from neopagan orthodoxy, then, the question is, What is to be done? How should they respond to Professor Tushnet's "hard-line" approach—an approach that will indeed be, and in fact is being, implemented by people who want to ensure that Christians never again get near the light switch and that they are properly punished for having switched off the lights to the party in the first place? It's a question that, for Christians, is as urgent as it is important. But to even begin answering it, we need a sober, penetrating, deeply insightful diagnosis of our condition and account of where we are and how we got here. Professor Smith deserves our deep thanks for providing it.

ROBERT P. GEORGE
McCormick Professor of Jurisprudence
Princeton University

Acknowledgments

This book has been a long while in the making, and I have benefitted from comments and conversations in so many different settings and with so many friends, colleagues, and cordial adversaries that I will surely fail to recognize people who have helped me in the project. My sincere apologies. But the inevitability of omissions is no reason not to thank some of the people who have read or commented on all or part of the book: Larry Alexander, Jim Allan, Harriet Baber, David Brink, Luis Pereira Coutinho, Marc DeGirolami, Patrick Deneen, Mike Devitt, Ross Douthat, Brian Dunkle, Chris Eberle, Stanley Fish, Bruce Frohnen, Bill Galston, Rick Garnett, Robby George, John Inazu, Mary Keys, Andy Koppelman, Tony Kronman, Thomas LeBien, Rachel Lu, James Martin, Jennifer Newsome Martin, Susannah Monta, Michael Moreland, Michael Perry, Jeff Pojanowski, Sam Rickless, Neville Rochow, Connie Rosati, Maimon Schwarzschild, Micah Schwartzman, Merina Smith, Nathan Smith, Adrian Vermuele, William Voegeli, John Witte, Robert Wilken, and George Wright.

Discussion conferences on the book were held at Notre Dame and the University of San Diego; these were tremendously helpful. Special thanks go to Rick Garnett and Larry Alexander for organizing those conferences. At the invitation of Father Louis Caruana, I was privileged to present a distillation of several of the chapters at a conference on "La Natura e il Naturalismo" at the Pontifical Gregorian University in Rome, and I benefitted significantly from the comments and questions there. At the invitation of Brad Wilson, I had the honor of giving a much scaled-down version of the book in the Charles E. Test Lectures for the James Madison Program at Princeton. The diverse and challenging questions from the audience at those lectures were again immensely helpful.

My students Jane Susskind and John Mysliwiec provided valuable help with the footnotes and index. Arlene Penticoff assisted in preparing the manuscript, patiently enduring my use of methods and word processing programs almost as archaic as the historical developments discussed in the book.

CHAPTER 1

A Portentous Question, a Quixotic Proposal

Consider, as an entry into our inquiry, two variations on an earnestly posed question—variations separated by almost two millennia. The first instance of the question was pressed in classical Rome. The second instance arises today in connection with the so-called culture wars. The recurring question is simple but fraught; if we could discern the answer to the question, we would likely be helped thereby to understand something important about the beginnings of our Western civilization, about our own perplexing and conflicted times, and maybe even about the kind of species we are.

Pliny's Question (and Tertullian's)

In the early second century, a literate and genial (and sycophantic)[1] Roman gentleman named Pliny—historians call him Pliny the Younger to distinguish him from his famous uncle, the encyclopedist who died in the eruption of Mount Vesuvius—wrote to his boss, the emperor Trajan, asking for legal advice.[2] At the time, Pliny was serving as governor for the province of Bithynia, in the north of present-day Turkey, and citizens of the province had accused some of their neighbors of being Christians.[3] In response, Pliny

---

1. Pliny's numerous letters to the emperor Trajan are filled with flattery. "I am well aware, Sir, that no higher tribute can be paid to my reputation than some mark of favour from so excellent a ruler as yourself." *The Letters of the Younger Pliny*, trans. Betty Radice (London: Penguin, 1963), 265. Such praise pervades the letters; see 260, 264, 277, 291, 296.

2. The letter is reprinted in *Letters of the Younger Pliny*, 293–95.

3. For a careful analysis of the episode, see Robert Louis Wilken, *The Christians as the Romans Saw Them*, 2nd ed. (New Haven: Yale University Press, 2003), 15–30.

had adopted what seemed to him a sensible procedure for dealing with such complaints. An accused person was brought before the governor and asked whether he or she was a Christian. Sometimes an accused person would answer yes. In such cases, Pliny would carefully explain that being Christian was a capital offense, and he would then repeat the question, twice. If the accused persisted in his or her affirmative answer, Pliny would sentence the confessing Christian "to be led away for execution."

Conversely, the accused might deny the charge or claim to have abandoned the Christian faith, and Pliny had devised a method to test such denials. Statues of the emperor Trajan and of pagan gods were provided, and the accused was ordered to worship the statues, to make an offering of wine and incense, and also to "[revile] the name of Christ." A defendant who satisfactorily complied with these requirements was released.[4]

This was Pliny's procedure, but he wasn't sure whether he was handling the cases correctly. He was especially concerned because the accusations seemed to be proliferating. So he wrote to ask the emperor's advice.

As part of his inquiry, Pliny also incidentally raised a more fundamental question: *Why* were Christians being subjected to legal sanctions at all? Was "the mere name of Christian . . . punishable, even if innocent of crime"? Or, instead, were only "the crimes associated with the name" to be punished?[5]

Pliny's working assumption, it seems, had been that merely being a Christian was a capital offense, because his investigations (conducted by interviewing some former or lapsed Christians, and also by examining under torture two slaves who were said to be deaconesses in the church) had revealed that the Christians, while practicing a "degenerate sort of cult," were not guilty of committing any actual crimes. True, they did exhibit an "unshakeable obstinacy" that Pliny found irritating. But "obstinacy" was not a criminal offense, and, in fact, Pliny had discovered nothing more culpable than this. "The sum total of their guilt or error amounted to no more than this: they had met regularly before dawn on a fixed day to chant verses alternately amongst themselves in honour of Christ as if to a god, and also to bind themselves by oath not for any criminal purpose, but to abstain from theft, robbery, and adultery, to commit no breach of trust and not to deny a deposit when called upon to restore it." Later they would "reassemble . . . to take food of an ordinary, harmless kind." And even the predawn services and the later gatherings had been discontinued after Pliny, in accordance

4. *Letters of the Younger Pliny*, 293.
5. *Letters of the Younger Pliny*, 293.

with a general Roman policy disfavoring private assemblies, had issued an edict forbidding such meetings.[6]

Despite their seemingly innocuous or even laudable behavior, Pliny had been sentencing people to death, evidently merely for being Christians. But he wondered whether he was doing the right thing.

In his response, Trajan expressed approval of Pliny's approach. Christians should not be aggressively "hunted out," Trajan cautioned, and they should be treated with due process in "keeping with the spirit of our age." But if brought before the governor, they "must be punished." Meaning, it seems, executed, since that was the punishment Pliny had been dispensing. There was no need to prove any independent offense; being Christian was enough. Accused persons could obtain pardon, though, by recanting and "by offering prayers to our gods."[7]

And *why* exactly should people be put to death merely for being Christian? Pliny had raised the question, but Trajan tendered no answer.

Just under a century later, the *why* question was raised again—albeit this time indignantly—by a feisty Christian lawyer living in Carthage. Addressed to the "rulers of the Roman Empire," Tertullian's *Apology* demanded some justification for "the extreme severities inflicted on our people."[8] In most respects, Tertullian insisted, Christians were no different from other Romans. "We sojourn with you in the world, abjuring neither forum, nor shambles [slaughterhouse], nor bath, nor booth, nor workshop, nor inn, nor weekly market, nor any other places of commerce. We sail with you, and fight with you, and till the ground with you; and in like manner we unite with you in your traffickings" (69).

Nor were Christians unfaithful citizens, Tertullian protested. On the contrary: Christians obeyed the law, cared for their poor (64), and supported the government. "Without ceasing, for all our emperors we offer prayer. We pray for life prolonged; for security to the empire; for protection to the imperial house; for brave armies, a faithful senate, a virtuous people, the world at rest, whatever, as man or Caesar, an emperor would wish" (54–55).

Tertullian acknowledged that Christian theological doctrines might seem far-fetched to sophisticated Romans. But these doctrines "are just (in that case) like many other things on which you inflict no penalties—foolish

---

6. *Letters of the Younger Pliny*, 294.

7. *Letters of the Younger Pliny*, 295.

8. Tertullian, "Apology," in *Selected Works* (Pickering, OH: Beloved, 2014), 1. Hereafter, page references from this work will be given in parentheses in the text.

and fabulous things, I mean, which, as quite innocuous, are never charged as crimes or punished" (80–81).

And yet, "with our hands thus stretched out and up to God, [you] rend us with your iron claws, hang us up on crosses, wrap us in flames, take our heads from us with the sword, let loose the wild beasts upon us" (55). And these savage punishments were inflicted merely because someone was Christian. "The mere name is made [a] matter of accusation, the mere name is assailed, and a sound alone brings condemnation" (8).

That punishments were inflicted merely for the status of being Christian was underscored, Tertullian thought, by the fact that, in stark contrast to how they treated other offenses, Roman authorities were quick to forgive anyone who renounced Christianity. "Certainly you give no ready credence to others when they deny [a criminal accusation]. When we deny you believe at once" (5). "Seeing, then, that in everything you deal differently with us than with other criminals, bent upon the one object of taking from us our name [of Christian], . . . it is made clear that there is no crime of any kind in the case, but merely a name" (6).

Roman persecution of the Christians may seem all the more puzzling in light of the Romans' reputation for broad-minded religious toleration. Under the empire, as we will see in chapter 3, a vast and diverse array of deities, rituals, cults, and temples flourished in relative harmony. As the Romans had conquered the various lands of the Mediterranean world, they had typically left intact as much of the local government, culture, and religion as possible: so long as the subjects accepted Roman rule, eschewed subversion, and paid their taxes, the Romans were generally content to leave well enough alone. Thus, the renowned and immensely erudite historian Edward Gibbon (with whom we will frequently consult) lauded the empire for its "universal spirit of toleration."[9] Jonathan Kirsch, a popular historian, describes the "open-minded and easygoing attitude of paganism."[10] The eminent Yale historian Ramsey MacMullen describes Rome as "completely tolerant, in heaven as on earth."[11]

9. Edward Gibbon, *The History of the Decline and Fall of the Roman Empire*, 2 vols. (London: Penguin, [1776] 1995), 1:56.

10. Jonathan Kirsch, *God against the Gods: The History of the War between Monotheism and Polytheism* (New York: Penguin, 2004), 63.

11. MacMullen quickly qualifies this description by noting that Romans were sometimes severe on Jews, Christians, Druids, and a few others, but he mitigates the observation with the explanation that in these instances "humanitarian views were the cause, not bigotry." Ramsay MacMullen, *Paganism in the Roman Empire* (New Haven: Yale University Press, 1981), 2. See

Why, then, did the Romans feel impelled to torture, banish, and execute people for, as Tertullian claimed, "the mere name" of Christ?

It might have been, of course, that Christianity was associated with subversive or antisocial conduct; "the mere name" might have been evidence of, or perhaps a rough proxy for, crime or subversion. Or at least the Roman authorities might have thought so. Could that have been the reason why they were torturing and executing people for being Christian?

But *what* other criminal or subversive behavior could be associated with the religion? In the first centuries of its existence, to be sure, Christianity was the source of shocking rumors. Christians were said to indulge in incest, cannibalism, and wild orgies. One story had it that Christians covered an infant with flour, then killed him, cut him up, and drank his blood. Another exotic rumor intimated that on their holy days, Christians of both sexes and of all ages mingled together to feast and drink; they then tied a dog to the lamp and provoked the dog to run, putting out the light, and in the darkness each Christian indiscriminately indulged in sexual intercourse with whomever happened to be nearest to him or her.[12]

Tertullian treated these sorts of slanders with contempt, and historians have generally given them little credence.[13] Rumors of cannibalism may have reflected uncomprehending and hostile inferences drawn from the Christian practice of eating the consecrated bread with the belief that it became the body of Christ; suspicions of incest might have arisen as a reaction to the Christian custom of calling each other (including spouses) "brother" and "sister."[14] In any case, it seems unlikely that Roman authorities believed such rumors. Pliny surely didn't; as noted, his investigations uncovered only innocuous or exemplary behavior.

---

also Ramsay MacMullen, *Christianity and Paganism in the Fourth to Eighth Centuries* (New Haven: Yale University Press, 1997), 2 (referring to classical paganism's "spongy mass of tolerance and tradition").

12. These rumors are reported in Minucius Felix, "Octavius," in *Ante-Nicene Church Fathers, Fathers of the Third Century*, trans. Philip Schaff (London: Aeterna Press, 2014), vol. 8, chap. 9, pp. 10–11. See also Keith Hopkins, *A World Full of Gods: The Strange Triumph of Christianity* (New York: Penguin, 1999), 209; Gibbon, *History of the Decline*, 1:522.

13. See, e.g., Stephen Benko, *Pagan Rome and the Early Christians* (Bloomington: Indiana University Press, 1984), 60–64; E. R. Dodds, *Pagan and Christian in an Age of Anxiety* (Cambridge: Cambridge University Press, 1965), 112. However, it is possible that one bizarre and renegade group associated with Christianity—the Carpocratians—did indulge in seriously licentious conduct. Benko, 64.

14. See James J. O'Donnell, *Pagans: The End of Traditional Religion and the Rise of Christianity* (New York: HarperCollins, 2015), 79.

And yet he executed Christians anyway. Pliny was a proper gentleman and official who wanted to do the right thing, and he had no deep-seated or idiosyncratic animosity toward Christianity. But he thought that as a Roman governor, his duty was to execute convicted Christians. And in this he was evidently correct, as the emperor's response to his query confirmed. But, once again, why?

We will return to the question in due course. For now, let us turn to another question, or perhaps to a different version of the same question, raised in a more contemporary setting.

Laycock's Question

Douglas Laycock is an agnostic, a libertarian, and a law professor who has been called "the preeminent lawyer-scholar of religious freedom over the last quarter-century";[15] and he raises a timely question that has surely occurred to others as well. Commenting on recent cases in which same-sex couples have sued marriage counselors or photographers or florists or other professionals who have objected on religious grounds to assisting with same-sex unions, Laycock observes that in most such cases these professionals' services are readily available from other counselors or providers who do not have any such objection. Moreover, he suggests, no sensible same-sex couple would actually want the services of, say, a counselor who is religiously opposed to their union.[16] Why, then, do these parties insist on suing people whose services they neither need nor want?

Here, though, a small correction is needed, and also an addition. Laycock presents the point I have just described not so much as a question but

15. True, he was called that by me. Steven D. Smith, "Lawyering Religious Liberty," *Texas Law Review* 89 (2011): 917. But although not everyone would give the same assessment, Laycock's stature in the field is undeniable. Thomas C. Berg, "Laycock's Legacy," *Texas Law Review* 89 (2011): 901 ("Douglas Laycock is a towering figure in the law of religious liberty").

16. See, e.g., Douglas Laycock and Thomas C. Berg, "Protecting Same-Sex Marriage and Religious Liberty," *Virginia Law Review* 99, in Brief 1 (2013): 9 ("Of course, no same-sex couple would ever want to be counseled by such a counselor. Demanding a commitment to counsel same-sex couples does not obtain counseling for those couples, but it does threaten to drive from the helping professions all those who adhere to other religious understandings of marriage"). On the practical futility of asking a counselor to counsel people contrary to the counselor's religious commitments, see Joseph Turner, "Counselors like Me Need Conscience Protections like Tennessee's," *Federalist*, May 3, 2016, http://thefederalist.com/2016/05/03/counselors-like-me-need-conscience-protections-like-tennessees.

more as an accusation. He says the plaintiffs in these cases are trying not to gain a needed remedy but rather to drive traditionally religious professionals out of business, and he says the plaintiffs are doing this because they are intolerant.[17] In addition, Laycock makes a similar accusation against Christians who oppose same-sex marriage or who favor other sorts of regulations of sexual activity: these Christians are also being intolerant. Laycock the libertarian is visibly frustrated with both sides in these culture-war issues: a perfectly good "live and let live" arrangement is available, he thinks, but each side rejects it. Each side persecutes the other even when there is no good reason to do so and nothing to gain. "Each side wants a total win."[18]

Laycock's "intolerance" interpretation of the contending parties and their motivations is contestable, to be sure.[19] But suppose he is right; even so, his accusation of intolerance is more a characterization than an actual explanation of the conflicts he is commenting on. Let us stipulate that it is intolerant to sue people you disagree with, or to restrict their private sexual behavior, when they are not interfering with your ability to live your own life. Fine. But the question still looms: *Why* would you do that? Except for the handful of perverse or opportunistic souls who revel in litigation or who hope to win some large damage award, becoming embroiled in a lawsuit is a highly unpleasant and unprofitable way to pass one's days. And it is costly and time-consuming to enact and enforce regulations of, say, sexual behavior you disapprove of. So if (as Laycock supposes) the same-sex couples have no legitimate interest in litigating and the Christians have no legitimate interest in regulating, why do they waste their time and money on these profitless activities?

Although the stakes are not presently as high as they were for Tertullian and his beleaguered coreligionists, this contemporary question seems to have much in common with the Christian apologist's complaint. In each case, people are using the law to crack down on a religion or a way of life that they disapprove of but that doesn't seem to be realistically harming them or interfering with their own lives in any obvious way. Why would they do that?

It is a large and important question, not amenable to any quick response. As with Pliny's and Tertullian's question, we will return to it in due course. First, though, let us shift our focus for a moment and consider a proposal

---

17. Laycock and Berg, "Protecting Same-Sex Marriage," 9.

18. Douglas Laycock, "Religious Liberty and the Culture Wars," *University of Illinois Law Review* 2014 (2014): 879.

19. See Steven D. Smith, "Die and Let Live: The Asymmetry of Accommodation," *Southern California Law Review* 88 (2015): 703.

that, if sound (as it will likely not appear at first to be), might circle back to offer some insight into these puzzles.

A Poet's Proposal

In the dark days just preceding World War II, the celebrated if often inscrutable poet T. S. Eliot presented a series of lectures at Cambridge University. Published under the title *The Idea of a Christian Society*,[20] Eliot's lectures advanced a thesis that, though it may seem prima facie implausible and even offensive to contemporary readers, is at least intriguing. For our purposes, the argument might be summarized in terms of three main claims—one predictive, one interpretive, one prescriptive.

The predictive claim was that the future of Western societies would be determined by a contest between Christianity and a rival that Eliot described as "modern paganism" (48). "I believe," he told his English audience, "that the choice before us is between the formation of a new Christian culture, and the acceptance of a pagan one" (10). Looking outward to America and the Dominions, similarly, Eliot declared that "if these countries are to develop a positive culture of their own, . . . they can only proceed either in the direction of a pagan or of a Christian society" (36).

The interpretive claim was that Western societies as of his time should be characterized as "Christian"—but not because they were deeply or consciously Christian in any substantial sense. On the contrary, Eliot looked out on the world and perceived a religious and cultural muddle. Regarding "the division between Christians and non-Christians," he observed, "the great majority of people are neither one thing nor the other, but are living in a no man's land" (39). In this muddled situation, people's self-labeling could not be taken at face value. "In the present ubiquity of ignorance, one cannot but suspect that many who call themselves Christians do not understand what the word means, and that some who would vigorously repudiate Christianity are more Christian than many who maintain it" (34–35). Still, Western societies had once been Christian, and "a society has not ceased to be Christian until it has positively become something else" (10). And that, he thought, had not happened. Not yet, anyway.

---

20. T. S. Eliot, "The Idea of a Christian Society," in *Christianity and Culture* (New York: Harcourt/Harvest, 1948), 36. Hereafter, page references from this work will be given in parentheses in the text.

Eliot's interpretive claim about a society's character was analogous to the law's treatment of domicile: you remain a domiciliary of a state until you establish domicile in a different state. So if you were born and raised in Kansas, say, then although you may have wandered the globe for the last half-century without in all that time setting foot in Kansas, until you establish a permanent residence somewhere else you will still be a domiciliary of Kansas.[21] In a similar way, Eliot thought that England and other Western societies had once been Christian, and until they became "positively something else," they would remain "Christian" societies—even if there was precious little Christianity left in them.

Eliot's prescriptive claim was that a Christian society is preferable to a pagan one. Not that a Christian society, or at least one that could possibly be achieved, would be any sort of Shangri-La. On the contrary. "We must remember that whatever reform or revolution we carry out, the result will always be a sordid travesty of what human society should be."[22] Eliot understood as well that his preference for a Christian society would not find ready acceptance with the kind of people who attend learned lectures at eminent universities like Cambridge—or, for that matter, anywhere else.[23] But he suggested that the other option was even less inviting. "A Christian society only becomes acceptable after you have fairly examined the alternatives."[24] And once those alternatives—the "pagan" alternatives—are considered, it becomes apparent, he thought, that "the only hopeful course for a society which would thrive and continue its creative activity in the arts of civilisation, is to become Christian. That prospect involves, at least, discipline, inconvenience and discomfort: but here as hereafter the alternative to hell is purgatory."[25]

There is little in this position that seems calculated to elicit assent or even sympathy in educated readers today. Such an audience will not merely disagree with Eliot's preference for a Christian society; it will likely find his description of the alternatives puzzling, or perverse. Perhaps with some less than welcome help from so-called Christian Reconstructionists,[26] we might

21. See, e.g., White v. Tennant, 31 W. Va. 790 (1888).

22. Eliot, "The Idea of a Christian Society," 47.

23. "Paganism," he acknowledged, "holds all the most valuable advertising space." Eliot, "The Idea of a Christian Society," 18.

24. Eliot, "The Idea of a Christian Society," 18.

25. Eliot, "The Idea of a Christian Society," 18–19.

26. See, e.g., Rousas John Rushdoony, *Christianity and the State* (Vallecito, CA: Ross House Books, 1986).

form some dim idea of what a modern Christian society might look like. And we can concoct imaginary scenarios—albeit fantastic and probably dystopian ones—by which such a society might come about.[27] But paganism? Seriously?

Indeed, what would it even mean to embrace, today, a "pagan" society? To revive the practice of sacrificing bulls to Apollo? To make important political and military decisions by poring over the entrails of animals, or by studying the flight patterns of birds? Nobody, surely nobody worth bothering about, wants anything like that. As Thomas Bulfinch wrote (with perhaps a tinge of regret?) in the introduction to his famous book of mythology: "The religions of ancient Greece and Rome are extinct. The so-called divinities of Olympus have not a single worshipper among living men."[28]

Nor need we turn to secularists to press this objection. Consider this observation from another lecture, also given at Cambridge by a literary Anglican, a decade and a half after Eliot's presentation. In a talk inaugurating a chair in Renaissance and medieval literature, C. S. Lewis commented:

> It is hard to have patience with those Jeremiahs, in press or pulpit, who warn us that we are "relapsing into Paganism." It might be rather fun if we were. It would be pleasant to see some future Prime Minister trying to kill a large and lively milk-white bull in Westminster Hall. But we shan't. What lurks behind such idle prophecies, if they are anything but careless language, is the false idea that the historical process allows mere reversal; that Europe can come out of Christianity "by the same door as in she went" and find herself back where she was. It is not what happens. A post-Christian man is not a Pagan; you might as well think that a married woman recovers her virginity by divorce. The post-Christian is cut off from the Christian past and therefore doubly from the Pagan past.[29]

Given such peremptorily dismissive criticism from a fellow in the faith, Eliot's thesis may seem hopeless. And if "paganism" is equated with sacrificing bulls to Zeus, or perhaps with fantastic stories about whimsical or lascivious deities, the thesis would indeed be irredeemable. (Although given

27. See, e.g., Margaret Atwood, *The Handmaid's Tale* (Boston: Houghton Mifflin Harcourt, 1985).

28. Thomas Bulfinch, *Bulfinch's Mythology* (New York: Collier Books, [1867] 1962), 13.

29. C. S. Lewis, "De Descriptione Temporum" (lecture, Cambridge University, Cambridge, 1954), https://archive.org/details/DeDescriptioneTemporum.

Lewis's ample use of fauns and dryads and satyrs and such in his own stories, one might wonder why *he* in particular should be so dismissive of paganism, even in this fairly literal sense.)

We might, but probably should not, deflect Lewis's criticism by speaking not of "paganism" but rather of something like a "classical" orientation or worldview. "Classical" is a more respectable quality, and it is possible to revere the "classical" culture of the ancient Greeks and Romans without endorsing the religious subcomponent described as "paganism." Indeed, this stance (manifest in, among many other sites, the celebrated epic history of Rome's decline by Edward Gibbon) is by now utterly familiar. Nor is there anything especially unsettling about the claim that the modern world has in many ways returned to a "classical" perspective and culture: as it happens, this is the central claim of a recent book by Ferdinand Mount explaining, as its subtitle suggests, "how the classical world came back to us."[30]

And yet, it would be a mistake to try to salvage Eliot's thesis through this kind of amendment. Though it may incite resistance, the term "paganism" is preferable to "classical," I think. Not merely because it is more provocative, nor because Eliot used it, but because it retains a recognition of something I think Eliot meant (and in any case, should have meant) to recognize: namely, that religion—or what *we* would call "religion"—was central to and *not* detachable from the much-admired classical approach to culture and sexuality and politics.

To be sure, Eliot referred not to "paganism" *simpliciter*, but rather to "modern paganism." That term might of course be nothing more than an unilluminating pejorative. Conversely, it might be that beneath the surface features or manifestations, there is some more substantive continuity perspicuously connecting the classical perspectives and practices we call "paganism" with modern movements and views. In that case, Eliot's thesis might provide insights that more conventional accounts of our situation do not. And it might turn out that just as Laycock's question seems to be a variation on the question urgently pressed almost two millennia ago by Tertullian, so the answer to the contemporary question will turn out to be a modern version of the classical explanation.

30. Ferdinand Mount, *Full Circle: How the Classical World Came Back to Us* (New York: Simon and Schuster, 2010).

The Inquiry

That, at least, is the hypothesis on which this book proceeds. The book grows out of a project that I have thought of as an extended reflection on Eliot's quixotic proposal. This project thus involves the consideration and defense of various claims that will seem counterintuitive, or worse, at least initially.

Why undertake such a project—one that is faced from the outset with daunting obstacles and entrenched incredulities? And why invite anyone else—namely, readers—to join in the project?

The answer, quite simply, is that Eliot's diagnosis may provide much needed illumination. At the beginning of his first lecture, Eliot explained that he was advancing his admittedly unconventional interpretation in response to "immediate perplexities that fill our minds."[31] He declared as well his "suspicion that the current terms in which we discuss international affairs and political theory may only tend to conceal from us the real issues of contemporary civilisation."[32] Indeed, "the current terms in which we describe our society . . . only operate to deceive and stupefy us."[33] I have a similar suspicion.

But *how* have "current terms . . . tend[ed] to conceal from us the real issues of contemporary civilisation"? Well, here is one possibility. Modern understandings of history and culture commonly work against the backdrop of a story in which history unfolds in stages, one replacing the other: once retired, past stages are gone for good. Been there, done that. More specifically, an ancient and classical world culturally dominated by what is often called "paganism" eventually gave way to a medieval world presided over by Christianity, which in turn was gradually superseded by a modern world characterized by "secularism." So we live today in "a secular age," as the title of a hefty book by the philosopher Charles Taylor has it.[34] History does not stop, and so we may move on—indeed, we may already be in a "postsecular" period, as some observers claim—but there is no going back to earlier stages of Christendom or paganism.

Something like this historical story and this "no going back" progressive conception of how history unfolds is taken as virtually axiomatic by educated people today. Thus, in culture-war controversies over matters like same-sex

---

31. Eliot, "The Idea of a Christian Society," 5.
32. Eliot, "The Idea of a Christian Society," 3.
33. Eliot, "The Idea of a Christian Society," 6–7.
34. Charles Taylor, *A Secular Age* (Cambridge, MA: Harvard University Press, 2007).

marriage, traditionalists and holdouts are frequently warned against being on "the wrong side of history." The progressive conception informs the confident dismissal of the possibility of modern paganism even by traditionalist religious thinkers like C. S. Lewis. The "historical process," Lewis declares, does not "[allow] mere reversal. . . . It is not what happens."

The conception of history as progressing—as moving from pagan to Christian to secular—widely informs our interpretations of current cultural struggles, which are often depicted as conflicts between progressive "secular" constituencies and holdover "religious" actors. And yet, this "secular versus religious" framework increasingly seems inadequate. That is because the parties and factions on all sides of the culture wars exhibit qualities standardly associated with "religion": an uncompromising zeal or passion, a tendency to view issues in "good versus evil" or "light versus darkness" terms, an eagerness to demonize opponents. These are the features that Laycock finds so dismaying in the current culture wars. Perhaps surprisingly, and distressingly, similar tendencies—and in particular, an eagerness to resort to the rhetoric of demonization—are starkly evident even in some decisions of the United States Supreme Court.[35]

At least a few observers have recognized that our current cultural struggles are most perspicuously described as a contest between competing religiosities.[36] But between *which* religiosities? One party, though complex, has a familiar feel to it—it is composed mostly of traditional Catholics and evangelicals and devout Jews, uneasily allied with Mormons and perhaps a few Muslims. But what sort of religiosity animates the other side?

This is where Eliot's proposal might provide some help. Both the implausibility and the potential illumination in his proposal derive from the fact that it implicitly departs from the standard, taken-for-granted view of Western history as a one-directional advance from one stage to another (pagan, to Christian, to secular, to . . . postsecular?) and instead discerns an ongoing contest between two contrasting and enduring religiosities or orientations. In the classical world, one of these orientations was most conspicuously (though not solely) manifest in Christianity; the competing orientation was manifest in what came to be called "paganism." And those contesting orientations remain active today—or so Eliot's diagnosis suggests—in shaping

---

35. See, e.g., United States v. Windsor, 133 S. Ct. 2675 (2013). For discussion, see Steven D. Smith, "The Jurisprudence of Denigration," *U.C. Davis Law Review* 48 (2014): 675–701.

36. See, e.g., William Voegeli, "That New-Time Religion," *Claremont Review of Books* 15, no. 3 (Summer 2015): 12 (reviewing several books that interpret current cultural conflicts as a clash of competing religiosities).

PAGANS AND CHRISTIANS IN THE CITY

our culture, our politics, and our world. They were and are foundational to the practices that provoked Pliny's question almost two millennia ago, and that provoke Douglas Laycock's question today. The investigation and defense of Eliot's proposal thus offer an oblique but potentially revealing way of addressing the questions noted earlier in this chapter.

That investigation and defense will require considerable work, as well as a willingness to examine and perhaps reconsider our ingrained attachment to some current assumptions that are often taken for granted. We have already noticed one of those entrenched assumptions—the assumption that history moves forward from one phase to another, leaving past phases irretrievably behind. Another common assumption that we will discuss is the widespread conception, pervasive and influential in the academy, of human beings as bearers of "interests" who live and act primarily to further those interests (and who, accordingly, need to be understood and explained as "rational interest-seekers"). In contrast to this conception (though not necessarily in contradiction to it) is the possibility that humans—or many humans—have an essential religious dimension, and that without appreciating this religious dimension we will not understand what people are or why they behave in the ways they do.

Such assumptions about the nature of human beings are presupposed in all discussions of human affairs, and so we will need to consider them at the outset. Then we will turn to the Rome of late antiquity and observe the struggles, sometimes inconspicuous and sometimes quite open, between "paganism" (as it came to be called) and Christianity. We will see how these contrasting religiosities reflected basic existential orientations that could not easily coexist in peace. The tension led to the back-and-forth political struggle of the fourth century between Christianity and paganism.

But although Christianity ultimately prevailed in that struggle *as an official and political matter*, we will see that the contrasting orientations endured: though officially defeated, paganism as a distinctive existential orientation persisted through the centuries in uneasy collaboration and contention with an official Christianity. And in recent decades, that position has become more open and confident. It is readily discernible, for example, in the work of respected and thoroughly "secular" thinkers like Ronald Dworkin, Sam Harris, and Barbara Ehrenreich.

Finally, we will return to the present and consider how the conflict between the kind of religiosity represented by Christianity and that reflected in paganism can help to make sense of our present situation.

Why go to the trouble? But I have already said: the motivation for the undertaking is the hope of illumination. My goal is the same as Eliot's—to see through and past "the current terms [that] only tend to conceal from us the real issues of contemporary civilisation."[37]

In addition, I should at the outset make, *a fortiori*, the same disclaimer Eliot did: "This is a subject which I could, no doubt, handle much better were I a profound scholar in any of several fields. But I am not writing for scholars, but for people like myself."[38] For people, scholars or not, who find our times perplexing, and troubling, and who find the standard "religious versus secular" interpretations and explanations unsatisfying. Perhaps Eliot will provide some help. We will see.

37. Eliot, "The Idea of a Christian Society," 3.
38. Eliot, "The Idea of a Christian Society," 5.

CHAPTER 2

Homo Religiosus

Our subject is T. S. Eliot's thesis that the future of Western societies will be determined by a contest between Christianity and "modern paganism." And so our first order of business, it might seem, would be to clarify just what "paganism" is, so that we could then consider what "*modern* paganism" might look like and how it might contrast with modern Christianity. Never fear: we will indeed address those matters in due course. But both paganism and Christianity are species within the genus of "religion," and so, with apologies for the delay, our comparison will be improved if we first step back and try to get a grasp on what sort of thing "religion" is.

But that step back calls for a second one, because saying what "religion" is turns out to be no quick and easy task. Indeed, some scholars have concluded that the very idea of "religion" as a distinct thing or category is an artificial modern invention, devised for political or academic purposes.[1] So, rather than attacking the question head-on, we may do better to sneak up on it from behind, so to speak, by starting with a different question that is closer to home—the question of human personhood. Not "What is *religion?*"—not to start off with—but rather, initially, "What are . . . *we?*"

---

1. See, e.g., William T. Cavanaugh, *The Myth of Religious Violence* (New York: Oxford University Press, 2009), 57–122. Cavanaugh notes that the eminent scholar Wilfred Cantwell Smith "was compelled to conclude that, outside of the modern West, there is no significant concept equivalent to what we think of as religion" (61). Cf. Jonathan Z. Smith, *Relating Religion: Essays in the Study of Religion* (Chicago: University of Chicago Press, 2004), 179 (describing "the major expansion of the use and understanding of the term 'religion' that began in the sixteenth century"); Nicholas Lash, *The Beginning and End of "Religion"* (Cambridge: Cambridge University Press, 1996), 13–17 (describing "the invention of 'religion'").

Persons and "Interests"

That question—"What are we?"—is one that law, politics, history, and the social sciences seldom ask but always answer, at least implicitly. All these disciplines are concerned with people—with *human beings*—and so they necessarily proceed on the basis of presuppositions about what sorts of entities we humans are.[2] Indeed, not only in academic studies but also in our day-to-day affairs, such presuppositions are implicit if mostly unnoticed in all our mundane discussions, decisions, and interactions. All these constantly involve people; all thus necessarily import assumptions about how people are constituted and what makes them—or rather *us*—behave in the sometimes comfortingly predictable, sometimes puzzling or bizarre, ways we behave.

Within legal studies (my own field), the subdiscipline that is probably most self-conscious in its assumptions about the nature of persons is law-and-economics. Economics, Richard Posner explains, "assum[es] that man is a rational maximizer of his ends in life, his satisfactions—what we shall call his 'self-interest.'"[3] This interest-seeking conception of the person is taken as axiomatic not only in economics, though, but also in many other academic neighborhoods, as in the virtually ubiquitous rational choice theory.

Perhaps more surprisingly, an interest-seeking conception can animate even thinking devoted not to maximizing satisfactions, but rather to articulating the meaning of justice. Thus, in the contractarian theory offered by John Rawls, probably the most influential political philosopher of the past half-century, the content of justice is derived from a thought experiment that conjectures about the political principles that would be selected by hypothetical persons in an "original position" situated behind a "veil of ignorance" that prevents them from knowing the particular situations they will occupy in life.[4] These contracting parties are presented as rational interest-seekers. Thus, Rawls describes "the principles of justice as those *which rational persons concerned to advance their interests* would consent to as equals."[5] These "rational persons" are motivated by a desire "to win for themselves the high-

2. See generally John H. Evans, *What Is a Human? What the Answer Means for Human Rights* (New York: Oxford University Press, 2016).

3. Richard A. Posner, *Economic Analysis of Law*, 5th ed. (New York: Wolters Kluwer Law and Business, 1998), 3–4.

4. John Rawls, *A Theory of Justice* (Cambridge, MA: Belknap Press of Harvard University Press, 1971).

5. Rawls, *A Theory of Justice*, 19 (emphasis added).

est index of primary goods."[6] And Rawls explains that the "rational person . . . follows the plan which *will satisfy more of his desires* rather than less."[7]

Usually the term "interests" is closely associated with "desires," as Rawls says, or with "satisfactions," as Posner puts it. What makes something an "interest," in other words, is that humans in fact desire or feel a need for it, and feel (or at least expect to feel) "satisfaction" upon attaining it. Understood in this way, "interests" seem to be, at least in principle, empirically verifiable facts—and thus compatible with a hardheaded scientific approach to social understanding and to public decision making.[8]

To be sure, the term is elastic enough to be adapted to other purposes and meanings. For example, a theorist will occasionally try to add a normative dimension by distinguishing between merely "subjective" and more "objective" interests—or between what we *do* in fact want and what we *should* want, or what we *would* want if we were properly reflective. In this vein, Ronald Dworkin contrasted what he called "experiential interests" that we value "because and when they feel good" with "critical interests" that "represent critical judgments rather than just experiential preferences."[9]

Nothing prohibits theorists from using the term in these expansive ways. If the term is construed too broadly, though, it risks becoming empty. For example, if the term is used in a more normative sense, as with Dworkin, the claim that "people should act to realize their (reflectively justifiable) interests" risks dissolving into the tautology that "people should act for the ends for which they should act." Which is true enough, no doubt, but not very illuminating. On the whole, therefore, the "interest-seeking" conception seems most rigorous and useful—even for normative projects, like Rawlsian justice or economics in its prescriptive mode—when "interests" are understood as referring to actual human desires and satisfactions.

If the conception of persons as interest-seekers is powerfully influential, one reason is that the conception has much to recommend it. It resonates with a great deal in our experience. All of us *do* have interests or desires

6. Rawls, *A Theory of Justice*, 144.

7. Rawls, *A Theory of Justice*, 143 (emphasis added).

8. "People who use the terms *preference, wants, needs*, and *interests*," Charles Lindblom observes, "often assume that they refer to some objective attributes of human beings, such as a person's metabolic rate. . . . These are bedrock facts about 'real' preferences or interests." Charles E. Lindblom, *Inquiry and Change: The Troubled Attempt to Understand and Shape Society* (New Haven: Yale University Press, 1990), 19.

9. See, e.g., Ronald Dworkin, *Life's Dominion: An Argument about Abortion, Euthanasia, and Individual Freedom* (New York: Vintage Books, 1993), 201–2.

that we try to satisfy as fully and efficiently as possible (subject to a variety of constraints, perhaps). And yet, although the interest-seeking conception seems realistic and useful for many purposes, it does not comfortably fit all aspects of human experience. Sometimes people deliberately act in ways that do not seem calculated to advance their subjective wants and needs.

The most striking examples, probably, are instances in which people knowingly sacrifice a great deal—including, sometimes, their lives—for some moral purpose or noble cause. Like Antigone in Sophocles's *Oedipus at Colonus*, a daughter or son gives up a satisfying life or a lucrative and fulfilling career in order to care for an aging parent. Or a person voluntarily sacrifices his or her life in defense of country, or to rescue someone in distress. At least in the ordinary sense of the term, these people do not appear to be acting to promote their own "interests."

To be sure, as we have already noticed, the term "interest" is elastic enough that it *can* be stretched to cover these instances. We can simply say that a particular moral or heroically altruistic person felt a subjective desire to care for a parent—he must have, or why would he have done what he did?—or that he felt an "interest" in risking and sacrificing his life in order to defend his country. But this is often not how it appears, either to the person or to others who observe. The person and we would say that she *sacrificed her own interests* to help another, or to do what was right, or from a sense of duty. As noted, moreover, if the concept of "interests" is expanded to cover all these cases, the idea risks becoming empty and tautological. To say that "people act to advance their interests" is just to say that "people act to do whatever they think or want their actions to do." Which is to say nothing at all of any substance.

Religion as we conventionally think of it is an area in which the interest-seeking conception fits awkwardly.[10] Even in an ostensibly "secular" age, millions of people still donate large sums of money to churches, or take time off from work or sacrifice recreation time to attend worship services that are often less than scintillating. They participate in church-sponsored service activities or regularly devote time to religious study, reflection, or prayer.[11] Once again, like all human conduct, religious conduct *can* be described

---

10. See Jonathan Haidt, "Forget the Money, Follow the Sacredness," *Campaign Stops* (blog), *New York Times*, March 17, 2012, http://campaignstops.blogs.nytimes.com/2012/03/17/forget-the-money-follow-the-sacredness/?_r=0.

11. Considerable data regarding religious practice in America is collected in Robert D. Putnam and David E. Campbell, *American Grace: How Religion Divides and Unites Us* (New York: Simon and Schuster, 2010).

in interest-seeking terms. "John goes to church because he wants to meet people," or "Susan donates to her church because she believes this will help her get to heaven." Scholars have accordingly applied economic analysis to religion; such analyses have been illuminating at least with respect to some aspects of the subject.[12] And yet, this sort of description does not capture all of religion; indeed, a purely interest-seeking piety is often thought to be a lesser or illegitimate kind of religion.

As an old saying has it, "man does not live by bread alone."[13] The interest-seeking conception captures and explains a good deal about humans and our dealings, but it does not seem to capture or explain *everything* about us. Perhaps not even the most important or essential things. Something—something that is arguably crucial—is left out, or is included only in distorted form. But what?

Persons and Meanings

Some thinkers suggest that an understanding of humans merely as interest-seekers fails to recognize that central part of human life that tries to discern *meaning* or *purpose* in life, and then to live in accordance with that meaning or purpose.[14] In this vein, the psychologist Viktor Frankl argued that "man's main concern is not to gain pleasure or to avoid pain, but rather to see a meaning in his life."[15]

Frankl's view grew out of his own horrific experiences in Nazi death camps (in which his wife, father, mother, and brother died). He observed

12. See, e.g., Paul Horwitz, "Freedom of the Church without Romance," *Journal of Contemporary Legal Issues* 21 (2013): 89–125; Michael W. McConnell and Richard A. Posner, "An Economic Approach to Issues of Religious Freedom," *University of Chicago Law Review* 56 (1989): 1.

13. Matt. 4:4.

14. As noted, the term "interest" is potentially broad and elastic; consequently, a proponent of the interest-seeking conception might try to annex or absorb the criticism by simply acknowledging a possible "interest" in living a meaningful life, or in searching for a "purpose" in life. But the annexation can run either way: if one side can say we have an "interest" in meaning or purpose, the other side can say that the "purpose" of life includes the satisfaction of interests. This sort of debate seems quite pointless. The important question is whether an exclusive focus on subjective "interests" functions to distort or shortchange the importance of "meaning."

15. Viktor Frankl, *Man's Search for Meaning* (New York: Washington Square Press, 1963), 179.

that the prisoners most likely to endure the grim brutalities of the camps were not necessarily those who were outwardly most healthy or fortunate, but rather those who had some purpose in their lives. Generalizing this insight, Frankl founded a school of psychology that he called "logotherapy." "According to logotherapy," he explained, "the striving to find a meaning in one's life is the primary motivational force in man."[16] What people most urgently need, he insisted, is a "why" for life;[17] given this *why*, "man is even ready to suffer, on the condition, to be sure, that his suffering has a meaning."[18]

Although developed in less excruciating circumstances, philosopher Susan Wolf's more recent reflections on meaning run parallel to Frankl's views. Wolf observes that many of the most important reasons we act do not fit with the psychology of self-interest—or, for that matter, in more purely "moral" imperatives. These reasons, rather, "engage us in the activities that make our lives worth living; they give us a reason to go on; they make our worlds go round. They, and the activities they engender, give *meaning* to our lives."[19] "What gives meaning to our lives gives us reasons to live even when the prospects for our own *well-being* are bleak."[20]

If meaning can give us reason to live even when conditions are grim, the reverse is also true: the lack of meaning can make life seem empty or intolerable even when we seem to be flourishing—when it seems that all our "interests" are being satisfied. The point is poignantly developed in an autobiographical account by Leo Tolstoy, who explained how his own life, though outwardly prosperous in every imaginable way, became unbearable to him precisely because it seemed so meaningless.

> My question, the one that brought me to the point of suicide when I was fifty years old, was a most simple one that lies in the soul of every person, from a silly child to a wise old man. It is the question without which life is impossible, as I had learnt from experience. It is this: what will come of what I do today or tomorrow? What will come of my entire life?

16. Frankl, *Man's Search for Meaning*, 154.

17. Frankl, *Man's Search for Meaning*, 121, 127, 164.

18. Frankl, *Man's Search for Meaning*, 179. The "mass neurosis" of the twentieth century, Frankl thought, was an "existential vacuum," or lack of meaning (204, 167).

19. Susan Wolf, *Meaning in Life and Why It Matters* (Princeton: Princeton University Press, 2010), 2 (emphasis added).

20. Wolf, *Meaning in Life*, 56.

Expressed another way the question can be put like this: why do I live? Why do I wish for anything, or do anything? Or expressed another way: is there any meaning in my life that will not be annihilated by the inevitability of death that awaits me?[21]

To his dismay, Tolstoy discovered that he had no answer to these questions. "I could not attribute any rational meaning to a single act, let alone to my whole life."[22] This condition left the novelist with feelings of "fear, abandonment, loneliness" until he found meaning in religious faith—the faith not of the theologians and churchmen, in his case, but of the ordinary working people.[23]

So people do not merely pursue "interests"; they also seek—and seek to live in accordance with—"meaning." But what *is* meaning, exactly? We talk about people having (or not having) a "meaningful" life, or about having (or not having) "purpose" in life. But what does "meaning" in this existential sense entail?

Sometimes the proponents of meaning appear to be contemplating something purely subjective and personal—something like the "projects" or "goals" that different people set for themselves. In this vein, Viktor Frankl sometimes described meaning as an "aim," a "purpose," or a "task";[24] these descriptions might suggest that the sort of meaning he had in mind was little more than a personally chosen goal that an individual might care about and pursue.[25] Susan Wolf, similarly, says that meaning does not need to come from anything grand or heroic; it can be supplied by humble activities like gardening or practicing the cello.[26]

21. Leo Tolstoy, "A Confession," in *A Confession and Other Religious Writings*, trans. Jane Kentish (London: Penguin, 1987), 34–35.
22. Tolstoy, "A Confession," 19. "This spiritual condition presented itself to me in the following manner: my life is some kind of stupid and evil joke that someone is playing on me. Despite the fact that I did not acknowledge any such 'someone,' who might have created me, this concept of there being someone playing a stupid and evil joke on me by bringing me into the world came to me as the most natural way of expressing my condition" (31).
23. Tolstoy, "A Confession," 63, 63–78.
24. Frankl, *Man's Search for Meaning*, 121–22.
25. Consistent with this subjective conception, Frankl emphasized that meaning is a personal matter that varies with the individual, not a monolithic universal imperative. See, e.g., *Man's Search for Meaning*, 122 ("These tasks, and therefore the meaning of life, differ from man to man, and from moment to moment. Thus it is impossible to define the meaning of life in a general way").
26. Wolf, *Meaning in Life*, 4.

On this view, claims about the need for meaning may seem to boil down to something quite platitudinous: "Your life will be happier and more fulfilling if you have goals that you're pursuing, or projects that you care about." And yet, this merely subjective conception was insufficient for both Wolf and Frankl. Although meaning is associated with subjective satisfaction, Wolf observes, not all activities that people find satisfying are meaningful. After all, some people get subjective satisfaction from "smoking pot all day, . . . doing crossword puzzles, or worse (as personal experience will attest), Sudokus."[27] These activities may provide subjective satisfaction. But they do not make for "meaning" in life, Wolf contends, because they lack objective value.[28] Wolf thus defends a "bipartite conception" in which "meaning" must have both a subjective and an objective dimension:[29] it "arises when subjective attraction meets objective attractiveness."[30]

And what is "objective" value or attractiveness, exactly? Wolf admits that she has no very satisfactory account of what "objective" value is; nor, she thinks, do other philosophers.[31]

While emphasizing the personal quality of meaning, likewise, Frankl stressed as well an objective, unchosen dimension of meaning. He disagreed with "some existentialist thinkers [like Sartre] who see in man's ideals nothing but his own inventions." Rather, "the meaning of our lives is not invented by ourselves, but rather detected."[32] Without some larger or more encompassing meaning, the more mundane and personal meanings would lose their efficacy: "The question which beset me [in the death camps] was, 'Has all this suffering, this dying around us, a meaning? For, if not, then ultimately

27. Wolf, *Meaning in Life*, 16. See also 47 ("People do the darnedest things. They race lawn mowers, compete in speed-eating contests, sit on flagpoles, watch reality TV").

28. For Wolf's defense of the requirement of objective value against objections, see "Response," in *Meaning in Life*, 102, 119–27.

29. Wolf, *Meaning in Life*, 20. On this bipartite view, for a life to be meaningful, both an objective and a subjective condition must be met; a meaningful life is a life that the subject finds fulfilling, and one that contributes to or connects positively with something that has value outside the subject.

30. Wolf, *Meaning in Life*, 62.

31. Wolf, *Meaning in Life*, 45–47.

32. Frankl, *Man's Search for Meaning*, 156–57. "We have to beware of the tendency to deal with values in terms of the mere self-expression of man himself. For *logos*, or 'meaning,' is not only an emergence from existence itself but rather something confronting existence. If the meaning that is waiting to be fulfilled by man were really nothing but a mere expression of self, or no more than a projection of his wishful thinking, it would immediately lose its demanding and challenging character; it could no longer call man forth or summon him" (156).

there is no meaning to survival; for a life whose meaning depends upon such a happenstance—as whether one escapes or not—ultimately would not be worth living at all.'"[33]

Frankl occasionally talked in almost mystical terms of an "ultimate meaning" that "necessarily exceeds and surpasses the finite intellectual capacities of man,"[34] or of an "infinite meaning of life" that "includes suffering and dying, privation and death,"[35] and hence that could work to redeem even the horrific and senseless savagery of the death camps. The focus on "ultimate meaning" became more overt in Frankl's later work. Neither in his earlier nor in his later work, however, could Frankl offer any very clear account of what "ultimate meaning" might be.[36]

Is "Meaning" Meaningful?

The difficulty of giving a good account of "ultimate meaning," or (as Wolf acknowledges) of providing a satisfactory explanation of the "objective value" that seems a necessary condition for meaning, may provoke a familiar objection: perhaps the very notion of "meaning," or of "ultimate meaning," is nothing more than a confusion of thought. More generally, the idea of "ultimate meaning" seems closely akin to the idea of a "meaning of meanings,"[37] as Terry Eagleton puts it, or of a "meaning of life"—notions much scoffed at by skeptical thinkers. Queries about the "meaning of life" can have an adolescent or even comical feel to them; they evoke associations of Douglas Adams's supercomputer ("Deep Thought") that calculates the meaning of life to be . . . 42.[38] Eagleton remarks that the very idea of a meaning of life "seems a quaint sort of notion, at once homespun and portentous, fit for satirical mauling by the Monty Python team."[39] The dedication of his book

33. Frankl, *Man's Search for Meaning*, 183.
34. Frankl, *Man's Search for Meaning*, 187.
35. Frankl, *Man's Search for Meaning*, 132.
36. In later work, Frankl linked "ultimate meaning" to religion—but to religion "in its widest sense," as he put it, and indeed in a sense "encompassing even agnosticism and atheism." Viktor E. Frankl, *Man's Search for Ultimate Meaning* (Cambridge, MA: Perseus Publishing, 2000), 153.
37. Terry Eagleton, *The Meaning of Life* (New York: Oxford University Press, 2007), 31, 77.
38. Douglas Adams, *A Hitchhiker's Guide to the Galaxy* (New York: Ballantine Books, 1979), 165.
39. Eagleton, *The Meaning of Life*, 53.

on "the meaning of life" reads "For Oliver, who found the whole idea deeply embarrassing." (Tellingly, Eagleton was not deterred by the embarrassment and did not stop at the dedication; instead he proceeded to write a book on the question—though not one that purports to disclose what the meaning of life really is.)

In the deconstructive vein, the Oxford philosopher Antony Flew methodically dissected Tolstoy's autobiographical account of his own angst-ridden quest for meaning and tried to show that the novelist was fundamentally confused.[40] It was appropriate enough for Tolstoy to ask "Why?" or "What for?" with respect to various particular activities in his life—writing a book, educating his son, and so forth. But Tolstoy had perfectly good answers to those particular and sensible questions, Flew thought. Unfortunately, Tolstoy "would not take an answer for an answer";[41] he persisted in asking the "What for?" question beyond the point where the question made sense. He was like the child who keeps asking "Why?" when the most basic and only possible kind of response has already been given.[42]

In a similar vein, another Oxford philosopher, R. M. Hare, described an incident in which a foreign student who had been living with Hare and his wife, and who was normally a "cheerful, vigorous, enthusiastic young man," became despondent after reading Camus and coming to the conclusion that, as the student put it, "nothing matters."[43] As Hare recalled the incident, he was able to restore the student to good spirits simply by pointing out that his existential despair was the result of a conceptual or semantic mistake.

> My friend had not understood that the function of the word "matters" is to express concern; he had thought mattering was something (some activity or process) that things did, rather like chattering; as if

40. Antony Flew, "Tolstoi and the Meaning of Life," in *The Meaning of Life*, ed. E. D. Klemke, 2nd ed. (New York: Oxford University Press, 1999), 209.

41. Flew, "Tolstoi," 210.

42. Flew's dismissive analysis would not have taken Tolstoy by surprise. Indeed, Tolstoy himself raised similar criticisms. Thus, in his "search for the overall meaning of life" (Tolstoy, "A Confession," 28), he tried to persuade himself that his questions were misconceived. "The questions seemed so stupid, simple, and childish. But the moment I touched upon them and tried to resolve them I was immediately convinced, firstly, that they were not childish and stupid questions but were the most important and profound questions in life, and secondly, that however much I thought about them I could not resolve them" (29).

43. R. M. Hare, "Nothing Matters," in Klemke, *The Meaning of Life*, 277.

the sentence "My wife matters to me" were similar in logical function to the sentence "My wife chatters to me." If one thinks that, one may begin to wonder what this activity is, called mattering; and one may begin to observe the world closely (aided perhaps by the clear cold descriptions of a novel like that of Camus) to see if one can catch anything doing something that could be called mattering; and when we can observe nothing going on which seems to correspond to this name, it is easy for the novelist to persuade us that after all *nothing matters*. To which the answer is, "Matters" isn't that sort of word; it isn't intended to describe something that things do, but to express our concern about what they do; so of course we can't observe things mattering; but that doesn't mean that they don't matter.[44]

So we should not confuse "matters" with "chatters." Dismissive analyses like those of Flew and Hare are in the spirit of the logical positivists, who argued that a sweeping set of beliefs and propositions—including virtually all moral, religious, and aesthetic propositions—are merely meaningless or nonsensical. Philosophers have come to view this as an inadequate response to genuine human questions and beliefs,[45] however, and some philosophers likewise suggest that the question of "the meaning of life" is a real one that cannot be deflected through analytical deconstruction. It is, as John Cottingham observes, "the question that will not go away."[46]

But then, what *is* the sense of that question—the one that will not go away?

Meaning and the Drama of Time

Another (fortuitously named) philosopher, John Wisdom, proposes a potentially helpful analogy. Sometimes we arrive at the theater late, or leave early, and thus see only part of the play. We might then ask what the play "means," and "in this case we want to know what went before and what came after

44. Hare, "Nothing Matters," 281.

45. See Hilary Putnam, *Reason, Truth, and History* (New York: Cambridge University Press, 1981), 105–6.

46. John Cottingham, *On the Meaning of Life* (London: Routledge, 2003), 1. Cf. Charles Taylor, *A Secular Age* (Cambridge, MA: Harvard University Press, 2007), 677 ("Lots of people don't want to ask the meta-question ['what is the meaning of it all']; but once it arises for someone they will not easily be put off by the injunction to forget it").

in order to understand the part we saw." But then again, sometimes we see the whole play and nonetheless ask, "What did it mean?" In this case also, "we are asking a question which has sense and is not absurd. For our words express a wish to grasp the character, the significance of the whole play." Similarly, when we ask about "the meaning of it all," "we are trying to find the order in the drama of Time."[47]

Of course, we might be asking something a bit more basic; we might be asking whether there *is* any "drama of Time." Wisdom acknowledges the question. "Is the drama of time meaningless as a tale told by an idiot? Or is it not meaningless? And if it is not meaningless is it a comedy or a tragedy, a triumph or a disaster, or is it a mixture in which sweet and bitter are forever mixed?"[48]

We can extend Wisdom's analogy by adopting the perspective not of the theater audience but rather of people who may be—or may *not* be—actors in a play. We find ourselves on what might be a sort of stage, and in the midst of people and scenes in which some sort of action seems to be unfolding, but we do not know for certain whether there is any overall script or drama or whether instead people are just milling around, pursuing their individual aims and projects—their "interests"—but without any larger encompassing plot or purpose. In this situation, we might want to know—and might ask, meaningfully—whether we are part of a drama or not.[49]

Something like that, it seems, is what the question of Meaning, or of "meaning" in its more ambitious forms, is typically asking. Beyond our purely human plans and finite projects, is there some larger Story—some "secret plot to it all,"[50] as Terry Eagleton puts it—in which we have somehow been placed?

Suppose we accept this as a (perhaps metaphorical) formulation of the question of Meaning. And suppose we venture an affirmative answer to the question, or at least acknowledge the possibility of an affirmative answer: there is—or there *may be*—a grand narrative or a "secret plot to it all." We are then, it seems, in the realm of religion. Indeed, the view that there is some larger Meaning in the cosmos, and that we ought to

47. John Wisdom, "The Meanings of the Questions of Life," in Klemke, *The Meaning of Life*, 257, 258–59.

48. Wisdom, "Meanings of the Questions," 260.

49. Cf. Robert M. Adams, "Comment," in Wolf, *Meaning in Life*, 75, 83 ("But judgments of meaning in life are assessments of something that does have a narrative structure").

50. Eagleton, *The Meaning of Life*, 106.

live in accordance with it, is a plausible candidate for an answer to the vexing question of what "religion" is, or of what the difference is between religious and nonreligious worldviews.[51] Sigmund Freud thus maintained that "the idea of life having a purpose stands and falls with the religious system."[52]

A thoughtful recent articulation of this view comes from Jonathan Sacks, formerly chief rabbi of the United Hebrew Congregations of Great Britain. Like Viktor Frankl and Susan Wolf, Sacks contends that meaning is central to human life. "We are meaning-seeking animals," Sacks asserts. Other animals do not ask the question, so far as we can tell, but *we* do. "It is what makes us unique. To be human is to ask the question 'Why?'"[53] Sacks adds that "by a meaningful life . . . I do not mean life as a personal project. I mean life with a meaning that comes from outside us, as a call, a vocation, a mission."[54] This conception has a religious quality, as Sacks explains.

> That is what religion for the most part is: the constant making and remaking of meaning, by the stories we tell, the rituals we perform, and the prayers we say. The stories are sacred, the rituals divine commands, and prayer a genuine dialogue with the divine. Religion is an authentic response to a real Presence, but it is also a way of making that presence real by constantly living in response to it.[55]

51. In this vein, Michael Perry associates "religion" with "religious or limit questions," such as: "Who are we? Where did we come from; what is our origin, our beginning? Where are we going; what is our destiny, our end? What is the meaning of suffering? Of evil? Of death? And there is the cardinal question, the question that comprises many of the others: Is human life ultimately meaningful or, instead, ultimately bereft of meaning, meaning-less, absurd?" Michael J. Perry, *The Political Morality of Liberal Democracy* (New York: Cambridge University Press, 2010), 43 (footnotes omitted).

52. Sigmund Freud, *Civilization and Its Discontents*, trans. James Strachey (New York: Norton, [1930] 1961). Scornfully dismissive of religion as "so patently infantile, so foreign to reality" (22), Freud endorsed the deflationary conclusion that "what decides the purpose of life is simply the programme of the pleasure principle" (25).

53. Jonathan Sacks, *The Great Partnership: Science, Religion, and the Search for Meaning* (New York: Schocken, 2011), 25. "We are the meaning-seeking animal, the only known life form in the universe ever to have asked the question 'Why?' There is no single, demonstrable, irrefutable, selfevident, compelling and universal answer to this question. Yet the principled refusal to ask it, to insist that the universe simply happened and there is nothing more to say, is a failure of the very inquisitiveness, the restless search for that which lies beyond the visible horizon, that led to science in the first place" (288–89).

54. Sacks, *The Great Partnership*, 104.

55. Sacks, *The Great Partnership*, 197.

In support of this interpretation, Sacks quotes the philosopher Ludwig Wittgenstein:

> To believe in God means to understand the question about the meaning of life.

> To believe in God means to see that the facts of the world are not the end of the matter.

> To believe in God means to see that life has a meaning.[56]

Wittgenstein's propositions may be misleading in one respect: not all religious understandings are theistic in character.[57] But a belief in Meaning, or in a Story, is the sort of belief that typically elicits the description of "religion." As William James observed, "If any one phrase could gather [religion's] universal message, that phrase would be 'All is *not* vanity in this Universe, whatever the appearances may suggest.'"[58]

The Limitations of "Meaning"

Our discussion thus far has suggested that although human beings are indeed interest-seeking organisms, we are more than that: we are also "meaning-seeking" beings who attempt to discern and live in accordance with both local and larger meanings. And on one view, religion engages this meaning-seeking dimension of our nature by offering a sort of Grand Story or metanarrative that confers meaning by explaining what the cosmic and human drama is all about.

But this account will generate objections. Let us notice two especially pertinent ones. One objection would contend that this "metanarrative" version leaves out a good deal of religion. Not all religions offer a metanarrative. And even in those that do, the metanarrative is arguably not what is most essential or fundamental. It may not have been there at the outset at all—not explicitly, at least; the metanarrative may have been elaborated as the religion

---

56. Sacks, *The Great Partnership*, 19.

57. William James, *The Varieties of Religious Experience*, rev. ed. (New York: Barnes and Noble, 2004), 39.

58. James, *Varieties of Religious Experience*, 44.

developed. When Moses kneels in awe before the burning bush,[59] he is not responding to any cosmic story telling him where he came from and where he is ultimately going. Christianity, similarly, offers a cosmic narrative in which the main chapters are creation, fall (into the world of pain and mortality, our present habitation), and redemption leading to eternal life. The metanarrative provides guidance with the usual questions of "meaning": Who am I? Why am I here? How should I live? What does the future hold for me? And yet when Jesus calls Peter, James, and John to leave their fishing boats and follow him, he does not expound any metanarrative into which this invitation might fit. He merely requests, or perhaps commands: "Come, follow me."[60]

A different objection would observe that the foregoing account grounds religion in human *needs*—more specifically, in a need for "meaning." But that version of religion seems problematic for at least two reasons. First, some people seem to feel no such need. At least to outward appearances, many people go through life working, sleeping, eating, drinking, loving, and grieving without worrying overmuch about "what it all means" or "what the point of it all is." Tolstoy's account of his existential crisis is intriguing, arguably, in part because Tolstoy himself was exceptional. More generally, it may be that accounts of religion explicitly in terms of its ability to provide "meaning" are mostly modern in character—responses to the widespread modern sense of a "loss of meaning" in a "disenchanted" world; we will say more about that condition in a later chapter.

A second problem with understanding religion by reference to a "need for meaning" is that the account can be subtly subversive of religion. The need-based account plays nicely into dismissive interpretations of religion as mere "wish fulfillment."[61] We may "need" lots of things—a loving home, a secure job, good health, world peace. It does not follow that we will get these things, or that there is anything in the world—anything real—that corresponds to these needs. The French philosopher Luc Ferry thus observes that "there is a strong likelihood that the need pushes us to invent the thing, and then to defend it, with all the arguments of bad faith at our disposal, because we have become attached to it. The need for God is, in this respect, the greatest argument against His existence that I know of."[62]

59. Exod. 3.

60. Matt. 4:19.

61. See, e.g., Sigmund Freud, *The Future of an Illusion*, ed. Todd Dufresne, trans. Gregory C. Richter (Toronto: Broadview Press, [1927] 2012).

62. Luc Ferry, *A Brief History of Thought: A Philosophical Guide to Living*, trans. Theo Cuffe (New York: HarperCollins, 2011), 230.

But for at least some religious believers, religion has not been primarily a response to any need or wish; rather, it arises from a perception of something that, like it or not, is real or true—perhaps uncomfortably or distressingly so. Once again, when Moses unexpectedly encounters God in the burning bush, the man is far from happy about this newly encountered Reality and the associated duties that have suddenly been thrust upon him.[63] When Saul of Tarsus suffers an epiphany on the road to Damascus, the experience is neither sought after nor pleasant.[64]

To notice these objections is not to dismiss or disparage the "meaning"-based account of religion, but rather to suggest that "meaning" and a need for meaning may not be the only or the most fundamental ground of religion. But what might a more fundamental ground be?

Starting Over, with Sublimity

Another Jewish thinker, Rabbi Abraham Heschel, suggested a different starting point. Like Frankl and Sacks, Heschel talked about "ultimate meaning,"[65] but that is not where he began. He maintained, rather, that religion commences with a sense of "wonder," or of "awe." "Wonder or radical amazement is the chief characteristic of the religious man's attitude toward history and nature."[66] This attitude is subjective, obviously, but it is not *merely* or reductively subjective. Rather, "awe . . . is more than an emotion; it is a way of understanding. Awe is itself an act of insight into a meaning greater than ourselves."[67]

Religious awe discerns that there is in the universe something that is "sublime," which is related to the beautiful but transcends it. "The perception of beauty may be the beginning of the experience of the sublime. The sublime is that which we see and are unable to convey. It is the silent allusion of things

63. Exod. 3.
64. Acts 9.
65. Abraham Joshua Heschel, *God in Search of Man: A Philosophy of Judaism* (New York: Farrar, Straus and Giroux, 1955), 107, 119.
66. Heschel, *God in Search of Man*, 45.
67. Heschel, *God in Search of Man*, 74. Cf. James, *Varieties of Religious Experience*, 61 ("It is as if there were in the human consciousness a sense of reality, a feeling of objective presence, a perception of what we may call 'something there,' more deep and more general than any of the special and particular 'senses' by which the current psychology supposes existent realities to be originally revealed").

to a meaning greater than themselves. It is that which all things ultimately stand for. . . . This is why the sense of the sublime must be regarded as the root of man's creative activities in art, thought, and noble living."[68]

So religion starts with a sense of the sublime—of the sublime not merely as a subjective emotion but as a reality independent of our perceptions of it. But where and what is that reality? In this respect, Heschel contrasted the attitude of ancient Greek religion with that of what he called "Biblical man." Greek religion identified the sublime with nature, and more generally with the world; in essence, it sacralized the world, or parts of it.[69] By contrast, biblical man understood the sublime as a manifestation of something—or of Someone—who stood behind and above nature and the world.[70]

Consider this account from the first-century Stoic philosopher Seneca:

> If you have ever come upon a grove that is thick with ancient trees which rise far above their usual height and block the view of the sky with their cover of intertwining branches, then the loftiness of the forest and the seclusion of the spot and your wonder at the unbroken shade in the midst of open space will create in you a feeling of the divine (*numen*). Or, if a cave made by the deep erosion of rocks supports a mountain with its arch, a place not made by hands but hollowed out by natural causes into spaciousness, then your mind will be aroused by a feeling of religious awe (*religio*). We venerate the sources of mighty rivers, we build an altar where a great stream suddenly bursts forth from a hidden source, we worship hot springs, and we deem lakes sacred because of their darkness or immeasurable depth.[71]

Seneca's articulation agrees with Heschel's account of religion as arising from awe or a sense of the sublime; it supports as well his claim that classical or pagan religion identified the sublime with nature or the world.

68. Heschel, *God in Search of Man*, 39.

69. Heschel, *God in Search of Man*, 88–89.

70. "To the Biblical man, the sublime is but a form in which the presence of God strikes forth. . . . To the Biblical man, the beauty of the world issued from the grandeur of God; His majesty towered beyond the breathtaking mystery of the universe. Rather . . . than praise the world for its beauty, he called upon the world to praise its Creator." Heschel, *God in Search of Man*, 95–96.

71. Quoted in Valerie M. Warrior, *Roman Religion: A Sourcebook* (Newburyport, MA: Focus Pub.; R. Pullins, 2002), 2.

In sum, both classical and biblical religion were awe-inspired responses to the sublime. But classical religion located the sublime *in* the world and treated *the world itself*—or at least some parts of it—as divine. By contrast, biblical religion posited that the sublime *transcended the world*. (This distinction will become centrally important in a later chapter.)

The Holy

In other passages, Heschel associated "the sublime" with "the holy."[72] In this respect, his view converged with the classic account by the German scholar Rudolf Otto in *The Idea of the Holy*.[73] The source of religion, Otto contended, was the direct experience of a transcendent reality: "the holy." This reality is not merely subjective; it is "felt as objective and outside the self" (11).

The holy is sui generis, Otto thought: neither the holy nor the experience of it is reducible or analyzable into anything else. At one point he impatiently declared that a reader who had never had "any deeply-felt religious experience" would be unable to understand his work and "is requested to read no further" (8). Nonetheless, Otto struggled to explicate the concept of the holy. He invented and analyzed suggestive terms (the "numinous," "mysterium tremendum" [7, 12]). And he offered a variety of imperfect analogies. The experience of the holy, he suggested, was akin to the sense of awe (14), or to the "horror and 'shudder' in ghost stories" (16), or to the sense of "the sublime" (42), or to the feeling of the erotic (48), or to the "blissful rejoicing" experienced when listening to beautiful music (49).[74]

In a similar vein, the historian of religions Mircea Eliade, in his influential book *The Sacred and the Profane*, connected religion to a sense of, and a commitment to, the "sacred." The sacred represents a different kind or order

---

72. E.g., Heschel, *God in Search of Man*, 117.

73. Rudolf Otto, *The Idea of the Holy: An Inquiry into the Non-Rational Factor in the Idea of the Divine*, trans. John W. Harvey, rev. ed. (Whitefish, MT: Kessinger Publishing, [1917] 2010). Hereafter, page references from this work will be given in parentheses in the text.

74. Otto contended that the holy designated both a transcendent reality and a category of value (Otto, *Idea of the Holy*, 52). "Especially as encountered by mystics, the holy is experienced in its essential, positive, and specific character as something that bestows upon man a beatitude beyond compare, but one whose real nature he can neither proclaim in speech nor conceive in thought. . . . It is a bliss which embraces all those blessings that are indicated or suggested in positive fashion by any 'doctrine of Salvation.' . . . It gives the Peace that passes understanding, and of which the tongue can only stammer brokenly" (33–34).

of being; it is "the manifestation of something of a wholly different order, a reality that does not belong to our world."[75] To the religious person, "the world becomes apprehensible as world, as cosmos, in the measure in which it reveals itself as a sacred world."[76]

Meaning and Sublimity, Need and Truth

We have considered two different accounts of what "religion" is and of how it grows out of human nature and experience. In one account, humans have a need for "meaning," and this need is satisfied, ultimately, by a metanarrative that explains what the point of the "drama of Time" is and how humans fit into that drama. In a second account, religion arises as a response to the human encounter, which might or might not be pleasant, with another Reality—a Reality typically described with terms like "sublimity," "sacred," or "holy," and contrasted with ordinary mundane or "profane" reality. A person is "religious" insofar as he or she discerns such a "sacred" reality, respects it, and tries to live in harmony with or in conformity to it.

This second sense is very close to the definition proposed by William James: "Religion . . . shall mean for us *the feelings, acts, and experiences of individual men in their solitude, so far as they apprehend themselves to stand in relation to whatever they may consider the divine.*"[77] James is sometimes criticized for defining religion in the purely individualist terms of "individual men in their solitude" (although in fact he acknowledged religion's communal dimension and explained that he was merely not focusing his lectures on that aspect).[78] We will return to the point, briefly. With that qualification, James's definition captures a central sense of religion as a relation to the holy or the sacred.

Though different, the "meaning" and "sacredness" accounts seem fully compatible, even convergent. In the religious view, the sacred Reality that is the source or locus of sublimity is also what confers "meaning" on the world; we will return to the point shortly. In addition, although the "meaning" ac-

---

75. Mircea Eliade, *The Sacred and the Profane: The Nature of Religion*, trans. Willard R. Trask (Orlando: Harcourt, 1957), 11.

76. Eliade, *Sacred and the Profane*, 64 (emphasis deleted).

77. James, *Varieties of Religious Experience*, 39. James acknowledged the institutional nature of religion.

78. James, *Varieties of Religious Experience*, 37.

count seems to arise from a human *need*—the need for meaning—while the sublimity account starts with *truth*, or the encounter with something that is Real, these approaches are in the end nicely complementary.

That is because, in the religious perspective, the observation that we need something can have evidentiary significance; it can be a clue to the nature of the drama in which we are acting. The fact of *need* is thus pertinent to the question of *truth*. The connection of need to truth—or, if you like, the evidentiary significance of human need—was perhaps most insistently and eloquently pressed in recent times by C. S. Lewis.[79] Lewis perceived in human loves and pursuits and emotions—in our pursuit of beauty, in our romantic or nostalgic yearnings for a purer time or better condition—a desire for a good that no merely mundane activities and achievements can ever fully supply.[80] This desire suggested to Lewis that we are creatures oriented to some higher good—to a "transtemporal, transfinite good [that is] our real destiny," or to "our own far-off country, in which we find ourselves even now."[81] And then Lewis confronted the objection that the *fact* of desire does not entail the possibility of any *satisfaction* of desire.

> We remain conscious of a desire which no natural happiness will satisfy. But is there any reason to suppose that reality offers any satisfaction to it? "Nor does the being hungry prove that we have bread." But I think it may be urged that this misses the point. A man's physical hunger does not prove that man will get any bread; he may die of starvation on a raft in the Atlantic. But surely a man's hunger does prove that he comes of a race which repairs its body by eating and inhabits a world where eatable substances exist. In the same way, though I do not believe (I wish I did) that my desire for Paradise proves that I shall enjoy it, I think it a pretty good indication that such a thing exists and that some men will. A man may love a woman and not win her; but it would be very odd if the phenomenon called "falling in love" occurred in a sexless world.[82]

79. For an exposition, see Peter J. Kreeft, "C. S. Lewis's Argument from Desire," in *The Riddle of Joy*, ed. Michael H. Macdonald and Andrew A. Tadie (Grand Rapids: Eerdmans, 1989), 249.

80. See, e.g., C. S. Lewis, "The Weight of Glory," in *The Weight of Glory and Other Addresses*, rev. ed. (New York: HarperCollins/HarperOne, 1949), 25–34.

81. Lewis, "The Weight of Glory," 29.

82. Lewis, "The Weight of Glory," 32–33.

To the skeptic, Lewis's argument will likely seem question begging. If we begin by assuming some overall purposeful design in the world, then the fact of desire may well be a clue to that purpose and design. Conversely, if we do not begin by assuming any such purpose or design, or if we look at the world as the product of random, evolutionary natural selection, then it is not hard to imagine that creatures (namely, us) might evolve with desires and needs for which there is no satisfaction. We evolve with a sense of enjoyment or appreciation of life, perhaps—that quality might well be survival enhancing—and so we naturally project that enjoyment forward and thereby conceive a desire, say, to live forever. But it would not follow that any such possibility exists.

So the skeptic will think that Lewis's argument from desire begs the questions. To be sure, the believer might make a parallel objection against the skeptic. Skeptics, that is, may triumphantly point out that religion satisfies a deep human need and suppose that they have somehow discredited religion or shown it to be mere wishful thinking.[83] But the epistemic inefficacy of human need follows only if one begins by assuming that there is *not* any overall drama or design.

In the end, the fact of a need—for meaning, for comfort, for guidance, . . . for everlasting life—seems compatible with either a believing or a skeptical position, but arguments *to* either position from the fact of need or desire seem to work by assuming what is at issue—namely, that there is or there is not some overall design, of which human desires might be one piece of evidence. The upshot is that the conception of religion as a truth-oriented response to a human encounter with a higher Reality—the sublime, the holy—seems more fundamental, while the need- and meaning-based account seems complementary to but dependent on that more fundamental account. A religious metanarrative may speak to the need for meaning, but that need does not in itself give us grounds to suppose that the metanarrative is actually true. Those grounds must come from elsewhere—perhaps from some sort of actual encounter with the holy.

The Imperative of Consecration

In either the "meaning" or "sublimity" versions, religion serves a similar function: it serves to *consecrate*. Consecration is typically thought of as something done to a priest, or perhaps a king, or to a ritual object, endow-

83. See Freud, *The Future of an Illusion*.

ing these with a sacred quality and setting them apart for the performance of sacred functions. Literally, the word "consecration" means "association with the sacred"; to "consecrate" is thus to "sacralize" or to sanctify—to bring something into alignment with the sacred.[84]

And why is consecration so imperative? In the "meaning" version of religion, the sacred is the source of "ultimate meaning" from which lower or more mundane realities gain their meaningfulness. Previously, we have explained the "meaning" that humans seek, or the Meaning, in terms of a metanarrative or cosmic drama. But that Meaning might also be thought of in terms of a sort of higher or more ultimate Reality that would serve to redeem or give significance—or "meaning"—to the otherwise ephemeral, quotidian, and apparently pointless occurrences of mortal life. Consecration, or association with the sacred, thus gives a thing—an object, an event, a life, a world—its purpose, its meaning.

In the religious perspective, William James explained, "the visible world is part of a more spiritual universe from which it draws its chief significance."[85] Consequently, "when we see all things in God, and refer all things to him, we read in common matters superior expressions of meaning. The deadness with which custom invests the familiar vanishes, and existence as a whole appears transfigured."[86] Unconsecrated reality, conversely, would become meaningless: "sound and fury signifying nothing."

In the "sublimity" account of religion, similarly, consecration endows the world and its contents—people, animals, mountains, seas, birds, flowers—with beauty, sublimity, enchantment. Conversely, if the world is unconsecrated, or desecrated, it becomes just a collection of brute facts without meaning or majesty. In this vein, Abraham Heschel asserted that "without [sublimity], the world becomes flat and the soul a vacuum."[87]

Heschel's analogy suggests a previously three-dimensional world now crushed down to two dimensions—the depths, the heights, the mountains and valleys now leveled away. As an alternative analogy, imagine a movie with the musical sound track deleted. Visually, the same actions occur, but something is missing—something that helped to endow the movie with mys-

84. See Otto, *Idea of the Holy*, 56; Eliade, *Sacred and the Profane*, 17, 30, 32.

85. James, *Varieties of Religious Experience*, 418.

86. James, *Varieties of Religious Experience*, 409. Cf. E. L. Mascall, *The Christian Universe* (London: Darton, Longman and Todd, 1966), 47–48 (suggesting that "behind and beyond the world that our senses perceive, there is another realm of being which, . . . in some way or another, confers explanation upon the world of our senses and gives meaning to human life").

87. Heschel, *God in Search of Man*, 36.

tery and joy, romance and suspense. An unconsecrated world would be a world with no musical score.

Mircea Eliade described what consecration adds to the world, for the religious, in even stronger terms—in terms of "being."

> Religious man can live only in a sacred world, because it is only in such a world that he participates in being, that he has a *real existence*. This religious need expresses an unquenchable ontological thirst. Religious man thirsts for *being*. His terror of the chaos that surrounds his inhabited world corresponds to his terror of nothingness. The unknown space that extends beyond his world—an uncosmicized because unconsecrated space, a mere amorphous extent into which no orientation has yet been projected, and hence in which no structure has yet arisen—for religious man, this profane space represents absolute nonbeing. If, by some evil chance, he strays into it, he feels emptied of his ontic substance, as if he were dissolving in Chaos, and he finally dies.[88]

In the religious perspective, in short, consecration or association with the sacred is imperative because it is what gives life and the world meaning, beauty, order—even being. A sense of the subtle and yet vast qualitative difference between a consecrated and an unconsecrated world is probably most evident to the person who has lived in both—who has gone over from unbelief to a genuine faith, or vice versa. Tolstoy's autobiographical account is an instance of the first kind of transition—from a paralyzing meaninglessness to a meaningful faith. Conversely, those who have felt pushed away from religion—by reflecting on the ubiquity of suffering, maybe, or by what they take to be the implications of science—will sometimes have a tragic sense of what has been lost. It may be as if a world that once resonated with music and glowed with color has lost these enchanting qualities, and has thus become drab and empty.

Conversely, to the person who has always lived comfortably in the unconsecrated world, the supposed difference is likely to seem unreal or illusory. The matter-of-fact world has whatever meaning we choose to give it; that is all it ever had, or could have. The world is beautiful in the only way it could be beautiful. And to say, as Eliade put it (not for himself but for "religious man"), that the unconsecrated world would decline into nonbeing will

88. Eliade, *Sacred and the Profane*, 64.

seem starkly absurd. Here that world is, all around us. Here we are, smack in the middle of it. No problem of "nonbeing" here! Rejection of the sacred and the constraints it imposes will seem not tragic but rather liberating—like waking up from a misty dream (even a pleasant dream) and seeing the world for the rich and solid if unenchanted reality it is.

And yet, even the comfortably unconsecrated person may at times have a sense that something is lost or missing. She may read old literature and sense with a twinge of regret the "disenchantment of the world," as Weber put it;[89] or be like a person who never heard music and was happy enough but who then, momentarily catching the strains of a distant melody, wonders whether there might in fact be some whole dimension of sublimity to which she has somehow not been privy. Even the confidently unconsecrated man may find himself paralyzed by a crisis of meaninglessness, as John Stuart Mill did.[90] And, like Mill, he may try to find some substitute for the sublimity of sacredness in nature or literature, or perhaps in some lover whom he heroically but implausibly endows with almost divine qualities (as Mill did with his lover and later wife, Harriet Taylor). Commenting on Mill's "Harriet-worship," A. N. Wilson quotes Mill's friend Alexander Bain, who observed that "no such combination [of virtues as Mill attributed to Taylor] has ever been realized in the whole history of the human race."[91] And Wilson adds that "as [Mill's] encomiums of Harriet Taylor remind us, the human race can easily deprive itself of Christianity, but finds it rather more difficult to lose its capacity for worship."[92]

Death is the stark, inescapable fact that sometimes brings on this sense of the need for . . . for what? For something beyond the profane facts of secular existence, perhaps. In a short essay called "An Awareness of What Is Missing," the philosopher Jürgen Habermas recalls attending the memorial service for the Swiss playwright Max Frisch. Frisch was an agnostic, and his service was accordingly conducted without any priest or prayer. The service was attended mostly by "intellectuals, most of whom had little time for church and religion." Nonetheless, at Frisch's direction the service was held

89. See, e.g., *From Max Weber: Essays in Sociology*, ed. and trans. H. H. Gerth and C. Wright Mills (New York: Oxford University Press, 1946), 155 ("The fate of our times is characterized by rationalization and intellectualization and, above all, by the 'disenchantment of the world'").

90. J. S. Mill, "A Crisis in My Mental History—One Stage Onward," in *The Autobiography of John Stuart Mill* (Rockville, MD: Arc Manor, [1873] 2008), chap. 5.

91. A. N. Wilson, *God's Funeral* (New York: Norton, 1999), 51.

92. Wilson, *God's Funeral*, 52.

at Saint Peter's Church in Zurich, and it included a statement from Frisch thanking the ministers of Saint Peter's for permission to use the church. Habermas surmises that Frisch's choice of a church amounted to a public declaration "that the enlightened modern age has failed to find a suitable replacement for a religious way of coping with the final *rite de passage* which brings life to a close."[93]

Or we might say that the church reflected a last, touching effort to *consecrate* the life being memorialized.

Divergent Desiderata

For those who (unlike Frisch and Habermas) affirmatively embrace a religious view of life, the imperative of consecration provides a different order of desiderata to direct and regulate life. In the interest-seeking conception, goods are additive in nature, and choices are instrumentalist and calculative. Making decisions about how to live is like filling in and adding up the credits and debits on a perpetual, ever-unfolding balance sheet. Hence the seemingly ubiquitous efforts of contemporary academics to explain human behavior in terms of rational choice calculations, game theory, and cost-benefit analyses.

In a religious perspective, by contrast, the crucial imperative is to maintain the association with the sacred that is the source of meaning, beauty, possibly even being, and this imperative gives rise to a different order of desiderata that must be honored in a wholly different way. The decisive consideration now is to become and remain in harmony with the holy—with the Reality that gives meaning and purpose and sublimity to life. "Were one asked to characterize the life of religion in the broadest and most general terms possible," William James observed, "one might say that it consists of the belief that there is an unseen order, and that our supreme good lies in harmoniously adjusting ourselves thereto."[94] And so the religious person strives for sanctity, or *purity*, which is necessary to sustain that harmony.[95]

93. Jürgen Habermas, "An Awareness of What Is Missing," in *An Awareness of What Is Missing: Faith and Reason in a Post-Secular Age*, trans. Ciaran Cronin (Cambridge: Polity Press, 2010), 15.

94. James, *Varieties of Religious Experience*, 57. See also 418 (summing up the religious life as founded in the beliefs that "the visible world is part of a more spiritual universe from which it draws its chief significance" and that "union or harmonious relation with that higher world is our true end").

95. James, *Varieties of Religious Experience*, 255–62.

The opposite of *consecration* is of course *desecration*, and so the religious person seeks to avoid impurity, or corruption, or pollution, that would negate or undermine the association with the sacred. Rather than a calculation of costs and benefits, life is more analogous to a cherished personal relationship, in which one strives to show loyalty and love—and to avoid even small insults, betrayals, or gestures of disrespect, however slight the material cost might be.

This emphasis on purity and fidelity naturally calls upon different sorts of cognitive operations than does a focus on interest satisfaction. As noted, the pursuit of interests invokes a calculating, instrumentalist kind of reasoning. But the religious vocation is not at its core calculative or instrumentalist. It may be more analogous to a sort of aesthetic judgment or sensibility, in which one discerns what colors in a painting or what chords in a musical composition would support or instead disrupt the desired harmony. Or, if one believes (as in many religions) that directives have issued from the holy—in a sacred scripture, perhaps—then the religious vocation may call for a hermeneutical reasoning that seeks the true interpretation of what the directives mean and entail.[96]

The divergences in the desiderata sponsored by the interest-seeking and religious conceptions help to explain two other, often noticed differences between secular and religious approaches to living. First, in the religious mode, feelings, or perhaps what William James described as a kind of "cosmic emotion,"[97] are likely to play a vital role.[98] Once again, the religious mode is anchored in the sense of sublimity, as Heschel contended, or in the discernment of "the holy." Such discernment, as Otto emphasized, is not a purely "rational" operation. It is not *irrational*, he stressed, and indeed the response to the holy is typically elaborated and developed in highly rational forms;[99] nonetheless, the basic experience of the holy is not a merely intellectual operation.

The imperfect analogies we have employed here would underscore Otto's claim. Thus, a personal relationship, with a friend or a spouse or a lover, may have a rational dimension, but it is unlikely to flourish unless it is also

96. Even here, though, a sort of quasi-aesthetic sensibility may be needed to separate the "spirit" from the "letter" of the directives. See, e.g., 2 Cor. 3:6.

97. James, *Varieties of Religious Experience*, 79.

98. See James, *Varieties of Religious Experience*, 36 (discussing "the many sentiments which religious objects may arouse . . . [including] religious fear, religious love, religious awe, religious joy, and so forth").

99. Otto, *Idea of the Holy*, 1–4.

grounded in and supported by the partners' affective or emotional nature. Similarly, the aesthetic response to a beautiful painting or a musical masterpiece is not a merely intellectual operation. We would be inclined to say that someone who can meticulously explain and analyze, say, a Bach concerto, but who feels no emotional response to it, has missed the real concerto altogether.

Second, the differences in the interest-seeking and religious desiderata help to explain why the latter are deemed to have a kind of priority over the former and a kind of categorical quality. To slight or neglect an "interest" means merely that a person has somewhat less of some good. He is a dollar (or a million dollars) poorer than he would have been. But to disobey or disregard the demands of the sacred—to "desecrate" it—is to disrupt a relation upon which meaning, beauty, even (as Eliade suggested) "being" depend. Religious pursuits thus display a kind of zeal and passion, and a kind of absolutist quality, that seems foreign—and perhaps puzzling or irrational—to the mundane pursuer of "interests."

Even for the devout, no doubt, much of life is still given over to the instrumentalist pursuit of "interests"—to building the house and planting the crops, to working to achieve health and wealth and power. But these interest-pursuing activities must be performed within the framework and subject to the constraints of the sacred, with its injunctions and prohibitions. After all, what good would it do to become wealthy and powerful while cutting oneself off from the source of meaning and beauty and even being? "What doth it profit a man if he shall gain the whole world and lose his own soul?"[100]

As an analogy, think of a scholar who travels to a distant city to participate in an academic conference. The scholar may attempt during the trip to satisfy various wants and needs—to stay at a comfortable hotel, to have dinner with friends at a recommended restaurant, to take in the scenic or historical attractions of the city—but these preferences must not be permitted to interfere with the central purpose of the trip. The scholar may make choices among hotels or restaurants on the basis of personal preferences. But if the real and central purpose of the trip is to participate in the conference, then one thing the scholar must *not* do is schedule scenic trips or get-togethers with friends during the crucial sessions of the conference; to do that would be to defeat the whole purpose of the trip. So that desideratum, in contrast to all the others, is categorical. In a similar way, devout believers may have any number of subjective "interests" that they will seek to satisfy, but insofar

100. Mark 8:36.

as they are faithful to their understanding, they will not let these "interests" interfere with their religious obligations.

These implications of "religion" are widely perceived, and they are reflected in everyday usages of the term "religion." "Do you attend the symphony?" I ask, and you respond, "Yes, I do. Religiously." I understand that you are thereby expressing a kind of extraordinary, almost categorical commitment—one you do not merely assent to but about which you also feel a kind of passion.

To be sure, this description simplifies, as any description of life does, and idealizes. The messier reality is that the believer holds that he *should* always prefer religious goods and duties over more mundane interests. That is the believer's conviction and aspiration. But like most aspirations, it is not fully realized. "There is no one righteous; not even one."[101] The believer thus covenants to practice her faith, fails, regrets her failure, resolves to reform, *does* reform, then fails again, regrets again, and so forth. Such is the familiar, bumpy career of the religious life. The believer's life is not primarily devoted to "interests" in the conventional sense—and yet interests are always crowding in.

But then we might ask: Is something similarly true of the nonreligious, interest-seeking life? The nonbeliever *thinks* he may pursue his interests unimpeded by (illusory) "religious" values or mandates. But do such desiderata influence him nonetheless?

Religion and Personhood

We will revisit the question. For now, though, the question touches on a possible criticism of the basic argument of this chapter. Setting out to propose an alternative to the "interest-seeking" conception of the person, the chapter has elaborated a different, "religious" conception—a conception of, as William James put it, "man's religious constitution."[102] But this conception doesn't seem to fit *all* human beings: some people are religious, we say, and others aren't. Can qualities that only some people have, but that cannot be attributed to persons generally, support an account of human personhood?

To this criticism, either an audacious or a more conciliatory response might be given. The audacious response would contend that whether they

101. Rom. 3:10.
102. James, *Varieties of Religious Experience*, 5.

know it or not, all people *are* religious. A religious impulse or inclination is lurking in everybody, perhaps in the person's subconscious, or in the inherited customs and habits that help to constitute the person. Viktor Frankl sometimes advanced the first version of this claim; Mircea Eliade sometimes proposed the second version.

Thus, just as his Freudian counterparts attributed much in human psychology to the repressed sexual urges, Frankl argued on the basis of his own clinical experience that many people repress their religious inclinations. But such inclinations surface in the course of sustained therapy; there is, Frankl asserted, an "unconscious religiousness" and a "latent relation to transcendence" discernible even in people who believe themselves to be wholly secular.[103] Frankl thus proclaimed the "omnipresence of religion": "a religious sense is existent and present in each and every person, albeit buried, not to say repressed, in the unconscious."[104]

Eliade perceived a continuing and widespread religiosity in people's customs and habits. While acknowledging the fact of secularization in the modern world, Eliade added that "nonreligious man in the pure state is a comparatively rare phenomenon, even in the most desacralized of societies. The majority of the 'irreligious' still behave religiously, even though they are not aware of the fact. . . . Modern man who feels and claims that he is nonreligious still retains a large stock of camouflaged myths and degenerated rituals."[105]

A version of the audacious response can be grounded in theological assumptions. Augustine famously began his spiritual autobiography, written in the form of a confession to God, by declaring that "thou hast made us for thyself, and restless is our heart until it comes to rest in thee."[106] Not everyone feels this restlessness with the same sharpness, perhaps—here Pascal's gloomy reflections on men's tendency to use diversions like gambling, sports, work, and warfare to avoid noticing their existential condition, or their "wretchedness," might be pertinent[107]—and of course, not everyone

103. Frankl, *Man's Search for Meaning*, 68. Frankl emphasized, however, that he used the term "religion" "in the widest possible sense" and in a way that "goes far beyond the narrow concepts of God promulgated by many representatives of denominational and institutional religion" (17).

104. Frankl, *Man's Search for Meaning*, 152, 151.

105. Eliade, *Sacred and the Profane*, 204–5.

106. Augustine, *The Confessions of St. Augustine*, ed. and trans. Albert Cook Outler, rev. ed. (New York: Dover, 2002), 1.1.

107. Blaise Pascal, *Pensées*, trans. A. J. Krailsheimer, rev. ed. (London: Penguin, 1995), 37–43.

who does feel such restlessness will connect it to the absence of the sacred. Augustine was perfectly aware of these facts; indeed, his *Confessions* is basically a record of how he himself made the connection only gradually and after repeated false starts, mistaken interpretations, and misguided choices. But, in this view, whether we know it or not, the connection to the sacred—to God—is necessary and real for all of us.

These assertions will seem uncompelling, of course, and possibly offensive, to unbelievers. More generally, the audacious claim that all persons have a religious dimension or inclination whether they know it or not will likely seem implausible and insulting to people (such as a friend and colleague with whom I was just yesterday discussing the question) who feel quite sure that they know their own minds, and that there is no religious belief, inclination, need, or gap anywhere there to be found. The theologian E. L. Mascall observed that "nothing . . . should prevent us, as believers, from holding that God is at work, so to speak anonymously, even in the minds and lives of those who disbelieve in him; but we must not exasperate them by refusing to take them seriously in their unbelief."[108]

For our purposes, fortunately, we need not try to decide whether the audacious claim is defensible (an issue on which agreement seems unlikely). It is enough, rather, to offer a weaker and more conciliatory claim—namely, that religiosity of the kind discussed here is a sufficiently important and widespread feature of *many* human beings that we will understand human history and behavior better by taking that feature into account than by ignoring it, or by trying to dissolve it without remainder into something else—like "interests" as usually conceived.

So let us stipulate, at least for the sake of argument, that the "religious" conception of human personhood does not apply to all individuals. In that respect, it is no different than other useful conceptions of personhood. Thus, the traditional assertion that "man is a rational animal" is not negated by the observable fact that many people often act irrationally, and that a few seem largely lacking in rational capacity. Similarly, claims that humans are "moral" beings,[109] or "economic" beings,[110] are not discredited by the existence of a few psychopaths or by the occasional ascetic hermit. In the same way, the conception of humans as "religious" beings who seek mean-

108. Mascall, *The Christian Universe*, 18.

109. See, e.g., Christian Smith, *Moral, Believing Animals* (New York: Oxford University Press, 2009).

110. See Posner, *Economic Analysis of Law*, 3-4.

ing and respond to perceptions of sublimity or the sacred is fully compatible with an uneven reality in which some humans are self-consciously and profoundly pious, others are tepidly and intermittently religious, and still others, as Thomas Nagel says of himself, "lack the *sensus divinitatus* that enables—indeed compels—so many others to see in the world the expression of divine purpose."[111]

Nor are the various conceptions of personhood in any way incompatible or mutually exclusive. *Homo religiosus* coexists with *homo economicus* . . . and with *homo ludens*, and *homo sociologicus*, and so forth—all of which descriptions fit some individuals better than others. Borrowing and adapting a formula, we might say that a human being is composed of two (or more) natures in one person. Moreover, the strength of these various natures surely varies from person to person. "Ought it to be assumed that in all men the mixture of religion with other elements should be identical?" William James asked, and then he replied to his own question: "I answer 'No' emphatically."[112]

Nonetheless, James concluded a celebrated lecture series by predicting that "religion, occupying herself with personal destinies and keeping thus in contact with the only absolute realities which we know, must necessarily play an eternal part in human history."[113] In a similar vein, the sociologist Émile Durkheim asserted that "the religious nature of man" is "an essential and permanent aspect of humanity."[114] If James and Durkheim were right, then an effort to understand our history and even our current situation—our so-called culture wars—that does not take full account of our religious dimension seems foreordained to fail, and to distort.

In sum, acknowledging the religious conception does nothing to negate the interest-seeking conception. That conception remains available, useful, powerful—but not exclusive. Recognition of the religious conception implies that some aspects of human behavior will be understood better in religious than in interest-seeking terms. Conversely, an insistence on explaining all aspects of behavior in interest-seeking terms is likely to lead to a distorted and impoverished understanding of human and social and political phenomena.

111. Thomas Nagel, *Mind and Cosmos: Why the Materialist Neo-Darwinian Conception of Nature Is Almost Certainly False* (New York: Oxford University Press, 2012), 12.

112. James, *Varieties of Religious Experience*, 419.

113. James, *Varieties of Religious Experience*, 431.

114. Émile Durkheim, *The Elementary Forms of the Religious Life*, trans. Karen E. Fields (New York: Free Press, [1912] 1995), 1.

The Communal Dimension

In this chapter, we have mostly followed William James in focusing on what religion is and does for individual human beings. It would be wrong to end the chapter, though, without acknowledging that religion often has a communal dimension—a communal dimension that, though perhaps neither necessary nor sufficient to constitute "religion," seems more than merely incidental or aggregative.

Community is not strictly necessary for religion, it seems, because a person *might* encounter the sacred and find meaning just on his or her own. Indeed, religion sometimes can produce a sort of *antisocial* impulse; the imperative of purity can drive the believer away from the corruptions of human society. Saint Antony leaves society and retreats into the desert.[115] Jesus had done the same thing—for a period.[116] Saint Simeon Stylites sits apart atop his Syrian pillar for thirty-seven years (though he depends on followers and admirers to bring him sustenance). Roger Williams, the great champion of freedom of conscience, though evidently gregarious by nature, is moved in his quest for purity to separate himself, first from the Church of England, then from his Massachusetts Bay brethren, then from his more religiously stringent Plymouth congregation, eventually from his wife.[117] Williams's progressive flight from community is reflected in the chapter headings of Edwin Gaustad's sympathetic biography: "Exile from England," "Exile from Massachusetts," "Exile in London," "Exile from the Church," "Exile from the World."[118]

More commonly, though, religion pulls the faithful together. They found a church, a monastery, a synagogue, a temple. They feel that they cannot fully realize their religious aspirations except in union. The reclusive monks of the desert, like Antony, are succeeded by orders of Benedictines, later of Dominicans and Franciscans and Jesuits, living and worshiping together.

Moreover, the religious union is more than merely a mutual assistance society, or an enterprise in which collective efforts can better achieve each person's individual goals. If you need to move a boulder, you will be prudent to enlist the aid of other people—especially other strong people—but the

---

115. See generally Athanasius, *The Life of Antony and the Letter to Marcellinus*, trans. and ed. Robert C. Gregg, Classics of Western Spirituality (Mahwah, NJ: Paulist, 1980).

116. Matt. 4:1–11.

117. See Steven D. Smith, "Separation and the Fanatic," *Virginia Law Review* 85 (1999): 238.

118. Edwin S. Gaustad, *Liberty of Conscience: Roger Williams in America* (Valley Forge, PA: Judson, 1991), vii.

value of the group effort is merely aggregative. One really strong man is just as good as two weak ones. The communal dimension of religion, it seems, is not like that. It is a union that is itself a sort of natural end or culmination of the believers' spiritual imperatives.

"Where two or three of you are gathered together," Jesus tells his followers, "there will I be in the midst of you."[119] And the church founded by and around Jesus is not just a voluntary association devoted to remembering him and attempting to live by his teachings. It in a sense *is* Christ; it is "the body of Christ." Or so the faithful believe.[120]

This communal dimension of religion can be viewed as a means of expressing or fulfilling one central aspect of human personhood—namely, sociality. Humans are naturally social animals, Aristotle observed, and the individual who feels no need of society is not quite a man but is "either a beast or a god."[121] Just in itself, though, this social dimension can be satisfied by all manner of groups—families, teams, business partnerships, political parties, bowling leagues, book clubs, bird-watching societies. A religious community is both like and unlike these other associations. It is a form of human society, yes. But it is a society in which the propensity to fellowship converges with the need for meaning and the sense of the holy.

Community, we might say, tends to perfect or complete religion, and, conversely, religion can serve to perfect or complete community. To *consecrate* community. A community bound together around a shared sense of meaning and a shared commitment to the sacred has a more profound connection than one committed, say, to some important but mundane goal, like making a profit or securing passage of a piece of legislation. Persons in a religious community are bound together, we might say, at a more fundamental level of their being.

This emphasis on the communal dimension may go against the grain of modern individualist thinking that sees religion as something for or by "the individual in his solitude," as William James put it. But the communal dimension would have seemed utterly obvious to peoples of the ancient world. For them, it was the isolated believer who would have seemed anomalous. Religion—or what *we* would call "religion" in their world, because they likely would not have used or perhaps even understood the term—was

---

119. Matt. 18:20.

120. E.g., 1 Cor. 12:27.

121. Aristotle, *Politics*, trans. Ernest Barker (New York: Oxford University Press, 1962), 1.1253a.

inherently connected to temples, rituals, processions, theatrical spectacles, mass gatherings and entertainments, and cultic initiations.

In short, religion tended and tends to culminate in community. In, we might say, a *city*. This natural culmination is perhaps obscured for us today by familiar notions of "separation of church and state." But two thousand years ago, humans suffered from no such obstruction. Religion and the city went hand in hand; both practically and conceptually, the city and its religion were essentially inseparable. In the next chapter, we will consider what was surely the most glorious example of this union.

CHAPTER 3

City of the Gods

If you were asked what was the best period of human history to live in, what time and place would you choose? Swinging New York in Gatsby's "Roaring Twenties"? The Elizabethan England of Shakespeare and Ben Jonson? The Florence of Leonardo, Michelangelo, and Lorenzo the Magnificent? Periclean Athens? Kublai Khan's resplendent Cathay? India under the wise and benevolent Ashoka?

For Edward Gibbon, celebrated eighteenth-century historian of the Roman Empire, friend of luminaries like Hume and Voltaire, and faithful representative of Enlightenment sensibilities, the answer was obvious:

> If a man were called upon to fix the period in the history of the world, during which the history of the human race was most happy and prosperous, he would, without hesitation, name that which elapsed from the death of Domitian to the accession of Commodus [i.e., from AD 96 to 180]. The vast extent of the Roman empire was governed by absolute power, under the guidance of virtue and wisdom. The armies were restrained by the firm but gentle hand of four successive emperors, whose character and authority commanded involuntary respect. The forms of the civil administration were carefully preserved by Nerva, Trajan, Hadrian, and the Antonines, who delighted in the image of liberty, and were pleased with considering themselves the accountable ministers of the laws. . . .
>
> The labours of these monarchs were over-paid by . . . the exquisite delight of beholding the general happiness of which they were the authors.[1]

---

1. Edward Gibbon, *The History of the Decline and Fall of the Roman Empire*, 2 vols. (London: Penguin, [1776] 1995), 1:103.

In short, the period was a "golden age."[2]

Gibbon was idiosyncratic in his intensity, perhaps, and also in his specificity, but not in his general sentiment. Adulation of the classical world—of "the glory that was Greece and the grandeur that was Rome"[3]—has been a recurring theme among Western thinkers.[4] Indeed, at least since the Renaissance, an effort to reclaim or reconstruct the ethos and *civitas* of classical antiquity has been—and continues to be (though perhaps less overtly, as Virgil, Ovid, and Cicero fade from the curriculum)—a shaping influence in the formation of the Western world.

But why? The Antonine emperors may have been admirable rulers, comparatively speaking; their reign may stand out as a relative bright spot in a world history that sometimes seems, as Gibbon put it, "little more than the register of the crimes, follies, and misfortunes of mankind."[5] Still, to assert without qualification that "a man"—any man, in other words; and, as we will see, the masculine gender is apt here—would "without hesitation" prefer that period over all others seems an audacious claim. So, what was it about the period that made it so "golden"? What was the basis of the "general happiness" that Gibbon discerned, or thought he discerned?

"Every Refinement of Conveniency, of Elegance, and of Splendour"

Gibbon's effusive declaration supplies one reason: the period was "prosperous." This prosperity was a natural result of the Pax Romana, and of the trade permeating the "vast extent of the Roman empire." In this respect, the empire achieved the same commercial goals sought after by international political and trade agreements today. On a material level, consequently, life was good in this period, at least for the affluent—for people, basically, of the same class to which Gibbon himself[6] and his

---

2. Gibbon, *History of the Decline*, 1:104.

3. Edgar Allan Poe, "To Helen," in *The Complete Poetry of Edgar Allan Poe* (New York: Signet Classics, 2008), 66.

4. Cf. Norman F. Cantor, *Antiquity: From the Birth of Sumerian Civilization to the Fall of the Roman Empire* (New York: HarperCollins, 2003), 28 ("Yet the Roman Empire of 150 A.D. was a glorious thing, to be long remembered as a golden age").

5. Gibbon, *History of the Decline*, 1:102.

6. See, e.g., Edward Gibbon, *Memoirs of My Life*, trans. Betty Radice (London: Penguin, 1984), 174 ("According to the scale of Switzerland, I am a rich man; and I am indeed rich, since my income is superior to my expense, and my expense is equal to my wishes").

readers belonged in their own eighteenth-century world. Nor was material affluence merely crass; it was matched by a kind of cultural abundance and elegance.

So let us suppose that you are so fortunate as to belong to the affluent class in the age of the Antonine emperors. Like Gibbon, you are wealthy enough, let's say, but not extravagantly rich—not so rich that you can afford a palazzo or a sprawling country villa. Even so, you might reside in an elegantly decorated home comparable to those that can be visited today in archeologically restored Pompeii[7]—a *domus* nicely adorned with stately columns, an interior decorative pool in the atrium just inside the front entrance, colorful mosaics and murals, sculptures imported from Greece, and graceful gardens ornamented with (as a more recent historian reports) "shrubs, fountains, decorative statuettes, and often frescoes on the enclosing walls" (737). The furniture filling out your home will include bronze or marble tables "supported by elaborate legs compounded of lions' paws, volutes, griffins' foreparts, and the like" (731).

On a warm summer evening, you and your guests might enjoy a leisurely dinner out of doors, in enchanting fashion. "Sheltered by an awning or a vine-arbour and cushioned by mattresses and pillows, the diners would recline on their elbows in the Greek manner, picking titbits from a central table or, like Pliny's guests, from floating dishes in the form of little boats and water-birds; as night drew on, lamps would be lit in surrounding candelabra, some of them . . . suspended from the hands of bronze statues" (739). The dinner fare is sumptuous, and exotic. "The guests were treated to a whole sequence of unnerving surprises: peahen's eggs containing beccaficos rolled in spiced egg-yolk, a wild boar containing live thrushes, a pig full of sausages and black puddings, cakes and fruit filled with liquid saffron, thrushes made of pastry and stuffed with raisins and nuts, quinces decorated with thorns to look like sea-urchins" (740).

And, of course, wine: "no meal was complete without a jar of a fine vintage." These culinary delights would be served up in "superb beakers, cups, bowls, and dishes decorated with repousse reliefs of plants, arabesques or mythological scenes, together with the simpler, but still elegant, spoons and ladles" (740).

---

7. For a nice description, see Roger Ling, "The Arts of Living," in *The Oxford History of the Classical World*, ed. John Boardman, Jasper Griffin, and Oswyn Murray (Oxford: Oxford University Press, 1986), 718. Hereafter, page references from this work will be given in parentheses in the text.

So far, what's not to like? (I admit with some embarrassment that I have no idea what beccaficos are, or quinces, or volutes—but I infer that they all would have been in impeccably good taste.)

If you feel like going out, you might join your fellow citizens and subjects as a spectator at a chariot race at the Circus Maximus. Or perhaps a stirring gladiatorial contest at the Flavian Amphitheater (later known as the Colosseum), where you will cheer wildly along with your fellow Romans at the hunt and slaughter of exotic animals imported from Africa; and you will feel the thrill and solidarity as you and your fellows collectively implore the emperor to give thumbs up or thumbs down to some hapless warrior.

But then again, maybe (like Gibbon, who shunned sports even as a clumsy schoolboy)[8] you are a more sedate soul, lacking a taste for these muscular and bloody spectacles. In that case, you might prefer to attend the theater. Or maybe relax at one of the vast and elegant public baths, designed for leisurely repose and conversation, with cold and warm baths, open spaces for exercising, and even libraries, and lavishly decorated with sculptures and intricate mosaics.

Returning home but not yet ready to sleep, you might curl up with a history by Tacitus or Livy, or with a play by Terence or Plautus (or of course, by one of the Greek masters). Or maybe a work of philosophy by Plato or Aristotle or, if you prefer, by a homegrown thinker—the estimable Cicero. Or perhaps some poetry—the majestic epics of Homer or Virgil, or if you are in the mood for something a little lighter, perhaps some amorous stanzas of Catullus to his lover Lesbia or the seduction poetry of Ovid.

Speaking of seduction: your sophisticated society perfectly understands and amply accommodates the more sensual necessities. Indeed, in the Roman idiom this is one popular euphemism for the male organ—"the necessity."[9] Overall, your world is, as Norman Cantor says, "a sexual paradise."[10] There are, to be sure, a few constraints. It is against the law to lie with your neighbor's wife, for example (though such indiscretions happen, possibly quite often), and although homosexual encounters are in themselves perfectly respectable, it is shameful and unmanly to take the passive role in such an exchange. We will say more about these restrictions in due course. For now, the important point is that there are no prudish or moralistic impedi-

8. Gibbon, *Memoirs*, 15, 18.
9. Kyle Harper, *From Shame to Sin: The Christian Transformation of Sexual Morality in Late Antiquity* (Cambridge, MA: Harvard University Press, 2013), 47.
10. Cantor, *Antiquity*, 29.

ments to sexual activity per se.[11] On the contrary, your society unashamedly celebrates—and stimulates, and amply provides for—sexual gratification.

So your own bedroom lamps or hand mirrors are most likely decorated with erotic images—quite imaginative ones, probably.[12] The walls in your atrium might exhibit a fresco similar to that restored in Pompeii—of the fertility god Priapus, with his enormous, ineluctable phallus straining to reach what appears to be a basket of fruit. Similar images adorn doorbells or doorposts, and also the walls of the changing rooms in the elegant public baths.[13] And the city maintains numerous, much-frequented brothels. In these establishments, sex is eminently affordable—about the price of a loaf of bread.[14]

True, as a member of the aristocracy, you may have reservations about taking your pleasures in brothels. Not because they are immoral, but because they are, well, "vulgar."[15] But not to worry: your Roman society smiles on the more elegant practice of having conjugal relations with slaves, which are plentiful—probably constituting about two-fifths of the city's population.[16] As an affluent Roman, you likely own an assortment of them, perhaps hundreds,[17] and since with slaves consent is conveniently not an issue,[18] the opportunities for sexual fulfillment are ample.[19]

We are assuming here, as is no doubt already apparent, that you are not only affluent but also male. For women, opportunities for sexual fulfillment are much more limited and the strictures for deviation more severe.[20] Much later—centuries later—this distinction will come to seem unfair. But the dif-

11. The point is emphasized in Geoffrey R. Stone, *Sex and the Constitution* (London: Norton, 2017), 4–12.

12. These would depict "one man and one woman on a bed . . . joined in carnal embrace," but also "same-sex pairings" and "elaborate sexual positions," or mythical scenes—Zeus posing as a swan with Leda—or perhaps "scenes of women with horses" or "scenes of men with donkeys." Harper, *From Shame to Sin*, 68.

13. See Keith Hopkins, *A World Full of Gods: The Strange Triumph of Christianity* (New York: Penguin, 1999), 209.

14. Harper, *From Shame to Sin*, 49.

15. Harper, *From Shame to Sin*, 49.

16. See Robin Lane Fox, *The Classical World: An Epic History from Homer to Hadrian* (New York: Basic Books, 2006), 461.

17. See Fox, *The Classical World*, 549 ("Pliny also had hundreds and hundreds of slaves, at least five hundred [to judge from his will] and no doubt many more").

18. See below, 77.

19. Harper, *From Shame to Sin*, 26–37, 45–46.

20. Harper, *From Shame to Sin*, 37–45.

ferent standards make excellent sense on the premises of your own society (which we will look at more closely in a few pages). Indeed, women themselves are among the most ardent defenders of the different sexual standards for men and women.[21]

So it all seems very gratifying. The criterion so often invoked by modern thinkers and ethicists to characterize the good life is "human flourishing." Just what "human flourishing" consists of is not obvious—the term is obligingly opaque—but whatever it means, wouldn't it seem amply to fit the sort of life in the Roman Empire that we have been observing? Gibbon thought so, at any rate; as he put it, "the favourites of fortune united every refinement of conveniency, of elegance, and of splendour; whatever could sooth their pride or gratify their sensuality."[22]

Of course, less laudatory assessments are also available. There will always be naysayers. So if we were to take our instruction from, say, the satirical poet Juvenal, writing during the period so admired by Gibbon, we might come away with a very different impression of Rome—as a city of perilous streets and fire-plagued tenement housing, a city pervasively indolent, hypocritical, and corrupt, stocked with licentious husbands and faithless, conniving wives, in which it is next to impossible to make an honest living.[23] A critic might also notice the pervasive, abject poverty. Robin Lane Fox observes that "the modern cardboard cities of refugees in Egypt or Pakistan are the nearest we can come to imagining this 'other Rome,' although they lack Rome's openly accepted slavery."[24] Rodney Stark describes the cities of the Roman Empire as "far more crowded, crime infested, filthy, disease-ridden, and miserable than are third world cities in the world today."[25]

Or we might focus more severely on the bloody gladiatorial spectacles, in which thousands of humans and wild animals were routinely slaughtered for the entertainment of, and with the delirious enthusiasm of, spectators both noble and plebeian. Gibbon did not approve of such shows—they "degraded a civilized nation below the condition of savage cannibals"[26]—but, always broad-minded, he did not allow this embarrassment to interfere with his overall favorable judgment.

21. See below, 76.
22. Gibbon, *History of the Decline*, 1:80.
23. Juvenal, *Satires*, trans. William Gifford (London: W. Bulmer and Co., 1802).
24. Fox, *The Classical World*, 462.
25. Rodney Stark, *The Triumph of Christianity: How the Jesus Movement Became the World's Largest Religion* (New York: HarperCollins, 2011), 106.
26. Gibbon, *History of the Decline*, 2:138.

There was also the widespread and socially accepted practice of exposure of infants: parents of unwanted or unhealthy children would abandon the babies on a street corner or outside the town, hoping that someone might come along to rescue the infants. The hope was not utterly unrealistic: in fact, a few such foundlings might be claimed, often to be brought up as slaves or prostitutes. But more often the babies perished.[27] Philo of Alexandria described how "all the beasts that feed upon human flesh visit the spot and feast unhindered on the infants."[28] Again, Gibbon did not approve[29]—but neither did he amend his laudatory assessment of the city. Other evaluators, of course, might be less lenient toward these societal blemishes.

But we need not try to adjudicate between Gibbon's extravagantly positive assessment and the bleaker depictions by critics like Juvenal. Our policy here, and throughout, will be to take a sympathetic view: we come to praise Rome, not to bury it. Classical Rome, like modern Rome—or modern New York or London or Paris—had the stuff to support both favorable and less favorable appraisals; it all depends on what we choose to look at or, conversely, to excuse or ignore. Our immediate purpose here is to understand what it was in that world that could elicit the Enlightenment historian's effusive judgment. And we see that by focusing on selected classes and aspects of the period, we can find material to support that assessment. For the "favourites of fortune," it seems to have been a pleasant time to be alive.

The Majesty of the City

The foregoing catalogue of material comforts and carnal indulgences has been seriously misleading, though, and it has in fact *understated* Rome's grandeur if it has left the impression that your life as an affluent Roman would have been entirely given over to self-gratification. On the contrary, you would have felt an acute sense of your relation and responsibilities to your city, to the public, and to the emperors (to whom you would have offered sacrifices, as deities). And you would have taken a magnanimous pride in being a citizen of Rome—the stern but benevolent master of the world.

27. See O. M. Bakke, *When Children Became People: The Birth of Childhood in Early Christianity* (Minneapolis: Augsburg Fortress, 2005), 26–33.

28. Quoted in Bakke, *When Children Became People*, 112.

29. E.g., Gibbon, *History of the Decline*, 1:494.

Of *Rome*. The almost mystical name reached to both the city and the empire, and it embraced powerful traditions and associations not only of military conquest but also of exemplary civic achievement.

Thus, in walking to the chariot races or the theater or the baths, you would have passed some of the magnificent public buildings and monuments whose ruined remains, a millennium and a half later—or, to be precise, on October 15, 1764[30]—would inspire Gibbon to undertake his epic historical project. These imposing edifices had been upgraded under the emperors; the founding emperor, Augustus, boasted that he had inherited a city made of brick and transformed it into a city of marble,[31] and later emperors built monuments, temples, baths, and of course the spectacular Flavian Amphitheater, or Colosseum. Gibbon himself was profoundly moved by the remains of these buildings and monuments; he was impressed also that most of them were erected at private expense for public use.[32] The buildings were thus elegantly tangible evidence of a public spiritedness—or of "civic virtue," as scholars say—that has been the envy of later generations into the present.

But spectacular buildings were only one substantial manifestation of a rich public life—a form of life that contrasts dramatically with the sort of self-regarding, inwardly turned "bowling alone" culture sometimes discerned in the contemporary world.[33] The fact is, as a modern historian observes, "it was not easy to be a recluse in an ancient town. Public life was conducted in specific locations, much of it out of doors in a particular area of the city (the *agora*, flanked by public buildings, temples, and the senate-house)." This public character was manifest in "explosions of colour, pageantry, and popular demonstrations that mark ancient games and entertainments" (although also in "ritualized violence, . . . disorder and rioting in the cities").[34] Nor was this public life limited to the capital city; it was diffused through numerous urban centers (which Gibbon enthusiastically inventoried) and spread throughout the empire from Syria to northern Africa to Britain, all connected by thousands of miles of roads built solidly enough to survive for centuries after the empire itself had collapsed.[35]

30. Gibbon, *Memoirs*, 63.

31. Fox, *The Classical World*, 460.

32. Gibbon, *History of the Decline*, 1:70–71.

33. See Robert Putnam, *Bowling Alone: The Collapse and Revival of American Community* (New York: Simon and Schuster, 2000).

34. John Matthews, "Roman Life and Society," in Boardman, Griffin, and Murray, *The Oxford History of the Classical World*, 748, 763–64.

35. Gibbon, *History of the Decline*, 1:75–77.

To be sure, the roads had initially been constructed to permit the rapid deployment of the legions, and they thus remind us that the far-flung lands that constituted the empire had been conquered by force of arms—mostly in the latter centuries of the Roman republic before Rome had made the transition to an empire under Augustus. But this fact need not darken our appreciation of the golden age. That is because Roman rule was not oppressive, but rather beneficent; it was a means by which the blessings of Roman law and civilization had been bestowed on less fortunate peoples. Or so Gibbon insisted. "All the . . . provinces of the empire," he declared, "were embellished by the same liberal spirit of public magnificence, and were filled with amphitheatres, theatres, temples, porticos, triumphal arches, baths, and aqueducts, all variously conducive to the health, the devotion, and the pleasures of the meanest citizen."[36]

Consequently, "the tranquil and prosperous state of the empire was warmly felt, and honestly confessed, by the provincials as well as the Romans."[37] (The Jews, whom Gibbon regarded with scarcely disguised contempt[38]—and whose revolts in AD 66, 115, and 130 were savagely crushed by the legions,[39] with Gibbon's hearty *post hoc* approbation[40]—perhaps constituted an exception?) As support for this sanguine assessment, Gibbon quoted the elder Pliny:

> They [i.e., the provincials] acknowledged that the true principles of social life, laws, agriculture, and science, which had been first invented by the wisdom of Athens, were now firmly established by the power of Rome, under whose auspicious influence, the fiercest barbarians were united by an equal government and common language. They affirm, that with the improvement of arts, the human species

36. Gibbon, *History of the Decline*, 1:74.

37. Gibbon, *History of the Decline*, 1:82.

38. See, e.g., Gibbon, *History of the Decline*, 1:447-49 ("A single people refused to join in the common intercourse of mankind." "The sullen obstinacy with which they maintained their peculiar rites and unsocial manners" "in contradiction to every known principle of the human mind, that singular people seems to have yielded a stronger and more ready assent to the traditions of their remote ancestors, than to the evidence of their senses").

39. See generally Martin Goodman, *Rome and Jerusalem: The Clash of Ancient Civilizations* (New York: Vintage Books, 2008).

40. See Gibbon, *History of the Decline*, 1:516 ("We are tempted to applaud the severe retaliation which was exercised by the arms of the legions against a race of fanatics, whose dire and credulous superstition seemed to render them the implacable enemies not only of the Roman government, but of humankind").

was visibly multiplied. They celebrate the increasing splendour of the cities, the beautiful face of the country, cultivated and adorned like an immense garden; and the long festival of peace, which was enjoyed by so many nations, forgetful of their ancient animosities, and delivered from the apprehensions of future danger.

Acknowledging that suspicions might be aroused by "the air of rhetoric and declamation" evident in Pliny's effusion, Gibbon maintained that nonetheless "the substance . . . is perfectly agreeable to historic truth."[41]

The "Image of Liberty"

In fact, the process of subjugation had extended not only to those foreign peoples who so "warmly felt" and appreciated Roman rule (as Gibbon supposed), but also to the original Romans themselves. By the time of the Antonine emperors, the republic, which had endured for almost five centuries from the expulsion of the Tarquins until the consolidation of power by Octavius (soon to be renamed Augustus), was only a distant memory, having long since been displaced by the autocracy of empire. True, the outward forms of the ancient republican constitution had been preserved. But these were a mere facade—a camouflage for the largely unconstrained power of the emperors. Thus, what Romans enjoyed in the golden age was not actually democratic liberty but rather, as Gibbon delicately put it, the "image of liberty."[42]

Gibbon himself was candid about the Romans' loss of self-governance, and he recounted how this loss had been incurred. For half a millennium after banishing the kings in the sixth century BC, the Romans had carefully guarded their rights of self-rule through a government composed of various assemblies, of which the Senate was the most central, and of officials elected by the citizens. The most important of these officials were the two consuls and the ten tribunes, who represented the common citizens. One-year terms served or at least sought to keep these officials from accumulating significant personal power. This system of governance had evolved and functioned over a period of centuries, and it sustained Rome in the conquest first of Italy, then (in the Punic Wars) of Carthage, then of the larger Mediterranean region.

41. Gibbon, *History of the Decline*, 1:82.
42. Gibbon, *History of the Decline*, 1:96, 103.

In the first century BC, however, Rome had been wracked by a succession of savage civil wars: the soldiers of Sulla fought those of Marius, the legions loyal to Julius Caesar engaged those commanded by Pompey, and the armies and navies of Octavius battled and eventually defeated those of Mark Antony. Under Sulla and again under Antony and Octavius, proscriptions had been issued authorizing the slaughter of large numbers of leading citizens. Among many others, a fleeing Cicero had been captured and executed under the latter proscription; his head, hands, and eloquent tongue had been cut off and nailed to the rostra in the Roman forum—and, according to one report, spat upon and stabbed repeatedly with hairpins by Antony's wife Fulvia.[43] (To his credit, perhaps, Augustus, formerly known as Octavius, later privately praised Cicero to a grandson as "a learned man and a lover of his country.")[44]

After defeating Antony at Actium in 31 BC, Octavius managed a skillfully orchestrated ceremony in which he submitted his resignation to the Senate but was then prevailed upon to accept ten-year (renewable, and renewed) appointments to a number of offices, including imperator (essentially commander in chief of the legions), proconsul, and tribune. It was then that Octavius was given his new, more majestic name. Soon thereafter were added the titles of supreme pontiff and censor; elevation to the even loftier position of god did not officially come until after Augustus's death. Gibbon explained that the various governmental offices, especially those of consul and tribune, had constituted a sort of separation of powers that constrained governmental authority. Once those offices were united in a single man, the holder's power became practically irresistible.[45]

The same arrangements were continued with Augustus's successors. The result, Gibbon explained, was "an absolute monarchy disguised by the forms of a commonwealth. The masters of the Roman world surrounded their throne with darkness, concealed their irresistible strength, and humbly professed themselves the accountable ministers of the senate, whose supreme decrees they dictated and obeyed" (1:93).

So, should this loss of freedom count against Gibbon's glowing assessment of the period as a golden age? The eccentric, incorruptible Cato the Younger would surely have thought so; he had famously fallen on his sword

43. Anthony Everitt, *Cicero: The Life and Times of Rome's Greatest Politician* (New York: Random House, 2003), 319.

44. Plutarch, "The Life of Cicero," in Loeb Classical Library edition, vol. 7, 49.5, http://penelope.uchicago.edu/Thayer/E/Roman/Texts/Plutarch/Lives/Cicero*.html#46.3.

45. Gibbon, *History of the Decline*, 1:91. In the next few paragraphs, page references from this work will be given in parentheses in the text.

and then pulled out his own bowels rather than submit to the impending dictatorship of Octavius's adoptive father, Julius Caesar. Gibbon's own response to the question of liberty was more nuanced. He acknowledged that under Augustus and his immediate successors, the loss of liberty "rendered [the Romans'] condition more completely wretched than that of the victims of tyranny in any other age or country" (1:104). But that wretchedness resulted from two contingent factors. First, the subjects of the early empire felt the loss of democratic freedom more acutely because "they for a long while preserved the sentiments, or at least the ideas, of their freeborn ancestors" (1:105). Second, Rome in that period had the misfortune of being ruled by a series of spectacularly bad emperors: "the dark unrelenting Tiberius, the furious Caligula, the feeble Claudius, the profligate and cruel Nero, the beastly Vitellius, and the timid inhuman Domitian" (1:104).

By the time of Trajan, by contrast, early in the second century, self-governance was little more than a distant memory, so its absence was no longer resented; the "image of liberty"—or the outward trappings of constitutionalism—was sufficient. Moreover, Romans in this period had the good fortune of being governed by rulers of "virtue and wisdom" (1:103). Indeed, the Antonine era was "possibly the only period of history in which the happiness of a great people was the sole object of government" (1:102). In the hands of such enlightened rulers, "absolute power" was a beneficent force; "virtue and wisdom" could rule without the tedious encumbrances of assemblies and elections.

To be sure, restoration of the republic might still have been desirable "had the Romans of their day been capable of enjoying a rational freedom" (1:103), but, alas, they lacked such capacity. In fact, echoing a contention of one of his favorite modern authors, Montesquieu[46]—a contention to which James Madison famously responded in Federalist 10—Gibbon ventured that self-governance might be possible in a small republic but was not feasible for "an unwieldy multitude" (*History of the Decline*, 1:61).

In addition, it would be unduly harsh to say that the "image of liberty" was nothing more than a sham. True, Romans no longer governed themselves as a people, or as a polity. But they did receive the blessings of Roman law (1:64). And they enjoyed almost complete freedom in matters of religion. Or so Gibbon thought (1:56–61); we will say more on that subject in due course.

Gibbon recognized that a good life wholly dependent on enlightened absolutism was precarious. A wise and benevolent ruler might be followed by

---

46. Gibbon, *Memoirs*, 36.

an unmoored and wicked one. And in fact, one was: the philosopher-emperor Marcus Aurelius was succeeded by his depraved son Commodus (1:108–11), thus bringing the golden age to an end. So the blessed prosperity of the Antonine age was not destined to endure. Still, it was glorious while it lasted.

"The Most Religious People in the World"

Thus far, in describing Gibbon's golden age, we have mentioned religion only obliquely (as in noting the god Priapus—he of the prodigious phallus—or the deification of the emperors). The deferral has been deliberate; after all, it was not Roman religion that led a skeptical and enlightened modern like Gibbon to regard the world under the Antonine emperors with such extravagant approval. (As a young man, Gibbon had converted to but then repudiated Catholicism; his contempt in his maturity for religion, or "superstition," was only thinly veiled, both in his historical and in his autobiographical writings.) Nor, we might think, was religion central to the life we have been describing—to the life of opulence, culture, public entertainment (such as the gladiatorial contests), military conquest, and civic commitment. Maybe the Romans also had religion, but that was incidental.

If we think this, though, we will be mistaken. Religion was not merely present in the Roman world, not merely important; it was essential, and indeed inseparable from the various forms of flourishing we have been appreciating.

Thus, Polybius, the Greek historian who as a youth had been taken as a captive to Rome, and who later accompanied the distinguished military commander Scipio Aemilianus in the campaign that resulted in the destruction of Carthage, wrote a history addressed to a fundamental and fascinating question: How had Rome risen in such a relatively short time from a sleepy provincial town to become the colossal conqueror and master of the Western world? Polybius's history pondered the question at length, exploring various dimensions of Rome's rise to dominance. In the course of these reflections, he called attention to one crucial but (to us) surprising factor: the Romans were *religiously* superior to their neighbors. Thus, "the sphere in which the Roman commonwealth seems to me to show its superiority most decisively is in that of religious belief."[47]

47. Polybius, *The Rise of the Roman Empire*, trans. Ian Scott-Kilvert (London: Penguin, 1979), 349.

Polybius's opinion was hardly idiosyncratic. When the Romans received an envoy from the Greek city of Teos, they sent an introductory message declaring that "we [Romans] have totally and consistently held reverence toward the gods as of the highest importance and the truth of this is proved by the favour we have received from them in return. We are also quite sure that our great respect for the divine has been evident to everyone."[48] In a similar vein, Cicero placed in the mouth of a central character in one of his dialogues the following assessment: "If we seek to compare our Roman ways with those of foreigners, we shall find that in other respects we merely match them or even fall below them, but that in religion, that is, in the worship of the gods, we are much superior."[49]

The historian J. A. North thus observes that "both the Romans themselves and the Greeks who came to observe them in the later Republican period regarded the Romans as the most religious people in the world."[50]

The Religion of the City

This interpretation may seem surprising or incongruous to modern observers, because in most respects (as the foregoing description reflects) the Romans come across as supremely, exquisitely worldly. But are "religious" and "worldly" necessarily incompatible? We might suppose they are—almost by definition. But are we imposing a more modern and inapt conception of "religion" on the Romans? As we will see, far from being contraries, "religious" and "worldly" were in the ancient world nicely integrated and mutually reinforcing. And the revolution by which these terms came to be divorced and even antagonistic to each other—a revolution effected, primarily, by Christianity—has been and continues to be a powerful (and divisive, and much-resented) feature of our modern world.

So we need to take a closer look at Roman religion and its integral connection to the city. In fact, Rome and Roman religion were inseparably bound together from the very beginning, at least in the official accounts. Thus, in the national epic by the poet Virgil, Rome's legendary ancestor Aeneas movingly recounts the events of the horrific night in which his native

---

48. J. A. North, *Roman Religion* (New York: Cambridge University Press, 2000), 76.

49. Cicero, *The Nature of the Gods*, trans. P. G. Walsh (Oxford: Oxford University Press, 1998), 2.8, p. 50.

50. North, *Roman Religion*, 76.

city of Troy was destroyed by Ulysses's wily Greeks, smuggled into the city in the infamous Trojan horse. Aeneas tells how, in desperate fury, he recklessly flung himself against the invaders and yearned for vengeance on Helen, the exquisite instigator of the tragedy, but he was reproved by his divine mother, Venus. "Think," she commanded. "It's not that beauty, Helen, you should hate, / not even Paris, the man that you should blame, no. / It's the gods, the ruthless gods who are tearing down the wealth of Troy."[51]

And why had the gods dealt so harshly with his city? Homer had conjectured that the gods brought about the fall of Troy mostly for poetic purposes, "weaving ruin there / so it should make a song for men to come!"[52] Virgil, by contrast, explained that the gods had a loftier, less purely lyrical aim in view. Thus, when Aeneas desperately rushes back into the burning city in search of his wife Creusa, who had fallen behind in the family's frantic flight, he is instead greeted only by Creusa's ghost, who offers the consolation that "it's not without / the will of the gods these things have come to pass"; but the specter goes on to explain that the gods' design is for Aeneas to cross the seas and found a new kingdom in a distant land "where Lydian Tiber / flows with its smooth march through rich and loamy fields, / a land of hardy people."[53]

In short, the gods had decreed that Troy must fall so that Rome might rise. Similarly, Rome grew from a humble beleaguered town to a world empire with the help of the gods, which was a reward for the Romans' extraordinary piety. According to the historian Livy, writing in the Augustan period, one of Romulus's first acts, after founding the city and defeating a consortium of enemies, was to erect a temple to Jupiter.[54] Later, faced with imminent destruction by the Sabines (whose daughters the Romans had abducted), Romulus desperately appealed to Jupiter again, once again promising a temple, and his troops promptly rallied, "obey[ing] what they believed to be the voice from heaven."[55]

Upon Romulus's somewhat mysterious death, the story came to be that he had been carried up to heaven as a deity (although Livy notes "a few dissentients who secretly maintained that the king had been torn to pieces by the

51. Virgil, *The Aeneid*, trans. Robert Fagles (New York: Penguin, 2010), 2.744–747, p. 95.

52. Homer, *The Odyssey*, trans. Robert Fitzgerald (New York: Farrar, Straus and Giroux, 1998), 8.619–620.

53. Virgil, *The Aeneid* 2.963–971, pp. 101–2.

54. Livy, *The Early History of Rome*, trans. Aubrey de Sélincourt (London: Penguin, 2002), 43.

55. Livy, *Early History of Rome*, 44.

senators").[56] His regal successor, Numa Pompilius, selected with the approval of the augur, was renowned for having established and regularized the religious rites and priesthoods.[57] Among the subsequent kings, as Livy retells the stories, some were more and others less pious; overall, though, the role of the gods in Rome's rise was pervasive, and their favor persisted in the republican period. But in the century of political chaos and violence that brought the republic to an end, the rites and temples may have been neglected, and many attributed Rome's troubles to such neglect.[58] Upon his accession to power, therefore, one of Augustus's political priorities was to restore the temples, to erect new ones, and to reinvigorate the worship of the gods.[59]

Of *the gods*, in the plural. The matter will turn out to be more complex, but at least on its face Roman religion sponsored hundreds and even thousands of gods. A character in a Ciceronian dialogue complains that "the number of gods is beyond counting."[60] So there were the Olympian deities—aegis-bearing Zeus, Hermes the Wayfinder, clubfooted Hephaistos, Poseidon the Earthshaker, and company—endowed now with Latin names: Jupiter, Mercury, Vulcan, Neptune, and so forth. There were numerous exotic gods imported from foreign lands like Egypt, Syria, and Persia; Isis, Serapis, and Cybele (the Mater Magna) were especially popular. Then there were the nature gods: sun, moon, stars, the various gods of rivers, woods, and fields. Also the household or family gods—the lares and penates. And of course, the divine emperors: except for a few who declined the honor (like Tiberius) or whose wickedness was especially egregious (like Nero), emperors were typically, upon their deaths, elevated to divine status and favored with cults and shrines.[61] Expiring, the emperor Vespasian sighed: "Oh dear. I think I'm becoming a god."[62]

In addition, there was a whole host of deities personifying what would seem to be human qualities (Felicity, Faith, Hope) or contingencies of life—Ops (abundance), Salus (physical and moral welfare), Fortuna. Or, as a Ciceronian dialogue puts it, mere "concepts" (Virtue, Honor, Safe-

56. Livy, *Early History of Rome*, 49.

57. Livy, *Early History of Rome*, 51–55.

58. See Fox, *The Classical World*, 427.

59. Fox, *The Classical World*, 427. See also Anthony Everitt, *Augustus: The Life of Rome's First Emperor* (New York: Random House, 2006), 242–43.

60. Cicero, *Nature of the Gods* 1.84, p. 32.

61. See, generally, Valerie M. Warrior, *Roman Religion: A Sourcebook* (Newburyport, MA: Focus Pub.; R. Pullins, 2002), 127–38.

62. Warrior, *Roman Religion*, 138.

ty).[63] Writing in the early fifth century, as Christianity was displacing overt paganism, Augustine would mockingly report that it took a whole field crew of gods just to raise an ear of corn—one (Proserpine) to germinate the seed, another (Seia) to tend the seed while under the ground, another (Segetia) to nurture the stalk once sprouted, still another (Tutilina) to keep the stalk safe, with Nodotus to protect the plant's stems and Voluntina, Patelana, Hostilina, Flora, Lacturnus, Matuta, and Runcina to superintend different aspects and phases of the ripening ear of corn.[64]

This sprawling pantheon provided poets with the characters and materials to create the assortment of captivating and fantastic stories that students of literature today continue to study, and that typically go under the heading of "Greek and Roman mythology." Homer's poems were of course a leading source of these stories, but they were fetchingly related for Romans of the Augustan period in Ovid's *Metamorphoses*. While regarding the stories as rank superstition, Gibbon nonetheless delighted in this literature, and read and reread it, both as a boy and as a mature adult.[65]

The crowds of gods had their own affairs to attend to, and they were for the most part not especially concerned about the mundane doings of mortals. And yet the gods did have the power either to bless or to blight, to help or to hinder, so it was essential to maintain good relations with them. The Romans thus devoted massive resources to honoring the gods and retaining their favor; it was in this sense that the Romans deemed themselves religiously superior to all other nations.

One essential component of this propitiatory investment was the regular ritual sacrifice of animals—of bulls, goats, sheep, pigs. In his early reign, before he became unhinged, Caligula sacrificed over 160,000 animals in less than three months' time—a display of piety publicly regarded as "splendid," as the historian Suetonius observed.[66] Sacrificial ceremonies were performed with rigorous exactitude; any deviation from the proper language and form would make the sacrifice unacceptable to the deity being addressed.[67] An

63. Cicero, *Nature of the Gods* 3.61, p. 129. See also John Scheid, *An Introduction to Roman Religion*, trans. Janet Lloyd (Bloomington: Indiana University Press, 2003), 155–57.

64. Augustine, *The City of God against the Pagans*, trans. and ed. R. W. Dyson (Cambridge: Cambridge University Press, 1998), 4.8, pp. 152–53.

65. Gibbon, *Memoirs*, 14, 35, 81.

66. Suetonius, "Gaius Caligula," in *The Twelve Caesars*, trans. Robert Graves (London: Penguin, 1957), 151.

67. James J. O'Donnell, *Pagans: The End of Traditional Religion and the Rise of Christianity* (New York: HarperCollins, 2015), 31.

emperor himself might on occasion recite the prayers and preside over the ceremony in which he and his attendants would anoint the sacrificial animal and then stun it with an axe blow before slitting its throat, collecting its blood, and carving up its body.[68]

Unlike a modern church service, a sacrifice was not merely a sober liturgy or a ponderous homily but also a feast, typically involving heavy eating and even heavier drinking by the devotees.[69] There were sights and smells to stimulate and assault the senses. Ramsay MacMullen quotes an ancient observer who reported that "the priest himself . . . stands there all bloody and like an ogre carves and pulls out entrails and extracts the heart and pours the blood about the altar."[70] The religious festivities spilled over beyond temple precincts into noisy and colorful processions that encircled and enthralled Roman cities and towns. The worship of the imported deities Atargatis, Isis, and Cybele, MacMullen observes, "made use of inspired, mad dancing and produced a great impression on observers and was also easily and often seen, since its practitioners wandered about in public in search of an audience. To the sound of rattles, tambours, and shrill pipes, with their heads tipped back or rolling wildly on their shoulders, accompanied by their own howls and yells, they whirled about and worked themselves into a state of frenzy."[71]

The stories about the gods were also regularly acted out, through plays and ballets, in theaters built to seat thousands of spectators. These were not stodgy performances; they were, as Robin Lane Fox remarks, "enormous fun."[72]

MacMullen explains that "the entire range of musical instruments . . . was called into the service of the gods in one cult or another, along with every conceivable style of dance and song, theatrical show, prose hymn, lecture or tractate philosophizing, popularizing, edifying, and so forth."[73] To a more prudish eye, in fact, the theatrical performances to the gods were so

68. For a vivid description of one such ceremony, see O'Donnell, *Pagans*, 28–42.
69. Ramsay MacMullen, *Paganism in the Roman Empire* (New Haven: Yale University Press, 1981), 39.
70. MacMullen, *Paganism in the Roman Empire*, 41. MacMullen explains that "the great bulk of meat (not fish or fowl) eaten in the ancient world had been butchered in temple precincts, most of which, ill-supplied with water, could not be swashed down easily, accumulated ugly piles of offal in corners and supported not only flies in clouds but stray mongrels as well" (41).
71. MacMullen, *Paganism in the Roman Empire*, 24.
72. Robin Lane Fox, *Pagans and Christians* (London: Penguin, 1986), 70.
73. MacMullen, *Paganism in the Roman Empire*, 24.

lascivious, so lewd, as to amount to a form of thinly sacralized pornography. That at least was Augustine's mature view[74] (although by his own account he had delighted in going to the theater as a younger man).[75]

Another vital element of the civic religion was divination, or the taking of the auspices, by which leaders sought to determine the will of the gods with respect to pending military or political decisions. The entrails of animals or birds were carefully scrutinized, and the portents or "prodigies" (such as lightning strikes, a deformed child at birth, or a mole with teeth on it)[76] were studied, in quest of clues to the divine agenda. Livy relates the story of an early and skeptical king, Tarquin, who sought "to ridicule the whole business of omens" by ordering an augur, Attius Navius, to say whether what the king was privately thinking at the moment was actually possible. The augur consulted the birds and then answered in the affirmative, upon which the king triumphantly declared that what he had been wondering was whether the augur could cut a whetstone in half with a razor. And then, Livy recounts, "Believe it or not: without a moment's delay Navius did it."[77] A statue was erected in honor of the feat, and Livy observes that "whatever we may think of this story, the fact remains that the importance attached to augury and the augural priesthood increased to such an extent that to take the auspices was henceforward an essential preliminary to any serious undertaking in peace or in war: not only army parades or popular assemblies, but matters of vital concern to the commonwealth were postponed, if the birds refused their assent."[78]

When Rome encountered more serious difficulties, so that deeper counsels were needed, a different guild of priests pored over the cryptic Sibylline texts (which in the murky past had been delivered to King Numa by a mysterious old crone).[79] Or unusual rites might be attempted—burying a few foreigners alive, for example.[80]

74. E.g., Augustine, *City of God* 2.8–9, pp. 59–61.

75. Augustine, *The Confessions of St. Augustine*, ed. and trans. Albert Cook Outler, rev. ed. (New York: Dover, 2002), 3.2, p. 32 ("Stage plays also captivated me, with their sights full of the images of my own miseries: fuel for my own fires").

76. Fox, *The Classical World*, 290.

77. Livy, *Early History of Rome*, 75–76.

78. Livy, *Early History of Rome*, 76. See also Cicero, "On Divination," in *Cicero on Old Age, on Friendship, on Divination*, trans. W. A. Falconer, Loeb Classical Library (Cambridge, MA: Harvard University Press, 1923), 213, 225 (reporting that "after the expulsion of the kings, no public business was ever transacted at home or abroad without first taking the auspices").

79. See Warrior, *Roman Religion*, 13, 22–23; O'Donnell, *Pagans*, 26, 92.

80. See Fox, *The Classical World*, 306.

The business for which the gods' help was sought emphatically included military affairs. A battle was not fought without consulting the sacred chickens: if the chickens ate the pellets scattered for them, good fortune awaited, but if they declined, defeat loomed. One impatient general, Publius Claudius, who during the first war with Carthage had rashly chosen to disrespect a flock of uncooperative chickens—he had them drowned, commenting in exasperation that since they refused to eat, they could instead drink—was duly paid with military disaster.[81] And upon approaching an enemy city, the Romans performed a ritual, called *evocatio*, calculated to lure the city's gods over to the Roman side with promises of superior cultic worship.[82]

The ritual sacrifices and the auspices were conducted by men who were at once high political officials and members of one or another public priesthood. Thus, the political leaders of the Roman state—the consuls, the prefects, later the emperors—simultaneously served as officials within the four major public priesthoods, with the emperor himself filling the role of head pontiff, or *pontifex maximus*.

The Romans' public religiosity was conspicuously manifest in their architecture. The capital city was rife with elegant temples dedicated to the various deities; as you walked from your *domus* to the baths or the games, you would surely have passed by any number of them. The same was true for other cities in the empire. Edward Watts illustrates the pervasiveness of these religious structures with the example of Alexandria in the later empire. A fourth-century catalogue, he notes, "lists almost 2,500 temples in the city, nearly one for every twenty houses."[83] In one sense, though, this estimate of one temple for every twenty houses is a gross understatement: the actual ratio was more like one to one. That is because every house was in a sense a minitemple containing its own shrine dedicated to the household gods: the lares and penates.[84] In *A World Full of Gods*, his imaginative portrayal of the Roman world, Cambridge historian Keith Hopkins has his fictional time travelers report back: "There were temples and Gods, and humans praying to them, all over the place: at the entrance to the town, at the entrance to the

---

81. Cicero, *Nature of the Gods* 2.7, p. 49.

82. O'Donnell, *Pagans*, 110.

83. Edward J. Watts, *The Final Pagan Generation* (Oakland: University of California Press, 2015), 18–19. Nor did religion end at the city limits. Watts reports that "the Roman countryside housed an even greater array of sacred sites. These included large temple complexes, grottoes and other rustic sacred locations, and a large category of rural structures that served, in effect, as temples run by the household that controlled the land" (19).

84. Warrior, *Roman Religion*, 25–26.

Forum; there were altars at crossroads, Gods in niches as you went along, with passersby just casually blowing a kiss with their hands to the statue of a God set in a wall. And of course, here in the Forum, the ceremonial center of the town, there were temples, altars, Gods, heroes just about everywhere we looked. . . . Our end of the square was filled by the grand Temple to Jupiter, with Vesuvius magnificently snowcapped behind. And all the rest of the buildings looked as though they could be temples too."[85]

Religion was pervasive not only spatially but also temporally. The calendar was structured around the major religious festivals—the Lupercalia, Parlia, Robigalia, Saturnalia, and various others—and was administered by the priestly college of pontiffs.[86] All in all, 177 days of the year were designated as holidays or festivals, in honor of thirty-three different gods or goddesses.[87]

But then, what about the images of worldliness we noted earlier—the gladiatorial games and chariot races? And the extravagant sexuality? We have already noted how military and political activities were infused with religion. The theatrical performances, likewise, were dedicated to the gods.[88] And odd though it may seem to moderns, the games were religious exercises as well; before the gladiators and the wild animals were brought out and cheered on as they slaughtered each other, the games were dedicated to the honor of the gods.[89] In hard times, when Roman leaders felt an urgent need for the gods' assistance, they would sometimes sponsor a special set of games ordained to the gods.[90] So for all their fatal ferocity, these were essentially religious rites.

Perhaps surprisingly, a similar description could fit the city's rampant sexuality—the brothels and the sex slaves and the ubiquitous phalluses. We will say more on that subject momentarily.

In sum, public or civic religion was pervasive in the Roman world. City and religion were thoroughly integrated, coextensive, inseparable. "There was a religious aspect to every communal action," the historian John Scheid explains, "and a communal aspect to every religious action."[91]

---

85. Hopkins, *World Full of Gods*, 13.

86. Scheid, *Introduction to Roman Religion*, 48–54; Warrior, *Roman Religion*, 59–69.

87. Watts, *The Final Pagan Generation*, 24.

88. Scheid, *Introduction to Roman Religion*, 106–8; Warrior, *Roman Religion*, 115–20.

89. Hopkins, *World Full of Gods*, 41.

90. See, e.g., Suetonius, "Divus Augustus," in Graves, *The Twelve Caesars*, 54.

91. Scheid, *Introduction to Roman Religion*, 20. See also Fox, *Pagans and Christians*, 82 (describing "the gods' role on every level of social life and their pervasive presence").

Sex and the City

Rome's pervasive and unembarrassed sexuality likewise had both a religious and a civic dimension. In the Roman Empire, sexual morality reflected two broad premises. First, sexual fulfillment is not only natural and pleasurable and presumptively acceptable; it is also a kind of ecstatic religious performance. But, second, sexual behavior and fulfillment are constrained by the city—or by the demands of social and political life.

The Divine Imperative. The historian Kyle Harper's recent study shows how these premises informed the attitudes and economy of the empire. "Male sexual energy was a definite quantity that had to be expended, somewhere," Harper explains;[92] consequently, "any hard restrictions on male sexual exertion in the years after puberty were considered implausible."[93] Sex provided sensual gratification, of course: the physician-philosopher Galen observed with clinical detachment that "a very great pleasure is coupled with the exercise of the generative parts, and a raging desire precedes their use."[94] Indeed, abstinence was deemed unhealthy (except by a few Stoics):[95] it could lead to nausea, fever, and poor digestion.[96] But sexual fulfillment was not merely a physical imperative, it was also a sort of religious performance or duty. "The figure of Eros himself, symbol of joy and life, was unfailingly popular," Harper observes, and "sexual passion was an immanent divine force"[97]—the "mysterious, indwelling presence of the gods."[98] In a similar vein, Kathy Gaca explains that "in antiquity, sexual arousal, activity, and reproduction were in part immanent divine powers, not simply human forms of energy."[99]

In the second century rom-com novel *Leucippe and Clitophon*, for example, the protagonist, Clitophon, reports that his passions were "inflamed" by a song about Apollo's attempted conquest of the lovely nymph Daphne, and he explains that "even if you school yourself into self-control, an example in-

92. Harper, *From Shame to Sin*, 47.

93. Harper, *From Shame to Sin*, 54.

94. Quoted in Peter Brown, *The Body and Society: Men, Women, and Sexual Renunciation in Early Christianity*, 2nd ed. (New York: Columbia University Press, 2008), 17.

95. Harper, *From Shame to Sin*, 70–78.

96. Harper, *From Shame to Sin*, 58.

97. Harper, *From Shame to Sin*, 68. See also 57–58 ("Wine, like sex, was an immanent divine force, and the wash of its warm ecstasy was experienced as a communion with Dionysus").

98. Harper, *From Shame to Sin*, 67.

99. See also Kathy L. Gaca, *The Making of Fornication: Eros, Ethics, and Political Reform in Greek Philosophy and Early Christianity* (Berkeley: University of California Press, 2003), 132.

cites you to imitate it, especially when that example is a divine one; in which case, any shame that you feel at your moral errors becomes an outspoken affront to the station of a higher being."[100] Later, when Clitophon is feeling apprehensive about his project to seduce the lovely Leucippe, his servant Satyrus reproves and encourages him. "[The god] Eros admits of no feebleness," Satyrus urges. "You observe the military nature of his accoutrements, the bow, the quiver, the missiles, the flame: all manly things, and crammed with courage. And you are cowardly and timorous with a god such as that inside you?" The worldly-wise servant thus urges his wavering master to go forth and seduce "as a soldier in the service of a manly god."[101]

But it was not only the male characters for whom sexual desire enjoyed a divine imprimatur. Harper explains that more generally, and especially through the female character Leucippe, the author Achilles Tatius conveys "an ambitious vision of conjugal eros, in which the most profound stirrings of the body not only connected man with the divine forces that replenished the earth but also offered personal transcendence."[102] More generally, Roman novels convey a picture of "a world keenly knit by the gods so that mankind might find in erotic fulfillment nothing short of salvation."[103]

Peter Brown expresses the characteristic attitude in poetic language that might have earned the admiration of the Romans themselves:

> The men we meet in the second century still belonged to the rustling universe of late classical polytheism. They knew that they had been knit, by the cunning of the gods, to the animal world. They felt pulsing in their own bodies the same fiery spirit that covered the hills every year with newborn lambs and that ripened the crops, in seasonal love-play, as the spring winds embraced the fertile ears. Above them, the same fire glowed in the twinkling stars. Their bodies, and their sexual drives, shared directly in the unshakable perpetuity of an immense universe through which the gods played exuberantly.[104]

This sacralization of sexuality helps explain the ubiquity of erotic imagery—paintings, mosaics, statues—in Roman culture. The explicit imagery

100. Achilles Tatius, *Leucippe and Clitophon*, trans. Tim Whitmarsh (Oxford: Oxford University Press, 2001), 7–8.
101. Achilles Tatius, *Leucippe and Clitophon*, 22.
102. Harper, *From Shame to Sin*, 80.
103. Harper, *From Shame to Sin*, 21.
104. Brown, *The Body and Society*, 27–28.

within homes—on lampshades, in wall frescoes—has already been men-tioned.[105] Similar depictions adorned the public spaces. Summarizing the findings of archeological research, Keith Hopkins has his fictional time trav-eler Martha report:

> Here in real Pompeii, in the only changing rooms of these upscale baths, used by women, men, and children, explicit pictures of sexual couplings confront you whether you like it or not. In [one depic-tion] the man was having the woman from behind, but [another] showed the woman on top, and [another] was a picture of a woman fellating a man, interrupted in his reading. These changing rooms were clearly aiming at an educated clientele. Then to balance mat-ters, there was cunnilingus by a man. . . . The next picture was more conventional, except that the woman had one leg athletically over the man's shoulder.
>
> After all that, the sexual combinations became rather more com-plicated. . . . Anyhow the next two pictures showed a trio of two men and a woman, and then a quartet of two men and two women in a homosexual and heterosexual chain.[106]

The stimulation of visual art was reinforced by erotic literature and the-atrical performances[107]—including, during the spring Floralia celebration, live inspirational sex shows.[108] Hopkins's time travelers report that "one lo-cal bar had a bronze bell hanging over the counter shaped as a hunchback pygmy, with several large penises and five bells. To get service, you just yanked on one of the penises. We saw bells like this all over Pompeii, and in grand houses too. Some quite artistically made."[109] Kyle Harper explains that "what modern cultures might regard as obscene or pornographic was an ordinary part of bourgeois and elite domesticity."[110]

---

105. See above, 54. See also Harper, *From Shame to Sin*, 66 ("Men, women, and children were surrounded by lush paintings of venereal acts in various stages of consummation").

106. Hopkins, *World Full of Gods*, 17–18.

107. Harper, *From Shame to Sin*, 48.

108. Sarah Ruden, *Paul among the People: The Apostle Reinterpreted and Reimagined in His Own Time* (New York: Random House, 2010), 19.

109. Hopkins, *World Full of Gods*, 21.

110. Harper, *From Shame to Sin*, 66. See also Fox, *The Classical World*, 537: "On doorbells, lamps or doorposts there had long been images of erect penises; there had also been sexual scenes, very explicit, on the surrounds of personal hand-mirrors and so forth. . . . When we

For the most part, Roman culture was indifferent to whether sexual fulfillment was achieved with a same-sex or opposite-sex partner.[111] Sex with boys at the right stage of maturity was looked on with favor, and celebrated in romantic poetry;[112] following Homer, boys were deemed most alluring in early adolescence, when the first soft hair appeared on their cheeks.[113] Some writers regarded pederasty as more pure and virtuous than sex with women: that was because the "'form, complexion, and image of the boy's beauty' was . . . a powerful reminder, sent by the gods, of heavenly beauty, a sensible impression of the incorruptible reality."[114] The emperor Hadrian, though married, was devoted to his young lover Antinous, who accompanied the emperor on his many travels; after Antinous's tragic death, perhaps by drowning (or perhaps by suicide, or even in a religious sacrifice), Hadrian had his beloved elevated to the status of a god and also named a city after him.[115]

One major qualification on this acceptance of pederasty and homosexual conduct, however, was that Roman sexuality was subject to an ethic of manliness—of machismo, if you like—and this ethic put limits on the kind of sexual conduct that a man could honorably engage in. More specifically, men were expected to play the penetrative or insertive role.[116] Conversely, "effeminate" men were reviled; it was disgraceful to be the passive partner in sexual relations, or to fulfill the function ascribed to a woman.[117] Sarah Ruden reports that "to keep it unmistakable that he had no sympathy with passive homosexuals, a man would tout his attacks on vulnerable young males."[118]

---

find paintings of a naked woman on top of a man in the colonnade round a central peristyle garden or numbered paintings of oral sex between men and women, including foursomes, in the changing-room of a set of public baths, we cannot explain somehow a painings to avert the 'evil eye' and assume good fortune. They are simply sexy."

111. Harper, *From Shame to Sin*, 24, 36.

112. See Amy Richlin, *The Garden of Priapus: Sexuality and Aggression in Roman Humor* · (New Haven: Yale University Press, 1983), 34–44.

113. Fox, *The Classical World*, 41.

114. Harper, *From Shame to Sin*, 29–30. See also Richlin, *The Garden of Priapus*, 41.

115. Anthony Everitt, *Hadrian and the Triumph of Rome* (New York: Random House, 2009), 283–94.

116. Harper, *From Shame to Sin*, 36.

117. Harper, *From Shame to Sin*, 32–37. "The viciousness of mainstream attitudes toward passivity," Harper explains, "is startling for anyone who approaches the ancient sources with the false anticipation that pre-Christian cultures were somehow reliably civilized toward sexual minorities" (37). For a vivid description of the revulsion felt against "effeminate" men, see Ruden, *Paul among the People*, 47–54.

118. Ruden, *Paul among the People*, 53.

Another corollary of manliness was the imperative of self-mastery. Excessive sexual indulgence was thought to be enervating and, like passive homosexuality, effeminate.[119] So sexual passions were to be gratified, certainly, but a man who allowed his sexual passions to gain control of him was to that extent less than virtuous, just as a man who could not control any other passion was worthy of criticism.

Civic Constraints. But if the ideal of manliness both encouraged and constrained sexual gratification, probably the most important constraints came from the demands of social life. In the Roman Empire, society was patriarchal and hierarchical.[120] And the Romans were constantly concerned, even obsessed, with the necessity of reproduction[121]—of reproduction within the patriarchal family. Hence the imperative—and the function—of marriage. It might be hoped that marriage would lead to love, but this was a luxury; the institution's understood purpose was "the reproduction of legitimate offspring."[122] This concern with reproduction was not merely neurotic, but was grounded in grim demographic realities. Peter Brown points out that the average life expectancy was less than twenty-five, and only four out of a hundred men, and fewer women, lived to age fifty.[123] Given the high mortality rate, "for civic elites of the second century . . . wholehearted commitment to sex and marriage was a call to arms against death, in a landscape that always appears to contemporaries (overshadowed by so many tombs of children and young wives) to be trembling on the brink of demographic collapse."[124]

The imperative of reproduction within the patriarchal family sponsored different roles for men (who worked, warred, and participated in politics and civic life) and for women (who tended to the household), and these different roles included radically different sexual standards for men and women. Men were expected to have sexual adventures before marriage—which typically

119. Harper, *From Shame to Sin*, 56; see also Brown, *The Body and Society*, 18–20.

120. Brown, *The Body and Society*, 9 ("In the second century A.D., a young man of the privileged classes of the Roman Empire grew up looking at the world from a position of unchallenged dominance. Women, slaves, and barbarians were unalterably different from him and inferior to him").

121. Harper, *From Shame to Sin*, 39–40. See also 78 ("The sexual economy of the high Roman Empire was dominated by the imperatives of social reproduction").

122. Harper, *From Shame to Sin*, 62.

123. Brown, *The Body and Society*, 6.

124. Brown, *The Body and Society*, xlvi. See also xliii ("Among the Greco-Roman notables . . . the bodies of men and women were mobilized against death. They were asked to produce, in an orderly fashion, orderly children to man the walls of those bright little cities whose entrance roads were lined with tombs").

occurred in their midtwenties—and to have ample opportunities for sexual expression thereafter.[125] By contrast, the sexual behavior of women—or at least of respectable women—was governed by an ideal of chastity. This ideal dictated virginity until marriage—an event that occurred as young as age twelve but typically in the midteens, and that was effectively mandatory for respectable women—and complete fidelity thereafter.[126] The norm against adultery was enforced by convention, by law (the so-called *lex Iulia*, titled after Augustus's daughter Julia, whose profligate conduct prompted her imperial father to promulgate the prohibition),[127] and, perhaps most effectively, by self-help. To have relations with another man's wife was tantamount to despoiling his property. At least in Roman literature, therefore, adulterers were subject to being killed, beaten, castrated, or raped at the election of the dishonored husband.[128] Upon assuming the office of consul during the reign of Septimius Severus, Dio Chrysostom found that there were two thousand trials for adultery in progress;[129] the number suggests that the prohibition was not a dead letter but also that violations were not rare.

Beyond its prohibition of actual adultery, Roman culture prescribed feminine modesty. "The Roman matron," Harper explains, "should dress only so nice as to avoid uncleanness, she should always be chaperoned in public, she should walk with her eyes down and risk rudeness rather than immodesty in her greetings, and she should blush when addressed."[130] But these norms of chastity and modesty were not simply imposed on women by men; at least to outward appearances, they were embraced by women and promoted "with verve." "Chastity was a badge of honor, separating the Roman matron from the slaves whose bodies she ostentatiously controlled."[131]

The Political Economy of Sexuality. This last observation begins to answer a question that the preceding discussion must have provoked: If men were expected to indulge their sexual desires and passions (albeit not to excess,

---

125. Harper, *From Shame to Sin*, 52–70.

126. Harper, *From Shame to Sin*, 37–52.

127. Harper, *From Shame to Sin*, 38–39. For discussion of the law and how it worked in practice, see Fox, *The Classical World*, 433–35; Richlin, *The Garden of Priapus*, 215–19; Aline Rousselle, *Porneia: On Desire and the Body in Antiquity*, trans. Felicia Pheasant (Eugene, OR: Wipf and Stock, 1988), 88–90.

128. Richlin, *The Garden of Priapus*, 216.

129. Rousselle, *Porneia*, 89.

130. Harper, *From Shame to Sin*, 41.

131. Harper, *From Shame to Sin*, 45.

and only in the penetrative, not the passive, role), and if women were enjoined to virginity before marriage and to a chaste fidelity afterward, then who were the men supposed to have sex *with* (beyond, of course, their wives, and the limited demographic of comely adolescent boys)? The answer, basically, was: with prostitutes and slaves.

Thus, in Roman cities, brothels dotted the cityscape like Starbucks or Taco Bells in a modern American city.[132] The historian Dio Chrysostom complained that brothels "are apparent everywhere in the city—at the governor's porch, in the marketplaces, by the buildings both civil and religious, right in the middle of what ought to be most revered."[133] The emperor Caligula sponsored an imperial brothel, "stocked it with married women and freeborn boys" (as Suetonius observed), "and then sent his pages around the squares and public places, inviting men of all ages to come and enjoy themselves"—on credit if necessary.[134] The brothels were supplemented by taverns, inns, and public baths that were well known as centers of sexual gratification.[135] Prostitutes, recruited (or, perhaps more accurately, conscripted by necessity) from the poorer classes outside the norms of respectability, were "ubiquitous."[136]

The other main source of sexual satisfaction was slaves, both male and female.[137] Slaves were especially favored by the more aristocratic classes, who looked down on prostitution—not as immoral but as "squalid." With their ownership of numerous slaves, fortunately, the well-off found it "unnecessary to share sexual receptacles."[138] Sex with slaves was deemed perfectly acceptable because, as one Roman author put it, "every master is held to have it in his power to use his slave as he wishes."[139]

Given the culture's elevation and pervasive stimulation of (male) sexual desire, it should not be surprising that Roman men sometimes found themselves unable to limit their gratification to the approved channels of prostitutes, slaves, consenting boys, and of course, their own wives. Though

132. Harper, *From Shame to Sin*, 47.
133. Harper, *From Shame to Sin*, 74 (quoting Dio).
134. Suetonius, "Gaius Caligula," 167–68.
135. Harper, *From Shame to Sin*, 47.
136. Harper, *From Shame to Sin*, 46. See also 48 (noting that "droves of poor women were forced to become prostitutes").
137. Harper, *From Shame to Sin*, 26. See also 27 ("The ubiquity of slaves meant pervasive sexual availability").
138. Harper, *From Shame to Sin*, 49.
139. Quoted in Brown, *The Body and Society*, 23.

forbidden, adultery occurred; it is hard to know how frequently.[140] According to the Roman historian Suetonius, the emperor Augustus, although he sternly forbade adultery and unflinchingly banished his daughter Julia for her delinquencies, regularly had affairs with the wives of Roman nobles—though more as a means of spying on potential rivals, Suetonius hastens to explain, than for lubricious reasons.[141] Other emperors were notoriously less discreet, gratifying themselves in extravagant sexual orgies involving siblings, colleagues' spouses, children and even infants, and multiple pairings.[142]

There also seems to have been a widespread practice of predatory sex with boys whom, because of age or social status or lack of consent, social norms deemed ineligible for such relations.[143] Ruden reports that "it was . . . normal for a family of any standing to dedicate one slave to a son's protection, especially on the otherwise unsupervised walk to and from school."[144] But safe arrival at school was no sure security; philosopher-teachers were widely suspected of taking liberties with their pupils.[145]

Through these various means, some deemed legitimate and some not, Roman culture contrived amply to satisfy the natural, divinely approved need for sexual gratification. Kyle Harper observes that "the Roman Empire was the most complete and most refined expression of a sexual economy that had its origins in the very birth of the classical Mediterranean city-state. If the disciplines of sexual self-knowledge were more rigorous in the high empire, the delivery of sexual pleasures was more efficient than ever."[146]

Consecrating the City

As we have seen, religion was integrated into every aspect of Roman society, government, and culture (including sexuality), and it served to sustain the city that contemporary Romans and later admirers like Gibbon have regarded with admiration sometimes bordering on reverence. Nearly all Ro-

140. Brown, *The Body and Society*, 42; Richlin, *The Garden of Priapus*, 215–19.
141. Suetonius, "Divus Augustus," 82.
142. See, e.g., Suetonius, "Tiberius," "Gaius Caligula," and "Nero," all in Graves, *The Twelve Caesars*, 127–28, 164–65, and 222–23, respectively.
143. Harper, *From Shame to Sin*, 29. See also Ruden, *Paul among the People*, 62–65.
144. Ruden, *Paul among the People*, 55.
145. Harper, *From Shame to Sin*, 29.
146. Harper, *From Shame to Sin*, 60.

mans, educated or not, would have said or simply assumed that religion—the religion of the gods—was essential to Rome and Roman life.

This assumption will likely seem quite contrary to modern sensibilities, accustomed as we are to a "separation of church and state." And so we might ask, and quickly review: *Why* did Roman society need religion? The question is crucial because it will bear importantly on the conflict between paganism and Christianity, to be discussed in later chapters.

At the crudest level, religion was deemed necessary because it helped keep the masses—and perhaps the elites as well—in line. A cynic might imagine that this was religion's principal use, that (as Cicero stated the position, without endorsing it) "belief in the immortal gods was a total invention of the sages in the interests of the state, so that those who could not be impelled by reason should be constrained by religious awe to a sense of duty."[147] In a similar vein, in asserting the importance of religion to Rome, the historian Polybius emphasized its function in inducing people to comply with their duties and reducing official corruption.[148]

For devout Romans, however, religion was essential to society and state in a more important way. In this perspective, the gods were real, and powerful, and prone to intervene for good or ill in the affairs of mortals. The pagan epics, the *Iliad*, the *Odyssey*, and the *Aeneid*, are full of episodes showing how imperative it was to cultivate the favor of the gods and, conversely, how disastrous to provoke the gods' ire. Hence the vital importance of performing the rituals and sacrifices and auguries regularly and exactly. The *Odyssey* relates, for instance, how in his return from the Trojan wars, Menelaus sacrificed to the gods but was stingy in the quantity of animals offered up. He was accordingly blown off course and delayed by years; and he would have been destroyed altogether had he not charmed a nymph daughter of Proteus into telling him how he could stealthily seize her father and force him to grant a special favor.[149] And we have already seen how a leader who disregarded the guidance of the gods—Publius Claudius, for example, the ill-fated general who disrespected the sacred chickens—could bring disaster upon himself and those under his command.

But religion was valuable for reasons that went beyond rendering the people submissive and law-abiding, and even beyond the imperative of enlisting the gods' aid in battles and political decisions. Cicero suggested, more

---

147. Cicero, *Nature of the Gods* 1.118, p. 44.
148. Polybius, *Rise of the Roman Empire*, 349.
149. Homer, *The Odyssey* 4.277–627.

broadly, that the worship of the gods helped maintain the "sense of the holy"; without this, "our lives become fraught with disturbance and great chaos."[150] The gods "were not simply up in heaven," as Oxford historian Robin Lane Fox explains, "but rather were all around—in the storm, in sickness, in battle, on the hillside, in the public spaces, in dreams, in stories." They imparted to the world a "shining beauty and grace."[151] These themes point directly to the consecration function discussed in the previous chapter. Consecration, or literally, "association with the sacred," prevents the world from falling into chaos and instead connects with ultimate meaning and sublimity.

This sense of beauty, and of a city that was consecrated to and by the gods, was surely essential to what gave the Roman world its splendor—a splendor perceived by contemporaries but also later by Gibbon and other like-minded observers and recollectors. True, Rome had conquered many lands, but there have been other, geographically vaster empires (think of the Mongol Empire, for instance, or the Soviet Union). Rome in the first and second centuries experienced relative peace (although the philosopher-emperor Marcus, for example, was often at the German front, fighting off the barbarians) and commercial prosperity, but there have been other civilizations that have enjoyed these benefits. The Romans inherited the cultural and literary achievements of Greece and contributed some of their own, but there have been other ages of literary and cultural fluorescence—the Renaissance, or the Elizabethan or Shakespearean age. The Romans elaborated a system of law, but other communities and states have developed legal systems, and have enjoyed considerably more political freedom than the "image of liberty"—Gibbon's deft phrase[152]— which was all the Romans could claim under the empire.

And yet Gibbon perceived, as others have, something stately or majestic in the Roman world—something beautiful, even sublime—that made it stand out as distinctively blessed. And although Gibbon himself may or may not have appreciated the fact,[153] the Romans themselves—Cicero, Augustus,

---

150. Cicero, *Nature of the Gods* 1.4, p. 4.

151. Fox, *The Classical World*, 50.

152. Gibbon, *History of the Decline*, 1:103.

153. Gibbon began the second chapter of his history with the observation that "it is not alone by the rapidity, or the extent of conquest, that we should estimate the greatness of Rome" (*History of the Decline*, 1:56). He then proceeded to discuss Roman law, government, and philosophy; but the first subject he addressed was Roman religion, which he affectionately portrayed as exemplifying "the mild spirit of antiquity" (1:57). And while describing the myths as "the idle tales of the poets," he acknowledged that "the elegant mythology of Homer gave a beautiful, and almost a regular form, to the polytheism of the ancient world" (1:58).

and, later, the fourth-century pagan emperor Julian, who tried desperately to revive a by-then-ailing paganism—would have attributed this quality in large part to the Romans' peculiar virtue. Namely, to their unrivaled reverence toward the gods.

In sum, Rome in late antiquity was somehow much more than just a relatively (and sporadically) peaceful polity with a thriving economy. It also provided, in some measure, the goods that in the previous chapter we associated with religion—meaning, sublimity, and communal connection to the sacred. A resident of Rome—an affluent citizen, but even a poorer subject—was part of a larger and glorious enterprise that had its grand narrative (one stirringly related in Virgil's *Aeneid*, among other places), its connection to sublimity and the sacred (as visibly manifest in the ubiquitous temples and sacrifices and processions), and its communal consecrations of these ancient and enduring sources of meaning and sublimity.

G. K. Chesterton famously described America as a "nation with the soul of a church."[154] Chesterton's description would have fit the Roman Empire as well. *A fortiori*. Indeed, Rome *was*, in a sense, a kind of magnificent megachurch.

It was, in short, the city of the gods.

And yet, without wanting to be impertinent, we might wonder: Did the Romans actually, well, believe in this swarming mass of disparate deities? Really, sincerely *believe* in them? For *us*, the question is inextricably connected to the subject of religion: people cannot talk seriously about a religion without asking, or at least quietly wondering: Ah, but is it actually . . . true? Would the Romans have raised the same question, or at least understood it? And if so, how would they have answered it? We will consider the matter in the next chapter.

---

154. G. K. Chesterton, "What I Saw in America: The Resurrection of Rome Sidelights," in *G. K. Chesterton Collected Works*, vol. 21 (San Francisco: Ignatius, [1922] 1990), 45.

CHAPTER 4

Believing in Paganism

The previous chapter described how religion pervaded Roman society and served to consecrate the city, not only sustaining its material prosperity and military dominance, but also endowing the city with a "shining beauty and grace."[1] Roman religion was, as we saw, populated by gods beyond counting. The worship of this vast and teeming pantheon occurred in and through a myriad of temples, shrines, public sacrifices and processions, theatrical performances, and regular solemn consultations with the auguries and oracles. The gods manifested themselves as well, and were honored, through sexuality—sexual ecstasy being understood as "the mysterious, indwelling presence of the gods."[2]

In our survey of Roman religion, however, we mostly passed by in silence a question that modern students might think crucial. Did Romans actually *believe* in all these gods and goddesses? Did they think that the gods were real, and that the stories about them were, well, for lack of a better word . . . true? We passed over this question, but we cannot simply ignore it, because the question is important for our purposes; in attempting to answer it, we will be pointed toward a deeper understanding of what pagan religiosity consisted of. And that understanding will in turn be vital to our larger objective, which is to grasp what it might mean, today, to confront the choice T. S. Eliot described—the choice between a "Christian society" and "modern paganism."

---

1. Robin Lane Fox, *The Classical World: An Epic History from Homer to Hadrian* (New York: Basic Books, 2006), 50.

2. Kyle Harper, *From Shame to Sin: The Christian Transformation of Sexual Morality in Late Antiquity* (Cambridge, MA: Harvard University Press, 2013), 109.

So in this chapter we will ask: (How) did pagans believe? We will see that the answer to the question cannot be a simple yes or no, or even a slightly less simple "some did and some didn't." The answer will need to take into account not only the differences in belief and disbelief from one class and one person to another, but also what French historian Paul Veyne calls "the modalities of belief."[3]

Despite these differences, we will see that many and perhaps most pagans did manage to maintain, in one form or another, a belief in the gods that served to consecrate their shining city. Sometimes their believing took a simple and straightforward shape; sometimes it adopted more sophisticated or subtle or perhaps contorted forms. These various approaches strengthened Roman religion by providing subjects with different strategies or "modalities" for maintaining it. But the approaches also conflicted with, and thus undermined, each other, thereby rendering the city's religion vulnerable. Vulnerable to the decay of belief, and hence to competing bodies of belief—like Christianity.

Pagan believing, in short, was at once a necessary, a robust, but also a variegated and precarious enterprise.

Was Believing Necessary?

First, though, we should notice a preliminary objection. The objection suggests that the question we have raised in this chapter—whether Romans actually believed in the pagan gods—is misconceived. Thus, some historians assert that for the Romans, the issues of *truth* and of *belief* somehow did not present themselves in any serious way. "It is a mistake to overemphasize any question of the participants' belief or disbelief in the efficacy of ritual actions," J. A. North argues. "These rituals are not saying things, but doing things."[4] In a similar vein, Robert Wilken observes that "in the cities of the ancient world . . . one did not speak of 'believing in the gods' but of 'having gods.'"[5]

---

3. Paul Veyne, *Did the Greeks Believe in Their Myths? An Essay on the Constitutive Imagination*, trans. Paula Wissing (Chicago: University of Chicago Press, 1983), xi.

4. J. A. North, *Roman Religion* (New York: Cambridge University Press, 2000), 84.

5. Robert Louis Wilken, *The Christians as the Romans Saw Them*, 2nd ed. (New Haven: Yale University Press, 2003), 58. See also Robin Lane Fox, *Pagans and Christians* (London: Penguin, 1986), 31 ("[Romans] did pay detailed acts of cult, especially by offering animal victims to their gods, but they were not committed to revealed beliefs in the strong Christian sense of the term"). See also John Scheid, *An Introduction to Roman Religion*, trans. Janet Lloyd

Maybe. The Romans were famous for performing ingenious feats of engineering. The celebrated Pantheon—the temple to all the gods—continues to exhibit the largest internally unsupported dome in the world. Did the Romans also manage to perform the ingenious intellectual feat of maintaining religious practices devoted to the pantheon of gods that were internally unsupported by actual belief?

Later thinkers have sometimes aspired to such a condition. Questions of belief and truth polarize, and sometimes paralyze; better, if we could manage it, just to, well, live—leaving questions of belief and truth to philosophers or scientists or whomever.[6] And yet in modern society, matters of belief seem always to be obtruding. The philosophizing of someone like John Rawls, as we will see in a later chapter, seeks to overcome this obstacle and to achieve a kind of civic harmony by distancing civic life from questions of truth, or of Truth—by making truth a less pressing imperative. If the Romans managed to avoid or deflect such questions, we might well envy them.

But did they? Could they?

It is surely true, as we will see in the next chapter, that Roman religion was not concerned with matters of truth in a precise propositional sense in the way Christianity later was. Pagans did not exhaust themselves in formulating creeds and ferreting out heresies.[7] It may also be that, then as now, most people manage to go about the duties and rituals and performances that life thrusts upon them—upon us—by complacently or carefully assuming, without worrying overmuch, that whatever needs to be true for our lives to make sense *is* true. The performances have to be done in any case, so what good could it do to worry about whether the premises that inform those performances are true or not? Perhaps in this spirit, Livy relates the ancient episodes of divine guidance and intervention with an air of nonjudgmental detachment; he occasionally notices the question of factuality—did this divine intervention *really* happen?—but seemingly sees no need to adopt any definite conclusion one way or the other.

And yet it is difficult just to banish the question of truth altogether. The question is always there, lurking in the corners, waiting to come out and

(Bloomington: Indiana University Press, 2003), 173 ("The religious system of the Romans was founded on ritual, not on dogma. Their religious tradition prescribed rituals, not what they should believe. So each individual remained free to understand and think of the gods and the world-system just as he or she pleased").

6. See, e.g., Jeffrey Stout, "Truth, Natural Law, and Ethical Theory," in *Natural Law Theory: Contemporary Essays*, ed. Robert P. George (New York: Clarendon, 1992), 71.

7. See Fox, *Pagans and Christians*, 31.

confront us. Our practices and performances work on implicit presuppositions. Those presuppositions *can* be brought into the open and subjected to scrutiny. And circumstances can occur that provoke such scrutiny—perhaps the appearance of an accosting Socrates who thinks "the unexamined life is not worth living," but more likely just the mundane frustrations or failures of life that will sometimes force us to ask, "What am I doing? Why? Does this make any sense?"

In the case of Roman religion more specifically, didn't "having gods" presuppose a belief that the gods . . . existed?[8] And didn't the enormous investment of time and resources in ritual obeisance to the gods presuppose that the gods were real, and responsive? How could the Romans entrust crucial political and military decisions to the auspices without believing that the auspices were efficacious as a means of discerning the divine agenda? And if the decisions or battles went wrong, as they sometimes did, how could Romans suppress the occasional question or doubt?

So it is hard to imagine that Romans could entirely preserve a cozy obliviousness to such presuppositions and their factuality, or lack thereof. And indeed, we have already noticed the unhappy king Tarquin, who questioned the efficacy of the auguries, and the ill-fated general Publius Claudius, who doubted the reliability of the sacred chickens.[9] We will shortly see how Romans of a philosophical temperament could subject polytheistic religion to searching examinations.

In short, the issues of truth and belief surely *did* arise—not every day, not for everyone, but to some people, sometimes. Much in the way that such issues arise today. So it seems that we may proceed with our question. Did Romans actually believe in the gods? In what sense?

Ignorant Believers, Cultured Despisers?

One recurring answer to that question is that the uneducated and gullible masses of Romans believed in the gods (and on that basis acquiesced in rule of the governing authorities who claimed the support of those gods), while more educated Romans were skeptics who found it best to leave the masses in their credulous ignorance. Enlightened thinkers of the eighteenth

---

8. Cf. Fox, *Pagans and Christians*, 89 ("Naturally, a person had to believe that the gods existed").

9. See above, 69

century like David Hume and Edward Gibbon often approached their own world in that way. Gibbon attributed a prudently concealed skepticism to contemporaries whom he respected, even against their own contrary professions[10]—they may have *said* they believed, but surely they couldn't *really* believe—and he contemplated the project of "writing a dialogue of the dead in which Lucian, Erasmus, and Voltaire should mutually acknowledge the danger of exposing an old superstition to the contempt of the blind and fanatic multitude."[11] So it would be natural for Gibbon to project a similar attitude back onto the Romans—and he did. Gibbon commented acidly that "the various modes of worship, which prevailed in the Roman world were all considered by the people, as equally true; by the philosopher, as equally false; and by the magistrate, as equally useful."[12]

True, even the more philosophical class of citizens might actively and publicly participate in the religious rituals and pageantry. But such participation did not signify actual belief, Gibbon thought; rather, these more enlightened celebrants "concealed the sentiments of an Atheist under the sacerdotal robes."[13]

Gibbon's interpretation would have deflationary implications for Eliot's thesis, and hence for our overall inquiry. That interpretation basically equates paganism with the mythical stories about the gods, and perhaps with some of the public rituals dedicated to those gods—the sacrificing of bulls to Jove, for example. Even in ancient times, only the ignorant could believe in such stories and sacrifices, and by now no one believes them. Eliot's "modern paganism" would thus become a virtual impossibility.

We will come across candidates for whom Gibbon's interpretation may seem to fit. Other historians, however, have found the sort of dismissive interpretation favored by Gibbon facile, and implausible.[14] J. A. North observes that "the idea that the whole college of *pontifices* and the whole Roman

10. Of one friend and frequent correspondent, he wrote, "I much suspect that he never showed me the true colours of his secret skepticism," and he surmised that "the more learned ecclesiastics will indeed have the secret satisfaction of reprobating in the closet what they read in the church." Edward Gibbon, *Memoirs of My Life*, trans. Betty Radice (London: Penguin, 1984), 102, 183.

11. Gibbon, *Memoirs*, 90.

12. Edward Gibbon, *The History of the Decline and Fall of the Roman Empire*, 2 vols. (London: Penguin, [1776] 1995), 1:56.

13. Gibbon, *History of the Decline*, 1:59.

14. See, e.g., James J. O'Donnell, *Pagans: The End of Traditional Religion and the Rise of Christianity* (New York: HarperCollins, 2015), 98; Ramsay MacMullen, *Christianity and Paganism in the Fourth to Eighth Centuries* (New Haven: Yale University Press, 1997), 79.

senate were engaged in a religious charade carried out for the benefit of the superstitious masses seems as unlikely as any hypothesis can be."[15] And just as it would be absurd to say flatly that educated people today believe such and such in matters of religion—in fact, educated people believe and disbelieve all manner of different and contradictory things—it is implausible to attribute any uniform belief to Romans of the classical world. Ramsay MacMullen observes that "as anyone would expect, the spectrum of attested beliefs is very wide even among the educated classes."[16]

This diversity should hardly come as a surprise. Asked what Americans today believe in matters of religion, we would have to say that both the forms of religion and the modes of belief vary drastically. "Religion" (assuming the term is meaningful, as some doubt) is not uniform or all of a piece; it is a vastly diverse phenomenon, ranging from the highly structured theology and offices and liturgies of traditional Catholicism to the more freewheeling and free-form spiritualities of New Age crystal-gazers. And people believe and disbelieve in different forms of religion in different ways; some believe in a fairly literal sense, some in a more abstract or metaphorical or sophisticated (or perhaps sophistical) sense, some not at all. In a similar way, Roman religion took diverse forms and operated on different cultural and intellectual levels; the modes of believing or disbelieving in these different forms of religion surely differed as well. As we will see.

The Central Dilemma

So then, can we make any useful generalizations at all about Roman religious beliefs? Acknowledging the diversity but recognizing the simplification necessary for any summary presentation, we might helpfully adopt a distinction proposed in the first century BC by the encyclopedic scholar

15. North continues: "[The hypothesis] also seems to rest on a profound mistake: the underlying idea has to be that, as Roman nobles became more educated and sophisticated, they easily turned away from belief in the gods and towards some form of scientific materialism, believing that the universe could be explained without recourse to the gods. But this assumption is an anachronistic one: easy scientific rationalism may be available in our time but it was not in theirs. There were some philosophical systems that disposed of the gods or marginalized them, and some of the Roman elite certainly understood or followed such systems; but to jump from that to the assumption that the elite were all scientific rationalists exploiting the ignorant masses is quite without any justification." North, *Roman Religion*, 31.

16. MacMullen, *Christianity and Paganism*, 79.

Marcus Varro (later described by Lactantius as one "than whom no man of greater learning ever lived, even among the Greeks, much less among the Latins").[17] Varro distinguished among three forms or levels of Roman religion: the mythical, the civic, and the natural or philosophical.[18] Varro himself was dismissive of the popular myths portraying the gods as lascivious, violent, jealous, and whimsical; these, he thought, were "ignoble tales" and "lying fables."[19] But he treated the civic and the philosophical forms of religion with respect.

Varro's opinions were probably common among educated Romans. Literalistic belief was for the "crude untaught raw yokels"[20] (MacMullen's description of the condescending opinion of the masses held by educated Romans). But even elite Romans typically revered or at least publicly supported the sacrifices and the auguries. And they affirmed that Roman successes had depended on and would continue to depend upon the favor of the gods. We will see specific examples of this combination of skepticism and affirmation as we proceed.

So the myths were false, at least if taken literally, but the religion of the sacrifices and auguries was . . . what? True? Necessary? Insulated against open public denial? In attempting to reject the mythical religion while preserving the civic religion on which the city depended, educated Romans faced a kind of dilemma. After all, the gods of the myths were the same deities to whom temples and sacrifices were dedicated. So then, how could the gods of the stories be fictional but the gods of the sacrifices be real? And real in what sense, if not in the sense conveyed in the ancient stories?

Augustine would later argue that "mythical" and "civic" religion were not severable. The gods of the myths—Jupiter, Apollo, Venus, and company—were the same gods who were propitiated in the sacrifices and consulted in the oracles. If they were unreal in one place, they were unreal in the other place as well. So if mythical religion was false and pernicious, civic religion was equally false and pernicious.[21] Augustine maintained that the Stoic phi-

17. Lactantius, *The Divine Institutes*, ed. Alexander Roberts et al. (Lexington, KY: CreateSpace, 2015), 1.6, p. 21.

18. Varro's books on this subject are not extant; his writings come to us through the report of Augustine. Augustine, *The City of God against the Pagans*, trans. and ed. R. W. Dyson (Cambridge: Cambridge University Press, 1998), 4.27, p. 176; 6.5, p. 246.

19. Augustine, *City of God* 4.27, p. 176; 6.5, p. 247.

20. Ramsay MacMullen, *Paganism in the Roman Empire* (New Haven: Yale University Press, 1981), 8.

21. Augustine, *City of God* 6.6, pp. 249–54.

losopher Seneca had understood and declared the point[22] (though others have doubted Augustine's interpretation of Seneca);[23] the bishop contended that Varro had also understood this point perfectly well, and had dissembled in pretending to respect the civic religion.[24] In this respect, Augustine's interpretation was not unlike Gibbon's.

Maybe Gibbon and Augustine were right. Varro and like-minded Romans didn't admit as much, but then of course they couldn't or wouldn't confess their true views: that was Gibbon's and Augustine's point. Maybe Romans like Varro simply lacked the courage to profess what they really believed—or rather disbelieved; Augustine suggested as much.[25] Or maybe it wasn't a lack of courage that stopped Varro and his class from asserting the falsity of the civic religion, but rather prudence, and a concern for the public good. If Rome was the source of order and stability in the world, and if Roman governance depended on a general popular belief in the gods, wouldn't a prudent, public-spirited citizen avoid subverting such belief? That was Gibbon's suggestion, actually; his interpretation reflects a curious mixture of cynicism and charity.

This charitable-cynical interpretation *might* be right. But it overlooks other, more sophisticated or subtle alternatives—alternatives that might offer a way out of the dilemma, and that at least some educated Romans seem to have embraced. We might describe two such leading alternatives as *philosophical religion*—this was the third category of Roman religion recognized by Varro—and *civic fideism*. These alternatives emerge in a treatise by Cicero called *On the Nature of the Gods* (a book addressed, incidentally, to the Brutus of *et tu Brute* fame in slightly happier days than the ones Shakespeare would narrate in *Julius Caesar*).[26]

The Philosophy of (Roman) Religion

In the treatise, Cicero mostly presents himself as a youthful recorder of a dialogue about religion that had occurred years earlier among three older men. But the treatise begins with a sort of prologue in which Cicero explains that

22. Augustine, *City of God* 6.10, pp. 261–64.
23. See North, *Roman Religion*, 82.
24. Augustine, *City of God* 4.31, pp. 182–84.
25. Augustine, *City of God* 6.10, p. 263.
26. Cicero, *The Nature of the Gods*, trans. P. G. Walsh (Oxford: Oxford University Press, 1998), 1.1, p. 3. Hereafter, references from this work will be given in parentheses in the text.

"on this question, the pronouncements of highly learned men are so varied and so much at odds with each other that inevitably they strongly suggest . . . that the Academics [i.e., Skeptics] have been wise to withhold assent on matters of such uncertainty."

> Most philosophers have stated that gods exist, the most likely view to which almost all of us are led by nature's guidance. But Protagoras expressed his doubts about it, and Diagoras of Melos and Theodorus of Cyrene believed that gods do not exist at all. As for those who have claimed that they do exist, their views are so varied and at loggerheads with each other that to list their opinions would be an endless task. Many views are presented about the forms that gods take, where they are to be found and reside, and their manner of life; and there is total disagreement and conflict among philosophers concerning them. (1.1, p. 3)

Despite this description-defying diversity, the ensuing dialogue conveys what Cicero evidently regarded as two of the most eligible alternatives, expounded in the exchange by a Stoic, Quintus Lucilius Balbus, and by an Academic or Skeptic, Gauis Aurelius Cotta, who was also a priest (and who was later elected consul). A third position, that of Gaius Velleius, an Epicurean, is dispatched so decisively, and with Velleius's apparent acquiescence, that it seems not to be a serious candidate.

Balbus, the Stoic, peremptorily rejects the various stories about boisterous and lascivious gods and goddesses as "idiotic," as "superstition" and "sacrilegious fables" (2.63, p. 69). In this respect, he follows Varro. He follows Varro as well, however, in supporting the civic religion. Thus, Balbus insists on the necessity and virtue of divination, deploring what he perceives as recent backsliding in the practice (2.8, 10, pp. 50–52; 2.163, p. 106).

In denouncing mythic religion while praising civic religion, Balbus thereby squarely encounters the challenge just noted: How can skepticism about the mythic gods be reconciled with respect for the gods—seemingly *the same* gods—inherent in civic piety?

Balbus's response combines two strategies: he offers a philosophical defense of the existence of the gods together with a philosophical reinterpretation of the character or mode of their existence.

In his philosophical defense, Balbus presents a series of ostensible proofs that the gods are real. Cumulatively, he thinks, the proofs are irresistible: "the existence of the gods is so crystal clear that I regard anyone who denies it as out of his mind" (2.44, p. 62).

Some of Balbus's proofs appeal to religious experience. "Voices of Fauns have often been overheard," he contends, "and apparitions of gods have often been seen; these have compelled each and everyone who is not dull-witted or sacrilegious to admit that gods were at hand" (2.6, p. 49). Other proffered proofs are more logical in character; some of these resemble familiar proofs later developed by Christian thinkers and sometimes called the ontological argument[27] and the argument from design.[28]

Balbus's version of the ontological argument (which he takes from the philosopher Zeno) goes basically like this: (1) The universe itself is necessarily greater and better than anything contained in it. (2) To have life and reason is better than to lack these attributes. (3) But men have life and reason. (4) Therefore, if the universe is greater and better than anything contained in it, then the universe must have life and reason as well; otherwise, the universe would be less than the men it contains—which would be absurd. On this basis, Balbus proceeds to the seemingly pantheistic conclusion that "the universe is god"[29]—though he does not expound or embrace pantheism in any overt or systematic way.

The argument from design is probably even more familiar: it reasons that the orderliness observable in the universe can be accounted for only by supposing some Mind or Intelligence that creates and maintains such order. A familiar modern instance is Voltaire's clock maker argument: a clock is an intricate thing that could not come into existence through mere accident; therefore, if there is a clock, there must be a clock maker.[30] For the same purpose, Balbus invokes the example not of a clock—there is nothing especially intricate about a sundial—but of "a large and beautiful house."[31] And he enthusiastically elaborates on "the uniform movement and undeviating rotation of the heavens, the individuality, usefulness, beauty, and order of the sun and moon and stars, the very sight of which is sufficient proof that they are not the outcome of chance."[32] Observing these facts, he asks: "What can

27. For a critical review of the argument, see Peter van Inwagen, "Necessary Being: The Ontological Argument," in *Arguing about Religion*, ed. Kevin Timpe (New York: Routledge, 2009), 101.

28. See Elliott Sober, "The Design Argument," in Timpe, *Arguing about Religion*, 161.

29. Cicero, *Nature of the Gods* 2.20–22, pp. 54–55.

30. See Anthony Kenny, *A New History of Western Philosophy* (Oxford: Clarendon, 2010), 571.

31. Cicero, *Nature of the Gods* 2.17, p. 53 ("Supposing your eyes lit upon a large and beautiful house. Even if you could not descry its owner, no one could force you to believe that it was built by mice and weasels").

32. Cicero, *Nature of the Gods* 2.15, p. 52.

be so obvious and clear, as we gaze up at the sky and observe the heavenly bodies, as that there is some divine power of surpassing intelligence by which they are ordered?"[33] His position in this respect closely resembles the kind of view later associated with natural theologians like William Paley.[34]

If these arguments are persuasive, they might seem to demonstrate the existence of gods, or perhaps of *a* god, but how would these gods or this god square with the personified deities of Roman religion—with Jove, Venus, Minerva, and company? How does the philosophical approach allow Balbus to escape the dilemma that suggested that it was necessary either to affirm mythic and civic religion together (which Balbus could not honestly do) or to reject them both together (which he also was not inclined to do)?

Here Balbus displays the second part of his philosophical strategy. More specifically, he proposes an elaborate account, supported by ingenious etymologies, of how the Greek and Roman gods can be understood as symbolic representations of the divine reality, so that "behind these sacrilegious fables lies a scientific explanation which is quite sophisticated."[35] Consequently, "though we reject these stories with contempt, we shall be able to identify and grasp the nature of the divinity pervading each and every natural habitat, as Ceres on earth, as Neptune on the seas, and as other deities in other areas; and we shall acknowledge the significance of the names which custom has imposed on them. These are the deities which we are to revere and worship; our worship of the gods is best and most chaste, most holy and totally devout, when we revere them with pure, sincere and untainted hearts and tongues."[36]

In short, the gods *are* real, after all—not in a popular and crudely literal sense, though, but in a deeper philosophical or spiritual or even "scientific" sense. In this respect, Balbus can be seen as practicing a kind of nonliteral hermeneutics similar to that later profusely employed by religious Neoplatonists,[37] by early Christian thinkers like Origen and Augustine and their numerous followers, and even by modern "demythologizing" theologians like Rudolf Bultmann.[38] In this way, Balbus reconciles (at least to his own satisfaction) rejection of the mythical gods, understood literally,

33. Cicero, *Nature of the Gods* 2.70, p. 72; 2.4, p. 48.

34. See William Paley, "The Argument from Design," excerpted and reprinted in *Faith and Reason*, ed. Paul Helm (New York: Oxford University Press, 1999), 189.

35. Cicero, *Nature of the Gods* 2.64, p. 69. See generally 2.60–71, pp. 68–72.

36. Cicero, *Nature of the Gods* 2.71, p. 72.

37. See R. T. Wallis, *Neoplatonism*, 2nd ed. (Indianapolis: Hackett, 1995), 130–37, 147–51.

38. See Rudolf Bultmann, *Kerygma and Myth* (New York: Joanna Cotler Books, 2000).

with continuing support for the gods of the city, understood more philosophically and metaphorically.

The Consecration of Philosophy

But Balbus's elaborate defense of the gods was not merely an arid philosophical exercise. His account served to support and amplify the function
of pagan religion in beatifying and consecrating the Roman world, and the
Roman city. We have noted the similarity of Balbus's proffered proofs to
what in the later Christian tradition are sometimes called the ontological
argument and the argument from design. But this description fails to capture
the full force of Balbus's presentation, which is more poetic and beatifying
than dryly philosophical.

Thus, over and over again Balbus emphasizes not merely the orderliness
of nature but its "beauty," its "harmony," its capacity to inspire "wonder."[39]
(Here he sounds not so different from Abraham Heschel, discussed in chapter 2.) "All things are subject to nature, and are most beautifully administered by her" (2.81, p. 75). Balbus waxes rhapsodic for pages on end about
"the beauty of the things which we declare have been established by divine
providence," resorting to lengthy quotations of poetry as the only way of
conveying his admiration (2.98–118, pp. 82–90).

This beautiful orderliness, evident in the sun and moon and stars, extends to and indeed achieves a kind of culminating perfection in human
beings, providentially endowed with "mind, intelligence, reason, prudence,
and wisdom" (2.147, p. 100).

Humans, in turn, use these providential endowments, "by the work of
our hands . . . striv[ing] to create a sort of second nature within the world
of nature" (2.152, p. 102). This "second nature" would outstandingly include
the human city with its various arts and occupations. The city is thus a sort
of image of the cosmic order, and vice versa. "The universe is, so to say, the
shared dwelling of gods and men, or a city which houses both, for they alone
enjoy the use of reason and live according to justice and law" (2.154, p. 103).

---

39. Cicero, *Nature of the Gods* 2.15, p. 52 ("the individuality, usefulness, beauty, and order
to the sun and moon and stars"); 2.17, p. 53 ("the highly adorned universe, with its huge variety
and beauty of heavenly bodies"); 2.19, p. 54 ("harmony," "harmonious activity"); 2.58, p. 67
("above all, that its beauty is outstanding in its universal adornment"); 2.75, p. 74 (noting "the
argument inspired by wonder at the things of heaven and earth"). Hereafter, references from
this work will be given in parentheses in the text.

In Balbus's position, we see a kind of philosophical paganism that was not identical to the mythic religion (which it scorned), but that nonetheless served to preserve the gods (understood in a more sophisticated, nonliteral sense), and thereby to support the consecrating religion of the city.

Civic Fideism

Balbus's philosophical paganism, however, provokes contempt from Cotta, the Skeptic—a disdain that is intellectual but also patriotic, or civic. Cotta thinks Balbus's arguments fail from a philosophical standpoint. But he also thinks the philosophical arguments threaten rather than sustain the civic religion that both Balbus and Cotta affirm, and on which the city depends.

On the intellectual level, Cotta not only rejects but also systematically deconstructs and ridicules Balbus's arguments and etymologies. He sarcastically disparages Balbus's experiential evidence. "As for the utterances of a Faun," Cotta comments mockingly, "I myself have never heard one, but I am willing to believe you if you say that you have, even though I have no idea what a Faun is" (3.15, p. 113). He argues that the same logic deployed in Balbus's ontological argument (the universe is greater than anything it contains; humans have life, which is good; therefore, the universe must have life as well) could as easily be used to prove that the universe is "adept at reading a book," or that the universe is a "musician" (3.22, p. 115). The orderliness that Balbus observes in the cosmos should be attributed not to gods but to "nature" (3.26–28, p. 117). And with respect to Balbus's effusive praise of the cosmos's beauty and usefulness, Cotta retorts: "What benefit . . . can be observed in mice or cockroaches or snakes, all of them troublesome and destructive to the human race?" (3.65, p. 132). He goes on to press the familiar argument from evil:

> Either God wishes to remove evils and cannot, or he can do so and is unwilling, or he has neither the will nor the power, or he has both the will and the power. If he has the will but not the power, he is a weakling, and this is not characteristic of God. If he has the power but not the will, he is grudging, and this is a trait equally foreign to God. If he has neither the will nor the power, he is both grudging and weak, and is therefore not divine. If he has both the will and the power (and this is the sole circumstance appropriate to God), what is the source of evils, or why does God not dispel them? (3.65, p. 133)

But Cotta protests as well, in a more apparently pious vein, that Balbus is actually *undermining* the civic religion. "By deploying all these arguments for the existence of gods, you succeed in casting doubt on what is in my view crystal-clear" (3.10, p. 111). And before beginning his aggressive debunking of Balbus, Cotta unapologetically affirms that he is a priest, and he insists that "I shall indeed defend [the gods], and I have always done so; no words from any person, whether learned or unlearned, will ever budge me from the views which I inherited from our ancestors concerning the worship of the immortal gods" (3.5, p. 109).

This fervent declaration of faith seems in tension with Cotta's exercise in deconstruction, and it is hard to square with his own admission, earlier in the dialogue, that "many troubling considerations occur to me which sometimes lead me to think that [the gods] do not exist at all" (1.61, p. 24). So, how to reconcile Cotta's vigorously expressed skepticism with his equally vehement professions of belief?

One obvious possibility is the one suggested by Gibbon (and one, incidentally, used by modern thinkers in the tradition of Leo Strauss in interpreting a whole variety of important philosophers).[40] Cotta, the priest, is "conceal[ing] the sentiments of an Atheist under the sacerdotal robes." He does not believe in the gods, but for personal or public purposes he pretends to believe. So he is willing to confess his skepticism in "a conversation conducted between friends," as he says, but he agrees that the existence of the gods should never be questioned "in public" (1.61, p. 24). Cotta, of course, does not explicitly confess to holding this position; on the contrary, he protests that he *does* believe in the gods. He avows that "I have never regarded any of these constituents of our religion with contempt," and he even affirms that "Rome could never have achieved such greatness without the supreme benevolence of the immortal gods" (3.6, p. 109). But Gibbon (and Leo Strauss) would respond, probably, that this is what Cotta, the prudently and patriotically dissembling priest, *has* to say: for civic and public purposes, he has to pretend to believe in the gods.

And yet the interpretation does not quite fit. After all, it is in the "conversation among friends," not in public, that Cotta expresses both his doubts and his support for the gods.

40. See Leo Strauss, *Persecution and the Art of Writing* (London: University of Chicago Press, 1952). For a succinct summary of Strauss's approach to interpretation, see Ian Ward, "Helping the Dead Speak: Leo Strauss, Quentin Skinner, and the Arts of Interpretation in Political Thought," *Polity* 41 (2009): 239-41.

Still, is there any other way to understand Cotta's seemingly conflicting and conflicted utterances? Perhaps there is. Here is a possibility. Perhaps Cotta thinks that the world—and hence our knowledge of the world—is divided into different epistemic domains that have their own proper truths and rules of belief. There is the natural world, perhaps, and the philosophical world; and then there is the civic world. Operating under the epistemic criteria proper to the natural and philosophical worlds, Cotta finds Balbus's arguments for the gods profoundly deficient. But in the civic world, different rules of truth and belief apply, and these lead to different conclusions. In *that* world—in the civic world—the gods are real. Speaking *as citizen and as priest*, Cotta can accordingly assert that truth in complete good faith and without hesitation.

Cotta affirms the existence of the gods in public, in other words, not because he needs to dissemble, but because in the world of the city, the gods *are* real. And he strenuously resists Balbus's effort to import philosophical reasoning to bolster the civic religion, because the importation reflects—and effects—a corruption of categories that can only be harmful, both to philosophy and to the city (3.5–10, pp. 109–11).

On this interpretation, Cotta is proposing and practicing what might be called civic fideism: the gods should be affirmed in the civic realm based on epistemic criteria appropriate to that realm, and should not be supported or judged by the kind of reasoning appropriate to other domains. Whether this interpretation accurately captures Cotta's meaning is uncertain, but everything he says seems consistent with it. Moreover, if this is how Cotta is negotiating the problem of civic religion, he would be employing a strategy that has been used repeatedly in other contexts.

In the Middle Ages, for example, a group of thinkers sometimes known as the Latin Averroists seem to have resisted suspicions of heterodoxy by proposing a "two truth" position under which what was true in one domain—philosophy—might be different from what was true in another—in particular, theology.[41] More recently, drawing on a Wittgensteinian perspective that understands knowledge and truth in terms of "language games," the philosopher Norman Malcolm has argued that religion is a distinctive kind of "language game" with its own rules that need not track the rules used in other epistemic contexts. Religion is "a form of life; it is language embedded in action." In this view, religious discourse needs no justification outside

---

41. See Frederick Copleston, SJ, *A History of Philosophy*, vol. 2 (New York: Doubleday, [1962] 1993), 436–37.

itself. And God can exist in and for the language game of "religion" even if he does not exist in other such games—philosophy, for example, or science.[42]

In a similar vein, the scientist and popular writer Stephen Jay Gould famously proposed that science and religion should be viewed as "nonoverlapping magisteria";[43] each could be true in its own realm and according to its own proper criteria. Contemporary legal philosophers have likewise proposed very similar strategies for defending the legitimacy of constitutional discourse,[44] or of legal discourse generally.[45] And although ordinary lawyers might find these theories overly subtle, these same lawyers instinctively act on a similar premise when they argue in court; they understand that in the courtroom they must limit themselves to "legal" reasoning, and that such reasoning may lead to conclusions that are taken to be true—true *in law*—that would not be adopted and would not be true in other domains based on other kinds of reasoning.[46]

In a similar way, it seems, Cotta wants to treat civic religion as a distinctive and valuable practice with its own epistemic rules and answerable only to itself. True, the priests and the augurs might not be able to satisfy the philosopher, but then, who appointed the philosopher to be the boss of the priests and augurs in the first place? Civic religion is its own domain, and it is safe and beyond challenge so long as it remains within its proper sanctuary.

This at least seems a plausible interpretation of Cotta. Moreover, it is unlikely that Cotta was the only ancient practitioner of this mode of believing. In his searching examination of the "modalities of belief" by which ancient pagans maintained their myths, Paul Veyne invokes the notion of "mental balkanization,"[47] and he attempts to identify and describe different "programs of truth"[48] in which the nature of reality and the criteria of truthfulness differ. "A Greek put the gods 'in heaven,'" Veyne observes, "but he would have been astounded to see them in the sky. He would have been no

42. Norman Malcolm, "The Groundlessness of Belief," in *Faith*, ed. Terence Penelhum (London: Macmillan, 1989), 193, 203.

43. Steven Jay Gould, "Nonoverlapping Magisteria," *Natural History* 106 (March 1997): 16, http://www.science.fau.edu/sharklab/courses/evolution/pdfs/non-overlapping%20magisteria.pdf.

44. See Philip Bobbitt, *Constitutional Fate: Theory of the Constitution* (New York: Oxford University Press, 1982).

45. See Dennis Patterson, *Law and Truth* (New York: Oxford University Press, 1996).

46. See generally Steven D. Smith, *Law's Quandary* (Cambridge, MA: Harvard University Press, 2004).

47. Veyne, *Did the Greeks Believe?*, 41. See also 90 ("Truth is Balkanized . . .").

48. Veyne, *Did the Greeks Believe?*, 21, 48, 128.

less astounded if someone, using time in its literal sense, told him that Hephaestus had just remarried or that Athena had aged a great deal lately. Then he would have realized that in his eyes mythic time had only a vague analogy with daily temporality."[49] It would be a mistake, though, to conclude that the accounts of the gods were merely lies, or even "fictions," and thus unreal.

Veyne offers an intriguing illustration from his own experience: "For my part, I hold ghosts to be simple fictions but perceive their truth nonetheless. I am almost neurotically afraid of them, and the months I spent sorting through the papers of a dead friend were an extended nightmare. At the very moment I type these pages I feel the hairs stand up on the back of my neck. Nothing would reassure me more than to learn that ghosts 'really' exist. Then they would be a phenomenon like any other, which could be studied with the right instruments, a camera or a Geiger counter."[50]

So Cotta may have been not a dissembling skeptic after the manner of Gibbon but rather a civic fideist who in his mode of belief anticipated the Latin Averroists and the neo-Wittgensteinian "language game" theorists. And what about Cicero himself? Cicero begins the dialogue by identifying himself with Cotta's philosophical school.[51] And he gives Cotta the last word in the debate. But then he concludes the book by declaring that "Cotta's argument seemed to Velleius [the Epicurean] to be more truthful, but in my eyes Balbus' case seemed to come more closely to a semblance of the truth."[52] So Cicero professes to be a religious believer in the philosophical sense, not a civic fideist (or, if that interpretation seems unpersuasive, a Straussian skeptic) like Cotta.

What to make of this? Is Cicero being disingenuous? Perhaps. He was, after all, a politician, and knew not to say things that would make political trouble for himself. In other writings Cicero ties moral duties closely to the good of the state, or of the public, arguing that while it is never permissible to dissimulate for private advantage, prevarication may be permissible if it serves the public good.[53] He also believes that worship of the gods is good for the state; thus, early on in the book about the gods, Cicero reports with seeming approval the view that "without devotion to the gods all sense of the holy and of religious obligation is also lost. Once these disappear, our lives

49. Veyne, *Did the Greeks Believe?*, 18.
50. Veyne, *Did the Greeks Believe?*, 87.
51. Cicero, *Nature of the Gods* 1.11, p. 6.
52. Cicero, *Nature of the Gods* 3.95, p. 146.
53. See Cicero, *On Obligations*, trans. P. G. Walsh (New York: Oxford University Press, 2000), 3.93–95, pp. 116–17.

become fraught with disturbance and great chaos. It is conceivable that, if reverence for the gods is removed trust and the social bond between men and the uniquely pre-eminent virtue of justice will disappear."[54]

So perhaps Cicero fits Gibbon's (and Augustine's) interpretation; perhaps he is lying—or dutifully dissembling—out of timidity, or for the public good. And yet, as with Cotta, this interpretation does not quite fit, because in the dialogue itself Cicero both expresses uncertainty and indicates that he is drawn to a belief in the gods. If the dialogue was private enough to allow for sincerity, in other words, why would a skeptical Cicero have professed belief in the gods; if it was public enough to require such a (disingenuous) profession, why did he openly acknowledge his doubts?

It seems, as James O'Donnell observes, that Cicero "was believer and skeptic, both at once."[55]

The Precarious Tenacity of Pagan Faith

Believer and skeptic, both at once. It was a precarious position—but not an uncommon one. Then or now.

Balbus's philosophical paganism and Cotta's pagan civic fideism might be seen as complementary in the sense that they both served, or at least sought, to sustain the civic religion that functioned to support and consecrate Roman life and the Roman city. Educated Romans who found it impossible to take the mythic religion at face value might choose one or the other of these alternatives. Some Romans surely did follow Balbus's path: later Neoplatonists like Plotinus, Porphyry, and Proclus would be outstanding examples. We will notice them again, briefly, in a later chapter. Gibbon remarked in a disdainful tone on the efforts of "new Platonicians" and "fashionable philosophers" who "prosecuted the design of extracting allegorical wisdom from the fictions of the Greek poets" and who "recommended the worship of the ancient gods as the emblems or ministers of the Supreme Deity."[56]

Other Romans likely followed Cotta's example, deliberately or intuitively. (By the nature of the position, it would be difficult to identify such fideists with confidence; they would be estopped by their philosophy from

54. Cicero, *Nature of the Gods* 1.4, p. 4.
55. O'Donnell, *Pagans*, 46.
56. Gibbon, *History of the Decline*, 1:561.

telling us who they were.) This was a different way of sustaining the faith necessary to support the city.

But although philosophical paganism and civic fideism could complement each other, they could also contradict each other, imperiling both. The way in which Cotta might undermine Balbus is obvious on the face of the dialogue. As noted, Cotta disparages and systematically deconstructs Balbus's philosophical arguments for the gods. If Cotta's refutations persuade (and in Cicero's presentation the refutations seem almost overwhelming, Cicero's own closing disclaimer notwithstanding), then Romans who might have depended on such philosophical bulwarks would find themselves unable to affirm the presuppositions and implicit tenets of pagan religion.

Because Cicero gives Cotta the last word, we do not know just what Balbus might have said in rebuttal. But we can imagine. Cotta's fideism, as we have seen, depended on the strategy of dividing truth and belief into discrete domains, so that the epistemic rules proper to one domain would have no jurisdiction in another domain. Thus, belief in the gods might be unjustified for philosophy but wholly warranted in the civic domain. Balbus might well object, though, that the approach is untenable. Truth is the accurate representation of what is real. If the gods exist, they exist; if not, not. The gods cannot be real in one epistemic domain but not in another. And if there is reason to believe the gods are real, that is what we should believe; if not, not.

Once it is conceded, in short, that the gods do not exist in general, or for philosophy, they are doomed to disappear altogether. To put the point differently, just as Augustine would later argue that the civic religion could not be severed from the mythic one, so Balbus would likely have contended that the civic religion could not be separated from the philosophical one.

This is a powerful objection. As we have seen, Cotta's two-truth approach has been common enough as a historical matter. It can provide a convenient strategy, for a time, to protect some necessary body of beliefs against corrosive objections. But the approach has also had its powerful critics. Thomas Aquinas energetically attacked the "two truth" strategies of the Latin Averroists.[57] And the philosopher John Hick argued persuasively that the neo-Wittgensteinian "different language games" approach employed by thinkers like Norman Malcom in fact "cuts the heart out of religious belief and practice."[58]

---

57. For a highly dramatic account of this confrontation, see G. K. Chesterton, *St. Thomas Aquinas: "The Dumb Ox"* (New York: Doubleday, [1933] 1974), 70-74.

58. Hick concedes that religious talk *is* a special kind of language, and that religionists

On the level of common sense, the critics surely have the more appealing argument. To most people, truth means the accurate representation of the world. And the world is what it is, and is not what it is not. A statement or a belief cannot be true in one domain but false in another.

In sum, the implausibility of the mythic religion to more educated Romans—of the religion of stories about lustful, vengeful, whimsical gods—created a challenge to believing in the civic religion. But the civic religion was what sustained and consecrated the city—the city of "shining beauty and grace" that Romans revered, and that gave their lives meaning and purpose and sublimity. So thoughtful and sophisticated Romans rose to the challenge, devising "modalities of belief," as Veyne puts it, that served for decades and centuries to provide the necessary support.

The resulting intellectual achievement was intricate and impressive. And yet the modalities of belief remained fragile. And they were in turn stoutly challenged not just by the kind of internal examination evident in Cicero's treatise but also, later, by a radically different form of religiosity—Christianity. To which we turn in the next chapter.

---

often use terms in distinctive ways—"as pointers rather than as literal descriptions." Even so, "the pointers are undoubtedly intended to point to realities transcending metaphors and myths; and to suppress this intention is to do violence to religious speech and to empty the religious 'form of life' of its central and motivating conviction." John Hick, "Seeing-as and Religious Experience," in Penelhum, *Faith*, 183, 184.

CHAPTER 5

Looking beyond the World:
The Christian Revolution

As we saw in previous chapters, Roman religion was diverse and capacious, both in the deities and cults that it recognized and in the different "modalities of belief" that it supported. But it did not encompass all faiths. Most importantly, it could not absorb or contain Judaism or Christianity. With Judaism, Rome maintained a fragile peace broken by periodic bouts of revolt and unsparing repression.[1] With Christianity, relations were even less congenial; the Romans sometimes grudgingly tolerated Christians and sometimes subjected them to ferocious persecutions. (We will look more closely at these persecutions in the following chapter.)

Why did these religions in particular resist absorption into the Roman cornucopia of cults, rituals, and devotions? The answer, it seems, is that the Jerusalem-centered faiths represented a radically different form of religiosity—indeed, a fundamentally different orientation to the world—that was unassimilable into the Romans' thoroughly worldly civic piety. In this vein, and with reference to Judaism and Christianity, the Israeli historian Guy Stroumsa argues that "the religious transformations of the Mediterranean and Near Eastern world in the first centuries of the Roman Empire are so radical" that they are properly described as "a 'paradigm shift' in the domain of the religious."[2] And he observes that "the conflict between paganism and Christianity is so fascinating" because it had "decisive consequences for the future of Western culture."[3] Cambridge historian Keith Hopkins explains

1. See generally Martin Goodman, *Rome and Jerusalem: The Clash of Ancient Civilizations* (New York: Vintage Books, 2008).

2. Guy Stroumsa, *The End of Sacrifice: Religious Transformations in Late Antiquity*, trans. Susan Emanuel (Chicago: University of Chicago Press, 2009), 2.

3. Stroumsa, *The End of Sacrifice*, 101. Cf. Paul Veyne, *When Our World Became Christian:*

that "it is difficult for us now to recapture how very strange and offensive [Christianity] must have seemed to pagans in the Roman world."[4]

In this chapter, we will attempt to discern the nature of the "revolution"[5] that divided Judaism and Christianity from Roman religion. We will see how Judaism and Christianity represented a fundamentally different kind of religiosity from paganism, so that the empire's eventual acceptance of Christianity would amount to a transformation—in aspiration and ideal if never fully in practice—not merely of "religion" (as if that were some discrete and severable compartment of life) but of the basic orientation of human beings toward the world, and toward the city.

Were Pagans and Christians Really So Different?

Recently, however, a few revisionist historians, whom we might think of as historical deconstructionists or perhaps as retrospective conciliators, have suggested that the supposed differences between pagans and Christians were not so fundamental after all, and that the conflicts were mostly constructed by sectarian Christians who needed a fearsome opponent to define themselves against.[6] If the deconstructionists-conciliators are right, the inquiry proposed for this chapter might seem misdirected. So before proceeding, we should pause to notice the principal arguments for doubting that the supposed conflict between paganism and Christianity was as significant as scholars like Stroumsa and Hopkins—and many, many others—have supposed.

Two main and interrelated arguments run through the deconstructionist-conciliating interpretations. First, as we have seen already, what others call

---

312-394, trans. Janet Lloyd (Cambridge: Polity Press, 2010), 19 (describing "the chasm that separated Christianity from paganism").

4. Keith Hopkins, *A World Full of Gods: The Strange Triumph of Christianity* (New York: Penguin, 1999), 76.

5. See Pierre Chuvin, *A Chronicle of the Last Pagans (Revealing Antiquity)*, trans. B. A. Archer (Cambridge, MA: Harvard University Press, 1990), 11 (describing the emergence of Christianity as "a political, intellectual, and religious revolution").

6. See Douglas Boin, *Coming Out Christian in the Roman World: How the Followers of Jesus Made a Place for Themselves in Caesar's Empire* (New York: Bloomsbury Press, 2015). Similar themes are discernible in James J. O'Donnell's *Pagans: The End of Traditional Religion and the Rise of Christianity* (New York: HarperCollins, 2015). In a generally similar vein is Candida Moss, *The Myth of Persecution: How Early Christians Invented a Story of Martyrdom* (New York: HarperCollins, 2013).

"paganism" was not a monolithic religious system; rather, the term is used to cover a sprawling panorama of deities, rituals, stories, and practices. Nor for that matter was Christianity, in the beginning (or ever), a monolithic, tightly defined and organized movement.[7] So there could not have been a genuine conflict between "paganism" and "Christianity"—or so it might seem—because neither term refers to any unitary or organized movement or form of religion at all. Second, and relatedly, the so-called pagans never thought of themselves as "pagans"; Christians invented if not the word then the category, mostly as a way of classifying, dismissively,[8] those who did not join up with their own movement.[9]

As a purely descriptive matter, these observations seem mostly accurate, and hardly novel. Indeed, even as he argues that the differences between Roman religion and Christianity as well as later Judaism were so "radical" as to constitute a "paradigm shift," Guy Stroumsa points out that "neither 'paganism' nor even 'Christianity' can be reduced to a factitious unity that represents anything. The forms of Christian existence in the first centuries are numerous—and the concept of 'paganism' is of course only the creation of Christian thinkers and does not correspond to any concrete reality."[10]

As a logical matter, however, the inference from these descriptive observations to the conclusion that there was no inherent and fundamental conflict between paganism and Christianity, or that the ostensible differences between them were artificial or constructed, seems a non sequitur. One can imagine an analogous argument maintaining that although pet lovers have from time immemorial contrasted and debated the relative merits of "dogs" as opposed to "cats," in reality the various and sundry organisms placed under the label of "dog" are enormously diverse in size, color, and behavior. Moreover, no animal ever identified itself as a "dog": the term and the category have been imposed entirely from the outside—by humans. Same for cats. Consequently, the supposed contrast between "dogs" and "cats" is profoundly misconceived.

---

7. Cf. Peter Brown, *The Body and Society: Men, Women, and Sexual Renunciation in Early Christianity*, 2nd ed. (New York: Columbia University Press, 2008), xxxvii (noting "the infinite variety of Christianity throughout this period"). The diversity of early Christianity is stressed in James D. G. Dunn, *Neither Jew Nor Greek: A Contested Identity*, vol. 3 (Grand Rapids: Eerdmans, 2015).

8. Although it is often suggested that the term was one of abuse, meaning something like "country bumpkin," a recent careful analysis casts doubt on this interpretation. See Alan Cameron, *The Last Pagans of Rome* (New York: Oxford University Press, 2011), 14–32.

9. See, e.g., O'Donnell, *Pagans*, 5–6, 159–64, 214; Boin, *Coming Out Christian*, 112–18.

10. Stroumsa, *The End of Sacrifice*, 2–3.

But this conclusion would be merely silly. Let us concede (although a philosophical realist might dispute the point) that "dog" and "cat," like most or all other general terms and categories by which we understand and engage with the world—germs, planets, rivers, islands, cities, animals, plants, etc.—are devised by humans for the purpose of describing diverse particulars that usually would not and could not claim the terms for purposes of self-description (often because such entities—dogs, cats, germs, plants, rivers, etc.—do not and could not engage in self-description to begin with). The question is whether such terms and categories usefully help *us* to address real similarities and differences in the world. Similarly, although the point can always be debated, the widespread use of the categories "pagan" and "Christian" from late antiquity to the present at least suggests that the terms have proven useful in this way.

One recent conciliating book seeks to shed light on the religious situation in late antiquity by drawing parallels between Christians of that time and the LGBT movement of today.[11] An impressive achievement is that from the book's title to its dedication to the text itself, the author manages to work allusions to the LGBT movement into virtually every page. And how does this relentlessly executed parallel illuminate the historical developments? The gist of the argument, it seems, is that although people then and now have often been mistrustful of perceived differences, once they get to know the supposedly different folks ("The New Neighbors Who Moved in Next Door," as one chapter title puts it), they come to realize that the differences are not of great importance and need not impede a cordial human fellowship. Thus, by quietly getting to know their neighbors, and getting to be known by them, Christians "made a place [for themselves] in Caesar's Empire."

For this story line to work, the author has to emphasize and elevate those mostly inconspicuous Christians—"The Quieter Ones"[12]—who were content to mingle unobtrusively, to join in the Roman religious festivities, and (in disregard of the minimal essential prohibitions declared by the Christian council of Jerusalem)[13] congenially to eat the meat sacrificed to pagan deities. In other words, the author elevates the Christians who, then and now, would be regarded by more rigorous Christians as lax or lapsed or "lukewarm."[14] Conversely, the author disapproves and attempts to mar-

11. See Boin, *Coming Out Christian*.
12. Boin, *Coming Out Christian*, 15–35.
13. Acts 15.
14. Cf. Rev. 3:15–16 ("I know thy works, that thou art neither cold nor hot: I would thou

ginalize, as unreasonable or "antisocial,"[15] those more fervent Christians—including nontrivial figures like Saint Paul, Saint John, Tertullian, Cyprian, Perpetua, Athanasius, Ambrose, Gregory of Nazianzus, Augustine, and John Chrysostom[16]—who stood out as leaders and exemplars of the Christian movement, who wrote and expounded its sacred texts, who defined its doctrines, and who sometimes persisted in professing it even though this meant going to the cross or the pyre or the lions. Other adjustments are also needed; we need not detail here the ways in which the historical record must be clipped and contorted to fit the conciliating story line.[17] Even with these adjustments of the historical record, moreover, the story runs amok after Christianity achieves political dominance in the fourth century. Once Christians had earned the acceptance of their neighbors in the empire, it

---

wert cold or hot. So then because thou art lukewarm, and neither cold nor hot, I will spue thee out of my mouth" [KJV]).

15. Boin, *Coming Out Christian*, 37.

16. Boin, *Coming Out Christian*; see, for Saint Paul, 38–40; for Saint John, 40; for Tertullian, 21; for Cyprian, 31; for Perpetua, 29; for Athanasius, 128; for Ambrose, 121–24; for Gregory of Nazianzus, 118–20; for Augustine, 128; for John Chrysostom, 128.

17. Here is one example that may suffice. In 362, the emperor Julian, in a campaign to restore paganism to dominance, issued decrees that effectively prohibited Christians from teaching in the schools. Oxford historian Averil Cameron explains that "this measure effectively debarred Christians from teaching altogether, since rhetoric and grammar constituted most of the education syllabus." Averil Cameron, *The Later Roman Empire* (Cambridge, MA: Harvard University Press, 1993), 94. Historians have recognized that this was a drastic and unprecedented step in excluding people whose Christian beliefs the pagan ruler disapproved of, and in attempting to exercise control over the formation of the culture. See, e.g., Edward J. Watts, *The Final Pagan Generation* (Oakland: University of California Press, 2015), 113–15. The projected effect of this ban, Princeton historian G. W. Bowersock observes, was that "within little more than a generation the educated elite of the empire would be pagan." G. W. Bowersock, *Julian the Apostate* (Cambridge, MA: Harvard University Press, 1978), 84. Even Julian's great admirer, the pagan historian Ammianus Marcellinus, found these decrees "intolerable." See Ammianus Marcellinus, *The Later Roman Empire (A.D. 354–378)*, ed. and trans. Walter Hamilton (London: Penguin, 1986), 298 ("The laws which [Julian] enacted were not oppressive, . . . but there were a few exceptions, among them the harsh decree forbidding Christians to teach rhetoric or grammar unless they went over to the worship of the pagan gods"). When Boin narrates the episode, however, he first converts the prohibition into a bland conditional—Christians "shouldn't be employed as teachers *if* they refused to educate children about the Greek and Roman gods"; Boin, *Coming Out Christian*, 119 (emphasis added). This makes it sound as if Christians were excluded from teaching only if they refused to teach the subject matter. Boin then blithely describes Christian resentment over the debilitating exclusion as much ado about nothing: "a debate over educational policy had turned into spiritual battle" (120).

seems, the faction of more militant and unsociable Christians then seized control, to the considerable detriment both of the pagans and of the more congenial and reasonable Christians.[18]

For anyone who finds the book's attempted parallel between ancient Christianity and the modern LGBT movement at all instructive, this outcome presumably ought to be ominous. In any case, both in the book's overall treatment and in its grim culmination, the real lesson seems directly contrary to the author's conciliatory intentions. It turns out that between Roman pagans and the more committed (or, if you prefer, more unsociable or unreasonable) Christians, there *were* real and profoundly consequential incompatibilities.

A different and more compelling qualification is noted by the historian Wayne Meeks, who points out that in early Christianity "the daily practice of most church members was doubtless indistinguishable in most respects from that of their unconverted neighbors."[19] But then, how could it have been otherwise? A person who heard and believed the message about Jesus naturally continued to speak the same language as before—Greek or Latin or whatever—and to work and dress and eat in much the same ways as she had always done. For similar reasons, Christians continued to talk about good and bad, virtue and vice, mostly in the same vocabulary that they had previously used, and that their non-Christian neighbors used.[20] Consequently, "it is curiously difficult to say exactly what was new about Christian morality, or to draw firm boundaries around it."[21] "The Christian language of virtue and vice is ordinary, so much so that it is sometimes hard to see what all the fuss was about on the part of its attackers or its defenders."[22]

And yet, beneath these surface similarities and continuities, Meeks shows, fundamental and transformative differences are discernible. The result was that "a tectonic shift of cultural values was set in motion by those small and obscure beginnings."[23]

So it seems that we may pursue the chapter's inquiry after all: In what fundamental if subtle ways did Christian religiosity differ from pagan religiosity?

---

18. Boin, *Coming Out Christian*, 110–37.

19. Wayne A. Meeks, *The Origins of Christian Morality: The First Two Centuries* (New Haven: Yale University Press, 1993), 2.

20. Meeks, *Origins of Christian Morality*, 15.

21. Meeks, *Origins of Christian Morality*, 2.

22. Meeks, *Origins of Christian Morality*, 66 (emphasis omitted).

23. Meeks, *Origins of Christian Morality*, 1.

While not precluding our inquiry, however, the acknowledgment of diversity within both paganism and Christianity, as well as of similarities between pagans and Christians, should warn us against expecting to find clean and simple categories. Different scholars suggest a variety of distinctions. Roman religion, it is said, was polytheistic; Judaism and Christianity were monotheistic.[24] Roman religion focused on ritual, not on creed; Christianity cared about truth, doctrine, and belief—and heresy.[25] Roman religion was a piety of outward performances; Judaism and especially Christianity were concerned with the inner person—with what was in the mind and the heart.[26] Roman religion was a thing of *this world*; Christianity in particular emphasized *the next world*.[27] The Roman gods demanded proper sacrifice but were otherwise mostly indifferent to (and far from exemplary of) morality; the God of Judaism and Christianity was intensely committed to the moral life.[28] Although these distinctions are not without a basis in the historical evidence, it may turn out that they do not hold categorically. To borrow a familiar contrast articulated by Wittgenstein, what we find may not be unvarying and immutable essences of two utterly different religiosities, but rather partially overlapping but nonetheless distinct and distinguishable "family resemblances."

We can begin to appreciate the important family differences, nonetheless, if we recall the discussion in chapter 2 suggesting that religion can be understood as a sense of and a relation to the sacred. We can then ask, both for pagan and for Jewish and Christian religion: What and *where* (so to speak) is the sacred?

24. See, e.g., Jonathan Kirsch, *God against the Gods: The History of the War between Monotheism and Polytheism* (New York: Penguin, 2004).

25. See, e.g., Scheid, *Introduction to Roman Religion*, 19, 173. See also Chuvin, *Chronicle of the Last Pagans*, 10; Veyne, *When Our World Became Christian*, 33–36; Hopkins, *World Full of Gods*, 80. Cf. Stroumsa, *The End of Sacrifice*, 90 (describing "the definition of religion in Rome as the observance of rites, without belief really playing an independent role"). Robin Lane Fox remarks that "there was . . . no pagan concept of heresy" (*Pagans and Christians*, 31).

26. In this vein, Stroumsa observes that "the idea of the transformation of the internal life remained unknown to the official religion of the ancient city, as well as to the mystery cults." And he suggests that "if one has to specify in a single word the nature of this change [from paganism to Christianity], I would accept the Hegelian analysis that stresses the *interiorization* of religion" (*The End of Sacrifice*, 15, 2). See also Wilken, *The Christians*, 63–65; O'Donnell, *Pagans*, 69.

27. See, e.g., Scheid, *Introduction to Roman Religion*, 19.

28. See, e.g., O'Donnell, *Pagans*, 66 ("[The gods] mostly didn't care whether or not human beings did the right thing. Ethical precepts, living the good life, avoiding sin: that was your business, not the gods'").

The Location of the Sacred

In this respect, the work of the German Egyptologist Jan Assmann provides valuable illumination. Like Stroumsa, quoted at the outset of this chapter, Assmann argues that the shift from the pagan religiosity of Egypt, Greece, and Rome to the monotheistic faiths of later Judaism and Christianity represented a radical and portentous transformation—one that "has had a more profound impact on the world we live in today than any political upheaval."[29] This shift brought "with it a new mentality and a new spirituality, which have decisively shaped the Western image of man."[30]

So, what exactly was the radical, transformative difference? Assmann does not make it easy for readers to ascertain his answer to that question. His most characteristic and frequent claim is that there was a fundamental and enormously consequential difference between the polytheism of paganism and the monotheism of Judaism and Christianity. Or so it seems. But then Assmann qualifies that position, and then qualifies it again.

As a descriptive matter, the assertion that paganism was polytheistic and Christianity was monotheistic is at best an oversimplification. Scholars find strains of monotheism in paganism: the various gods are understood by some pagans as different faces of a single divinity.[31] The fourth-century Christian apologist Lactantius listed and quoted an assortment of pagan poets and thinkers who had understood the various pagan deities essentially as different masks or manifestations of one divine being.[32] We saw one expression of this view already in the religious articulation of Balbus, the Stoic character in Cicero's dialogue on the gods. Balbus, recall, defended the gods, plural, in a metaphorical sense but also asserted at one point that "the universe is god,"[33] with the various deities representing different aspects of that divinity. Noting such expressions, Assmann observes that "God's oneness

---

29. Jan Assmann, *The Price of Monotheism*, trans. Robert Savage (Stanford: Stanford University Press, 2010), 1.

30. Assmann, *The Price of Monotheism*, 2.

31. See, e.g., Stroumsa, *The End of Sacrifice*, 103 (noting "the existence of a pagan monotheism"), and 5 ("For example, the Platonist Celsus seems to be more strictly monotheistic than the Christian Origen"). See generally Garth Fowden, *Empire to Commonwealth: Consequences of Monotheism in Late Antiquity* (Princeton: Princeton University Press, 1994).

32. Lactantius, *The Divine Institutes*, ed. Alexander Roberts et al. (Lexington, KY: CreateSpace, 2015), 1.5, pp. 18–20.

33. See above, 91.

is not an invention of monotheism, but the central theme of polytheistic religions as well."[34]

Conversely, the monotheism of Christianity was at least complicated, and contestable. Christians believed in one God, yes, but that one God was somehow constituted as three persons.[35] Christians also came to believe in angels, and in a host of saints that in some ways replaced the functions of paganism's subordinate deities.[36] Thus, Assmann asserts that "as an instrument for describing and classifying ancient religions, the opposition of unity and plurality is practically worthless."[37]

So if the portentous difference was not actually between polytheism and monotheism, as much of Assmann's writing on its face seems to suggest, what then *was* the vital distinction? "What seems crucial," Assmann first explains, "is not the distinction between One God and many gods but the distinction between truth and falsehood in religion, between the true god and false gods, true doctrine and false doctrine, knowledge and ignorance, belief and unbelief."[38] In this respect, Assmann suggests, "biblical religion" (including "ancient Israelite, Jewish, and Christian religions") contrasted with "all the alien and earlier cultures that knew nothing of the distinction between true and false religion."[39] The concern of biblical religion with truth and falsity was "a revolutionary innovation in the history of religion."[40]

Perhaps. Still, if the real transformation was from pagan indifference to Jewish and Christian obsession with truth, why make so much of the distinction between polytheism and monotheism? The contrasts seem quite independent of each other. Why couldn't a polytheistic religion be concerned with questions of truth? (The discussion in the previous chapter of Cicero's dialogue on the gods shows that at least some pagans *were* interested in such questions.) Conversely, couldn't a religion devoted to a single deity nonetheless take a tolerant or relaxed stance toward propositional truth? We might

34. Assmann, *The Price of Monotheism*, 31.

35. Paul Veyne remarks (with less than complete theological precision, to be sure) that "given that it presents two or even three supernatural objects to be worshipped, namely God, Christ and—later—the Virgin, the Christian religion was, quite literally, polytheistic" (*When Our World Became Christian*, 20).

36. See Peter Brown, *The Rise of Western Christendom: Triumph and Diversity, A.D. 200–1000*, rev. ed. (West Sussex, UK: Wiley-Blackwell, 2013), 161–65.

37. Assmann, *The Price of Monotheism*, 31.

38. Assmann, *The Price of Monotheism*, 31.

39. Assmann, *The Price of Monotheism*, 5, 11.

40. Assmann, *The Price of Monotheism*, 23.

think of modern instances—Unitarianism, perhaps, or the familiar irenic invocations of the story of the six blind men of Indostan and the elephant.

So Assmann complicates the matter still further—but also clarifies it—by offering a second qualification: the really important distinction, he now says, is not so much either in the number of deities or in the concern about truth per se, but more in the character or location of divinity. More specifically, and crucially, the pagan gods were actors (albeit powerful and immortal actors) *of and within this world.* The God of Judaism and Christianity, by contrast, is "the *creator* of the world, which he guides in its course and maintains in its existence—an invisible, hidden, spiritual god who dwells *beyond time and space.*"[41]

In short, the ultimately crucial difference is not so much that the Jewish and Christian God is solitary while the pagan gods are plural. What matters, rather, is the relation of those deities to the world and even, we might say, their metaphysical status.[42] Jupiter, Juno, Apollo, and company are *part of* the world; they are creatures of time and space. As James O'Donnell explains: "The gods . . . were mainly the mightiest part of the world itself, not beings that somehow stood outside it all. When Olympus came to feel too earthen, then the planets were thought to be the homes of the gods, and the domains of space beyond were thought to be the highest and most perfect places in the world—but emphatically *in* the world."[43]

Conversely, the God of later Judaism and of Christianity can create and maintain the world because he is *not* merely part of the world, and is *not* contained within time and space.

So if we understand religion as a relation to the sacred, as suggested in chapter 2, then pagan religion differs from Judaism and Christianity in its placement of the sacred. Pagan religion locates the sacred *within* this world. In that way, paganism can consecrate the world from within: it is religiosity relative to an *immanent* sacred. Judaism and Christianity, by contrast, reflect a *transcendent* religiosity; they place the sacred, ultimately,

41. Assmann, *The Price of Monotheism*, 39 (emphasis added).

42. Paul Veyne observes that "the originality of Christianity lies not in its so-called monotheism, but in the gigantic nature of its god, the creator of both heaven and earth: it is a gigantism that is alien to the pagan gods." The Christian god was a "metaphysical god." Veyne, *When Our World Became Christian*, 20.

43. O'Donnell, *Pagans*, 67. See also Wilken, *The Christians*, 91 ("God, in the Greek view, dwelt in a region above the earth, but he did not stand outside of the world, the *kosmos*. Earth and heaven are part of the same cosmos, which has existed eternally. The world is not the creation of a transcendent God").

outside the world—"beyond time and space." To be sure, a simple and stark distinction between "immanent" and "transcendent" cuts a bit too cleanly (as theoretical distinctions on this level of generality inevitably do), in part because the Christian deity is both transcendent *and* immanent, even incarnate. Acknowledging the simplification inevitable in any such distinction, however, we can appreciate along with Assmann, Heschel,[44] and others the distinction's value in illuminating a fundamental difference between pagan and Christian (or, more generally, biblical) religiosities.

This contrast in the conceptions of deity may help to explain what otherwise seems the puzzling and accidental connection with monotheism and polytheism. A transcendent God of the kind professed by Jews and Christians would necessarily be singular, for reasons articulated by Greek thinkers and later by Christian theologians.[45] Aristotle had taught that it is matter that individuates things otherwise similar in form;[46] my pen is not the same thing as your pen, even though they have the same shape, color, and function, because my pen is made of different matter or, if you like, of different atoms. But on this logic, it would make no sense to talk in the plural of *immaterial* beings possessing the same form or divine features; there would be nothing to individuate one god from another. Such reasoning had already persuaded a thinker like Xenophanes in the fifth century BC of the necessary unity of god.[47]

In addition, we can appreciate how questions of truth would come to assume greater importance in Judaism and especially in Christianity. If there are many gods, all with a good claim to some sort of divinity, then it probably doesn't make much difference which or what sort of deity you choose to worship. Most likely, these are really just the same family of gods, going by different names in different places[48]—or maybe even just different names for different manifestations or aspects of the same divine Reality. Why would that Reality care under which of its names you choose to address it? Conversely, if there is only one supreme deity, who is the ruler of the universe,

44. See the discussion above, in chap. 2.

45. See, e.g., Saint Thomas Aquinas, *Summa Theologica*, trans. Fathers of the English Dominican Province (New York: Benziger Brothers, 1948), I, q. 2, arts. 2–3.

46. See A. C. Lloyd, "Aristotle's Principle of Individuation," *Mind* 79 (October 1970): 519.

47. See Jonathan Barnes, *Early Greek Philosophy* (London: Penguin, 1987), 95–97.

48. See Robin Lane Fox, *The Classical World: An Epic History from Homer to Hadrian* (New York: Basic Books, 2006), 50 ("As polytheists, the Greeks accepted many gods, and the gods which they met abroad were usually worshipped and understood as their own gods in yet another local form").

and if all the other supposed deities are either fictions or (as the early Christians believed) imposters and devils,[49] then it becomes much more urgent that you know the truth about what—or Whom—you are worshiping. Who wants to be caught worshiping and sacrificing to something or someone who doesn't exist or, worse, who is actually demonic and malevolent?

No Longer at Home in the World?

These distinctions in the conceptions of the metaphysical status of the divine and the location of the sacred may seem rarefied and academic, accessible mostly to theologians and philosophers, and of no conceivable interest to ordinary folk. If we were to stop the average religious devotee on his way to a pagan temple or a Christian service and ask, "Do you place your faith in a transcendent or a merely immanent sacred?," we might expect to receive an uncomprehending "Sorry, but I don't understand the question." Suppose we follow up by asking, "Do you believe that God or the gods created the world out of nothing, or rather that God or the gods are themselves part of the natural world?" Perhaps this question would lead to a meaningful and confident response—but probably not. And should that be a decisive question anyway? Would the answer make any real difference in the way people actually feel and live and worship?

We can press the doubt further. Christians might say that God is an entity beyond time and space, even beyond "being" (whatever that means). God is transcendent. But, the Christians would say, he is also immanent—and thoroughly involved in this world. Moreover, as humans in this world, Christians will necessarily and inevitably picture God in human images and terms[50]—as a muscular, majestic, white-haired figure, perhaps (as in countless medieval and early modern sculptures and paintings including, most famously, the depiction of God on the Sistine Chapel ceiling). What else could they do? Could *we* do? We humans are, well, human; so we will inevitably engage with the world in human terms and images.

In the end, in short, do abstract theological claims about God's transcendence of the natural world—which is, after all, the world we inhabit

---

49. Edward Gibbon, *The History of the Decline and Fall of the Roman Empire*, 2 vols. (London: Penguin, [1776] 1995), 1:459–60.

50. Cf. E. L. Mascall, *The Christian Universe* (London: Darton, Longman and Todd, 1966), 53 ("It has become customary in some circles to ridicule the use of images in religion, but it is difficult to see how we can avoid them").

and the only one we can really conceive of in any concrete way—have any practical significance?

Well, yes, actually. Perhaps not immediately and directly; it is not as if the typical farmer or cobbler learns one day that God is transcendent and promptly revises his opinions and his way of life. And yet, what may seem like abstract differences in the location of the sacred support fundamentally different orientations or attitudes toward the world—different orientations with effects and profound implications for even the most mundane aspects of life. First let us consider the difference in orientations; later we will look at a few of the divergent practical implications of these different orientations.

The function of paganism, once again, is to consecrate or sacralize nature and the world. As we saw in chapter 2, Abraham Heschel argued that the Greeks "regarded the elemental powers of nature as holy" and treated "nature" as an "object of ultimate adoration."[51] In a similar vein, Jan Assmann explains that "a world of gods does not stand opposed to the world made up of the cosmos, humankind, and society, but endows them with meaning as a structuring and ordering principle." In this way, "a world of gods constitutes the world of human destiny, which in its joys and sorrows, its crises and resolutions, its epochs and transitions, presents itself as a meaningful whole only in relation to the destinies of the gods."[52]

By locating the sacred within the world, in short, pagan religion gave life in the world shape and meaning, and sublimity. It helped to consecrate the world—to make the world a fit, orderly, even beautiful home for human habitation (assuming, of course, that the gods were rendered cooperative through proper propitiation). The polytheistic religion of antiquity, says Assmann, "seeks to make its votaries at home in the world."[53] Insofar as the city is part of that world, and indeed is a sort of "second nature" or image of the world (as Balbus argued),[54] paganism served to sacralize the city as well. And as we saw in chapter 3, this sacralization was no mere academic hypothesis; it was embodied, rather, in a host of buildings, rituals, performances, processions, and holidays.

For pagans, in sum, this city and this world were, and are, our home—the only home we have. This life, and the good things of this life, are the only ones we need to concern ourselves with.

51. Abraham Joshua Heschel, *God in Search of Man: A Philosophy of Judaism* (New York: Farrar, Straus and Giroux, 1955), 88, 90.

52. Assmann, *The Price of Monotheism*, 40–41.

53. Assmann, *The Price of Monotheism*, 9.

54. See above, 93.

An atheist might say much the same thing, of course. Or at least he might utter much the same words. But there is a crucial difference. The pagan could make those affirmations in an appreciative or laudatory or even rapturous tone, because our home in this city and this world and this life is a consecrated home—consecrated by its association with the gods. This world is our home not merely in the atheist's sense that, however shabby, it's the only one we've got, but rather in the sense of acknowledging how the gods have endowed this home with a "shining beauty and grace."[55]

The pagan orientation, in short, accepts this world as our home, and does so joyously, exuberantly, worshipfully. (Or at least that is one part of the pagan orientation; we may encounter other, darker aspects as we proceed.)

The transcendent monotheism of Judaism and Christianity, by contrast, disrupts this comfortable sense of being at home. Though created and sustained by God, the world is now also separated from God—a separation aggravated, in Christian doctrine, by the Fall. Christians (and also Jews) effectively undid the pagan sacralization of the world, and instead effected a "desanctification of nature," as Heschel explained.[56] As a result, Assmann observes, the monotheist "does not feel entirely at home in the world any more."[57] Judaism and Christianity are religions "of distantiation, in contrast to religions of complete immersion in the world."[58]

In Christianity, this distantiation generated an orientation that was complex—one that was, and is, difficult for non-Christians (and, often, Christians as well) to understand, and even more difficult for Christians actually to maintain. Matters would have been simpler if Christianity had simply and starkly rejected "the world" as a fallen realm to be resisted and escaped. Some Christian heretics took this view.[59] And indeed, even what became the canonical Christian Scriptures repeatedly warned disciples to keep themselves "unspotted from the world,"[60] sometimes coming close to what sounded like flat condemnation of the world.[61] Saint Simeon Stylites sitting for years atop

55. Fox, *The Classical World*, 50.

56. Heschel, *God in Search of Man*, 91.

57. Assmann, *The Price of Monotheism*, 42.

58. Assmann, *The Price of Monotheism*, 43.

59. See Everett Ferguson, *Church History*, vol. 1 (Grand Rapids: Zondervan, 2005), 98; Paul Tillich, *A History of Christian Thought: From Its Judaic and Hellenistic Origins to Existentialism*, ed. Carl E. Braaten (New York: Touchstone, 1967), 34–35.

60. James 1:27; 4:4. See also, e.g., John 15:16–19; Gal. 1:4; 1 John 5:19.

61. E.g., 1 John 2:15–17 (KJV): "Love not the world, neither the things that are in the world. If any man love the world, the love of the Father is not in him. For all that is in the world, the

his pillar, or Saint Antony dwelling in the desert, living on bread and water consumed only after sunset once a day, or once every few days,[62] would seem to embody this sort of contempt of the world.

At the same time, Christianity early on condemned as a heresy the view that the world is simply evil. Although fallen, the world is a creation of the true God, and hence good. It is to be appreciated as a blessing, not shunned or despised as an affliction.[63] We can try to appreciate this complex and challenging stance by considering how the desacralization of the world influenced the way Christians thought (or aspired to think) on an assortment of related topics: nature, the goods of this world, sexuality, and the city.

Nature

As noted, paganism sacralized nature—every mountain, valley, and stream had its proper deity—while Christianity revoked this sacralization. And yet Christianity also taught that nature was God's good creation. Though not "sacred" in the way it was for pagans, the world as God's creation continued to have a "sacramental" quality. The delicate prescription was thus neither to deny the beauty of the natural world (which would be ungratefully to disparage God's work), nor to rest in any adoring appreciation of that beauty (which would be a form of idolatry), but rather to appreciate natural beauty while looking beyond it to its source in the Creator.

Addressing the emperor Marcus Aurelius, Athenagoras the Athenian used analogies to illustrate the distinction and explain why "Christians do not worship the universe." When people visit the imperial family, "if they chance to come upon the royal residence, they bestow a passing glance of admiration on its beautiful structure," Athenagoras pointed out. "But it is to you yourselves that they show honour." Likewise, "at the musical contests the adjudicators do not pass by the lute-players and crown the lutes." In the

---

lust of the flesh, and the lust of the eyes, and the pride of life, is not of the Father, but is of the world. And the world passeth away, and the lust thereof: but he that doeth the will of God abideth for ever."

62. Athanasius, *Life of Antony* 2.7.

63. See Robert Louis Wilken, *The Spirit of Early Christian Thought: Seeking the Face of God* (New Haven: Yale University Press, 2003), 136–38; Colin Gunton, "The Doctrine of Creation," in *The Cambridge Companion to Christian Doctrine*, ed. Colin E. Gunton (Cambridge: Cambridge University Press, 1997), 141, 147–48; Tillich, *History of Christian Thought*, 41–43.

same way, "beautiful without doubt is the world." And "yet it is not this, but its Artificer, that we must worship."[64]

Augustine made the point in poetic terms.

> And what is this God [that I love]? I asked the earth and it said: "I am not he"; and everything in the earth made the same confession. I asked the sea, and the deeps and the creeping things, and they replied, "We are not your God; seek above us." I asked the fleeting winds and the whole air with its inhabitants answered, "Anaximenes was deceived; I am not God." I asked the heavens, the sun, moon and stars; and they answered, "Neither are we the God whom you seek." And I replied to all these things which stand around the door of my flesh: "You have told me about my God, that you are not he. Tell me something about him." And with a loud voice they all cried out, "He made us." My question had come from my observation of them, and their reply came from their beauty of order.[65]

In the abstract, these attitudes toward nature are importantly different. And yet, the practical significance of the difference still may not be obvious. The pagan thinks nature is divine; the Christian claims that nature itself is not divine but rather a creation and reflection of the divine. So the pagan gazes up at the starry sky and exclaims, "How *divine!*" The theologically fastidious Christian looks up and says, "What a sublime *manifestation* of the divine!" As a practical matter, how important is this difference? The pagan might praise nature in poetry—as in Virgil's *Georgics*, for example—but the Christian might do the same. Think of Saint Francis's famous "Canticle of the Creatures." Or Gerard Manley Hopkins's "Pied Beauty."

> Glory be to God for dappled things. . . .
> All things counter, original, spare, strange; . . .
>   With swift, slow; sweet, sour; adazzle, dim;
> He fathers-forth whose beauty is past change.
>   Praise him.[66]

64. Athenagoras, *A Plea for the Christians*, trans. B. P. Pratten (Pickerington, OH: Beloved, 2016), 18.

65. Augustine, *The Confessions of St. Augustine*, ed. and trans. Albert Cook Outler, rev. ed. (New York: Dover, 2002), 10.9, p. 176.

66. Gerard Manley Hopkins, "Pied Beauty," *Poetry Foundation*, accessed July 1, 2017, https://www.poetryfoundation.org/poems-and-poets/poems/detail/44399.

If the differences in pagan and Christian attitudes to nature did not have hugely different practical implications, however, the divergences become more conspicuous when we come to the other topics.

Goods

In the pagan conception, the gods' assistance is sought in the pursuit of a variety of this-worldly goods. Life. Health. Wealth and power. Glory and fame. Peace. Happiness. These are by and large the same kinds of goods that the "interest-seeking conception" of the person that we looked at in chapter 2 recognizes as the desiderata that govern human pursuits and that inform the instrumental reasoning by which personal and public decisions are made.

Christianity recommended a complex but fundamentally different attitude toward these goods. It did not deny their goodness. The world, once again, is a creation of the true God, and hence good; its pleasures and beauties are genuine goods. But they are not the ultimate good. That more ultimate good is something often described as "eternal life." To this the worldly goods needed to be subordinated; otherwise they would lose their goodness.

"Eternal life." The term recurs repeatedly in the New Testament to describe the goal and reward of Christian faithfulness.[67] The Apostles' Creed repeats the theme: "I believe in . . . the life everlasting." For his part, Augustine over and over emphasized that "eternal life is the Supreme Good."[68]

And what is "eternal life"? For Christians, the term connoted two things. As its literal meaning suggests, it meant life that goes on forever—that continues or resumes after death in a physical resurrection. But eternal life also meant something like the life of and with God, the Eternal. "For, impelled by the desire of the eternal and pure life," Justin Martyr declared, "we seek the abode that is with God, the Father and Creator of all."[69]

In both respects, the Christian orientation contrasted sharply with paganism. To be sure, many Greeks and Romans surely *hoped* for some sort of existence beyond the grave.[70] And some of the so-called mystery cults did

---

67. E.g., Matt. 19:16; Rom. 2:7; 1 Tim. 6:12; Titus 1:2; 1 John 1:2; Jude 21.

68. Augustine, *The City of God against the Pagans*, trans. and ed. R. W. Dyson (Cambridge: Cambridge University Press, 1998), 19.4, p. 918.

69. See, e.g., "The First Apology of Justin Martyr," in *The First and Second Apologies of Justin Martyr*, trans. Alexander Roberts and James Donaldson (Cumming, GA: St. Polycarp, 2016), chap. 8, p. 23.

70. See, e.g., Fox, *The Classical World*, 48.

seek to prepare their initiates for life in the next world. Even so, as the historian John Scheid explains, the mystery cults were not "religions of salvation and spirituality." "The wellbeing or salvation sought by these cults was of a nature just as material as that offered by the traditional cults: it had to do with this world, the here and now. True, they showed that death was not an evil, and offered hope for the beyond, but above all they set out to achieve a happy life in this world and possibly even to prolong it and help the deceased after their deaths."[71]

Scheid concludes that "there is no similarity between these cults and Christianity. They conveyed no message of triumph over death nor did they offer any fundamentally new revelations."[72] In particular, pagans rejected the idea of physical resurrection and of a final judgment. Indeed, Guy Stroumsa observes that this was "one of the characteristics of Christianity that would repel intellectual pagans the most."[73]

In addition, while hoping that the gods would assist them in achieving the goods of this world, pagans typically did not imagine any higher good—anything like union with the gods—that transcended earthly flourishing.[74] For pagans, the goods of this world—of the here and now—would be, so to speak, as good as it gets. By contrast, Christians looked for a blessedness that "eye hath not seen, nor ear heard, neither hath entered into the heart of man."[75] Once again, it did not follow that for Christians the goods of this world were not authentic goods. But if they were pursued as the ultimate goods, then they would, paradoxically, lose their goodness and turn to evils.

The idea is tirelessly and eloquently elaborated as the central theme of Augustine's *Confessions*. The spiritual autobiography relates how, as a boy, Augustine is immersed in childish games, and then in sexual adventures and carousing with friends.[76] Slightly later, as a talented and ambitious young man, Augustine leaves his provincial African town and travels to Rome and Milan in search of prosperity and eminence. Sexual gratification continues to be important to him (bk. 5).

71. Scheid, *Introduction to Roman Religion*, 186–87.

72. Scheid, *Introduction to Roman Religion*, 188.

73. Stroumsa, *The End of Sacrifice*, 9.

74. But see Fox, *Pagans and Christians*, 102–67 (describing ways in which pagans did expect to see and encounter the gods).

75. 1 Cor. 2:9.

76. Augustine, *Confessions* 1–3. Hereafter, references from this work will be given in parentheses in the text; the page references are to the Outler edition.

Gradually, however, he becomes convinced, at least in the abstract, that wisdom is to be preferred to sensual gratification. This conviction is reinforced by the sudden death of a dear companion. As friends, they had enjoyed everything together; now everything reminds Augustine of what has been lost beyond hope of recovery. "My heart was utterly darkened by this sorrow," he recalls, "and everywhere I looked I saw death" (4.9, p. 51).

Generalizing, he concludes that "every soul is wretched that is fettered in the friendship of mortal things—it is torn to pieces when it loses them, and then realizes the misery which it had even before it lost them" (4.11, p. 52).

Nonetheless, thoroughly immersed in careerism and the gratifications of sexuality, Augustine finds it difficult to relinquish the pursuit of these mundane goods. Even after he becomes intellectually convinced of the truth of Christianity, the allure of the world is strong. "But wait a moment," he tells himself, resisting conversion.

> This life also is pleasant, and it has a sweetness of its own. . . . We must not abandon it lightly. . . . See now, it is important to gain some post of honor. And what more should I desire? I have crowds of influential friends, if nothing else; and if I push my claims, a governorship may be offered me, and a wife with some money. . . . This would be the height of my desire. . . . I talked about these things, and the winds of opinions veered about and tossed my heart hither and thither. (6.19–20, p. 99)

Sexual gratification in particular is difficult to forswear. "Lord, make me chaste," Augustine famously prays, "but not yet" (8.17, p. 139).[77]

Eventually, though, in part through study and mystical experience, and in part through the influence and example of prominent Christians like Ambrose, the eloquent and erudite bishop of Milan, and Victorinus, a philosopher and Christian convert, Augustine is able to embrace the Christian faith more fully. That faith points him to a higher good—eternal life, or union with God—that is fulfilling, not shallow and transitory in the way earthly goods are. This new understanding culminates in a mystical experience that Augustine enjoys with his mother, Monica, shortly before her death. Mother and son are "discussing together what is the nature of the eternal life of the saints: which eye has not seen, nor ear heard, neither has entered into

---

77. This is a paraphrase; the actual quotation is "Grant me chastity and continence, but not yet."

the heart of man." Their conversation gradually brings them "to the point where the very highest of physical sense and the most intense illumination of physical light seemed, in comparison with that life to come, not worthy of comparison, even of mention" (9.23–24, p. 163). Looking back on the experience, Augustine would recall that "this world, with all its joys, seemed cheap to us even as we spoke." And he would add: "If this [experience] could be sustained, . . . and . . . should so ravish and absorb and envelop its beholder in these inward joys that his life might be eternally like that one moment of knowledge which we now sighed after—would not *this* be the reality of the saying: 'Enter into the joy of thy Lord'?" (9.25–26, p. 164).

And yet the worldly goods, once again, *are* authentically good. "Now there is a comeliness in all beautiful bodies, and in gold and silver and all things. The sense of touch has its own power to please and the other senses find their proper objects in physical sensation. Worldly honor also has its own glory, and so do the powers to command and to overcome. . . . For these inferior values have their delights, but not at all equal to my God, who hath made them all. For in him do the righteous delight and he is the sweetness of the upright in heart" (2.10, p. 25).

In short, Christians were—are—faced with a delicate challenge. They must live in the world, rejoicing in its beauties and blessings; in that respect, their mode of life seems not so different from that of the pagans. And yet they must not forget that the ultimate good is God, not the world, and that this world is not their true home.[78]

Sex and the City, Sex and the Cosmos

As noted, one aspect of the pagan orientation that Augustine found especially difficult to relinquish was its easy, open sexuality. As we saw in chapter 3, the pagan approach to sexuality was characterized by two main assumptions. First, sexual fulfillment, whether heterosexual or homosexual, and whether within or outside of marriage, is inherently natural and good (for men at least); it is a manifestation of the "mysterious, indwelling presence of the gods."[79] Opportunities for sexual satisfaction abounded, not only or mainly with spouses, but also with the hosts of prostitutes and slaves that

---

78. Heb. 13:14.

79. Kyle Harper, *From Shame to Sin: The Christian Transformation of Sexual Morality in Late Antiquity* (Cambridge, MA: Harvard University Press, 2013), 67.

the city maintained. But, second, sexual activity must be subordinated to the needs of the city—which was a principal reason why respectable women were expected to marry and to remain chaste before marriage and celibate afterward.

Within this matrix of assumptions, the Christian view of sexuality was not only radically alien; it was close to incomprehensible.[80] To be sure, assertions about "Christian" views of sexual morality are simplifications; then, as now, Christian thinkers differed in their understandings of sexuality. Moreover, Christian views of sexuality were not hermetically sealed off from ideas prevalent in their world; they were influenced by, among other things, the doctrines of the Platonists, Stoics, and Pythagoreans.[81] With these caveats, though, we can still say that Christian sexual ethics represented, as Kyle Harper explains, a "paradigm shift" and a "deep earthquake in human morality."[82]

The most obvious change was in the specific rules and prohibitions. For Christians, sex was permissible only within marriage—for both men and women: no more "double standard."[83] Same-sex sexual relations were condemned, as was pederasty.[84] Prostitution was regulated and discouraged[85] (though never actually eliminated). Even more important than the specific prohibitions, though, was the "new foundational logic of sexual ethics"[86] that supported the specific rules. In its underlying logic, Christian sexual morality did not rely on the assumptions that informed Roman attitudes and practices, but instead was grounded in an entirely different set of premises.

80. Harper, *From Shame to Sin*, 101 (describing the "vast gulf between Christian standards and contemporary sexual practice"). See also Kathy L. Gaca, *The Making of Fornication: Eros, Ethics, and Political Reform in Greek Philosophy and Early Christianity* (London: University of California Press, 2003), 293 ("Paul's unconditional imperative to flee fornication was radically new to the Greeks and other Gentiles, and its aim was to supplant religious sexual existence as they lived it, or, in the case of the philosophers, as they conceived it should be lived").

81. Both points are developed in Gaca, *The Making of Fornication*. Gaca nonetheless emphasizes the discontinuities between Christian and non-Christian understandings of sex. Even when Christians were influenced by Stoic or Pythagorean ideas, these ideas were radically transformed in the Christian understanding.

82. Harper, *From Shame to Sin*, 8, 18.

83. Sarah Ruden, *Paul among the People: The Apostle Reinterpreted and Reimagined in His Own Time* (New York: Random House, 2010), 15.

84. Harper, *From Shame to Sin*, 155–56.

85. Harper, *From Shame to Sin*, 186–88.

86. Harper, *From Shame to Sin*, 8.

We might note the essential pagan assumptions that Christianity did not share. The view that sexual activity was a necessity and that, as Kyle Harper puts it, "mankind might find in erotic fulfillment nothing short of salvation"[87] emphatically did not apply to Christianity; on the contrary, Christians tended to believe that the celibate life was not only possible but also commendable. So sexual renunciation became a prominent theme in Christian thinking.[88] In addition, Christian sexual ethics shared none of the typical Roman assumptions about manliness—assumptions that encouraged sexual gratification as natural and necessary but sternly condemned men who acted as the passive partners in sexual encounters.[89] Nor were Christian sexual ethics primarily based on social or political exigencies, such as the need for orderly reproduction within the family.[90] In the Christian view, Kyle Harper explains, "the cosmos replaced the city as the framework of morality."[91]

Thus, in the Christian view, the human body was, as the apostle Paul put it, a "temple of the Holy Spirit."[92] In Paul's understanding, the body became "a consecrated space, a point of mediation between the individual and the divine."[93] Unsanctioned sex functioned to pollute or desecrate that space.[94] By contrast to the Roman and Greek encouragement of sex in moderation, in the Christian view "the sexual machinery of the body was something to be protected from contamination, not simply to be kept in proper balance."[95] And "the harmless sexual novitiate that was an unobjectionable part of sexual life in antiquity" now became "an unambiguous sin, a transgression against the will of God, echoing in eternity."[96]

To the detached modern critic, this logic may seem like question begging. Let us grant for argument's sake that the human body is a temple, and

---

87. Harper, *From Shame to Sin*, 21.

88. The theme is developed at length in Brown, *The Body and Society*.

89. Harper, *From Shame to Sin*, 99 ("Similarly, early Christian literature—with one exception—offers none of the vicious attacks on passivity . . . , because the precise synthesis of machismo and sexual moralism was wholly absent from Christian discourse"). See also Ruden, *Paul among the People*, 66–67.

90. Harper, *From Shame to Sin*, 87.

91. Harper, *From Shame to Sin*, 8.

92. Harper, *From Shame to Sin*, 87.

93. Harper, *From Shame to Sin*, 93.

94. Harper, *From Shame to Sin*, 87–92. See also Gaca, *The Making of Fornication*, 144 ("Christian bodies, [Paul] states, are the temple of the holy spirit and fornication is a sin 'against the body' [1 Cor. 6:18–19], not unlike the desecration of a temple").

95. Harper, *From Shame to Sin*, 91.

96. Harper, *From Shame to Sin*, 92.

thus at least in a derivative sense holy; even so, unless one begins by assuming that sexual relations are somehow presumptively impure, why should they be perceived as compromising that holiness? To the pagans, as we have seen, just the opposite description seemed to apply: sexual passions were not impure but rather the "indwelling presence of the gods."[97]

But then, from a Christian perspective, that proposition only aggravated the problem. Let us suppose that sexual passion reflects the "indwelling presence of the gods"; we must then ask, *Which* gods? And the pagan answer, it seems, would be Eros, or perhaps Venus,[98] or (if sexual passion is supplemented with wine) maybe Dionysus, or perhaps Priapus of the prodigious phallus. Foreign or false gods, in other words.

The observation helps to explain why early Christians commonly equated fornication with idolatry.[99] The confinement of sex to one partner within the sanctified bonds of matrimony was correlated with monotheism; conversely, the Roman practice of a more wide-ranging sexual prodigality was the manifestation of a kind of polytheism. Consequently, "for Paul the sexual disorder of Roman society was the single most powerful symbol of the world's alienation from God."[100]

In this way, sexual morality "came to mark the great divide between Christians and the world."[101] That divide did not become operative immediately upon the political acceptance of Christianity under Constantine. Harper reports, rather, that the implementation of the new sexual morality was not effectively implemented until the reign of the emperor Justinian in the mid-sixth century. Still, looked at from afar, the change was dramatic, amounting to "a revolution" not only in rules of behavior but also in conceptions of the human person and his or her relations to the state and the cosmos.[102] And "sex was at the center of it all."[103]

Harper seems unhappy, or at least ambivalent, about the transformation. Although he is harsh in his descriptions of the brutal exploitation of prostitutes and slaves in the Roman system, his account of the new Christian morality is censorious as well. The change was recklessly effected, he suggests:

97. Harper, *From Shame to Sin*, 67.

98. Brown, *The Body and Society*, 18.

99. Harper, *From Shame to Sin*, 94. This point is developed at length in Gaca, *The Making of Fornication*, 119–46.

100. Harper, *From Shame to Sin*, 94.

101. Harper, *From Shame to Sin*, 85.

102. Harper, *From Shame to Sin*, 18.

103. Harper, *From Shame to Sin*, 1.

"Christian norms simply ate through the fabric of late classical antiquity like an acid, without the least consideration for the well-worn contours of the old ways."[104] And he strikes a wistful tone about what was lost. "The tradition of frank eroticism withers, and the visual depictions of lovemaking slowly recede. Gone is the warm eroticism of the Pompeian fresco, vanished is the charmed sensuality of the Greek romance."[105] Justinian's implementation of the new Christian morality reflected "the haze of ruin and violent puritanism."[106]

As we will see, a similar censoriousness toward the new Christian regime, and a similar wistfulness at the loss of the pagan world, are themes that have resonated through the centuries and continue to influence attitudes and agendas even today.

One City or Two?

Though pagan and Christian sexual morality were starkly different, they were not necessarily incompatible as a practical matter,[107] at least so long as Christians remained a powerless minority. If Christians chose to refrain from sex with prostitutes and slaves, and to confine sex to marriage, such restraint did nothing to impede pagan sexual expression. But in another area the differences were more likely to lead to conflict—namely, in what we might think of as their civic sensibilities, or their attitudes toward the city.

As we saw in chapter 3, Roman government and Roman religion were intimately intertwined. In Rome and elsewhere, paganism generally was at its core a religion of the city—of the earthly city: the Greek polis, the city of Rome, later the empire.[108] John Scheid observes that the founders of Rome or of other cities of antiquity also founded the religions of those cities and

---

104. Harper, *From Shame to Sin*, 12.

105. Harper, *From Shame to Sin*, 14–15.

106. Harper, *From Shame to Sin*, 1. In a similar vein, see Gaca, *The Making of Fornication*, 304–5.

107. But see Gaca, *The Making of Fornication*, 293 ("The antifornication social order that Paul aspired to form could never peacefully coexist with the religious sexual heritage of any Gentile gods").

108. Jan Assmann explains that "all the great [pagan] deities are gods of their respective cities." And "the cult is nothing other than the tribute owed the gods as civic overlords." Assmann, *The Price of Monotheism*, 41.

dictated the rules of those religions.[109] Consequently, "in trying to understand the religious behaviour of the ancient Romans, we should never forget the fundamental importance of *city ideology*. . . . That ideal of collective life determined most aspects of religious practice."[110]

More specifically, we have already seen in chapter 3 how Roman religion was thoroughly integrated into Roman political and civic life. Through a melding of religion, politics, and civic culture, the full majesty of the gods was deployed in support of the political community and its rulers—and vice versa. The community was religious; religion was communal.[111] And that religious life served to enlist the subjects' full loyalty to the city and its rulers. Patriotism and paganism were coextensive.

By contrast, although most Christians likewise believed that they could and should pay allegiance to the political community and its rulers, that belief was grounded in an entirely different and more complicated set of premises. Pagan Romans paid their devotions and performed their propitiating rituals to immanent gods who were in and of this world. Christians, by contrast, worshiped a transcendent God. Although actively concerned with and involved in mundane affairs (to the point that he had actually— and from the pagan perspective shamefully[112]—condescended to become a mortal human being, subject to pain and death), the Christian God was ultimately beyond time and space. This theological difference generated different attitudes toward the world: whereas pagans were fully at home in the world, Christians aspired to live for eternity—to be in but not of the world.

These conceptual and attitudinal differences in turn manifested themselves in radically different conceptions of the relation of persons to the political community and its rulers. Paganism sacralized the city, while Christianity did the opposite. And although Christians lived in and felt loyalty to the city, they could not be citizens of it in the same full and exclusive sense that pagans could. On the contrary, to invoke a metaphor often used by Augustine (significantly, used even *after* the empire had embraced Christianity), Christians were more like "pilgrims" in the world, and in the city.

This attitude was firmly rooted in Christian Scripture. The epistle to the Hebrews, ascribed to the apostle Paul, reminded Christians that the patriarch Abraham had left the city of his birth and had "made his home in the prom-

109. Scheid, *Introduction to Roman Religion*, 20.
110. Scheid, *Introduction to Roman Religion*, 16.
111. Scheid, *Introduction to Roman Religion*, 20.
112. See Wilken, *Spirit of Early Christian Thought*, 102–3.

ised land [of Palestine] like a stranger in a foreign country. . . . For he was looking forward to the city with foundations, whose architect and builder is God."[113] In this he had been joined by his wife and progeny. These venerated ancestors had "admitted that they were aliens and strangers on earth. People who say such things show that they are looking for a country of their own. If they had been thinking of the country they had left, they would have had opportunity to return. Instead, they were longing for a better country—a heavenly one. Therefore God is not ashamed to be their God, for he has prepared a city for them."[114]

The conclusion of this reasoning was that "here we do not have an enduring city, but we are looking for the city that is to come."[115]

Later Christian writers reiterated and elaborated on the theme. In a metaphor enthusiastically taken up by some twentieth-century theologians,[116] one anonymous early Christian expressed the basic stance in a letter to someone named Diognetus by affirming that Christians were "resident aliens" in the earthly cities they temporarily inhabited. "Yet while they dwell in both Greek and non-Greek cities . . . and conform to the customs of the country in dress, food, and mode of life in general, the whole tenor of their way of living stamps it as . . . extraordinary. They reside in their respective countries, but only as aliens. They take part in everything as citizens and put up with everything as foreigners. Every foreign land is their home, and every home a foreign land. . . . They spend their days on earth, but hold citizenship in heaven."[117]

In a different and even more influential metaphor, Augustine famously conveyed a similar idea with the image of the two cities.[118] We Christians, Augustine taught, are pilgrims in the earthly city, which performs a necessary and valuable function and hence deserves our support. But our ultimate

113. Heb. 11:9–10 NIV.

114. Heb. 11:13–16 NIV.

115. Heb. 13:14 NIV.

116. See, e.g., Stanley Hauerwas and William H. Willimon, *Resident Aliens: Life in the Christian Colony* (Nashville: Abingdon, 1989). See also George Weigel, *Soul of the World: Notes on the Future of Public Catholicism* (Grand Rapids: Eerdmans, 1996), 32–36.

117. "Epistle to Diognetus," in *Ancient Christian Writers: The Works of the Fathers in Translation*, trans. James A. Kleist, SJ (New York: Newman Press, 1948), 135, 139.

118. Augustine, *City of God*. See, e.g., 14.28, p. 632: "Two cities, then, have been created by two loves: that is, the earthly by the love of self extending even to contempt of God, and the heavenly by love of God extending to contempt of self. The one, therefore, glories in itself, the other in the Lord: the one seeks glory from men, the other finds its highest glory in God."

connection and our deepest loyalties must be to the heavenly city, or the city of God.[119]

We might express the fundamental difference by saying that, perhaps paradoxically, pagan *religious polytheism* was consistent with a sort of *political monism*; Christian *monotheism*, conversely, led to a kind of political polytheism—or at least to *political dualism*. Pagan religion thus served to support and consecrate the earthly city: the polis, or Rome, or the Roman Republic, or, later, the empire. Under the auspices of the diversity of gods, human beings were subjects of *one city*—the only city that mattered, the city served by a carefully integrated blend of politics and priesthoods. Christians, by contrast, though they worshiped *one God*, were subjects of *two cities*—an earthly city and a heavenly city. Both cities were real; both were valuable; both were ordained of God. But the Christians' true home was in—and thus their ultimate loyalty was to—the heavenly city. To the city of God, which provided the title for Augustine's magnum opus.

The fact that Christians considered themselves residents of two cities, not one, with their primary loyalty to the heavenly city, had important though complicated practical implications. The position could support a kind of quietism, or resignation. Our life in this city and this world is only for a brief moment in the span of eternity, so why fret overmuch about conditions here? Though it seems particularly prominent in the early years when Christians expected Christ's second coming to bring a quick end to the temporal city, this quietistic theme would resonate through the centuries.[120]

Conversely, the belief in a heavenly city—and, more generally, in a transcendent reality or truth against which this world might be judged—gave Christians a critical perspective and standard that pagans whose reality was limited to this world did not have. That transcendent standard could be used to criticize—and, in time, to reform—practices that were taken for granted in the pagan world: infanticide, slavery, inequality, the neglect of the poor and the diseased. It is not by accident that the idea that history and society should be progressing toward some sort of ideal condition comes with the emergence of transcendent religion and, in particular, Christianity.[121]

More immediately, though, and more problematically, their commitment to two cities meant that Christians did not and could not give the same

---

119. See, e.g., Augustine, *City of God* 19.17, pp. 945–47; 19.26, pp. 961–62.

120. See H. Richard Niebuhr, *Christ and Culture* (New York: HarperCollins, 2001), 45–82.

121. See generally Karl Löwith, *Meaning in History: The Theological Implications of the Philosophy of History* (Chicago: University of Chicago Press, 1949).

total, undivided allegiance to the earthly city that pagans could offer—and that pagan authorities sometimes demanded. In the first Christian centuries, this division in allegiance would prove to be a source of serious, sometimes ferocious, conflict and persecution.

In sum, Christianity amounted, as scholars like Guy Stroumsa and Pierre Chuvin and Jan Assmann have explained, to a "religious revolution." And regimes in place typically do not treat revolutionaries kindly. The Romans were no exception. As we will see in the next chapter.

CHAPTER 6

The Logic of Pagan Persecution

We began this book by noticing a question posed in the early second century by the provincial governor Pliny and again some decades later by the Christian lawyer and apologist Tertullian: Why did the Roman authorities persecute, prosecute, and often execute people just for being Christian? Pliny, the governor, found the Christians to be irritatingly inflexible and superstitious, but his investigations uncovered no criminal conduct on their part. And yet he sentenced to death anyone brought before him who confessed to being a Christian, without proof of any other crime. And his emperor, Trajan, approved this policy. For his part, Tertullian, the apologist, insisted that Christians were exemplary citizens who obeyed the laws, took care of themselves and their needy, and prayed without ceasing for the welfare of the empire and the emperor. And yet, he protested to the Roman authorities, "[you] rend us with your iron claws, hang us up on crosses, wrap us in flames, take our heads from us with the sword, let loose the wild beasts upon us."[1]

Why? Why would the Romans, much admired (by modern historians, at least, if not by early Christians like Tertullian) for their religious and cultural tolerance,[2] imprison, enslave, torture, and kill people just for being Christian? Pliny wasn't sure; he inquired of Trajan but got no answer. Tertullian was convinced that there was no adequate justification—hence his vehement protest to the "rulers of the Roman world."

Having raised but deferred this question in the first chapter, we are now in a position to consider an answer. Extrapolating and synthesizing, we will be able to see how it might have seemed both to pagans like Pliny and to Christians

---

1. Tertullian, "Apology," in *Selected Works* (Pickering, OH: Beloved, 2014), 55.
2. See above, 3–4.

like Tertullian that peaceful and mutually respectful coexistence *should* have been possible, if only the other side would be less unreasonable. It seemed that way, though, because each side misunderstood and misjudged the other. Both pagans and Christians in effect held out terms of mutual accommodation that seemed fair and reasonable *to them*, but that for discernible reasons were not—and could not be—accepted by the other side. The failure to achieve mutually acceptable terms of coexistence meant that so long as the pagans were in power, Christians were naturally treated with suspicion and were often persecuted.

In this chapter we will consider the terms of peaceful coexistence that Christians offered to pagans, and the alternative terms that pagans offered to Christians. And we will see why neither party could embrace the other party's terms without sacrificing or betraying its own beliefs and commitments. Hence the Roman persecution of Christians. Hence the centuries-long struggle between paganism and Christianity. (Hence also, at some removes, the contemporary culture wars—but that is for later chapters.)

The Fact of (Episodic) Persecution

Although the fact that Christians were persecuted will hardly seem a shocking observation, opposing misconceptions make it useful to note at the outset, first, that persecution did in fact occur—contrary to a recent, much-noticed book, it was not a "myth" that was "invented" by Christians[3]—but, second, that such persecution was episodic, not constant.

The earliest persecutions of Christians are recorded in the New Testament. Thus, Jesus warned his followers that "men shall revile you, and persecute you, and shall say all manner of evil against you falsely, for my sake."[4] The Gospels go on to explain how Jesus himself was crucified, at the instigation of Jewish authorities but with the consent and assistance of the Roman procurator, Pontius Pilate.[5] The Acts of the Apostles records additional public and private persecution carried out under the oversight if not the direction of Roman authorities: the stoning of Stephen, the execution of James, the imprisonment of Peter, the sundry prosecutions and extralegal sanctions inflicted on Paul and his evangelizing associates.[6]

3. Candida Moss, *The Myth of Persecution: How Early Christians Invented a Story of Martyrdom* (New York: HarperCollins, 2013).

4. Matt. 5:11 KJV.

5. Matt. 27.

6. Acts 7:57–60; 12:1–3; 14:4–6, 19; 16:19–24; 17:5–9; 21:30–32.

Paul himself elaborated on these afflictions in various epistles addressing persecutions suffered by different Christian communities. In these letters, Paul attempted to strengthen those communities in the faith so that they would be able to endure such punishments.[7] The strange, often inscrutable book of Revelation, or the Apocalypse, attributed to the apostle John, has been interpreted by scholars as an allegorical response to severe ongoing persecution.[8]

Later Christian traditions confidently recollected that the church's principal early leaders, Peter and Paul, were executed in Rome, probably during the reign of Nero.[9] Somewhat hazier traditions, later gathered and provocatively presented to the English-speaking world in Foxe's influential *Book of Martyrs*, recount the gruesome executions of many or most of the other leading original disciples. In addition to Simon Peter, two other Simons—the brother of Jude, and the Zealot—were crucified.[10] Mark, the Evangelist, "was beaten down with staves, then crucified; and after . . . beheaded."[11] Matthew, another Evangelist, was run through with a spear. Philip was "crucified and stoned to death."[12] And so forth. So at least related John Foxe.

In later decades, the official persecution of Christians was episodic but, when it occurred, horrific. Christians would be sent into the Colosseum, or the arenas in other cities, to be devoured by wild animals. Or they might be sentenced to labor under the appalling conditions of the imperial mines. Christian women were consigned to work in brothels.[13] Some Christians were roasted alive in the "iron chair."[14] Under Nero, the Roman historian Tacitus reported, Christians were "dressed in wild animals' skins," to be "torn to pieces by dogs" or "made into torches to be ignited after dark as substitutes for daylight."[15]

---

7. 2 Cor. 1:1–10; Phil. 2:17–18; 2 Thess. 1:1–10; 2 Tim. 3:10–14.

8. See, e.g., Steven J. Friessen, *Imperial Cults and the Apocalypse of John: Reading Revelation in the Ruins* (New York: Oxford University Press, 2001).

9. See Diarmaid MacCulloch, *Christianity: The First Three Thousand Years* (London: Penguin, 2009), 134, 161; P. G. Maxwell-Stuart, *Chronicle of the Popes: The Reign-by-Reign Record of the Papacy over 2000 Years* (London: Thames and Hudson, 1997), 12–16.

10. *Foxe's Book of Martyrs* (New Kensington, PA: Whitaker House, 1981), 6.

11. *Foxe's Book of Martyrs*, 7.

12. *Foxe's Book of Martyrs*, 9.

13. Adrian Goldsworthy, *How Rome Fell: Death of a Superpower* (New Haven: Yale University Press, 2009), 98–99.

14. Eusebius, *The Church History*, trans. Paul L. Maier (Grand Rapids: Kregel Academic, 1999), 175.

15. Tacitus, *The Annals of Imperial Rome*, trans. Michael Grant (London: Penguin, 1959), 365.

The fourth-century church historian Eusebius recorded numerous instances of such persecution, carefully and even tediously listing his sources—sometimes "tradition," sometimes letters or writings of earlier periods.[16]

Most of the postapostolic martyrs have passed into comparative anonymity; the city of Rome contains dozens of churches named after (and sometimes claiming relics of) ancient martyrs whom hardly anyone today has heard of. But a few—Ignatius, Polycarp, Perpetua, Justin, Origen, Cyprian—achieved legendary status.

Historians both ancient and modern have agreed that the persecution of Christians was sporadic, at least at the imperial level.[17] Eusebius chronicled in sometimes lurid terms the persecutions Christians had endured, but he also made it clear that not all the emperors engaged in persecution.[18] Before the so-called Great Persecution of the early fourth century that he himself lived through, Eusebius related, the Christian religion "was accorded honor and freedom by all men, Greeks and non-Greeks alike. Rulers granted our people favors and even permitted them to govern provinces, while freeing them from the agonizing issue of [pagan] sacrifice. In the imperial palaces, emperors allowed members of their own households—wives, children, and servants—to practice the faith openly. . . . All governors honored the church leaders, mass meetings gathered in every city, and congregations worshiped in new, spacious churches."[19]

Eusebius's contemporary, the Christian scholar Lactantius, wrote in a similar vein. In a book devoted to describing the horrors endured by Christians and the gruesome deaths suffered by some of their persecutors, Lactantius was also explicit that "while many well-deserving princes

16. In an introduction to Eusebius, *The Church History*, Paul Maier observes: "His sources, which Eusebius often quotes, paraphrases, or condenses . . . , need not be listed here, since he is always scrupulous about crediting the fonts of his information. His debt to Josephus, Hegesippus, Justin, Irenaeus, Dionysus of Alexandria, and others is open and acknowledged. He may have borrowed too heavily for modern tastes, but much of his material owes its very survival to its felicitous incorporation in Eusebius's record. He found much of his material in the vast library at his own Caesarea, founded by Origen and tended by Pamphilus, and that at Jerusalem established by Bishop Alexander, which accounts for the Greek and East emphasis in his pages" (16).

17. E.g., Robert Louis Wilken, *The Christians as the Romans Saw Them*, 2nd ed. (New Haven: Yale University Press, 2003), 24; Keith Hopkins, *A World Full of Gods: The Strange Triumph of Christianity* (New York: Penguin, 1999), 109–10.

18. Eusebius, *The Church History*, 107, 120–22, 146–55, 289–315.

19. Eusebius, *The Church History*, 289.

guided the helm of the Roman empire, the Church suffered no violent assaults from her enemies."[20]

To be sure, most governmental business occurred at the provincial or local levels, and a dearth of evidence makes it difficult to determine the extent of persecution by local authorities—or by mobs acting without official mandate but sometimes with official acquiescence.[21] The provincial governor Pliny was a loquacious sort of official who wrote often to the emperor Trajan, and whose correspondence was preserved; we accordingly know much more about what he did as governor than about the doings of almost any other similar Roman official.[22] One thing we know is that Pliny was executing people merely for being Christians, not because of any idiosyncratic anti-Christian animus but rather because he assumed that this was what a governor was supposed to do. Were other provincial officials acting similarly on the same assumption? It would be surprising if some were not.[23]

Thus, a few years after Pliny, in a protest to the Roman Senate, Justin Martyr described executions imposed on people merely for being Christian by a Roman prefect named Urbicus.[24] Justin added that similar measures "are likewise being everywhere unreasonably done by the governors."[25] It seems unlikely that Justin would have complained to the senators about official executions occurring in their own city if there had been no factual basis for the complaint.

Still, the lack of solid evidence makes it difficult to quantify how many Christians may have been punished or executed. Estimates of the number of Christians killed under Nero alone range from a few hundred to just under a thousand.[26] Guesses as to the total number of Christians martyred

20. Lactantius, *On the Manner in Which the Persecutors Died, Addressed to Donatus*, ed. Alexander Roberts et al. (Lexington, KY: CreateSpace, 2015), chap. 3, p. 8.

21. See W. H. C. Frend, *The Rise of Christianity* (Philadelphia: Fortress, 1984), 181 (noting that while due-process protections might discourage official indictments, "there was no protection, however, against mob violence backed by all sections of opinion"). See also 294.

22. Wilken, *The Christians*, 2–15.

23. But see Hopkins, *World Full of Gods*, 120 ("By no means all Roman governors were executing Christians. One governor dismissed a case because he thought the accusation vexatious; another told a crowd of overenthusiastic would-be martyrs that if they wanted to die they should hang themselves or jump over a cliff").

24. "The Second Apology of Justin Martyr," in *The First and Second Apologies of Justin Martyr*, trans. Alexander Roberts and James Donaldson (Cumming, GA: St. Polycarp, 2016), chap. 2, pp. 122–23.

25. "Second Apology of Justin Martyr," chap. 1, p. 121.

26. Rodney Stark, *The Triumph of Christianity: How the Jesus Movement Became the World's Largest Religion* (New York: HarperCollins, 2011), 138.

under Roman rule vary radically from under ten thousand to almost one hundred thousand.[27] Not surprisingly, Christian apologists (like John Foxe) have often offered inflated accounts; historians hostile to Christianity have inclined to more depreciating estimates. Edward Gibbon, with his contempt for the Christians and his admiration bordering on adulation for the Romans, treated the stories of Christian martyrs as "an undigested mass of fiction and error";[28] the Enlightenment historian wrote a long chapter drawing every possible inference that might serve to reduce the extent and severity of the persecutions.

Gibbon was explicit about his interpretive assumptions. The Romans were possessed of "the universal toleration of Polytheism";[29] their officials "were actuated, not by the furious zeal of bigots, but by the temperate policy of legislators."[30] Such a civilized people would not have been inclined to persecute: it just wasn't in their character. (Gibbon, of course, had not lived to witness the atrocities carried out under the Third Reich in the land of Goethe, Kant, and Bach.) The Christians, conversely, were credulous and superstitious, so their own reports should be discounted.[31] If Christians reported intolerance by the Romans (who we know, or at least Gibbon knew, were *not* intolerant), the Christians were probably misrepresenting the facts;

27. "Body Count of the Roman Empire," last updated March 2011, http://necrometrics.com/romestat.htm.

28. Edward Gibbon, *The History of the Decline and Fall of the Roman Empire*, 2 vols. (London: Penguin, [1776] 1995), 1:515. More recent, but in a similar vein, is the work of Candida Moss. Moss's eye-catching claim that persecution is a "myth" that was "invented" by the early Christians is deeply misleading, not only with respect to the historical facts but also with respect to the content of Moss's own presentation. Thus, while arguing that Christian martyr stories are historically unreliable, she adds that this fact "does not mean . . . that there were not martyrs at all or that Christians never died. It is clear that some people were cruelly tortured and brutally executed for reasons that strike us as profoundly unjust." Moss, *The Myth of Persecution*, 124–25. Her deflationary treatment of the persecutions depends largely on a series of baffling distinctions that serve to narrow what counts as "persecution" almost to the vanishing point. Thus, Moss distinguishes between "persecution" and "prosecution" (14, 159), and she excludes from the category of "persecution" punishments inflicted under general laws against subversion (as opposed to laws or edicts specifically targeting Christians) as well as punishments inflicted not from "blind hatred" but rather for what authorities believed to be legitimate reasons. See, e.g., 164 ("Just because Christians were prosecuted or executed, *even unjustly*, does not necessarily mean that they were persecuted. *Persecution* implies that a certain group is being unfairly targeted for attack and condemnation, usually because of blind hatred").

29. Gibbon, *History of the Decline*, 1:514.

30. Gibbon, *History of the Decline*, 1:524.

31. E.g., Gibbon, *History of the Decline*, 1:526, 576–77.

indeed, they were probably just projecting onto their adversaries the "implacable and unrelenting zeal which filled their own breasts."[32] Gibbon did not deny that *some* Christians had been executed by the Romans, but he thought the number was probably much smaller than Christians themselves supposed.

Whatever the body count may have been, though, it seems clear enough that over the first three centuries of the religion's existence, thousands of Christians, including a significant number of church leaders, were tortured, imprisoned, or killed for the offense of being Christian. Which once again raises the question: Why?

Christianity and Civic Allegiance

As we saw in the previous chapter, pagan religiosity served to secure the subjects' support for a city deemed to be consecrated by its association with the gods. Christians had an entirely different conception: they regarded themselves as pilgrims in the world, or as "resident aliens" whose higher loyalty was not to the earthly city but rather to their heavenly abode. Despite these differences in pagan and Christian conceptions of the relation of the individual to the city, it would not necessarily follow that the conceptions were incompatible in practice. And indeed, both Christians and pagans could and sometimes did propose that peaceful coexistence should be possible on fair and mutually acceptable terms. In proposing this, however, both sides failed fully to grasp and credit the other side's commitments.

Let us begin by considering the Christian position. Although Christians believed that their ultimate commitment was to a divine sovereign and a heavenly city, they insisted that they could still be loyal subjects of the earthly city. They could say this in complete good faith, because in fact their own Scriptures commanded as much. Albeit in cryptic fashion, perhaps, Jesus had enjoined his followers to "render unto Caesar the things that are Caesar's."[33] The apostle Paul had reached a similar though seemingly even more categorical conclusion through a remarkable or at least inventive (albeit contestable) piece of logic: he had deduced the obligation to respect earthly rulers from the very fact of divine sovereignty: "Everyone must submit himself to the governing authorities, for there is no authority except

32. Gibbon, *History of the Decline*, 1:539.
33. Matt. 22:21.

that which God has established. . . . Therefore, it is necessary to submit to the authorities, not only because of possible punishment but also because of conscience. This is also why you pay taxes, for the authorities are God's servants, who give their full time to governing. Give everyone what you owe him: If you owe taxes, pay taxes; if revenue, then revenue; if respect, then respect; if honor, then honor."[34]

In the spirit of these teachings, Tertullian insisted, as we saw in chapter 1, that "without ceasing, for all our emperors we [Christians] offer prayer. We pray for life prolonged; for security to the empire; for protection to the imperial house; for brave armies, a faithful senate, a virtuous people, the world at rest, whatever, as man or Caesar, an emperor would wish."[35] In a similar vein, Athenagoras the Athenian maintained to the emperor Marcus Aurelius that "[we Christians] are of all men most piously and righteously disposed toward the Deity and towards your government."[36] Justin Martyr protested to the emperor Antoninus Pius that "everywhere we [Christians], more readily than all men, endeavour to pay to those appointed by you the taxes both ordinary and extraordinary, as we have been taught by Him."[37]

Tertullian, Athenagoras, and Justin were in effect proposing terms for peaceful coexistence. Normally, Tertullian argued, addressing the "rulers of the Roman Empire,"[38] you let people believe as they are so inclined, however nonsensical their beliefs may seem to you,[39] so long as the believers pay allegiance to the government and do not behave subversively. All we Christians are asking for is to be treated under that benign policy. We obey the laws, take care of our own, and support and pray for the emperor and the empire. Why isn't this enough?

Had he been preternaturally prescient, Tertullian might have tried to phrase his proposal in Rawlsian terms. Given religious and cultural diversity (which the Roman Empire had in abundance), a just political com-

34. Rom. 13:1, 5–7 NIV. To be sure, not all Christians embraced this logic. Steven Friessen argues that the Apocalypse of John conveys a different message—that "Roman imperial authority was demonic." Friessen, *Imperial Cults*, 202.

35. Tertullian, "Apology," 54–55.

36. Athenagoras, *A Plea for the Christians*, trans. B. P. Pratten (Pickerington, OH: Beloved, 2016), 5.

37. "First Apology of Justin Martyr," in *First and Second Apologies*, chap. 17, p. 38.

38. Tertullian, "Apology," 1.

39. Tertullian argued that even if Christian doctrines struck Romans as absurd, they "are just (in that case) like many other things on which you inflict no penalties—foolish and fabulous things, I mean, which, as quite innocuous, are never charged as crimes or punished." Tertullian, "Apology," 80–81.

munity should be grounded in an "overlapping consensus" among citizens whose "comprehensive doctrines" are significantly divergent.[40] The pagan and Christian worldviews or "comprehensive doctrines" were obviously very different, but they converged in prescribing allegiance to earthly rulers and obedience to the laws adopted by those rulers. That convergence supplied the "overlapping consensus"—not at that time a "liberal" consensus, to be sure, but one supportive of imperial authority—on which a just, mutually respectful political community should be maintained.

So, could Romans accept these terms of coexistence? Sometimes they could and did, at least as a practical matter.[41] Robert Wilken observes that "in most areas of the Roman Empire Christians lived quietly and peaceably among their neighbors, conducting their affairs without disturbance."[42] As we have seen, Eusebius made the same point: during much of their existence Christians were "accorded honor and freedom by all men, Greeks and non-Greeks alike."[43] But such coexistence was more a matter of pragmatic accommodation than of agreement on principles. Then, as now, people could often manage to live together precisely by *not* fully appreciating and forthrightly declaring their own basic beliefs, and thus by overlooking or ignoring the fundamental incompatibilities of theirs and their neighbors' outlooks.[44] In sum, pagans might often put up with Christians, but they could not truly and understandingly embrace the Christian terms of political cooperation.

We noticed briefly in the previous chapter a recent book that argues that as they got to know Christians better, pagans were able to accept Christians as fellow subjects of the empire.[45] In reality, the truth is closer to the opposite. So long as Christianity remained a remote and little-understood sect, Roman authorities might have little practical reason to suspect or repress it. After

40. See John Rawls, *Political Liberalism* (New York: Columbia University Press, 1996), 133–72.

41. Hopkins, *World Full of Gods*, 111 (observing that Roman authorities' policy toward Christianity "fluctuated, if we can trust our sources, from cruel oppression to legal protection to benign neglect").

42. Wilken, *The Christians*, 16.

43. Eusebius, *The Church History*, 259.

44. Cf. Ramsay MacMullen, *Paganism in the Roman Empire* (New Haven: Yale University Press, 1981), 133: "Inside people's minds the most contrary beliefs might coexist, at some moment suddenly to be recognized as mutually intolerable. In that same fashion, Christians and pagans lived together for generations in the cities of the Empire, in peace disturbed rarely by spasms of frightful violence, both before and after 312."

45. See Douglas Boin, *Coming Out Christian in the Roman World: How the Followers of Jesus Made a Place for Themselves in Caesar's Empire* (New York: Bloomsbury Press, 2015).

all, they were used to putting up with all manner of exotic cults. But as the doctrines and commitments of the new faith were more clearly and forcefully presented, the incompatibility of Christianity with the pagan religiosity on which Rome was founded could become more conspicuous.

We can consider the reasons for this incompatibility under four general headings: allegiance, subversion, desecration, and liberty.

Ineffective Allegiance

Christians like Tertullian may have been perfectly sincere in professing their support for the empire and the emperor. But the Romans were concerned not merely with internal or subjective sincerity; they had also developed a formal and empirically verifiable way for subjects to manifest their allegiance. More specifically, subjects were expected to make formal, visible sacrifices to the gods and to the divine emperors. Pliny's method of testing accused Christians drew on this practice; to exonerate themselves, indicted persons were required to make sacrificial offerings to the gods.[46]

The exact patterns in which sacrifices were offered seem to have varied from region to region and city to city. Following the triumph of Augustus, cults to the divine emperors proliferated; some were regional, some municipal, some even more localized.[47] But in one form or another, as Steven Friessen explains, "imperial cults in Asia permeated Roman imperial society, leaving nothing untouched. So it is almost impossible to separate imperial cults from public religion, from entertainment, from commerce, from governance, from household worship, and so on."[48] Bruce Winter observes that "participation in these cultic activities in the Greek East and the Latin West in the first century provided the opportunity for everyone to express publicly undivided loyalty to those who brought them the divine blessing

46. See above, 1–2.

47. See Friessen, *Imperial Cults*, 25–131. See also 75: "Imperial cults permeated community life. Various temples and small shrines for the imperial family were found in towns and cities, and imperial cults were part of worship at many temples of other deities as well. Municipal imperial cults were part of many institutions besides temples, such as the agora, the bouleuterion [or assembly house], the gymnasium, and the baths. Festivals normally involved processions beyond the sites of the sacrifices themselves, so all public spaces were involved in such activities at different intervals. Imperial cults were an aspect of urban life encountered often and in diverse forms."

48. Friessen, *Imperial Cults*, 203.

of *pax romana*."[49] But "opportunity" is not quite the right word, because the expression of loyalty was not optional. "All citizens were *required* to express loyalty to emperors who . . . were addressed with same titles that the Christians used of Jesus."[50]

For Christians, this requirement presented a serious theological and practical problem. They of course did not believe in the gods—or rather, they believed the "gods" were in reality demons[51]—nor did they believe that the emperors were divine. Could they nonetheless perform the ritual sacrifices, on the assumption that no real harm was done in pretending to sacrifice to ostensible deities that were not in fact real, or at least not really deities? Some Christians drew this convenient conclusion.[52] But others regarded such performances as a betrayal of the faith and a forbidden performance of idolatrous worship.[53]

An early Christian document of uncertain authorship seeks to describe how this process worked in the case of Justin Martyr and several companions.[54] The men were brought before a Roman prefect named Rusticus and asked whether they were Christians. They answered that they were. After some follow-up examination, Rusticus then proposed that the men sacrifice to the gods.[55] Justin declined, observing that "no right-thinking person falls away from piety to impiety."[56] His companions did likewise. Rusticus then pronounced sentence: "Let those who have refused to sacrifice to the gods and to yield to the command of the emperor be scourged, and led away to suffer the punishment of decapitation, according to the laws."[57] And the sentence was duly carried out. Records of the trial and execution in the next century of the influential African bishop Cyprian reveal a very similar procedure.[58]

---

49. Bruce W. Winter, *Divine Honours for the Caesars: The First Christians' Responses* (Grand Rapids: Eerdmans, 2015), 59.

50. Winter, *Divine Honours*, 277 (emphasis added).

51. Gibbon, *History of the Decline*, 1:459–60.

52. Winter, *Divine Honours*, 196, 222; Boin, *Coming Out Christian*, 30.

53. Winter, *Divine Honours*, 222–25.

54. "Martyrdom of the Holy Martyrs Justin, Chariton, Charites, Paeon, and Liberianus, Who Suffered at Rome," trans. M. Dods, in *The Ante-Nicene Fathers*, ed. A. Roberts and J. Donaldson, 10 vols. (Peabody, MA: Hendrickson, 1994), vol. 1, http://www.clerus.org/clerus/dati/2001–02/19–999999/Tmarty.html.

55. "Martyrdom of the Holy Martyrs," 4.

56. "Martyrdom of the Holy Martyrs," 4.

57. "Martyrdom of the Holy Martyrs," 5.

58. See Robert Louis Wilken, *The First Thousand Years: A Global History of Christianity* (New Haven: Yale University Press, 2012), 72–74.

In the early decades, Christians sometimes managed to be excused from the sacrificial rites by claiming an exemption that the Jews had received based on the assumption that sacrifices performed in the temple in Jerusalem could substitute for the standard sacrifices normally required of Roman subjects.[59] The earliest Christians were Jews, after all, and it is likely that some early Christian leaders—the ones with whom Paul carried on a famous and fierce contention—insisted that even converted Greeks and Romans should be required to adopt Jewish customs and practices, such as circumcision, precisely so that Christians could continue to claim this Jewish exemption, thereby avoiding the requirement of sacrificing to the emperors and the other gods.[60] But as the divide between Christians and Jews became more conspicuous,[61] Christians forfeited their claim to the Jewish exemption, and thereby faced the daunting dilemma: to sacrifice (and thereby betray the faith) or not to sacrifice (and thereby face severe legal sanctions, including execution).

Sometimes the dilemma arose in connection with commercial activity. Bruce Winter explains that "as a prerequisite to engaging in any commercial transaction [Christians] had to give specific divine honours to the Caesars. Without doing so they would not have been able to secure provisions for their daily needs, as all goods could only be bought or sold through the authorized markets in a first-century city."[62] Subjects had to be certified for economic activity: "Then, and only then, could they sell or purchase essential commodities."

But sanctions for noncompliance were not limited to exclusion from the marketplace; they could include exile or "summary execution."[63] Nor was it only commercial activity that placed Christians in this precarious situation. Gibbon observed that "the innumerable deities and rites of polytheism were closely interwoven with every circumstance of business or pleasure, of public and of private life; and it seemed impossible to escape the observance of them, without, at times, renouncing the commerce of mankind, and all the offices and amusements of society." With characteristic sarcasm, Gibbon went on to observe that "the Christian, who with pious horror avoided the abomi-

---

59. Winter, *Divine Honours*, 117, 243.

60. Winter, *Divine Honours*, 192–95.

61. Just when and how this divide occurred presents a complicated historical question. See generally James D. G. Dunn, *Neither Jew Nor Greek: A Contested Identity*, vol. 3 (Grand Rapids: Eerdmans, 2015).

62. Winter, *Divine Honours*, 286.

63. Winter, *Divine Honours*, 286.

nation of the circus or the theatre, found himself encompassed with infernal snares in every convivial entertainment, as often as his friends invoking the hospitable deities, poured out libations to each other's happiness."[64]

Some Christians submitted to the relentless pressure and complied with the requirements—by performing the pagan sacrifices. But others refused. To the Romans, this refusal signified a failure of allegiance; persecution and punishment predictably followed.

Subversion

But Christians did not merely fall short in their demonstration of allegiance; intentionally or not, they actively and affirmatively subverted the foundations of Roman authority.[65] That is because the doctrines that Christians preached to the world fundamentally contradicted and thus undermined the basis of civic allegiance and obligation in the Roman political system. "By embracing the faith of the Gospel," Gibbon explained, "the Christians . . . dissolved the sacred ties of custom and education, violated the religious institutions of their country, and presumptuously despised whatever their fathers believed as true, or had reverenced as sacred."[66]

Pragmatic authorities, to be sure, might overlook these contradictions. They might be content to leave Christians undisturbed, so that the city could benefit from their industry and their taxes, so long as the Christians were content to leave the subversive implications of their faith implicit—in other words, so long as they were willing to practice their faith in secret or in silence. This was more or less Trajan's advice to Pliny, as we have seen: if Christians are brought before the ruler and affirmatively accused, they "must be punished";[67] but don't go around actively seeking them out. Cambridge historian Keith Hopkins remarks that "the very small size of Christianity helps explain why the Roman state paid so little attention to suppressing it effectively."[68]

Unfortunately, Christians often were not content to remain inconspicuous. They had been commanded by their Founder, after all, to go forth

64. Gibbon, *History of the Decline*, 1:460–61.
65. Cf. Wilken, *The Christians*, 125 ("It was, however, not simply that Christians subverted the cities by refusing to participate in civic life, but that they undermined the foundations of the societies in which they lived").
66. Gibbon, *History of the Decline*, 1:518.
67. See above, 3.
68. Hopkins, *World Full of Gods*, 82.

and preach the gospel to every creature.[69] And although the early dramatic evangelizing efforts of the apostle Paul and associates were not replicated in the immediately ensuing generations, many Christians still no doubt felt impelled to share the "good news"—the news that was surpassingly good, that is, in *their* perspective but that was openly destructive of pagan practices and commitments.[70] Gibbon relates an incident in which a centurion named Marcellus, during a public festival, suddenly threw down his arms and accouterments, renounced war and pagan idolatry, and declared that he would obey only Jesus. The man was promptly condemned and beheaded, and Gibbon placidly remarks that "it could scarcely be expected that any government should suffer" such conduct.[71]

Foxe's Book of Martyrs recounts a story taken from Jerome that (whether or not historically accurate) illustrates the problem. According to the story, Andrew, the apostle and the brother of Peter, was evangelizing in Achaia, and the governor, Aegeas, became concerned that the apostle's work was undermining the civic religion. A confrontation ensued, in which Andrew

> did plainly affirm that the princes of the Romans did not understand the truth and that the Son of God, coming from heaven into the world for man's sake, hath taught and declared how those idols, whom they so honored as gods, were not only not *gods*, but also most cruel *devils*; enemies to mankind, teaching the people nothing else but that wherewith God is offended, and, being offended, turneth away and regardeth them not; and so by the wicked service of the devil, they do fall headlong into all wickedness, and, after their departing, nothing remaineth unto them, but their evil deeds.[72]

Is it surprising that Aegeas took umbrage and ordered Andrew crucified?

A decisive vindication of pagan suspicions was ultimately provided in Augustine's epic work, *The City of God*. By the time Augustine's book was written, in the early fifth century, the empire had become officially Christian. But pagans were still plentiful, and the sack of Rome by the

---

69. Matt. 28:19–20.

70. Cf. Gibbon, *History of the Decline*, 1:451–52 ("It became the most sacred duty of a new convert to diffuse among his friends and relations the inestimable blessing which he had received, and to warn them against a refusal that would be severely punished as a criminal disobedience to the will of a benevolent but all-powerful Deity").

71. Gibbon, *History of the Decline*, 1:562.

72. *Foxe's Book of Martyrs*, 7–8.

Goths in 410 prompted critics to argue that the city's tragic plight was a consequence of abandoning the traditional gods. Augustine responded with a no-holds-barred attack on paganism. The pagan gods were demons.[73] They had never deserved credit for Roman political or military successes, but rather had worked only to insinuate wickedness into the Roman character.[74] In fact, the Roman state had never really been a true commonwealth at all in the fullest sense, because, as Cicero himself had asserted, a "true commonwealth" depends on justice, and the false pantheon of iniquitous demons had never been capable of supporting a just regime.[75] As Augustine's treatise proceeded, pointed criticisms evolved into savage mockery.[76]

In this ferocious condemnation of pagan religion, and of the state's reliance on such religion, Augustine was arguably just articulating content that had been implicit or less elaborately explicit in Christian thinking all along. In fact, very similar if somewhat less extensive indictments of paganism had been made by earlier Christian thinkers, including Justin Martyr, Athenagoras, Tertullian, Origen, and Lactantius. And when articulated, those indictments were boldly and emphatically subversive with respect to the pagan foundations of the pre-Christian Roman state.[77]

73. Augustine, *The City of God against the Pagans*, trans. and ed. R. W. Dyson (Cambridge: Cambridge University Press, 1998), 7.33, p. 307 (asserting that pagan gods are "demons: demons who, in the guise of spirits of the dead, or under the appearance of creatures of this world, desire to be thought gods").

74. Augustine, *City of God*, bks. 2, 4.

75. Augustine, *City of God* 2.21, pp. 76–80. However, under a less ambitious definition, Augustine conceded that Rome had been a commonwealth (19.21, pp. 950–51; 19.24, pp. 960–61).

76. Augustine, *City of God*, bks. 4, 6, 7. In one passage, for example, Augustine ridicules the pagan assignment of a variety of deities to assist in the consummation of a marriage— Jugatinus to help with the wedding; Domiducus to lead the bride home; Domitius to install her in the house; Manturna to ensure that she stays with her husband; Virginensis, Subigus, Prema, Pertunda, Venus, and Priapus to assist with different phases of the consummating intercourse. "Why fill the bedchamber with a swarm of deities when even the wedding attendants have departed?" Augustine asks mockingly: "If, at any rate, the man, labouring at his task, needed to be helped by the gods, might not some one god or goddess have been sufficient? Would not Venus alone have been equal to the task? . . . Why, when a newly married couple believe that so many gods of both sexes are present and viewing the proceedings, are they not so overcome with modesty that he is less aroused, and she made even more reluctant?" (4.9, p. 258).

77. See also Wilken, *The Christians*, 124–25 (explaining Celsus's criticism that Christians "undermined the foundations of the societies in which they lived").

Desecration

Even a modern, thoroughly secular observer can presumably appreciate the Roman concern with Christians like Andrew who went about undermining the pagan assumptions on which the Roman state was founded, however implausible those assumptions may seem today. Even a broad-minded and pragmatic Roman official who personally doubted the gods—the kind of official described or at least hypothesized by Gibbon, in other words[78]—might well have objected to this kind of subversiveness.

But, of course, many Romans would not have looked at the matter in this merely pragmatic way. Many honestly believed in the gods, either in a literal sense or in the more philosophical sense elaborated by the Stoic character Balbus in Cicero's dialogue. If you were a Roman of this mind, you would have believed that the gods were real, and that they were willing and able to guide the state so long as they were properly honored and propitiated. Conversely, if the gods were insulted or offended, they might visit ruin on the community (as they so often had done in the pagan classics of Homer and Virgil).

From this perspective, again, Christianity would inevitably appear as a profoundly subversive force—not merely because its doctrines contradicted the religious premises on which the state was founded but, even more importantly, because Christians defied and insulted the gods. The very existence of Christianity, with its perverse and sacrilegious doctrines—sacrilegious relative to pagan piety, that is—was a kind of desecration, or "desacralization." In sum, Christianity did not merely undermine people's *belief in* the gods; even more importantly, it interfered with the actual relation between the people and their rulers and their gods. It disrupted the *pax deorum*—the peace of the gods.[79]

The Roman concern with Christian desecration is evident in the fact that persecution of Christians typically picked up during difficult times. Gibbon observed that "if the empire had been afflicted by any recent calamity, by a plague, a famine, or an unsuccessful war; if the Tiber had, or if the Nile had not, risen beyond its banks; if the earth had shaken, or if the temperate order of the season had been interrupted, the superstitious Pagans were convinced that the crimes and the impiety of the Christians . . . had at length provoked the Divine Justice."[80]

78. See above, 86.

79. See Moss, *The Myth of Persecution*, 175.

80. Gibbon, *History of the Decline*, 1:537.

Here Gibbon's Enlightenment contempt for anything "superstitious," normally directed against the Christians, is applied to the pagans. But in fact, the pagan attribution of calamities to Christianity was not merely irrational scapegoating; under the premises of pagan piety, at least, the attribution was logical enough. Indeed, it was not only pagan premises that supported this logic. In the Bible, a transgression by a single individual can sometimes bring down God's wrath on the entire community of Israel.[81]

Under this logic of desecration, the "Great Persecution" under the emperor Diocletian was initially provoked—or so contemporaries related—when frustrated augurs blamed their failures on Christians who had made the sign of the cross. In fury, Diocletian directed his wrath against all Christians in the immediate vicinity,[82] and what became the most savage of all persecutions was unleashed.

Liberty (and Dignity)

The considerations discussed thus far—the Christians' refusal to register their allegiance by performing required sacrifices, Christianity's contradiction of and thus subversion of the beliefs on which the Roman state rested, Christianity's effective desecration of the relation between the Romans and their gods—seem more than sufficient to explain why Romans could not accept coexistence on the terms offered by Christian apologists like Tertullian. In addition, though, there was another, more amorphous but also in one sense even more fundamental consideration that helps to complete the picture—and that illuminates as well the ongoing tension between Christianity and the kind of immanent religiosity reflected in Roman paganism. That consideration can be explained by reference to a value that in modern times might be articulated in terms of liberty—of religious, intellectual, and moral liberty—or perhaps also of "dignity."

As noted in chapter 5, modern scholars have sometimes tried to explain the difference between Christianity and paganism by asserting that Christianity was and paganism was not concerned with *truth*, or that Christianity was and paganism was not concerned with *morality*.[83] Our survey suggested

---

81. See, e.g., Josh. 7.

82. See Lactantius, *On the Manner*, chap. 10. See also Averil Cameron, *The Later Roman Empire* (Cambridge, MA: Harvard University Press, 1993), 45.

83. See above, 108.

that hard-and-fast distinctions in these terms are overdrawn. Nonetheless, Christianity did manifest a commitment to formulating theological truths in precise creeds and doctrines, and to identifying and proscribing theological falsehoods or heresies, that was wholly foreign to a pagan mentality. As Robin Lane Fox remarks, "There was . . . no pagan concept of heresy."[84] Similarly, Christians exhibited an intense, perhaps puritanical concern for morality—sexual morality, for example—that was alien to pagan sensibilities.[85]

These Christian commitments followed from the belief in a transcendent deity who stood outside the contingencies of this-worldly time and space, and who prescribed the "straight and narrow path" to "eternal life."[86] In the Christian view, all of human life transpired "under the aspect of eternity"—and thus under and subject to a transcendent standard. We might say that all of human life was subject to *judgment*.

For devout Christians, this fact of a transcendent standard or judgment was not an infringement of liberty. On the contrary. "You shall know the truth," Jesus had taught, "and the truth shall make you free."[87] Augustine concurred: it was the gospel that brought "true liberty."[88] "[A] good man is free," he explained, "even if he is a slave, whereas the bad man is a slave even if he reigns: a slave, not to one man, but, what is worse, to as many masters as he has vices."[89] By contrast, the mere absence of moral restrictions would amount to "a vagrant liberty."[90]

Moreover, it was the belief in a transcendent standard that in time would permit Christians to pronounce a practice—infanticide, gladiatorial combat, eventually slavery—to be unjust and immoral even if it had been widely practiced and accepted by all known human cultures. "Man is the measure of all things," Protagoras had declared.[91] On that premise, if a practice (like slavery or infanticide) was widely accepted by human beings, what other

84. Fox, *Pagans and Christians*, 31.

85. See above, 108.

86. See above, 118–21.

87. John 8:32.

88. Augustine, *City of God* 2.29, p. 92.

89. Augustine, *City of God* 4.4, p. 147. See also 14.11, p. 605: "The choice of the will, then, is truly free only when it is not the slave of vices and sins. God gave to the will such freedom, and, now that it has been lost through its own fault, it cannot be restored save by Him Who could bestow it. Hence, the Truth says, 'If the Son therefore shall make you free, ye shall be free indeed.'"

90. Augustine, *The Confessions of St. Augustine*, ed. and trans. Albert Cook Outler, rev. ed. (New York: Dover, 2002), 3.5, p. 34.

91. Plato, *Theatetus*, trans. Harold North Fowler (London: W. Heinemann, 1921).

evaluative criterion was there to appeal to? But Christianity emphatically rejected the Protagorean premise. Not man but rather God was ultimately the measure of all things,[92] and hence even a universally accepted practice—like slavery—might be deeply wrong.

In a different and thoroughly understandable sense, though, the assertion of a perpetual, all-encompassing divine standard of truth and morality could be viewed—and resented—as an oppressive limitation on a man's liberty to think and to worship and, within legal limits, to live as he pleased. (The masculine gender remains apt here.) Within a pagan framework, a man was free to choose what to believe, which deities to worship, and, within broad limits, how to conduct himself sexually. In Christianity, conversely, *this* kind of freedom was denied. Or rather, the freedom might formally persist, but some exercises of the freedom would be approved while others would be condemned as incorrect, even damnable. It was as if a stern Big Brother was watching with a censorious eye your every deed, your every word, your every wayward or lustful thought. Keith Hopkins remarks on the pagans' adverse reaction to "early Christians' magnification of guilt."[93]

Even if the Christians' censorious views were not implemented in law (and of course, they could hardly be legally enforced while Christians remained a powerless minority), so that liberty was not restricted through legal sanctions, the condemnation of pagan views and practices might nonetheless be resented as an offense against what in modern terms might be described as the pagans' "dignity." The possibility is displayed in a third-century dialogue called the *Octavius* written by the Christian apologist Minucius Felix. The dialogue purports to relate a conversation between two of Minucius's friends—one (Octavius) a committed Christian and the other (Caecilius) a pagan. As the three are walking to enjoy the baths at Ostia, just outside Rome, they pass an image of the god Serapis, and Caecilius follows the pagan custom of pressing a kiss with his hand to the image's lips.[94] Octavius immediately reproves Minucius, in Caecilius's hearing, for allowing his friend "in broad daylight . . . to give himself up to stones."[95] Caecilius is predictably

92. Cf. Jan Assmann, *The Price of Monotheism*, trans. Robert Savage (Stanford: Stanford University Press, 2010), 55 ("Only in the context of a religion in which god appears as both lawgiver and judge does the thought first become thinkable that man's judgment and god's can diverge significantly").

93. Hopkins, *World Full of Gods*, 88.

94. Minucius Felix, "Octavius," in *Ante-Nicene Church Fathers, Fathers of the Third Century*, trans. Philip Schaff (London: Aeterna Press, 2014), vol. 8, chap. 2, p. 3.

95. Minucius Felix, "Octavius," chap. 3, pp. 3–4.

resentful, protesting that "Octavius' speech has bitterly vexed and worried me,"[96] and he goes on to argue that the Christians' god "runs about everywhere, and is everywhere present: they make him out to be troublesome, restless, even shamelessly inquisitive, since he is present at everything that is done, wanders in and out of all places."[97]

In the dialogue, the breach between Octavius and Caecilius is healed, almost miraculously, when Octavius, in a long speech, convinces the pagan of the truth of Christianity. Caecilius thanks the Christian for this service, and the friends depart "glad and cheerful."[98] For social interactions not culminating in such an improbably happy conclusion, though, it is understandable that Christian censoriousness might be resented as an irksome or even intolerable curtailment of liberty, or (as advocates today would likely put the point)[99] as an offense against the "dignity" of the censured pagans. Gibbon observes that "the Pagans were incensed at the rashness of a recent and obscure sect, which presumed to accuse their countrymen of error, and to devote their ancestors to eternal misery."[100] And there is at least a hint of this kind of objection in Pliny's criticism of Christians as given to "unshakeable obstinacy," and in his assertion that they were on that basis worthy of chastisement even though he had not found them guilty of any actual crime.[101]

During Christianity's first three centuries, of course, Romans were entirely free to ignore or reject Christianity, and hence to reject the constraints on pagan liberty that Christianity entailed;[102] and that is precisely what the vast majority of Romans did. Even so, resentment of the seemingly unreasonable restrictions that Christianity sought to impose—unreasonable from a pagan perspective—and of the Christians' perceived censorious and dogmatic attitudes, likely reinforced the reasons why Roman pagans were suspicious of Christianity and unwilling to embrace peaceful coexistence on the terms proposed by Christians such as Tertullian.

96. Minucius Felix, "Octavius," chap. 4, pp. 4–5.

97. Minucius Felix, "Octavius," chap. 10, p. 12.

98. Minucius Felix, "Octavius," chaps. 40–41, pp. 48–49.

99. For discussions of the increasing significance on the idea of "dignity" in contemporary law and advocacy, see Mark L. Movsesian, "Of Human Dignities," *Notre Dame Law Review* 91 (2016): 1517; Jeremy Waldron, "Dignity, Rights, and Responsibilities," *Arizona State Law Journal* 43 (2012): 1107; James Q. Whitman, "The Two Western Cultures of Privacy: Dignity versus Liberty," *Yale Law Journal* 113 (2004): 1191.

100. Gibbon, *History of the Decline*, 1:560.

101. See above, 2.

102. See Hopkins, *World Full of Gods*, 82–83.

Paganism's (Unacceptable) Terms of Coexistence

Although pagans could not accept the terms of the Christian proposal for coexistence, they could and did make a counteroffer. In effect, pagans proposed their own terms for peaceful coexistence. And these terms would have seemed entirely fair—from a pagan perspective, anyway. So the Christians' obstinate dismissal of the eminently reasonable pagan proposal would have provided further justification for repression of Christianity.

In essence, the possibility held out by paganism was that Christians and Christianity might be accepted on the same terms under which a vast variety of other cults and rituals were embraced within the broad canopy of paganism. For the most part, Romans had managed to accommodate a wide range of cults and deities on terms of reciprocity: I will respect your preferred deity if you will respect mine. Why couldn't Christianity be accepted on the same basis?[103] After all, the family of "the gods" could be extended almost without limits. It could include not only the original Roman deities but also the entire Greek pantheon, as well as deities imported from Egypt and Syria and elsewhere. It could surely have been augmented to include the god of the Christians on these same embracingly ecumenical terms. Or so it might have seemed, from a pagan perspective.

Thus, according to the church historian Eusebius (who took the report from Tertullian), the emperor Tiberius had heard of Jesus and had *sua sponte* proposed to add him to the pantheon of deities; the senators declined to approve the emperor's proposal only on the ground that they were insufficiently informed regarding the new religion.[104] The accuracy of this report may well be doubted;[105] even so, the story describes a development that, under proper circumstances and with proper solicitation, *might* have been possible. Later, the empress Mammaea sought out the learned Christian philosopher and apologist Origen to converse about theological matters. And her ecumenical son, the emperor Alexander Severus, placed a statue of Jesus in his private chapel (alongside statues of Abraham, Orpheus, and Apollonius); there was even a rumor that Alexander intended to erect a temple to Jesus. Another rumor had it that the emperor Philip the Arab had actually con-

---

103. To be sure, as noted already, subjects were expected to make a small gesture of respect to the divine emperor and to "the gods." But, seriously, how much of a burden was this? How hard was it to recite a short, *pro forma* loyalty oath, or to sprinkle a splash of wine or flick a pinch of incense on an altar? Wilken, *The Christians*, 25–27.

104. Eusebius, *The Church History*, 59–60.

105. See, e.g., Gibbon, *History of the Decline*, 1:550.

verted to Christianity.[106] The erudite pagan philosopher Porphyry, though one of Christianity's most vehement critics, wrote a treatise that included Jesus among human sages who had been elevated to divinity after his death.[107]

Other Roman authorities would likely have been willing to extend the same terms of acceptance if Christians had been agreeable.[108] And in fact, some Christians *were* agreeable; as noted, some performed the small sacrificial gestures to the gods and otherwise mingled congenially with their pagan neighbors.[109] One modern historian who enthusiastically approves of such conciliatory conduct suggests that Christians who were willing to accept these terms seem to have gotten along well enough in the Roman world.[110]

We saw earlier that the Christian proposal for coexistence might be articulated in a Rawlsian vocabulary: though Christian and pagan "comprehensive doctrines" differed radically, both positions converged in prescribing obedience to earthly rulers, and that convergence might provide the "overlapping consensus" on which a just political community could be constructed. But the pagan proposal for coexistence might equally or even more persuasively be cast in Rawlsian terms. In effect, the pagan approach attempted to ground community not in claims of truth, or of Truth, but rather in what we could call "reasonableness"—of reasonableness understood in terms of sociability and willingness to accept others' practices and commitments on terms of reciprocity and mutual respect.[111]

In this spirit of "reasonableness," the Roman demands of allegiance would have seemed inoffensive and easy to comply with. All that was required, really, was a simple and innocuous gesture. "If [the Christians] consented to cast a few grains of incense upon the altar," Gibbon explained, "they were dismissed from the tribunal in safety and with applause."[112] "Why

106. These episodes are recounted in Gibbon, *History of the Decline*, 1:553–54.
107. See Wilken, *The Christians*, 148–53.
108. It is true that Pliny required accused Christians not only to worship the Roman gods but also to "revile the name of Christ." See above, 2. Other Roman rulers may have done the same. But the latter requirement quite likely was imposed on the (correct) assumption that Christians insisted on viewing their God as the exclusive deity. Had Christians been willing to treat Christ as one god among many, the Roman response would likely have been different.
109. See Boin, *Coming Out Christian*, 29–31. See also Gibbon, *History of the Decline*, 1:549 ("In every persecution there were great numbers of unworthy Christians who publicly disowned or renounced the faith that they had professed").
110. See generally Boin, *Coming Out Christian*.
111. For a discussion of this tendency in contemporary political thought, see Jody S. Kraus, "Political Liberalism and Truth," *Legal Theory* 5 (1999): 45.
112. Gibbon, *History of the Decline*, 1:537–38. See also Robin Lane Fox, *The Classical World:*

can't you compromise?" Keith Hopkins has an educated pagan press on a Christian friend. "It surely wouldn't be too dreadful if someone told you Christians to take an oath 'by an emperor,' or pour a simple libation 'to the emperor's health.' Could you just participate in our public festivals, for the sake of form . . . ?"[113]

And yet the more fervent Christians were unwilling to make this seemingly innocent gesture, or to enter into this "reasonable" and fair arrangement for cooperation. On the contrary, they refused the sort of respectful reciprocity by which most other cults had been assimilated into the Roman religious system. Christians insisted, rather, that their God was the one true God, and that the various Roman deities were false gods, or demons. From a distance, it is easy to see why from the pagan perspective the Christian stance would have seemed arrogant, unsociable, and unreasonable. "The Christians were seen as religious fanatics," Robert Wilken explains, "self-righteous outsiders, arrogant innovators, who taught that only their beliefs were true."[114]

And yet it is understandable as well why devout Christians (like the Jews before them)[115] did not and could not view the matter in these terms—why they could only view the ostensible reciprocity of the Roman arrangement as a sham. The Christian faith taught, after all, that Jesus was the one true God. So any pagan offer to accept Jesus as one god among many was not really an invitation of inclusion; it was instead a proposal that the Christians renounce their faith and become polytheistic pagans instead. A Christ understood as one god among many would no longer be the Christ that Christians believed in and worshiped. As Lactantius explained, "If the honour paid to Him is shared by others, He altogether ceases to be worshipped since His religion requires us to believe that He is the one and only God."[116] So the general Roman policy, understood by Romans as "We'll accept you and your god if you'll accept ours," inevitably sounded to the Christians like disingenuous or

---

An Epic History from Homer to Hadrian (New York: Basic Books, 2006), 548 (noting that "they were not being asked to do much, only to offer the gods a pinch of incense, but if they refused they should be killed").

113. Hopkins, *World Full of Gods*, 210.

114. See Wilken, *The Christians*, 63. See also Gibbon, *History of the Decline*, 1:536–37 ("The Christians alone abhorred the gods of mankind, and by their absence and melancholy on these solemn festivals, seemed to insult or to lament the public felicity").

115. See Assmann, *The Price of Monotheism*, 19 ("For the Jews, Yahweh could not be translated into 'Assur' 'Amun' or 'Zeus.' This was something the 'pagans' never understood").

116. Lactantius, *The Divine Institutes*, ed. Alexander Roberts et al. (Lexington, KY: CreateSpace, 2015), 1.19, p. 46.

at least ignorant double-talk: "We'll accept your religion if you will effectively renounce it and accept our pagan religion instead."[117]

A modern (imperfect) analogy may help. Proponents of including creationism in the school curriculum sometimes use the language of inclusion and reciprocity. "You evolutionists and we creationists have different theories about how life came about," they suggest, "so let's just teach both theories— on equal terms."[118] From one point of view, this can seem like an eminently reasonable, broadly tolerant proposal. But for many scientists and educators, the proposal reflects a spurious reciprocity, because the "theories" are not comparable: one theory is scientifically supported and the other is not. So the "equal time" proposal is analogous to a shady trader's offer: "I'll accept your (legally valid) money if you'll accept my (counterfeit) currency." Treating evolution and creationism as competing "theories" would amount to a travesty and indeed a betrayal of science. That, in any case, is how evolutionists often see the matter.

Christians in the Roman Empire were in an analogous position—even if pagans applying their own religious perspective could not understand the fact, and thus perceived the Christians as inflexible, dogmatic, and undeserving of accommodation. Athenagoras tried to explain the Christian perspective to the emperor Marcus Aurelius as one philosopher speaking with another.[119] To conceive of divinity in terms of a host of finite and changeable deities who often behave in ways that would be shameful even for humans is obviously unacceptable. Isn't it? Conversely, even pagan philosophers and poets have acknowledged that, ultimately, God must ultimately be one. Why then, Athenagoras pleaded, should Christians be punished for declining to worship the finite deities and instead confining their worship to the one, true, infinite God?

Repeatedly flattering the emperor's philosophical acumen, Athenagoras was hopeful that Marcus would see the justice in this position. His hope was not rewarded.

Augustine later explained the ultimate conflict in lucid terms. Both Christians and pagans, he said, "make common use of those things which are necessary to this mortal life." The heavenly city, or the community of Christians, "must of necessity make use of this [earthly] peace also," and

117. Cf. MacMullen, *Paganism in the Roman Empire*, 94 (observing that "Christ and Iaveh were drawn into polytheism on the latter's terms, simply as new members in an old assembly").

118. For a description of this "balanced treatment" position, see Edward J. Larson, *Evolution: The Remarkable History of a Scientific Theory* (New York: Random House, 2004), 257–59.

119. See generally Athenagoras, *A Plea for the Christians*.

"for as long as it does so, it does not hesitate to obey the laws of the earthly city." And hence "a harmony is preserved." The problem arises when pagans insist on the worship of multiple gods. "But the Heavenly City knows only one God who is to be worshipped. . . . Because of this difference, it has not been possible for the Heavenly City to have laws of religion in common with the earthly city. It has been necessary to dissent from the earthly city in this regard, and to become a burden to those who think differently. Thus, she has had to bear the brunt of the anger and hatred and persecutions of her adversaries."[120]

How Tolerant Were the Romans Really?

We noted earlier the judgment of many modern historians that Roman authorities were admirably tolerant, particularly in matters of religion.[121] Indeed, even the Christians could acknowledge the broad range of religious cults that flourished, and were freely allowed to flourish, under Roman rule. "Among every nation and people [subject to Roman rule], men offer whatever sacrifices and celebrate whatever mysteries they please," Athenagoras acknowledged to the emperor. "The Egyptians reckon among their gods even cats, and crocodiles, and serpents, and asps, and dogs. And to all these both you and the laws give permission so to act, deeming . . . that it is necessary for each man to worship the gods he prefers."[122]

And yet, as we have also seen (and as Athenagoras bitterly complained), Romans also engaged, episodically, in the savage persecution of Christians— even though Christians professed allegiance to and even prayed for the emperors and for the most part behaved peaceably and responsibly. To be sure, the Roman policy of persecution was not gratuitously vindictive or malicious; it was, as we have seen, entirely rational (on pagan premises at least). Even so, does the Roman practice call for a revision of the familiar judgment of the Roman Empire as religiously tolerant?

The question itself is elusive, and probably misconceived. A first observation, though, is that the Romans themselves would not have explained or defended their own practices in terms of toleration. For them, tolerance was not an ideal, or an established virtue. As J. A. North ob-

120. Augustine, *City of God* 19.17, pp. 945–46.
121. See above, 4.
122. Athenagoras, *A Plea for the Christians*, 5.

serves: "If there was tolerance it was not tolerance born of principle. So far as we know, there was no fixed belief that a state or individual ought to tolerate different forms of religion; that is the idea of far later periods of history. The truth seems to be that the Romans tolerated what seemed to them harmless and drew the line whenever there seemed to be a threat of possible harm; only, they saw no great harm in many of the cults of their contemporary world."[123]

Indeed, toleration did not come to be viewed as a positive value or virtue until relatively recently. Prior to a modern "transvaluation of values," tolerance of error or wrongdoing would be viewed mostly as an indication of weakness, lack of integrity, or lack of courage. Thus, Ethan Shagan explains that "before the 1640s, the state's prerogative to punish religious deviance was almost unanimously praised as moderate, while broad claims for religious toleration were almost unanimously condemned as extremist."[124]

And indeed, in other contexts, that earlier logic is readily understandable even today. A school principal who acquiesces in bullying, or a manager who puts up with sexual epithets, jokes, and innuendos in the workplace, will not gain sympathy by invoking the value of "toleration." On the contrary, for such evils the contemporary attitude confidently and righteously prescribes "zero tolerance."

Still, granting that "religious toleration" is *our* value, not theirs, can *we* nonetheless describe the pagan world as religiously tolerant? Yes and no—but probably more no than yes. Roman paganism surely did manage to encompass and accommodate a vast diversity of deities and cults. But then again, it accommodated religions that were willing to accept *its* terms. Indeed, the Roman approach might more accurately be described as one not of *tolerance* but of a combination of *indifference* and *assimilation*—policies today not typically associated with toleration.

Thus, for the most part, as J. A. North notes, Roman authorities simply didn't care which deities people worshiped, or how. Jan Assmann observes generally that "it . . . makes no sense to talk of 'tolerance' with regard to the polytheisms of pagan antiquity, since here the criterion of incompatibility is missing; as far as other peoples' religion is concerned, there is nothing

---

123. J. A. North, *Roman Religion* (New York: Cambridge University Press, 2000), 63.

124. Ethan Shagan, *The Rule of Moderation: Violence, Religion, and the Politics of Restraint in Early Modern England* (Cambridge: Cambridge University Press, 2011), 288. See generally Alexandra Walsham, *Charitable Hatred: Tolerance and Intolerance in England, 1500–1700* (Manchester: Manchester University Press, 2008).

that would need to be 'tolerated.' "[125] Moreover, the Romans did not so much tolerate diverse or foreign deities as annex them into the Roman system. In this vein, Rodney Stark suggests that rather than speaking of a collection of *different* religions, it is more cogent to think of Roman paganism as constituting a religious "system."[126] The cults devoted to the different gods and goddesses were parts of a single expansive religion, much in the way that different Catholics today might feel special attachments to a multitude of different saints while still belonging to the same capacious faith.

To say this, though, is not to criticize the Romans for accommodating diverse cults only on Roman terms. What else could they do? What else could anyone do? Accept and accommodate strange religions on the basis of terms and assumptions they did *not* hold?

In the end, it thus seems misconceived to evaluate Roman paganism in terms of toleration, either for praise or for blame. What we can say is that pagan religion had resources for including or accommodating a variety of deities and cults, but there were limits to what could be accommodated. In troubled times, at least, Christianity fell outside those limits. For pragmatic reasons it might sometimes be put up with, so to speak, but it could not really be respected or tolerated. In a similar way, Christianity had its own, different resources for permitting or accommodating various beliefs and religiosities, but again there were limits (as would become apparent after Christianity became the preferred religion of the empire). In the long run, Christian dualism—or its commitment to two cities, each with its proper jurisdiction—would evolve into acceptance of a "separation of church and state" that has functioned to permit a vast diversity of faiths and antifaiths to coexist more or less peacefully. But it would take centuries for that kind of separation to develop. And whether it can survive the erosion or rejection of its Christian foundations remains uncertain.[127]

---

125. Assmann, *The Price of Monotheism*, 18. See also H. A. Drake, *Constantine and the Bishops: The Politics of Intolerance* (Baltimore: Johns Hopkins University Press, 2000), 453 ("If pagans did not preach compulsion, that was only because there was nothing to compel—the belief system shared by all peoples of their empire was polytheistic, with local variations only in the names of particular deities and the specifics of particular practices").

126. Stark, *The Triumph of Christianity*, 10.

127. See below, chaps. 10 and 11. See also Steven D. Smith, *The Rise and Decline of American Religious Freedom* (Cambridge, MA: Harvard University Press, 2014); Steven D. Smith, "Discourse in the Dusk: The Twilight of Religious Freedom" (review essay), *Harvard Law Review* 122 (2009): 1869.

When we set aside unilluminating labels like "tolerance," what seems clear is that although in the early centuries paganism and Christianity sometimes operated side by side as a matter of practical convenience or necessity, they did not manage to work out mutually acceptable terms of peaceful coexistence. Their experience stands as a testament to the difficulty of "just getting along"—a difficulty that persists today (as we will discuss in later chapters).

CHAPTER 7

The Struggle for the City

Pagans and Christians struggled for mastery in Rome during the first centuries of what is often called (spoiling the suspense) the Christian era. Initially subdued and utterly one-sided, the struggle became a genuine contest in the fourth century, as the emperor Constantine's conversion tipped the balance in favor of the previously impotent Christians. Even so, the struggle persisted, with both sides experiencing unanticipated triumphs and reversals in their respective fortunes. By century's end, though, the contest was effectively over: Christianity had prevailed.

Or at least so it may appear in hindsight. Contemporaries would have had a different perception.[1] Few discerned any struggle in the early centuries; paganism enjoyed an overwhelming preeminence, while a marginal and virtually powerless Christianity was intermittently persecuted and suppressed (as we saw in the preceding chapter). Even after Constantine's historic conversion gave Christianity a new importance, and even after Constantine and his imperial successors began issuing decrees constricting the practices of paganism, what Edward Watts has called "the final pagan generation," including prominent pagans like the orator Libanius and the Roman prefect Praetextatus, failed to discern any actual struggle for dominance. Mostly overlooking a few irksome but largely unenforced religious restrictions, "the elite of the final pagan generation had better things to worry about. There was money to be made, honors to be gained, and fun to be had by those who could cooperate openly with the regime, even if they chose to criticize

---

1. Peter Brown argues that the "struggle" version was articulated by late fourth- and early fifth-century Christian authors. Peter Brown, *Power and Persuasion in Late Antiquity: Towards a Christian Empire* (Madison: University of Wisconsin Press, 1992), 128–29.

it privately."[2] These leading pagans lived in a world, as they saw it, "that was full of gods, had always been full of gods, and always would be full of gods."[3] They could not imagine that the world could ever be essentially different in that respect.

By century's end, though, the world *was* different. Christianity was now officially in control; paganism was officially (if not in practice) banished.

How did this unimaginable transformation—unimaginable to the pagans—come to pass? And, most important for our purposes, what did the official triumph of Christianity and the official defeat of paganism mean for the future of these two religiosities, and of the orientations (toward transcendence, and toward a merely immanent sacredness) that they represented?

The first of these questions—how Christianity came to prevail over paganism—has commanded the attention of numerous able historians, among them our Enlightened friend Edward Gibbon (who described the question as "an important, though perhaps tedious, inquiry");[4] but the historians have disagreed about the answers. We revisit the question here, in comparatively summary fashion, not to offer answers that are either novel or definitive—in fact, we will see that definitive answers are almost surely unavailable—but because the question and its possible answers are directly relevant to the second question, and to our assessment of the modern condition. More specifically, the questions of whether and how and in what sense Christianity prevailed over paganism will be closely relevant to our assessment of T. S. Eliot's proposition that modern Western societies face a choice between Christianity and "modern paganism."

Two Accounts (and a Third That We Cannot Consider)

Leading accounts of the political triumph of Christianity have fallen into two main families. One family of interpretations stresses what we might call the "*displacement*" theme; the other emphasizes what could be called the "*suppression*" theme. The first kind of interpretation emphasizes cultural or intellectual or spiritual factors; the second focuses more on the political, and the coercive.

2. Edward J. Watts, *The Final Pagan Generation* (Oakland: University of California Press, 2015), 89.

3. Watts, *The Final Pagan Generation*, 36.

4. Edward Gibbon, *The History of the Decline and Fall of the Roman Empire*, 2 vols. (London: Penguin, [1776] 1995), 1:497.

According to the first kind of interpretation (which was more or less Gibbon's view),[5] Christianity naturally came to displace paganism because the newer religion was more responsive to the needs of the empire's peoples. By the fourth century, the Oxford historian E. R. Dodds asserts, "paganism appears as a sort of living corpse, which begins to collapse from the moment when the supporting hand of the State is withdrawn from it."[6] And so paganism came to be challenged by a diverse array of new or imported cults and faiths. Christianity ultimately turned out to be the winner among those challengers; it thereby displaced paganism because of some intrinsic quality that made it more appealing or efficacious.

Displacement interpretations can emphasize different features of pagan and Christian religions; these different emphases may reflect different assumptions about human psychology and motivation. A *communitarian* or cultural version suggests that Christianity provided a more satisfying and inclusive sense of community than paganism did.[7] What we might call the *creedal* version suggests that Christian doctrines and teachings came to seem more believable than pagan stories and themes.[8] A *spiritual* version suggests that Christianity did a better job than paganism did in satisfying people's spiritual needs[9]—needs for meaning, for example, of the kind we discussed in chapter 2. These different interpretations are of course not mutually exclusive; it is conceivable that Christianity did better in more than one of these dimensions.

Or perhaps not. The other major family of interpretations, more political in its emphases, emphatically denies that paganism was dying out of its own force in the later empire, or that Christianity displaced paganism because of any cultural or creedal or spiritual superiority.[10] Far from a steady decline into senility, Ramsay MacMullen asserts, "a general refreshing [in paganism] can be seen over the course of the second and third

5. Gibbon, *History of the Decline*, 1:497–99.
6. E. R. Dodds, *Pagan and Christian in an Age of Anxiety* (Cambridge: Cambridge University Press, 1965), 132.
7. See below, 178–79.
8. See below, 179–82.
9. See below, 183–88.
10. See Ramsay MacMullen, *Paganism in the Roman Empire* (New Haven: Yale University Press, 1981), 62–73 (presenting evidence of the vitality of paganism); Ramsay MacMullen, *Christianity and Paganism in the Fourth to Eighth Centuries* (New Haven: Yale University Press, 1997), 13 ("The real vitality of paganism is instead recognized; and to explain its eventual fate what must also be recognized is an opposing force, an urgent one, determined on its extinction").

centuries."[11] So what happened, rather, is that the convert Constantine and his imperial successors were true believers; in a demonstration of what MacMullen calls "the murderous intolerance of the now dominant religion,"[12] they used their authority and might to crush paganism.

It seems unlikely that either of these interpretations will ever finally and decisively defeat the other. After all, can we really know whether the appeal of paganism was waning in the second and third and fourth centuries? Temples were still open, perhaps. Sacrifices were still being performed. Auguries were still being taken. But what does all this activity demonstrate?

Consider an analogous contemporary question: Is traditional Christianity in decline in America today? True, people continue to attend church, to declare their affiliations with one or another denomination, to make monetary contributions to their churches. And yet, does this behavior reflect authentic Christian faith? Or is it something more superficial—mere habitual or inherited repetition perhaps? Or maybe a defensive reaction to the confounding challenges of the modern world, and thus perhaps more reflective of a desperate *crisis* of faith and meaning than of genuine conviction? Is Christianity alive and vibrant, or is it "a sort of living corpse," to borrow Dodds's phrase? In addressing such questions, pundits and social scientists and theologians today have vast amounts of evidence to work with—voluminous statistics quantifying declared faith and church attendance and financial contributions[13]—and yet they vary widely in what they take away from those vast and murky oceans of data.[14]

For the ancient world, by contrast, we have only the tiniest fraction of evidence available for measuring contemporary religiosity. How likely is it, then, that we can reliably ascertain what Romans and Greeks really felt and believed with respect to the received pagan religiosity? Ramsay MacMullen confidently declares that paganism was thriving until it was violently suppressed by Christian rulers and Christian mobs. And then he concedes

11. MacMullen, *Paganism in the Roman Empire*, 106.

12. MacMullen, *Paganism in the Roman Empire*, 14.

13. See, e.g., Robert D. Putnam and David E. Campbell, *American Grace: How Religion Divides and Unites Us* (New York: Simon and Schuster, 2010).

14. Compare, e.g., Peter L. Berger, "The Desecularization of the World: A Global Overview," in *The Desecularization of the World*, ed. Peter L. Berger (Washington, DC: Ethics and Public Policy Center; Grand Rapids: Eerdmans, 1999), 1–19; with Steve Bruce, *Religion in the Modern World: From Cathedrals to Cults* (New York: Oxford University Press, 1996).

that "we cannot poll the past; and adequately self-revealing moments in our sources are too few to support much generalization about what any given [religious] act meant to the participants."[15]

In any case, given these disagreements among able historians, it seems improbable that any satisfactory resolution is achievable in a book like this one. Fortunately, for our purposes we need not try to decide whether the "displacement" interpretations or the "suppression" interpretations contain a greater measure of truth. We *do* need to consider some of the arguments and evidence associated with each family of interpretations, however, because these will bear upon the questions that *are* central to our inquiry. Namely, in what sense *did* Christianity prevail (if it did), and in what sense was paganism actually extinguished (if it was)?

Before considering this evidence, though, we note a wholly different kind of explanation of Christianity's rise, not because scholars or students today would think to propose or ponder it, but because to the fourth-century Christians this might have seemed to be *the* decisive account of the crucial political and cultural developments. We could call this the *providential-demonic* account. From a Christian perspective, as Gibbon noted, the reason why Christianity came to prevail over paganism was because Christianity was *true* and paganism was not.[16] But this description understates the claim. The idea was that the struggle between Christianity and paganism represented only one mundane theater in a larger, cosmic war between the forces of good and the legions of evil. Moreover, in speaking of the battle between good and evil, we are not (or rather, they were not) being merely metaphorical. The hosts of demons that beset Antony in the desert—and that he managed to fend off with, as he said, "much prayer and asceticism"[17]—were not poetic personifications, according to the account of Saint Athanasius; they variously appeared in the forms of wild animals—"lions, bears, leopards, bulls, and serpents, asps, scorpions and wolves"—but also as female temptresses and even devout though devious monks.[18] Keith Hopkins remarks on "how pervasive demons were in the thought world of Jews, pagans, and Christians alike."[19]

15. Cf. MacMullen, *Christianity and Paganism*, 149.

16. Gibbon, *History of the Decline*, 1:447.

17. Athanasius, *The Life of Antony and the Letter to Marcellinus*, trans. and ed. Robert C. Gregg, Classics of Western Spirituality (Mahwah, NJ: Paulist, 1980), 47.

18. Athanasius, *Life of Antony*, 38, 48, 50.

19. Keith Hopkins, *A World Full of Gods: The Strange Triumph of Christianity* (New York: Penguin, 1999), 207.

This war between good and evil agents occurs here on earth, but even more importantly it is being waged in the celestial sphere. And the triumph of Christianity comes about because God's armies eventually vanquish the hosts of Satan. Peter Brown explains that

> the conflict between Christianity and paganism was presented, in fourth- and fifth-century Christian sources, as having been fought out in heaven rather than on earth. The end of paganism occurred with the coming of Christ to earth. It was when He was raised on the Cross on Calvary—and not, as we more pedestrian historians tend to suppose, in the reign of Theodosius I—that heaven and earth rang with the crash of falling temples. The alliance of the Christian church with Christian emperors, to abolish sacrifice and to close and destroy the temples, was not more than a last, brisk mopping-up operation, that made manifest on earth a victory already won, centuries before, by Christ, over the shadowy empire of the demons.[20]

Possibly. But any assessment of such a proposition—probably, indeed, any accurate *presentation* of the proposition—exceeds the jurisdiction of modern academicians (like myself). Whether there is a cosmic battle between good and evil, or between God and his followers against the devil and his minions, and how that battle has fared at any particular time, are questions about which the modern academic must humbly confess abject incompetence. In declining to consider whether Christianity's triumph was due to its truth and to providential assistance, Gibbon coyly explained that his own discussion would focus on what might be deemed "secondary causes."[21] In this respect, we have little choice, in this venue at least, but to follow Gibbon's lead.

And so, acknowledging that everything said here might seem to the actual combatants wholly to miss the most important facts, and to treat eternally foreordained events as fortuitous contingencies, we will limit ourselves to considering the two major contemporary accounts of the ancient conflict between paganism and Christianity—namely, the displacement and the political or suppression accounts.

---

20. Peter Brown, *Authority and the Sacred: Aspects of the Christianisation of the Roman World* (Cambridge: Cambridge University Press, 1995), 4–5 (footnote omitted).

21. Gibbon, *History of the Decline*, 1:447.

How the West Was (and Wasn't) Won for Christianity

The Political Struggle. Despite significant differences in historical interpretations, some aspects and episodes of the sometimes latent and sometimes open struggle between paganism and Christianity can be recalled with tolerable confidence. Whether or not these episodes constitute the *explanation* for Christianity's success, they will at least provide an acceptably secure framework for our inquiry.

Thus, as we have seen, in the early centuries of the Christian era, and for understandable reasons that we considered in the previous chapter, Roman authorities generally looked on Christianity with suspicion and disfavor, and they often expressed their disapproval with repressive measures, including, sometimes, harsh methods of punishment and execution. Exactly how many Christians were punished or executed is, as we saw, unknowable. What we can say with confidence is that the persecution of Christians was intermittent, not constant or ubiquitous, but that it did occur, repeatedly; and when it did, the repression could be savage.

In the middle of the third century, in the midst of what many historians perceive as a "time of troubles"—of grave political, military, and economic challenges that threatened the very survival of the empire[22]—the emperors Decian and Valerian promoted campaigns of severe repression. Then again in the early fourth century, under the emperor Diocletian, his imperial associate Galerius, and his successor Maximinus Daia, Roman authorities instituted what came to be known as "the Great Persecution." The Christian thinker and rhetorician Lactantius, who lived through that harrowing period, reported that

> presbyters and other officers of the Church were seized, without evidence by witnesses or confession, condemned, and together with their families led to execution. In burning alive, no distinction of sex or age was regarded; and because of their great multitude, they were not burnt one after another, but a herd of them were encircled with the same fire; and servants, having millstones tied about their necks, were cast into the sea. Nor was the persecution less grievous on the rest of the people of God; for the judges, dispersed through all the temples, sought to compel every one to sacrifice. The prisons were crowded; tortures hitherto unheard of, were invented; and lest

22. See Michael Grant, *The Climax of Rome* (London: Weidenfeld and Nicolson, 1968), 5–6.

justice should be inadvertently administered to a Christian, altars were placed in the courts of justice, hard by the tribunal, that every litigant might offer incense before his cause could be heard.[23]

Under these circumstances, "to be beheaded was an indulgence shown to very few."[24] Lactantius, to be sure, seemed almost to find a morbid pleasure in detailing the horrifically slow and excruciating methods devised to execute Christians, and he took even more delight in lingering over the gruesome deaths of the persecuting emperors Galerius and Daia.[25] Although Lactantius insisted that his accounts were all based on "the authority of well-informed persons," and that he had "commit[ted the events] to writing exactly as they happened,"[26] surely the details are subject to doubt—for example, whether the stench from the dying Galerius's worm-addled intestines could have been so potent as to "pervade . . . the whole city." And once again, it is impossible to quantify how many Christians were condemned, tortured, and killed.

Still, the fact of the persecution is plain enough. Robert Markus observes that "in the Great Persecution at the beginning of the fourth century, the forces of Roman conservatism rallied in a last attempt to eliminate a dangerous threat to the traditional consensus."[27]

Reversal came relatively suddenly, after an ambitious upstart named Constantine somewhat ambiguously embraced Christianity (following a

23. Lactantius, *On the Manner in Which the Persecutors Died, Addressed to Donatus*, ed. Alexander Roberts et al. (Lexington, KY: CreateSpace, 2015), chap. 15, p. 21.

24. Lactantius, *On the Manner*, chap. 22, p. 31.

25. Lactantius, *On the Manner*, chap. 33, p. 44.

And now, when Galerius was in the eighteenth year of his reign, God struck him with an incurable plague. A malignant ulcer formed itself low down in his secret part, and spread by degrees.

[H]is bowels came out, and his whole seat putrefied. . . . The humours having been repelled, the distemper attacked his intestines, and worms were generated in his body. The stench was so foul as to pervade not only the palace, but even the whole city; and no wonder, for by that time the passages from his bladder and bowels, having been devoured by worms, became indiscriminate, and his body, with intolerable anguish, was dissolved into one mass of corruption.

On the painful death of Daia, see chap. 49, pp. 62–63.

26. Lactantius, *On the Manner*, chap. 52, p. 65.

27. Robert Austin Markus, *Christianity and the Secular* (Notre Dame: University of Notre Dame Press, 2006), 21.

vision that he claimed to have experienced in 312), proceeded to win a decisive battle against numerically superior forces near the Milvian Bridge just
outside Rome, and went on to make himself first joint and later sole emperor
over the realm. Constantine (along with his coemperor Licinius) initially declared, in the so-called Edict of Milan, that Christianity would be tolerated.
But he soon went further, favoring Christian churches and Christian bishops
with influence and lavish endowments.[28]

Exactly *why* he did all this is a subject of much dispute. Some historians
have viewed the man as a "cynical opportunist"[29] who embraced Christianity for crass political purposes. The eminent Swiss historian Jacob Burckhardt
pronounced Constantine an "essentially unreligious" man who was "driven
without surcease by ambition and lust for power."[30] The dominant view today,
by contrast, seems to be that Constantine was a sincere and even zealous convert—albeit a somewhat irregular one: Christians, after all, are normally discouraged from slaughtering their wives and children—who gained no political
advantage from his conversion to Christianity.[31] Either way, within a generation
Christianity had passed from being a persecuted to a preferred faith.

While favoring Christianity, however, Constantine himself maintained
a policy of religious toleration. The French historian Paul Veyne explains
that "despite his deep desire to see all his subjects become Christians, . . .
[Constantine] never persecuted pagans or denied them the right to express
themselves; nor did he disadvantage them in their careers: if superstitious
people wished to damn themselves, they were free to do so."[32]

28. See W. H. C. Frend, *The Rise of Christianity* (Philadelphia: Fortress, 1984), 484–88,
503–5.

29. Adrian Murdoch, *The Last Pagan: Julian the Apostate and the Death of the Ancient
World* (Stroud, UK: Sutton, 2003), 5.

30. Jacob Burckhardt, *The Age of Constantine the Great*, trans. Moses Hadas (New York:
Pantheon, [1852] 1949), 292.

31. For an overview of the debate and an argument that Constantine *was* genuinely Christian, see Peter J. Leithart, *Defending Constantine: The Twilight of an Empire and the Dawn of
Christendom* (Downers Grove: InterVarsity, 2010), 79–96. See also Diarmaid MacCulloch,
Christianity: The First Three Thousand Years (London: Penguin, 2009), 191 ("There is no doubt
that [Constantine] came to a deeply personal if rather capricious involvement in the Christian faith"). Cf. Paul Veyne, *When Our World Became Christian: 312–394*, trans. Janet Lloyd
(Cambridge: Polity Press, 2010), 121 ("All in all, the Christianization of the ancient world
constituted a revolution set in motion by a single individual, Constantine, with motives that
were exclusively religious").

32. Veyne, *When Our World Became Christian*, 8. See 11 ("He did not force anyone to
convert; he appointed pagans to the very highest of state offices; he never legislated against
the pagan cults . . . and he allowed the Roman Senate to continue to fund the official priests

In fact, insofar as imperial rigor was exercised in religious matters, it was mainly toward the Christians themselves,[33] who upon the cessation of persecution promptly became mired in intricate theological disputations. Constantine was dismayed by this contentiousness. "He attributes the origin of the whole [Trinitarian] controversy," Gibbon commented, "to a trifling and subtle question, concerning an incomprehensible point of law, which was foolishly asked by the bishop, and imprudently resolved by the presbyter."[34] Disgusted, the emperor reproved a group of bishops: "Even the barbarians . . . know God and have learned to reverence him, . . . [while the bishops] do nothing but that which encourages discord and hatred and, to speak frankly, which leads to the destruction of the human race."[35] For pagans, however, the Christians' theological quarrels were a welcome distraction of the emperor's attention. "The divisions of Christianity suspended the ruin of *paganism*," Gibbon observed.[36]

Still, Constantine was not wholly forgetful of, or permissive toward, the pagans. At least according to Eusebius, the emperor did order the closure of several pagan temples.[37] (Other evidence suggests the contrary: the pagan orator Libanius later reported that "Constantine made absolutely no changes in the traditional form of worship.")[38] While discounting a report that Constantine prohibited pagan ceremonies, Gibbon noted that the emperor did suppress some practices of divination, and that while promising his subjects religious freedom, he also exhorted them to follow his example in accepting Christianity. "Without violating the sanctity of his promise [of religious freedom], without alarming the fears of the pagans, the artful monarch advanced, by slow and cautious steps, to undermine the irregular and decayed fabric of polytheism."[39]

Constantius, Constantine's son and eventual successor (following a turbulent series of events, including a massacre of potential family rivals, a

---

and public cults of the Roman state; these continued as before and did so until almost the end of the century") (footnotes omitted).

33. See Hugo Rahner, *Church and State in Early Christianity*, trans. Leo Donald Davis, SJ (San Francisco: Ignatius, [1961] 1992), 46–49.

34. Gibbon, *History of the Decline*, 1:789.

35. Quoted in H. A. Drake, *Constantine and the Bishops: The Politics of Intolerance* (Baltimore: Johns Hopkins University Press, 2000), 4.

36. Gibbon, *History of the Decline*, 1:827.

37. Watts, *The Final Pagan Generation*, 48.

38. Quoted in Watts, *The Final Pagan Generation*, 49.

39. Gibbon, *History of the Decline*, 1:825.

civil war, and the untimely deaths of his two brothers), took after his father in favoring Christianity, albeit under an Arian interpretation condemned by many bishops as heretical. A good deal of sometimes violent tension between the emperor and the Christian church accordingly ensued. Instead of being persecuted by pagan authorities, Trinitarian Christians were now being hounded and harassed by a nominally Christian emperor.[40]

Even so, a species of Christianity remained ascendant. In 341, moreover, Constantius issued an order that by its terms forbade pagan sacrifices; fifteen years later, he prescribed actual penalties, including capital punishment, for the violation of this prohibition and also ordered the closure of temples. These seemingly draconian orders nonetheless appear to have gone entirely unenforced, and were scarcely noticed by pagan officials.[41] Gibbon concluded that the prohibition was "either composed without being published, or was published without being executed."[42] Indeed, when visiting Rome in 357, Constantius himself (who, like his father and his Christian successors up until the emperor Gratian, retained the traditional imperial title of *pontifex maximus* over the pagan priesthoods)[43] made a friendly tour of the city's pagan temples.[44] Edward Watts reports that "most temples remained open despite the laws, statues and images of the gods stared down from every corner of the cities, public sacrifices continued to be offered in many parts of the empire (including in Rome itself), and the traditional religious routines of households throughout the empire could continue unaffected."[45]

Despite lax enforcement, however, antipagan laws and precedents were slowly and quietly accumulating. Then, in 361, fortunes flipped again. Constantius unexpectedly died, cutting short yet another incipient civil war, and he was succeeded by his learned and colorful cousin Julian (who as a child had been deemed too youthful and innocuous for inclusion in the earlier family massacre). The new emperor promptly came out and declared himself a pagan. "I feel awe of the gods," he exuded. "I love, I revere, I venerate them."[46] Gibbon

40. See Rahner, *Church and State*, 49–60.

41. Watts, *The Final Pagan Generation*, 86–89.

42. Gibbon, *History of the Decline*, 1:827.

43. Gibbon, *History of the Decline*, 1:827n172.

44. Watts, *The Final Pagan Generation*, 89; Alan Cameron, *The Last Pagans of Rome* (New York: Oxford University Press, 2011), 33.

45. Watts, *The Final Pagan Generation*, 102.

46. Quoted in G. W. Bowersock, *Julian the Apostate* (Cambridge, MA: Harvard University Press, 1978), 16.

observed that a "devout and sincere attachment for the gods of Athens and Rome, constituted the ruling passion of Julian."[47]

And the gods rewarded this devotion—or so the new emperor believed.

> Notwithstanding the modest silence of Julian himself, we may learn from his faithful friend, the orator Libanius, that he lived in a perpetual intercourse with the gods and goddesses; that they descended upon earth, to enjoy the conversation of their favourite hero; that they gently interrupted his slumbers, by touching his hand or his hair; that they warned him of every impending danger, and conducted him, by their infallible wisdom, in every action of his life; and that he had acquired such an intimate knowledge of his heavenly guests, as readily to distinguish the voice of Jupiter from that of Minerva, and the figure of Apollo from that of Hercules.[48]

Acting on his newly declared faith in the old religion, Julian reinstituted the imperial sacrifice of animals on a massive scale. A contemporary quipped that if Julian were to enjoy a long tenure as emperor, "the breed of horned cattle must infallibly be extinguished."[49] While purporting to embrace religious toleration, Julian gave preference to pagans for high office,[50] declined to discipline a mob that had rioted and murdered the Christian bishop of Cappodocia[51] (though the emperor did appropriate the bishop's much-admired library),[52] and required that churches that had been built on pagan sites be demolished so that the temples could be rebuilt.[53]

Probably his most controversial measure, however, was his edict banning Christians from teaching in the schools on the grounds that, since they did not believe in the gods, they were morally unfit to teach the classics.[54] The projected effect of this ban, Princeton historian G. W. Bowersock observes, was that "within little more than a generation the educated elite of the

---

47. Gibbon, *History of the Decline*, 1:864.

48. Gibbon, *History of the Decline*, 1:873.

49. Gibbon, *History of the Decline*, 1:878.

50. Cf. Gibbon, *History of the Decline*, 1:892 (asserting that "it was the object of the insidious policy of Julian, to deprive the Christians of all the temporal honours and advantages which rendered them respectable in the eyes of the world").

51. Bowersock, *Julian the Apostate*, 80–81.

52. Gibbon, *History of the Decline*, 1:901n120.

53. Gibbon, *History of the Decline*, 1:895.

54. Bowersock, *Julian the Apostate*, 83–85.

empire would be pagan."[55] The law was "a masterstroke," Adrian Murdoch observes: it "marginalized Christianity to the point where it could potentially have vanished within a generation or two, and without the need for physical coercion."[56] The exclusion provoked outrage, including from Julian's fervent admirer, the pagan soldier and historian Ammianus Marcellinus (who served in Julian's army).[57] Edward Watts observes that Julian's educational exclusions were the first instance in Roman history of citizens being legally sanctioned purely because of their beliefs.[58]

Government-sponsored paganism was back, it seemed, with a vengeance.[59]

Julian was and has remained a fascinating figure; in modern times he has inspired not only extensive historical study but also novels, plays, and poems.[60] Bookish, slovenly, bearded (in imitation of the philosophers but in defiance of the fashions of the day), mystical, ascetic, and sexually abstemious, he proved to be an unlikely but capable military commander, crushing opposition to the empire in Gaul and Germany.[61] In addition to performing his governmental and military duties, he wrote books on philosophy, history, and religion, including the virulently anti-Christian *Against the Galileans*. His paganism (or "Hellenism," as he preferred) mixed academic learning and philosophical refinement with an old-fashioned devotion to the gods and the auguries.[62]

55. Bowersock, *Julian the Apostate*, 84.

56. Murdoch, *The Last Pagan*, 139.

57. See Ammianus Marcellinus, *The Later Roman Empire (A.D. 354–378)*, ed. and trans. Walter Hamilton (London: Penguin, 1986).

58. Watts, *The Final Pagan Generation*, 113–14.

59. G. W. Bowersock argues that Julian "never contemplated any other solution to the religious problem than total elimination. His view of the Christians was totally intolerant from the start." Bowersock, *Julian the Apostate*, 85.

60. See Murdoch, *The Last Pagan*, 206–18.

61. See generally Bowersock, *Julian the Apostate*, 12–20, 33–45. On Julian's slovenliness, see Gibbon, *History of the Decline*, 1:854–55.

62. Consider Ammianus's description of Julian on the eve of his accession to power. "Preparing to battle Constantius for supreme authority, Julian busied himself with the inspection of the entrails of sacrifices and with observation of the flight of birds. He was eager to discover how things would end, but the answers were ambiguous and obscure and left him in doubt about the future. At last the Gallic rhetorician Aprunculus, a master of this branch of divination, . . . announced that he had discovered what was to come by the inspection of a liver, which he had found covered with a double layer of skin. Julian was afraid that this might be an invention designed to flatter his hopes and was in consequence depressed, but he then experienced himself a much more convincing omen, which clearly symbolized the

Had Julian's reign been extended, some historians surmise,[63] he might have succeeded in repressing Christianity and reestablishing paganism as the official and dominant religion of the realm (albeit in a reformed version that attempted to incorporate some of Christianity's advantageous features, including a disciplined priestly hierarchy and a commitment to caring for the poor).[64] But after less than two years as emperor, in uncharacteristic defiance of the omens but in accordance with his intense identification with Alexander the Great, Julian resolved on a military campaign into Persia.[65] Having reached the Tigris River, to the dismay of his soldiers, and in a decision that has perplexed observers both ancient and modern, the emperor ordered the supporting ships—more than a thousand of them—to be burned.[66] Their means of convenient retreat having been destroyed, the legions then proceeded with the invasion, marching now into territory unknown to them.

Soon the ill-advised and badly executed invasion was floundering, and the armies were faced not only with hostile forces but also with scanty supplies and scorching heat.[67] Forced to acknowledge the failure of his campaign, Julian attempted to lead his exhausted and demoralized troops back to friendlier country, but in the retreat the emperor was killed by a stray arrow. One legend had it that just before expiring, Julian gasped, "Thou hast won, O Galilean."[68] Ammianus, by contrast, depicts the emperor on his

---

death of Constantius. At the very moment when the latter died in Cilicia [a fact not yet known to Julian] the soldier whose right hand was supporting Julian as he was mounting his horse slipped and fell to the ground, whereupon Julian was heard by a number of people to exclaim that the man who had raised him to high station [i.e., Constantius] had fallen." Ammianus, *The Later Roman Empire*, 234.

63. See Peter Brown, *The World of Late Antiquity, AD 150–750* (San Diego: Harcourt, 1971), 93; Veyne, *When Our World Became Christian*, 99 (asserting that but for the early death of Julian, "Christianity might have constituted no more than a historical parenthesis, opened by Constantine in 312, which would now close forever"); Murdoch, *The Last Pagan*, 139. Gibbon was more skeptical. See Gibbon, *History of the Decline*, 1:879, 908.

64. Bowersock, *Julian the Apostate*, 87–88. Julian was not the first emperor to try to regularize and reform the pagan priesthood. See Lactantius, *On the Manner*, chap. 37 (describing reform efforts by Maximin Daia).

65. On Julian's identification with Alexander, see Bowersock, *Julian the Apostate*, 15, 78, 101. On his defiance of the omens, see Bowersock, 107–11. For a different interpretation, see Murdoch, *The Last Pagan*, 157–59.

66. See Bowersock, *Julian the Apostate*, 114–15; Murdoch, *The Last Pagan*, 179–80; Gibbon, *History of the Decline*, 1:937–38.

67. Gibbon, *History of the Decline*, 1:940–43.

68. Murdoch, *The Last Pagan*, 190.

deathbed discoursing in good Socratic fashion with pagan philosophers on the immortality of the soul.[69]

Needing a leader to conduct the desperate retreat, the embattled legions hastily selected a distinguished pagan officer, Salutius, who refused the perilous appointment; and so they turned to another senior officer named Jovian, who happened to be Christian.[70] Jovian managed to get the army out of Persia (in part by striking a disastrous deal that relinquished a sizable piece of territory to the Persians), and though his reign was short, he was succeeded by a series of Christian rulers. Jovian favored a policy of religious toleration, as did his immediate successors, Valens and Valentinian.[71] Gradually, however, and perhaps (as one historian argues)[72] acting on fears lingering from "the Great Persecution" and reawakened by Julian's anti-Christian campaign, the emperors, and in particular the Spanish and severely orthodox emperor Theodosius, adopted a harsher series of laws closing temples and forbidding pagan sacrifices.[73]

Although the scope of these measures and the extent of their enforcement continue to provoke disagreement among historians,[74] the clear overall trend was toward the official elevation of Christianity and the repression of paganism. And when emperors stopped short in these efforts, mobs of militant monks and other faithful sometimes stepped in to carry out the task[75]—hence the destruction of the famous temple of Serapis in Alexandria and the murder of the distinguished female pagan scholar Hypatia.[76]

The Politics of Symbolism. In explaining how and when Christianity prevailed over paganism, it is tempting to point to some watershed edict or law that signaled the change and that effectively suppressed the older religion. Perhaps the alleged closing of several pagan temples under Constantine? Or the law under Constantius that purported to make pagan sacrifice a capital offense? Or the edicts of Theodosius in 391 and 392 that expanded prohibitions on pagan worship?[77]

69. Ammianus, *The Later Roman Empire*, 294–95.

70. Bowersock, *Julian the Apostate*, 118.

71. Watts, *The Final Pagan Generation*, 116; Gibbon, *History of the Decline*, 1:980.

72. See Drake, *Constantine and the Bishops*, 409.

73. Watts, *The Final Pagan Generation*, 182, 207.

74. For a careful review of the evidence on these questions, see Alan Cameron, *The Last Pagans*, 33–92.

75. Drake, *Constantine and the Bishops*, 408; Averil Cameron, *The Later Roman Empire* (Cambridge, MA: Harvard University Press, 1993), 76.

76. Drake, *Constantine and the Bishops*, 401, 409–11; Brown, *Power and Persuasion*, 89–103, 119.

77. Watts, *The Final Pagan Generation*, 207.

But these explanations encounter a puzzle. Despite the apparent severity of some of these measures taken at face value, it seems that they had little actual effect on the practice of pagan religion. Indeed, as Edward Watts explains, prominent and politically involved pagans like Libanius and Praetextatus seem scarcely to have noticed them.[78] These seem to have been paper prohibitions that went largely unenforced. And even while adopting such antipagan measures, emperors like Constantine, Constantius, and Theodosius continued to tolerate or even support paganism in various ways,[79] and to appoint substantial numbers of known pagans to high positions within the empire. Gibbon, never charitable toward Christianity, nonetheless acknowledged that even under Theodosius, "the profession of Christianity was not made an essential qualification for the enjoyment of the civil rights of society, nor were any peculiar hardships imposed on the sectaries, who credulously received the fables of Ovid, and obstinately rejected the miracles of the Gospel. The palace, the schools, the army, and the senate, were filled with declared and devout Pagans; they obtained, without distinction, the civil and military honors of the empire."[80]

What, then, to make of the apparent legal prohibitions issued by Constantius, Theodosius, and other Christian emperors of the period? Were these simply empty gestures, made to appease more aggressive Christian critics perhaps but not intended to have any real effect? There is no certain answer to such questions. But what seems clear is that however negligible their actual coercive effect may have been, such measures had a symbolic impact. Together with other overtly symbolic measures, these laws and pol-

---

78. E.g., Watts, *The Final Pagan Generation*, 89, 102, 207–9.

79. See, e.g., Brown, *World of Late Antiquity*, 88: "Constantine . . . accepted pagan honours from the citizens of Athens. He ransacked the Aegean for pagan classical statuary to adorn Constantinople. He treated a pagan philosopher as a colleague. He paid the traveling expenses of a pagan priest who visited the pagan monuments of Egypt."

80. Gibbon, *History of the Decline*, 2:88–89. Gibbon added: "Theodosius distinguished his liberal regard for virtue and genius by the consular dignity which he bestowed on [the pagan senator] Symmachus; and by the personal friendship which he expressed to [the pagan orator] Libanius; and the two eloquent apologists of Paganism were never required either to change or to dissemble their religious opinions. The Pagans were indulged in the most licentious freedom of speech and writing; the historical and philosophical remains of Eunapius, Zosimus, and the fanatic teachers of the school of Plato, betray the most furious animosity, and contain the sharpest invectives, against the sentiments and conduct of their victorious adversaries. If these audacious libels were publicly known, we must applaud the good sense of the Christian princes, who viewed, with a smile of contempt, the last struggles of superstition and despair" (88–89).

icies gradually came to induce subjects to conceive of the empire in more Christian terms.

Thus, Edward Watts explains that Constantius's facially tough but practically feckless edicts against pagan sacrifice amounted to "largely symbolic policies."[81] But this is not to minimize their importance: symbolism can be important. An admired modern scholarly study argues that political communities are "imagined."[82] They exist not as physical facts, but as constructs in the minds of their citizens. And public symbols are the matter around and by which such imaginings occur. The competing pagan and Christian parties at least implicitly understood this point.

Thus, when the Christian emperors of the later fourth century cut off funding for the support of the temples and the vestal virgins, it was not merely the withdrawal of material resources that Christians applauded and pagans resented; it was the denial of support that was perceived to be *public* in nature.[83] Gibbon explained that for the pagan senatorial faction, "the Roman sacrifices would be deprived of their force and energy, if they were no longer celebrated *at the expense, as well as in the name, of the republic.*"[84]

It was precisely this public sponsorship that Ambrose, feisty bishop of Milan and perhaps the most powerful figure in the church at the time, found most objectionable. Responding to the pagan senator Symmachus's argument that monies for the temples had originally been bequeathed for that purpose by "dying persons,"[85] Ambrose argued to the emperor that even if the funds technically came from past donations by private parties, they had long been deemed part of the public treasury; hence, if the emperor were to restore the monies for pagan worship, "you will seem to give rather from your own funds," and thus to be giving imperial approval to pagan worship.[86] The optics, as modern pundits say, were crucial.

Other symbolic changes were more purely visual, and perhaps even more salient to average Roman subjects. Pagan temples served, Edward

81. Watts, *The Final Pagan Generation*, 102.

82. Benedict Anderson, *Imagined Communities* (London: Verso, 2006).

83. Watts, *The Final Pagan Generation*, 183 ("Part of this had to do with the idea that the state needed to pay for the public rituals if those rituals were to represent true expressions of collective devotion").

84. Gibbon, *History of the Decline*, 2:75 (emphasis added).

85. Symmachus, *Relation* 3, para. 13, reproduced at https://people.ucalgary.ca/~vandersp /Courses/texts/sym-amb/symrel3f.html (introduction by J. Vanderspoel).

86. Ambrose, *Epistle* 17, para. 3, reproduced at https://people.ucalgary.ca/~vandersp /Courses/texts/sym-amb/ambrepf.html (introduction by J. Vanderspoel).

Watts explains, "to visually overwhelm people."[87] So when these temples were converted into Christian churches, the symbolism of displacement was starkly on display—as it was when Christian mobs, sometimes with imperial approval or at least acquiescence, destroyed those same temples.[88] No wonder that the emperor Julian, in his short-lived pagan revival, required that the churches be taken down and the pagan temples rebuilt in their place.

Similarly, the magnificent new Christian churches and basilicas dominated city skyscapes[89] (as they still do in places like Rome and Florence). These edifices and the ceremonies conducted in them "left visitors amazed," Peter Brown reports. One traveler of late antiquity reported back to his correspondent: "You simply cannot imagine the number and the sheer weight of the candles, tapers, lamps and everything else they use for the services. . . . They are beyond description." Brown observes that "the churches spoke far more loudly and more continuously of the providential alliance of Church and empire than did any imperial edict."[90] Understanding the importance of this visual and tangible message, Milan's powerful bishop Ambrose built, and fought tenaciously to retain, impressive basilicas—sometimes against imperial edicts and imperial troops—as part of his campaign not only against paganism but also against the Arian heresy that for a period dominated the imperial family.[91]

Perhaps the most sustained struggle over a public symbol concerned the so-called Altar of Victory—a shrine to the goddess Victory that had been placed next to the door of the Senate House by the first emperor, Augustus. Gibbon explains that the altar "was adorned by . . . a majestic female standing on a globe, with flowing garments, expanded wings, and a crown of laurel in her outstretched hand. The senators were sworn on the altar of the goddess to observe the laws of the emperor and of the empire: and a solemn offering of wine and incense was the ordinary prelude of their public deliberations."[92] In 357, Constantius ordered the altar removed. The pagan emperor Julian had

---

87. Watts, *The Final Pagan Generation*, 137.

88. See Drake, *Constantine and the Bishops*, 409; Gibbon, *History of the Decline*, 2:78–87.

89. See Brown, *Power and Persuasion*, 120–21.

90. Peter Brown, *The Rise of Western Christendom: Triumph and Diversity, A.D. 200–1000*, rev. ed. (West Sussex, UK: Wiley-Blackwell, 2013), 77.

91. Ambrose's efforts in this respect are described in Garry Wills, *Font of Life: Ambrose, Augustine, and the Mystery of Baptism* (New York: Oxford University Press, 2012). See also Averil Cameron, *The Later Roman Empire*, 78 (observing "the practical impact of church building").

92. Gibbon, *History of the Decline*, 2:73.

it restored. Then, in 382, the Christian emperor Gratian again had the altar taken down. Whereupon the pagan senator and Roman prefect Symmachus wrote an eloquent plea to Emperor Valentinian II requesting restoration of the altar—a plea that was in turn stoutly opposed by Ambrose the bishop.

All the disputants in this controversy recognized the symbolic importance of the shrine. While arguing that removal of the altar had led to "misfortunes," including a poor harvest,[93] Symmachus primarily emphasized that the maintenance of the shrine was a way of preserving a continuity of identity with Rome's pagan past. "We ought to keep faith with so many centuries, and to follow our ancestors, as they happily followed theirs."[94] For his part, Ambrose acknowledged the existence of "altars in all the temples, and an altar also in the temple of Victories." In fact, the pagans "celebrate their sacrifices everywhere."[95] But Symmachus's proposal was different: the senator and his allies were demanding a pagan shrine "in the Senate House of the city of Rome,"[96] where Christian senators as well as pagans met to deliberate, and where "an altar is so placed for this purpose, that every assembly should deliberate under its sanction."[97] To place a pagan altar in that centrally important public spot would be to "insult the Faith."[98] Such a symbolic gesture would be intolerable: Ambrose thus threatened that if the emperor were to approve the restoration of the altar, he would betray the faith and would be denied worship privileges. "You indeed may come to the church, but will find either no priest there, or one who will resist you."[99]

In this fierce polemical struggle over a central symbolic manifestation of the empire, Ambrose prevailed: Symmachus's plea was rejected. As all sides recognized, a symbolic victory was significant in defining the empire as Christian or pagan. And in winning the fight over this and other symbols, Christians managed to create a conception of the city—of the "imagined community"[100]—as Christian, not pagan.

93. Symmachus, *Relation* 3, para. 14.

94. Symmachus, *Relation* 3, para. 8.

95. Ambrose, *Epistle* 18, para. 31, reproduced at https://people.ucalgary.ca/~vandersp /Courses/texts/sym-amb/ambrepf.html (introduction by J. Vanderspoel).

96. Ambrose, *Epistle* 18, para. 31.

97. Ambrose, *Epistle* 17, para. 9. Pressing the point, or perhaps overarguing it, the bishop went on to depict how "the smoke and ashes from the altar, the sparks from the sacrilege, the smoke from the burning might choke the breath and throats of the faithful" (para. 9).

98. Ambrose, *Epistle* 17, para. 31.

99. Ambrose, *Epistle* 17, para. 13.

100. See Anderson, *Imagined Communities*, and above, 174.

The Cultural-Spiritual Struggle. But was the eventual triumph of Christianity a purely top-down development, the result of the emperors' halfhearted coercive and somewhat more consistent symbolic support of the new religion? At least some historians have suggested that the emperors were not so much causing and guiding cultural developments as responding to and reflecting them.

Thus, the seminal work of the Belgian scholar Franz Cumont discerned a kind of corruption and a waning of credibility in the classical paganism of the second through fourth centuries; this decline was reflected in the increasing popularity of imported Oriental cults like those dedicated to Isis, Serapis, and Mithra.[101] "The gods and heroes of mythology had no longer any but a purely literary existence," Cumont argues. "The old national religion of Rome was dead."[102] Other scholars have agreed. Norman Cantor declares that "by 150 AD whatever vitality had once existed in ancient polytheism had mostly declined, and the gods played little or no role in individual lives. The state temples to the old gods became civic centers rather than religious entities."[103] Antonia Tripolitis contends that "confidence in the traditional cults and their gods that served as the basis of the political, social, and intellectual life was waning. The general populace no longer placed its hope or faith on the ancient gods."[104]

As noted, however, other historians dispute this interpretation.[105]

101. See Franz Cumont, *The Oriental Religions in Roman Paganism* (Chicago: Open Court, 1911), 196–212. See also Brown, *World of Late Antiquity*, 63 ("The spread of the oriental cults in western Europe . . . is a notorious feature of the first and second centuries. There cults spread because they gave the immigrant, and later the local adherent, a sense of belonging, a sense of loyalty that he lacked in the civic functions of his town").

102. Cumont, *Oriental Religions*, 203, 204.

103. Norman F. Cantor, *Antiquity: From the Birth of Sumerian Civilization to the Fall of the Roman Empire* (New York: HarperCollins, 2003), 39. See also Jonathan Kirsch, *God against the Gods: The History of the War between Monotheism and Polytheism* (New York: Penguin, 2004), 93 (asserting that "by the first century of the Common Era, . . . the classical paganism of Greece and Rome was already in decline").

104. Antonia Tripolitis, *Religions of the Hellenistic-Roman Age* (Grand Rapids: Eerdmans, 2002), 2. As noted, E. R. Dodds described the paganism of the fourth century as "a sort of living corpse." Dodds, *Pagan and Christian*, 132.

105. See, e.g., MacMullen, *Paganism in the Roman Empire*. See also Robin Lane Fox, *Pagans and Christians* (London: Penguin, 1986), 115 ("Far into the second and third centuries AD, this piety of the majority survived the wit of poets and philosophers"), 123 ("By the early Christian period, the forms of religious life had grown, but the idea of divine encounters [with pagan deities] had not faded: it had grown with them"), 669 (arguing that "the pagan cults were not quick to die away").

Even with vastly more evidence, it would likely be difficult to resolve this disagreement; given the paucity of data, resolution seems impossible. We can nonetheless consider the paganism of late antiquity relative to the emerging Christianity to appreciate the intellectual and spiritual strengths and limitations of each. Our consideration can take note of three dimensions on which the advantages of paganism and Christianity might be compared: the communal, the creedal, and the spiritual or existential.

From the outset, caveats are in order. Not everyone has the same need for community, or for the same kind of community. Then, as now, some people will find association in a closely knit congregation of like-minded people to be comforting or fulfilling; others will experience it as stifling. Similarly, evaluations both of the believability of creeds and of spiritual efficacy will differ from person to person, just as religiosity itself varies greatly among people. What strikes one person as a self-evident and ennobling truth will appear to another as a demeaning absurdity.

So although partisans of each orientation did confidently and aggressively proclaim paganism or Christianity spiritually superior, and although modern scholars occasionally offer similar assessments,[106] we will refrain here from pretending to render any final judgment. For our purposes, it will be enough to observe how both paganism and Christianity had their profound and discernible strengths. One pertinent consequence of this more tentative assessment will be that although particular aspects or features of paganism might fade or be repressed, it was unlikely that paganism did or could simply disappear; and in fact, it didn't.

So, let us start with community. Norman Cantor argues that "the [Christian] Church provided a sense of community and institutions of friendship and caring within the largely joyless, anomic world of the Roman Empire."[107] In a similar vein, Peter Brown contends that the "appeal of Christianity lay in its radical sense of community: it absorbed people because the individual could drop from a wide impersonal world into a miniature community, whose demands and relations were explicit."[108] A distinctive feature of this new community was its egalitarian quality: "the Church included a powerful

106. See generally MacMullen, *Christianity and Paganism* (generally depicting paganism as tolerant and attractive and Christianity as oppressive); Veyne, *When Our World Became Christian*, 19, 22 (asserting Christianity's clear superiority over paganism) (see below, 188).

107. Cantor, *Antiquity*, 39.

108. Brown, *World of Late Antiquity*, 68.

freedman chamberlain of the emperor; its bishop was the former slave of that freedman; it was protected by the emperor's mistress, and patronized by noble ladies."[109] And the community was notable for caring for its poor and sick; even the pagans, Gibbon points out, admired this feature of the Christian community.[110]

Then, as now, of course, the more close-knit a community may aspire to be, the more distressing internal dissensions and jealousies can become. This problem is already painfully evident in New Testament epistles chastising the various churches for their internal divisions and for their tendency to favor richer over humbler members.[111] Making an exception to his usual policy of discounting the testimony of Eusebius, Gibbon comments in a jaundiced tone that during Diocletian's reign, "fraud, envy, and malice, prevailed in every [Christian] congregation."[112] Moreover, admission into the Christian community might seem to be a sacrifice of full participation in the convivial pagan associations, entertainments, and festivities that devout Christians were taught to shun as idolatrous: in gaining one community, a person might be losing another.

In addition, even insofar as Christian communities approximated their ideals, and even for those who might yearn for the community that the church could offer, entrance might still be deterred by the fact that admission was conditional on the affirmation of a creed—one that pagans often regarded as, well, offensive and preposterous. Which brings us to the question of believability—a concern that could be an issue both for pagans and for Christians.

We have already seen how even in the pre-Christian era, many educated Romans found the myths about the gods incredible, and this difficulty likely increased in ensuing centuries as cults proliferated and new deities swelled the pantheon.[113] Paul Veyne contends that by the time Christianity arrived, "for six or seven centuries already, paganism had been in crisis. It

109. Brown, *World of Late Antiquity*, 66.
110. Gibbon, *History of the Decline*, 1:493. For elaboration of the point, see Rodney Stark, *The Triumph of Christianity: How the Jesus Movement Became the World's Largest Religion* (New York: HarperCollins, 2011), 112–19.
111. See, e.g., 1 Cor. 1:10–17; James 2:1–9.
112. Gibbon, *History of the Decline*, 1:559.
113. See Dodds, *Pagan and Christian*, 133: "The religious tolerance which was the normal Greek and Roman practice had resulted in a bewildering mass of alternatives. There were too many cults, too many mysteries, too many philosophies of life to choose from: you could pile one religious insurance on another, yet not feel safe."

was crammed with too many fables and naiveties; a pious and educated pagan no longer knew what he should believe."[114]

One remedy for this embarrassment among traditional but educated pagans was to interpret the myths more metaphorically. We have already seen this allegorical-philosophical approach employed by Balbus, the Stoic character in Cicero's dialogue on the gods;[115] later thinkers developed the method with dedicated ingenuity.[116] So the story of Saturn eating his children might be taken as a sort of allegory representing the fact that seeds return to the earth from which they grew, or perhaps as a poignant poetic expression of the existential truth that Time (i.e., Saturn, aka Cronos) inexorably destroys all that it begets.[117] In a more philosophical vein, Jupiter might represent heaven, Juno earth, and Minerva the Platonic ideas: "heaven being that *by which* anything is made; earth being that *of which* it is made; and the ideas being the form *according to which* it is made."[118] Gibbon commented scornfully: "As the traditions of Pagan mythology were variously related, the sacred interpreters . . . could extract from any fable any sense which was adapted to their favorite system of religion and philosophy. The lascivious form of a naked Venus was tortured into the discovery of some moral precept . . . ; and the castration of Atys explained the revolution of the sun between the tropics, or the separation of the human soul from vice and error."[119]

To critics (like the proto-Humean character Cotta of Cicero's dialogue), this philosophizing strategy might seem a futile maneuver. Indeed, Cotta said as much.[120] In their attacks on paganism, Christian thinkers like Athenagoras, Lactantius, and Augustine pressed the point. If the divine reality is one, and is spiritual rather than corporeal, why not forthrightly acknowledge and worship that divine reality or Being? What is the point of fragmenting divinity into a thousand tiny anthropomorphized

114. Veyne, *When Our World Became Christian*, 43–44. Veyne adds, however, that "among the simple masses, paganism was generally accepted and was therefore solidly rooted; it could have endured indefinitely" (44).

115. See above, chap. 4.

116. See R. T. Wallis, *Neoplatonism*, 2nd ed. (Indianapolis: Hackett, 1995), 130–37, 147–51.

117. These interpretations, attributed to Varro, are discussed and criticized in Augustine, *The City of God against the Pagans*, trans. and ed. R. W. Dyson (Cambridge: Cambridge University Press, 1998), 6.8, p. 255; 7.19, p. 290.

118. This was Varro's interpretation, as described by Augustine, *City of God* 7.28, p. 303 (emphasis added).

119. Gibbon, *History of the Decline*, 1:869.

120. See above, 94.

subdeities, each of which is deemed not exactly real but only a metaphor, or an analogy?[121]

But then Jewish and Christian Scripture sometimes provoked comparable embarrassments, which Christian thinkers sometimes tried to escape through the same philosophizing or analogizing strategy. Christians were after all committed to a sacred Scripture that contained many ancient stories that challenged devotees' credulity or assaulted their moral sensibilities in the same way the pagan myths did. And sophisticated Christians like Origen and Augustine sometimes responded to this difficulty by adopting analogical or metaphorical interpretations.[122] In this spirit, Adam's sons Abel and Seth and his descendant Enos could be taken as symbols of Christ, and of the church,[123] as could Noah's ark.[124] Abel's murderous brother Cain (who was said in Scripture to have founded a city), Abraham's concubine Hagar, and Hagar's son Ishmael were all symbols of the earthly city. Conversely, Abraham's wife Sarah and the city of Jerusalem were symbols of the heavenly city.[125]

The symbolism could become intricate and multilayered, one symbol serving to symbolize another.[126] Indeed, it was his discovery of this hermeneutical possibility that allowed Augustine to embrace the Bible and Christianity after years of incredulity;[127] he later wrote a treatise expounding in detail the rich assortment of methods by which Scripture should be interpreted.[128]

For Christians, to be sure, there were limits to this strategy. Pagan critics attacked the most central historical-theological claims of the Gospels—that God had condescended to become incarnate in the man Jesus, that Jesus was born of a virgin, that after his crucifixion he was resurrected—but on these essential claims Christian apologists needed to, and did, stand firm. The debate over such historical and hermeneutical issues between learned

---

121. Augustine, *City of God* 7.28–30, pp. 303–6. See also generally Athenagoras, *A Plea for the Christians*, trans. B. P. Pratten (Pickerington, OH: Beloved, 2016).

122. For a discussion of the similarities in pagan and Christian allegorical interpretation, see Dodds, *Pagan and Christian*, 130–31.

123. Augustine, *City of God* 4.18, pp. 670–71.

124. Augustine, *City of God* 15.26, p. 686.

125. Augustine, *City of God* 15.1–3, pp. 634–37.

126. Augustine, *City of God* 15.2, p. 637.

127. Augustine, *The Confessions of St. Augustine*, ed. and trans. Albert Cook Outler, rev. ed. (New York: Dover, 2002), 5.24–25, pp. 81–82; 6.8, p. 89.

128. Augustine, *On Christian Doctrine*, trans. J. F. Shaw (New York: Dover, 2009).

apologists like Origen or Augustine and astute pagan critics like Celsus or Porphyry was as vigorous and sophisticated as more modern debates on the same subjects with which contemporary believers and skeptics are familiar.[129] Still, many of the less theologically central biblical stories could be, and were, reinterpreted in more spiritual or metaphorical terms.[130]

But although both pagans and Christians might offer spiritual or philosophical readings to domesticate stories that would otherwise seem offensive or far-fetched, this philosophizing turn favored Christianity over the long run. That is because philosophy tended to push the sacred in a transcendent direction. Plato's idea of the Good, unlike the pagan deities but like the God of the Hebrews and the Christians, was not in and of this corruptible and corrupted world. So there was an implicit incongruity in the efforts of Stoics and Neoplatonists to use philosophy to shore up a pantheon of gods who definitely *were* in and of this world. It was as if enfeebled gods were being treated with a regimen that was in fact slowly lethal to them. With respect to the Neoplatonist Iamblichus and the later Athenian School, R. T. Wallis observes that "among [the school's] unintended results was the draining of the traditional gods of such personality as they still retained; hence in seeking to establish traditional worship on a philosophical basis the post-Iamblicheans ironically ensured the triumph of Christianity."[131]

Augustine mocked without mercy the incongruities and the arbitrariness in thinkers like Varro who tried through allegorical interpretations to reconcile pagan deities with the loftier teachings of the philosophers.[132] And while praising Plato effusively and at length[133]—by his own account, after all, Platonic books had played a major role in his own transition to Christianity[134]—Augustine hammered on the implausibilities and inconsistencies in later philosophies that attempted to use Plato to justify worship of the pagan gods.[135]

129. For an insightful study of such debates, see generally Robert Louis Wilken, *The Christians as the Romans Saw Them*, 2nd ed. (New Haven: Yale University Press, 2003).

130. Gibbon, not surprisingly, had no more patience for this approach when employed by Christians than when it was used by pagans. He commented scornfully that "acknowledging that the literal sense is repugnant to every principle of faith as well as reason, they deem themselves secure and invulnerable behind the ample veil of allegory." Gibbon, *History of the Decline*, 1:457.

131. Wallis, *Neoplatonism*, 137.

132. Augustine, *City of God*, bks. 6–7.

133. Augustine, *City of God* 8.5–9, pp. 318–25.

134. Augustine, *Confessions* 7.13, p. 114.

135. Augustine, *City of God*, bks. 8–10.

We will return to the question of believability, but let us first consider the matter of spiritual or existential efficacy. Which form of religiosity—pagan or Christian—was better able to give meaning to people's lives, and sublimity to the world in which they passed their days?

Each position had its manifest advantages. We have already seen, in chapter 3, how paganism served to consecrate and beatify the world and the polity. Robin Lane Fox observes that the gods endowed the world with a "shining beauty and grace."[136] In the philosophical renderings of paganism, E. R. Dodds explains, "the whole vast structure [of the cosmos] was seen as the expression of a divine order; as such it was felt to be beautiful and worshipful."[137] In a similar vein, Fox observes that "everywhere, the gods were involved in life's basic patterns, in birth, copulation, and death[, in] adolescence, marriage and childbirth."[138] The beatification was not limited to the philosophically trained; it was extended to the multitudes in vivid forms—in the sights and smells of the sacrifices, the music and swirl of the pagan theater, the pomp and rhythm of the processions, the press and roar and tumult of the games and the races. And also, of course, in the ecstasy of sexual intimacy, experienced and understood as the "mysterious, indwelling presence of the gods."[139]

In short, paganism sacralized the world and rendered it beautiful—for some, hauntingly beautiful. Noting "the echo of divine beauty which had been rendered visible and so mysteriously potent, by the material image of a pagan god," Peter Brown suggests that "it was the sense of the intimate and intangible presence of the unseen that consoled the last pagans."[140] There were, however, limitations to this pagan beatification of life and the world, among which two stand out.

First, and most starkly, for every actual man and woman, it would all precipitously end with, as Homer had put it, "the dark mist of death."[141] What came after death was murky, but there was no general expectation that it would be happy. Homer had spoken of the "hateful darkness," and of "the

---

136. Robin Lane Fox, *The Classical World: An Epic History from Homer to Hadrian* (New York: Basic Books, 2006), 49–50.

137. Dodds, *Pagan and Christian*, 6.

138. Fox, *Pagans and Christians*, 83.

139. See above, 71.

140. Brown, *World of Late Antiquity*, 78.

141. Homer, *The Odyssey*, trans. Robert Fitzgerald (New York: Farrar, Straus and Giroux, 1998), 4.192.

houses of the dead—the dank, moldering horrors that fill the deathless gods themselves with loathing."[142] Virgil observed mournfully:

> Ah! life's best hours are ever first to fly
> From hapless mortals; in their place succeed
> Disease and dolorous eld; till travail sore
> And death unpitying sweep them from the scene.[143]

And Catullus sadly intoned:

> When the sun sets, it sets to rise again,
> But for us, when our brief day is over,
> There is one endless night that we must sleep.[144]

Second, although the gods might serve to endow the world with beauty and enchantment, their doings and purposes were not actually concerned with *us*—with humans. True, a god or goddess might occasionally take a liking, or a loathing, to some particular mortal (especially if that mortal, like Achilles, or like Rome's ancestor Aeneas, happened to be the offspring of some momentary tryst between the god or goddess and a mortal woman or man), or even to a nation. In the *Iliad*, the various gods intervene aggressively, as Zeus intermittently permits, for the Greeks or for the Trojans. For the most part, though, the gods were out for themselves, so to speak. They were mostly indifferent to the joys and sorrows of all the Marcuses, Gaiuses, and Juliuses of this world.

How much if at all did these features detract from the ability of paganism to provide meaning to the matters of mortal life? As usual, no single or manifestly correct answer is forthcoming. Attitudes toward death vary. The Stoical emperor Marcus Aurelius found in the inexorability of death a sort of morose comfort against the vicissitudes of life. Why worry about misfortunes when you know that "within a very little time . . . you . . . will be dead; and soon not even your names will be left behind."[145]

---

142. Homer, *The Iliad*, trans. Robert Fagles (New York: Penguin, 1998), 13.776, p. 363; 20.78–79, p. 505.

143. Virgil, *Georgic III*, in *The Georgics of Virgil*, trans. James Rhoades, 2nd ed. (London: Kegan Paul, Trench, Trubner and Co., 1891), 66.

144. Catullus, *Carmina* 5, quoted in E. L. Mascall, *The Christian Universe* (London: Darton, Longman and Todd, 1966), 20.

145. Marcus Aurelius, *Meditations* (New York: Dover, 1997), bk. 4, p. 21

Odysseus opts to reject the promise of immortality with the lovely nymph Calypso in favor of returning to his home and his wife, Penelope.[146] And it can be argued—it sometimes *is* argued—that the inevitable fact of death is what gives human life its shape and meaning, and what makes possible courage and nobility of character.[147] The warriors in the *Iliad* may come across as more interesting and admirable figures than the gods themselves. That is precisely because Achilles and Hector and their comrades, knowing that they must unavoidably go down to the House of Death, and soon, understand that their only hope of immortality lies in winning glory for themselves; and they accordingly exert themselves to demonstrate valor and resourcefulness. There is an unmistakable nobility in their exertions, and in their defiance in the face of death.

And yet there also remains a tragic sense, and a kind of profound futility, in the Homeric assumption that the best a man can hope for is to kill gloriously and die gloriously, so that his name will be recalled in the lyrics chanted by bards when the man himself is no longer around to hear the songs. "Then what's the good of glory, magnificent renown," Sophocles has the aged Oedipus ask, "if in its flow it streams away to nothing?"[148] Marcus Aurelius agreed: "Fame after life is no better than oblivion."[149] A hero may grimly make the best of mortality, but, given the chance, wouldn't he eagerly exchange it for a life of endless contentment? And so in the midst of battle on the plains outside Troy, the gallant warrior Sarpedon confesses to his comrade Glaucus:

> Ah my friend, if you and I could escape this fray
> and live forever, never a trace of age, immortal,
> I would never fight on the front lines again
> or command you to the field where men win fame.
> But now, as it is, the fates of death await us,
> thousands poised to strike, and not a man alive
> can flee them or escape—so in we go for attack!
> Give our enemy glory or win it for ourselves![150]

---

146. Homer, *The Odyssey* 5.212–234.

147. Cf. Fox, *The Classical World*, 47 ("In Homer's poems, the dominant image is that there is no life beyond the grave. . . . This superb view of man's condition heightens the poignancy of a hero's life. We are what we do; fame, won in life, is our immortality").

148. Sophocles, "Oedipus at Colonus," in *Sophocles: The Three Theban Plays*, trans. Robert Fagles (London: Penguin, 1982), lines 274–75, p. 299.

149. Aurelius, *Meditations* 2.15.

150. Homer, *The Iliad* 12.374–381, pp. 335–36.

The tragic futility of this mortal condition leads Homer's Apollo to remark on

> wretched mortals . . .
> like leaves, no sooner flourishing, full of the sun's fire,
> feeding on earth's gifts, than they waste away and die.[151]

And Zeus, preeminent among the gods, echoes the sun god's judgment:

> There is nothing alive more agonized than man
> of all that breathe and crawl across the earth.[152]

When Odysseus, visiting the underworld, attempts to console the shade of Achilles with the observation that he seems to be a lord among the dead, the renowned warrior responds:

> No winning words about death to *me*, shining Odysseus!
> By god, I'd rather slave on earth for another man—
> some dirt-poor tenant farmer who scrapes to keep alive—
> than rule down here over all the breathless dead.[153]

Christianity offered an utterly different picture of humans' lives and destinies. Like the pagan poets, Christian authors could comment wistfully on the brevity of life. "All flesh is like grass," says an apostolic epistle, "and all its glory like the flower" that fades.[154] "For every man dies in a little while," remarks Augustine, "nor is that to be deemed a benefit which vanishes like a mist in a moment of time."[155] But men and women would not linger in the grave; rather, they would be resurrected and, if their lives had been faithful, would go on to enjoy eternal life with God. This was the good news of the gospel, which Christians eagerly proclaimed to the world.

"O death, where is thy victory?" Paul exults. "O grave, where is thy sting?"[156] Luc Ferry asserts that "the entire originality of the Christian mes-

---

151. Homer, *The Iliad* 21.528–530, p. 535.
152. Homer, *The Iliad* 17.515–516, p. 457.
153. Homer, *The Odyssey* 11.255–258.
154. 1 Pet. 1:24–25.
155. Augustine, *City of God* 4.5, p. 149.
156. 1 Cor. 15:55.

sage resides in 'the good news' of literal immortality—*resurrection*, in other words and not merely of souls but of individual human bodies."[157]

The historian Paul Veyne contends that its message of eternal life gave Christianity a huge spiritual advantage over paganism. Under Christianity, a person's life "suddenly acquired an eternal significance within a cosmic plan, something that no philosophy or paganism could confer."[158] To Edward Gibbon, the idea of a life after this one was "an idle and extravagant opinion, which was rejected with contempt by every man of a liberal education and understanding."[159] The Enlightened historian nonetheless argued that its promise of immortality was a major selling point for Christianity.[160] He could appreciate the point, perhaps, because he himself was not immune to a sort of poetic despondency when contemplating the brevity of life. "The present is a fleeting moment, the past is no more; and our prospect of futurity is dark and doubtful."[161] The illustrious historian's memoirs conclude with the observation that "I must reluctantly observe that two causes, the abbreviation of time, and the failure of hope, will always tinge with a browner shade the evening of life."[162]

Veyne's and Gibbon's assessment finds support, it seems, in the fact that even some pagans came to embrace the notion of an afterlife. We have noted Ammianus's report that on his deathbed the pagan emperor Julian was solemnly affirming the immortality of the soul.[163] In response to such later pagan thinking, Augustine, after savaging the more popular idea that the gods conferred benefits in this life, went on to devote four books in his magnum opus to a critique of later pagan philosophies that taught that the gods could provide blessings after death.[164]

Veyne adds that Christianity had another important advantage over paganism because it taught that God cared about—indeed, was essentially devoted to—human beings. "The pagan gods live above all for themselves," Veyne observes. "In contrast, Christ, the Man-God, sacrificed himself for his

---

157. Luc Ferry, *A Brief History of Thought: A Philosophical Guide to Living*, trans. Theo Cuffe (New York: HarperCollins, 2011), 84–85.

158. Veyne, *When Our World Became Christian*, 19.

159. Gibbon, *History of the Decline*, 1:464.

160. Gibbon, *History of the Decline*, 1:447. See also 1:510 ("Minds afflicted by calamity and the contempt of mankind cheerfully listen to the divine promise of future happiness").

161. Edward Gibbon, *Memoirs of My Life*, trans. Betty Radice (London: Penguin, 1984), 175.

162. Gibbon, *Memoirs*, 175.

163. See above, 172.

164. Augustine, *City of God*, bks. 6–10.

men."[165] Thus, "Christianity owed its success as a sect to a collective invention of genius . . . namely, the infinite mercy of a God passionate about the fate of the human race, indeed about the fate of each and every individual soul, including mine and yours, and not just those of the kingdoms, empires and the human race in general."[166]

Although declaring himself "an unbeliever,"[167] Veyne asserts that in consequence of these doctrines, Christianity's "spiritual superiority over paganism was blindingly clear."[168] "Thanks to the historical-metaphysical epic of Creation and Redemption, . . . one now knew where one came from and for what one was destined."[169]

This ostensible spiritual superiority, of course, turned on the assumption that the Christians' "good news"—about the resurrection, about eternal life, about an infinitely loving God—was actually true. Which brings us back to the question of believability. For pagans, the idea that a god would become human (not just for purposes of a momentary coupling with a comely maid, but for the full, tedious, painful, humiliating duration of a life), would be born of a woman, would allow himself to be seized and subjected to a horrendous and humiliating death, this in order to save a pathetic race of mortals—all this was contemptible nonsense. Lactantius summarized the pagan objection:

> They say . . . that it was unworthy of God to be willing to become man, and to burthen Himself with the infirmity of flesh; to become subject of His own accord to sufferings, to pain, and death. . . . Why, then (they say), did He . . . render Himself so humble and weak, that it was possible for Him both to be despised by men and to be visited with punishment? why did He suffer violence from those who are weak and mortal? why did He not repel by strength, or avoid by His

---

165. Veyne, *When Our World Became Christian*, 22.

166. Veyne, *When Our World Became Christian*, 21. Cf. Brown, *World of Late Antiquity*, 51–52 (arguing that Christianity appealed to "a need for a God with whom one could be alone: a God whose 'charge,' as it were had remained concentrated and personal rather than diffused in benign but profoundly impersonal ministrations to the universe at large").

167. Veyne, *When Our World Became Christian*, 24.

168. Veyne, *When Our World Became Christian*, 15. Cf. Hopkins, *World Full of Gods*, 78 ("The Christian revolution promoted a radical message of love and charity, flaunted the idea that even the foolish and uneducated could be wise, that the virtuous simpleton could outargue learned philosophers, that the rich should be generous to the poor, that the holy should care for the sick").

169. Veyne, *When Our World Became Christian*, 29.

divine knowledge, the hands of men? why did He not at least in His very death reveal His majesty? but He was led as one without strength to trial, was condemned as one who was guilty, was put to death as one who was mortal.[170]

And so the Christian conception was unworthy of a deity, and the Christian promises of meaning and sublimity were hollow. Worse than hollow, in fact: because in offering the false promise of eternal bliss, Christianity in fact deprived *this* world—the world we actually inhabit, and the only world we can count on—of the sublimity (transitory and tinged with tragedy as it might be) that paganism provided. With Christianity's suppression of the gods, a beauty passed out of the world, a beauty all the more poignant because so fleeting, to be replaced by a grim, censorious emptiness.

"Why should I desire to live in a world void of gods?" the emperor Marcus Aurelius had asked.[171] With the triumph of Christianity, the question ceased to be hypothetical.

Existential Orientations

The competing strengths and weaknesses of paganism and Christianity are thus reflective of two different orientations to life in the world—orientations that were discernible then and are discernible now. (These are of course ideal types, so to speak, rarely encountered in their purity; and they are not the only possible orientations; we will consider a third major possibility in a later chapter.) We, all of us, find ourselves in the world for a brief interval. How should we regard this life, and this world? What stance or attitude should we take?

According to one orientation, life in the world is sufficient unto itself—as it needs to be, because it is our only life in the only world that we have any reason to believe in. Life is—or at least can be—a beautiful and sometimes sublime thing, but its beauty and sublimity are finite and immanent to this world. The sacred exists, but it exists *here*—in the here and now. There is not, and there need not be, anything else. Not for us mortals, at least.

The other orientation can acknowledge the beauty and sublimity of life in the world. It can go so far, as in much Christian thought, as to insist that

170. Lactantius, *The Divine Institutes*, ed. Alexander Roberts et al. (Lexington, KY: CreateSpace, 2015), 4.22, p. 194.
171. Aurelius, *Meditations* 2.8.

although not actually divine, the world has a sacramental quality. In this view, however, the world is not sufficient unto itself. Rather, its blessed qualities of beauty and sublimity are reflective of a more transcendent Reality, and they point beyond themselves to a beatified existence that "eye hath not seen, nor ear heard, neither have entered into the heart of man."[172] Cut off from that transcendence, life in the world would become empty, pointless, devoid of meaning. And humans, who, unlike animals, are aware of their looming dissolution into nothingness, would be (in the words of Homer's Zeus) the most "agonized . . . of all that breathe and crawl across the earth."[173]

Perhaps no Christian thinker expressed this perspective more poignantly than Augustine. As discussed in chapter 5, his classic *Confessions* was in essence a narrative of how he arrived at the understanding famously expressed in the first pages—that "thou hast made us for thyself, and restless is our heart until it comes to rest in thee."[174] The goods of this world may entice and entertain, but their appeal is ephemeral. Augustine himself was acutely aware of the pleasures of sexual intimacy, and loath to forgo them; hence his famous conflicted plea, "Lord, make me chaste, but not yet" (8.17, p. 139).[175] Ultimately, though, worldly goods cannot satisfy us. They are "glowing fantasies"—like food consumed in dreams, by which "the sleepers are not nourished" (3.10, p. 37). They "do not abide. They flee away" (4.15, p. 55). Taken by itself, this life is actually a "life-in-death" or a "death-in-life" (1.6, p. 4).

So the world is good, yes, but it is not sufficient unto itself. "For wherever the human soul turns itself, other than to you," Augustine says, addressing God, "it is fixed in sorrows, even if it is fixed upon beautiful things external to you and to itself, which would nevertheless be nothing if they did not have their being from you" (4.15, p. 61).

Whether Christianity or paganism was more spiritually efficacious, or whether the immanent or transcendent orientation to life in the world was more true and satisfying, may ultimately boil down to the question of whether Augustine was right on this crucial point.

When paganism and Christianity are understood in terms of these existential orientations, it becomes apparent why neither form of religiosity

172. 1 Cor. 2:9.

173. Homer, *The Iliad* 17.515–516.

174. Augustine, *Confessions* 1.1, p. 1. Hereafter, references from this work will be given in parentheses in the text.

175. This is a paraphrase; the actual quotation reads "Grant me chastity and continence, but not yet."

could ultimately and decisively vanquish the other. Probably there has not been a time in which each orientation has not claimed its constituency—whatever labels might be applied. Indeed, it seems likely that most human beings have, as individuals, felt the power and pull of—and have at times inclined toward—each orientation.

So the beauties of the world and gratifications of life seem precious, and sufficient. "A book of verses, a jug of wine . . . , and thou beside me . . . , is paradise enough."[176] What more is needed? What more could anyone want? And then . . . a dullness sets in. Life is fleeting, and empty. Food is flat; music is mere sound; physical beauty does not arouse. "The long, looming days lay up a thousand things closer to pain than pleasure," the Sophoclean chorus chants mournfully, "and the pleasures disappear, you look and know not where."[177] Or even if pleasures retain their pungency, we know that they will soon cease. Can this really be all there is? And if so, what is the point?

The sensually satiated soul seeks more spiritual delights—and perhaps, turning to faith, finds them. For a while, at least. And yet . . . doubt persists. Is this faith, this hope of "eternal life," mere delusion, mere wishful thinking? Is the spiritual seeker exchanging the only real satisfactions available to mortals, limited and transitory though such satisfactions are, for an illusion?[178]

"You Christians deny yourselves all the satisfying pleasures," Keith Hopkins's scornful pagan complains, "and for what? For a 'dream of posthumous immortality.' For a vain hope—because 'No one knows the secret of the universe.'"[179] In a similar vein, while noting that "our devout predecessors, vainly aspiring to imitate the perfection of the angels, . . . disdained, or they affected to disdain, every earthly and corporeal delight," Gibbon recommended a different course: "In our present state of existence, the body is so inseparably connected with the soul, that it seems to be our interest to taste, with innocence and moderation, the enjoyments of which that faithful companion is susceptible."[180]

In the face of this commonsensical view, the Christian movement has been a centuries-long struggle to assure its devotees of the superiority of

---

176. *The Rubaiyat of Omar Khayyam*, trans. Edward Fitzgerald, ed. Stanley Appelbaum (New York: Dover, 1990), para. 12, p. 27.

177. Sophocles, "Oedipus at Colonus," lines 1381–1383, p. 358.

178. Cf. Gibbon, *History of the Decline*, 1:520 ("The Pagan multitude, reserving their gratitude for temporal benefits alone, rejected the inestimable present of life and immortality, which was offered to mankind by Jesus of Nazareth").

179. Hopkins, *World Full of Gods*, 216.

180. Gibbon, *History of the Decline*, 1:478–79.

the goods of the spirit over the more tangible but transitory pleasures of the world. In his *Confessions*, Augustine recounted that struggle in his own soul; in *City of God* he projected it onto the sweep of history. The struggle is one that must be perpetual, one that is always a struggle against natural inclinations. Augustine recognized this fact as well. Consequently, there are many who identify with the earthly city but will ultimately end up in the heavenly kingdom. And vice versa.[181] The saint was uncertain of the ultimate outcome even in himself.[182]

And so emperors like Domitian and Decius and Diocletian could execute Christians, but they could not thereby deprive the believers of their heavenly hope. Conversely, emperors like Theodosius and, later, Justinian could use the force and violence of law to suppress the incidents of paganism. They could close temples and prohibit animal sacrifice. But if paganism is not exhausted by these outward manifestations but rather is understood in terms of the immanent orientation that sacralizes life in this world, denying or at least remaining practically noncommittal toward any other, then it seems that neither Christian emperors nor bishops could or did abolish the substantial essence of paganism. Not even within themselves (as their own extravagantly worldly conduct sometimes exhibited).

If anything could achieve that abolition, it would not be Christianity, but rather science and secularism: but we will defer that prospect to a later chapter.

181. Augustine, *City of God* 1.35, p. 49; 18.49, p. 896.
182. Augustine, *Confessions* 10.48, p. 200.

CHAPTER 8

Under a Christian Canopy

We saw in the last chapter that by the end of the fourth century, Christianity had triumphed over paganism, at least in the political realm. Emperors like Theodosius—and, later, Justinian—tightened legal restrictions on pagan worship and practice. And thus began the long period of Christian political dominance often described—or deprecated—as "Christendom." The nations of Christendom were the Christian societies that T. S. Eliot perceived as the historical antecedents for the more confused modern situation that by inertia or default was still vaguely Christian but was vulnerable to being displaced by "modern paganism."

But was paganism actually extinguished, or was it merely driven underground? Or perhaps hidden in plain sight? Surely a deeply rooted religiosity that had flourished for centuries could not be simply and finally extinguished with the issuance of a few imperial edicts and the smashing of a few temples. Thus, Peter Brown reports that "even a century and a half after the battle for the public faith of the empire was lost to Christianity, the philosopher Proclus would be writing, in the mood of a still evening after thunder, intimate hymns to the gods and a totally pagan *Elements of Theology*."[1] And historians observe that paganism lingered on both in the countryside and in enclaves like Athens for decades, even centuries.[2]

---

1. Peter Brown, *The World of Late Antiquity, AD 150–750* (San Diego: Harcourt, 1971), 73.

2. Peter Brown, *Power and Persuasion in Late Antiquity: Towards a Christian Empire* (Madison: University of Wisconsin Press, 1992), 129 (describing "polytheists firmly established in small cities all over the eastern empire . . . up to and beyond the end of the sixth century"). Cf. Henry Chadwick, *The Early Church*, rev. ed. (London: Penguin, 1993), 168–69: "In rural districts the country folk were deeply attached to old pagan customs, especially those associated with birth, marriage, and death. In the Western provinces the pastoral problem for centuries

193

Even so, by the end of the fifth or sixth century, paganism had for the most part been effectively suppressed. Or so historians say.[3] And if we think mostly of what Varro had described as the mythical and civic forms of classical paganism,[4] the obituaries are probably accurate enough. But if we instead consider paganism not just in terms of these concrete public manifestations but also as an existential orientation or as the form of immanent religiosity that sacralizes this world, a different judgment will emerge.

In this chapter, we will briefly survey how, under the public supervision of official Christianity, paganism continued to flourish in a number of senses. Our survey will begin with the most conspicuous though perhaps least important mode in which paganism persisted: many of the external features of classical paganism—the "badges and incidents" of paganism, to borrow a phrase from American constitutional law[5]—were preserved, either in their own forms or as incorporated into the official Christian faith and culture. Next we will consider how paganism endured as a powerful, evocative, shaping force in the historical memory and imagination of the West. It persisted both in a positive form—in wistful memories of (and attempts to recapture) the beauty and freedom that had ostensibly been lost with the suppression of paganism—and in the more negative form of a lingering anger or resentment toward the force that had supposedly defeated and suppressed it—namely, Christianity.

Finally, we will consider how the substantial essence of paganism (namely, as an orientation that sacralizes this world and its goods) survived and flourished. Usually, to be sure, this orientation did not and does not identify itself as "paganism." But then, ancient paganism did not identify itself as "paganism" either.

The combination of these modes of pagan persistence leads to a different, perhaps surprising question: Far from being eradicated, did paganism in fact remain the dominant cultural position even after the ostensible triumph

---

was to stamp out pagan superstitions among the peasants on the land. But in the towns, even in such Christian citadels as Syria and Asia Minor, clandestine rites, including occasional sacrifices, continued to be practiced as late as the seventh century."

3. See, e.g., Peter Brown, *Authority and the Sacred: Aspects of the Christianisation of the Roman World* (Cambridge: Cambridge University Press, 1995), 11–19; Edward Gibbon, *The History of the Decline and Fall of the Roman Empire*, 2 vols. (London: Penguin, [1776] 1995), 2:71.

4. See above, 88.

5. See Jones v. Alfred H. Mayer Co., 392 U.S. 409, 439 (1968) (explaining that the Thirteenth Amendment allows Congress to regulate to address the "badges and incidents" of slavery).

of Christianity? The answer to that question, it will turn out, is complicated. In a certain sense, the Western world has arguably always remained more pagan than Christian. In some ways Christianity has been more of a veneer than a substantial reality. Perhaps the most emphatic testimony to this fact has come from Christian priests, preachers, and prophets, who have consistently held that the world—the ostensibly Christian world—is very far from actually understanding and accepting the transcendent Reality proclaimed by Christianity. And yet the Christian veneer, if that is what it is, has been important in its own right, because it has represented a sort of canopy within which paganism has survived and even flourished. Less metaphorically, Christianity has supplied the regulative ideal, or authoritative standard, under which culture and political discourse have functioned.

The widespread acceptance of that ideal, despite failures in realization, suggests that descriptions of the centuries between the fall of Rome and the rise of the modern world as "Christian," or as "Christendom," are not false. In an attenuated but crucial sense, these *were* "Christian" societies, as T. S. Eliot and so many others have supposed.

And so, both the pagan and Christian alternatives have persisted. Paganism has not needed to be reinvented; it has been with us all along. Remove the Christian canopy, repudiate the Christian regulatory ideal and aspiration, and what remains would be . . . paganism. In this way, the choice between a Christian and a pagan society has remained very much a live possibility.

The Enduring Incidents of Paganism

Just because Christianity became officially preeminent, it could hardly be expected that people would promptly relinquish practices and modes of speech and thought that had grounded and shaped their lives for centuries. And in fact, the practices and features of ancient paganism survived, in two basic ways.

First, although pagan sacrifices might be abolished and pagan temples torn down, other indicia of paganism persisted. Magical and astrological practices reminiscent of paganism continued to flourish for centuries.[6] So did the terms and names of paganism; though scarcely anyone pauses to notice the fact, even today the days of our week trace their names back

---

6. See generally Keith Thomas, *Religion and the Decline of Magic: Studies in Popular Beliefs in Sixteenth and Seventeenth Century England* (Oxford: Oxford University Press, 1971).

to Greco-Roman or Nordic deities (the sun, the moon, Tiw, Wodan, Thor, Frige, and Saturn).[7] Likewise for our months: January is named for the Roman god Janus, March for the god Mars, April for Aphrodite, May for Maia, June for Juno, July and August for the first two of the divinized Caesars.

Second, many pagan notions and practices managed to become baptized, so to speak, and thus to persist and even flourish in a sort of *converso* existence. They were incorporated, in only slightly altered form, into Christian religion and culture. A symbol of this process is the majestic Roman building called the Pantheon, still intact (and still visited by millions every year). The building, whose customary name refers to the array of pagan deities, survived although or because it was rechristened as a church dedicated to Christian martyrs. The same thing happened to innumerable pagan temples, shrines, and practices.

In this vein, Keith Thomas recalls

the notorious readiness of the early Christian leaders to assimilate elements of the old paganism into their own religious practice. . . . The ancient worship of wells, trees, and stones was not so much abolished as modified, by turning pagan sites into Christian ones and associating them with a saint rather than a heathen divinity. The pagan festivals were similarly incorporated into the Church year. New Year's Day became the Feast of the Circumcision; May Day was SS. Philip and James; Midsummer Even the Nativity of St John the Baptist. Fertility rites were converted into Christian processions and the Yule Log was introduced into celebrations of the birth of Christ.[8]

Ramsay MacMullen likewise describes how Christianity incorporated or annexed large chunks of pagan practice.[9] Christian holidays were adjusted

---

7. Cf. Brown, *World of Late Antiquity*, 80 ("Throughout the Middle Ages, the stars still hung above Christian Europe, disquieting reminders of the immortality of the gods. The gods had left their names on the days of the week").

8. Thomas, *Religion and the Decline of Magic*, 54.

9. Ramsay MacMullen, *Christianity and Paganism in the Fourth to Eighth Centuries* (New Haven: Yale University Press, 1997), 150–59. See also Peter Hunter Blair, *The World of Bede* (Cambridge: Cambridge University Press, 1990), 63: "The [pagan] temples were by no means to be destroyed, but only the images which they housed. If the temples were well built they were to be consecrated to the service of God so that the people might continue to worship in familiar places. They should not be deprived of their customary sacrifices of oxen, but on appropriate days they should build wooden booths in the neighbourhood of former temples,

to correspond with traditional pagan celebrations, so that people could continue to parade and party as they had always done. Liturgical services adopted and adapted pagan practices of lighting candles, ringing bells, bowing or bestowing a reverential kiss on entrance into a church. The content of lay prayers and petitions continued mostly unchanged, although they were now directed to one among a swelling host of saints instead of to some member of a pantheon of deities.[10]

MacMullen concludes that "the triumph of the church was one not of obliteration but of widening embrace and assimilation."[11] Of the Renaissance period, a thousand years after the official demise of paganism, Jacob Burckhardt observed that "many local and popular usages, which are associated with religious festivals, are forgotten fragments of the old pre-Christian faiths of Europe."[12] In fact, "the popular faith in Italy had a solid foundation," Burckhardt thought, "just in proportion as it was pagan."[13]

To be sure, insofar as pagan practices were successfully "baptized," they ipso facto became Christian, not pagan. And yet a forced conversion is susceptible of being sloughed off. In which case, the incidents of paganism remained, ready to revert to their former character.

The Persistence of Paganism in the Western Imagination

As names (like the days of the week) and practices were assimilated into newly emerging forms of culture and liturgy, their pagan origins might eventually be forgotten by most practitioners. One might thus argue that history and the fading of memory have purged these references and practices of any real pagan content (much in the way that no one today thinks of Los Angeles as the city of the angels). Thus, with respect to so-called "pagan survival," Robin Lane Fox argues that "almost all of this continuity is spurious. Many

---

now converted to Christian use, and celebrate with religious feasting, their animals no longer sacrificed to devils, but killed for their own food with thanksgiving to God."

10. On the proliferation of saints and their function in restoring sanctity to nature, see Peter Brown, *The Rise of Western Christendom: Triumph and Diversity, A.D. 200–1000*, rev. ed. (West Sussex, UK: Wiley-Blackwell, 2013), 161–65.

11. MacMullen, *Christianity and Paganism*, 159.

12. Jacob Burckhardt, *The Civilization of the Renaissance in Italy*, trans. S. G. C. Middlemore (London: Penguin, [1860] 1990), 306.

13. Burckhardt, *Civilization of the Renaissance*, 307.

of [paganism's] details were set in Christian contexts which changed their meaning entirely."[14]

Often, however, just the opposite has happened: Western thinkers and cultures have self-consciously attempted to remember and even revive the classical past—including the pagan elements of that past. And they have harbored a deep, active resentment of Christianity for obliterating the freedom and beauty associated with paganism. Indeed, a good deal of Western art, literature, and academic or popular polemics on political or religious or cultural subjects amounts to the relentless reenactment and rearticulation of these positive and negative themes. In these ways, paganism—even classical paganism—has maintained a prominent and revered place in the historical imagination of the West. .

Although both the positive and the more negative or accusatory dimensions of paganism's legacy have reverberated throughout Western history, in fact each dimension is conveniently associated with a particular era or movement. The positive dimension, or the effort to recall and recover the positive virtues of the classical past (including its paganism), is identified with—indeed, it is the essence of—what we call "the Renaissance." The negative or accusatory dimension was a central theme of what we call "the Enlightenment."

Yearning for the World That Was Lost. Regret or nostalgia for what was lost with the ostensible demise of paganism has been manifest in a variety of forms. One is poetry. Thus, Owen Davies observes that "the great German poets Goethe and Johann von Schiller fell in love with the gods of Rome and Greece, and the harmonious beauty of the sacred groves and pools where they were worshipped. In Britain, the Romantic poets Wordsworth, and particularly Keats and Shelley imbued the landscape with pagan enchantment."[15] Thus Wordsworth's "Great God! I'd rather be a pagan, suckled in a creed outworn,"[16] reacting against what he perceived as the spiritual barrenness of the modern, commercialized world.

Or Heinrich Heine's whimsical and yet wistful story "Gods in Exile." Heine's story tells how, with the coming of Christianity, the gods had been forced to "take flight, seeking safety under the most varied disguises and

---

14. Robin Lane Fox, *Pagans and Christians* (London: Penguin, 1986), 22.

15. See Owen Davies, *Paganism: A Very Short Introduction* (Oxford: Oxford University Press, 2011), 91.

16. William Wordsworth, "The World Is Too Much with Us," in *Six Centuries of Great Poetry: A Stunning Collection of Classic British Poems from Chaucer to Yeats*, ed. Robert Penn Warren and Albert Erskine (New York: Dell, 1955), 364.

in the most retired hiding places. Many of these poor refugees, deprived of shelter and ambrosia, were now forced to work at some plebeian trade in order to earn a livelihood [and] . . . to drink beer instead of nectar."[17] Nonetheless, these gods would occasionally come out of hiding, albeit sometimes in disguise, and would appear to mortals. Heine described "a pale assemblage of graceful phantoms, who have risen from their . . . hiding-places amid the ruins of ancient temples, to perform once more their ancient, joyous, divine service; . . . with sport and merry-making . . . to dance once more the merry dance of paganism, the *can-can* of the antique world—to dance it without any hypocritical disguise, without fear of the interference of the police of a spiritualistic morality, with the wild abandonment of the old days, shouting, exulting, rapturous. Evoe Bacche!"[18]

Sometimes the yearning has gone further, generating active efforts to recover that pagan past. Probably the outstanding manifestation of this impulse is what we call the Renaissance. The name itself means rebirth, and the thing for which the thinkers and artists of the period were seeking a rebirth was, of course, the classical heritage of ancient Greece and Rome.

The Renaissance has generated any number of historical interpretations, some of which deny that it is useful to talk about a "Renaissance" at all.[19] But what seems clear is that fourteenth-, fifteenth-, and sixteenth-century thinkers and artists, first in Italy and then elsewhere in Europe, made a vigorous effort to recover the writings, the ideas, and the artistry of antiquity—and to model their own writing, thinking, art, and governance on those ancient precedents. In this "new civilization" of the Renaissance, Jacob Burckhardt asserted, "its active representatives became influential because they knew what the ancients knew, because they tried to write as the ancients wrote, because they began to think, and soon to feel, as the ancients thought and felt."[20] The recovery effort was hardly limited to ancient religion; it included Greek and Roman rhetoric, law, politics, poetry, architecture, sculpture, and painting. But the pagan elements came as part of the package.

Probably this pagan dimension is most vividly manifest in the painting and sculptures of Renaissance artists. Hundreds of depictions of episodes from the stories of Greek and Roman gods by masters like Botticelli, Ve-

---

17. Heinrich Heine, "Gods in Exile," in *The Prose Writings of Heinrich Heine*, ed. Havelock Ellis (Lexington, KY: CreateSpace, 2013), 155, 156.

18. Heine, "Gods in Exile," 159.

19. Charles G. Nauert, *Humanism and the Culture of Renaissance Europe*, 2nd. ed. (Cambridge: Cambridge University Press, 2006), 3.

20. Burckhardt, *Civilization of the Renaissance*, 136.

ronese, Titian, and many others make up an essential part of the cultural outpouring that distinguishes this period.[21] Of Botticelli, for example, Paul Johnson observes that "he was the first great Renaissance artist to make full use of ancient mythology not merely for subject matter—*The Birth of Venus, Primavera*, et al.—but to give his works spiritual content." For Botticelli, "paganism was his forte and myth his inspiration."[22] More generally, "the Renaissance was in one important respect a celebration of the artistic and intellectual virtues of pagan antiquity to modern civilized life."[23]

A doubt arises, though: Does all this artistic rejoicing in pagan deities and stories reflect actual paganism, or merely the appropriation of pagan images and themes for more modern purposes? It is hard to be certain; indeed, it is hard to know whether the question even makes sense.

We might conjecture that in painting his airy and alluring Venuses, Botticelli surely did not actually believe that the goddess was physically real, gracefully embodied and actively intervening in the affairs of mortals and even mating with them, as she does in the *Iliad* and the *Aeneid*. Pico della Mirandola wrote a book defending the literary and artistic use of pagan deities and themes on the premise, as Paul Strathern explains, that "the early classical and pagan gods should be seen as embodiments of more abstract metaphysical ideas. . . . Seen in this light, the goddess Venus thus became the abstract ideal of beauty."[24] Similarly, the Apollo and the Calliope in Raphael's *Parnassus*, painted in a Vatican chapel for Pope Julius II, were understood to be symbols of knowledge and poetry, not actual and active beings hanging out on a holy mountain.

But then, as we have seen, many educated Roman pagans of late antiquity would likely have said much the same thing. The gods are real, yes—but not literally, as depicted in the myths. Rather, they are symbols of the sublime reality that animates the world and manifests itself in nature.[25]

21. Giovanni Boccaccio had made the pagan deities accessible in the fourteenth century with his book *The Genealogies of the Pagan Gods*. See Paul Johnson, *The Renaissance: A Short History* (New York: Random House, 2002), 31.

22. Johnson, *The Renaissance*, 142. See also Paul Strathern, *Death in Florence: The Medici, Savonarola, and the Battle for the Soul of a Renaissance City* (New York: Pegasus Books, 2015), 61 (observing that after Botticelli met Ficino and the poet Poliziano, his work "underwent a profound transformation. Instead of religious scenes he began to depict pagan subjects from classical mythology").

23. Johnson, *The Renaissance*, 179.

24. Strathern, *Death in Florence*, 83.

25. See above, 91, 109, 180–81.

Consequently, as to whether the Renaissance was predominantly Christian or pagan, the historical evidence can yield different interpretations, depending on the perspective and commitments of the historian. Burckhardt, whose seminal book gave impetus to modern thinking about the Renaissance, suggested that in response to pervasive corruption in the church, many or most Italians had largely lost their Christian faith. How could they not have? "That the reputation attaching to the monks and the secular clergy must have shattered the faith of multitudes in all that is sacred is, of course, obvious."[26] And Burckhardt perceived a strong, genuinely pagan dimension to much of the thought and art of the period. "This [Renaissance] humanism was in fact pagan, and became more and more so as its sphere widened in the fifteenth century."[27]

True, public shows of Christian religiosity by rulers were common enough. But in the spirit of Edward Gibbon, Burckhardt supposed that these were mere matters of political calculation, not of genuine Christian belief.[28] And even "the worship of the saints among the educated classes often took an essentially pagan form."[29] The pagan tendencies manifested themselves, among other ways, in the widespread respect among many Renaissance figures for astrology, and for omens and auguries.[30]

Maybe. And yet the thinkers of the time did not admit to having declined (or ascended) from Christianity back into paganism. When they were accused of having done so, as sometimes happened, they responded with denials, and with defenses asserting their Christian orthodoxy.[31] The defenses *might* have been duplicitous, as the Burckhardt-Gibbon–Leo Strauss type of interpretation would intimate. But can we really be so sure?

Thus, other historians have emphasized the continuing commitment to Christianity by influential Renaissance figures. Charles Nauert contends that Renaissance thinkers like Petrarch and Ficino, while challenging medieval scholastic methods and conceptions, remained sincere and committed

26. Burckhardt, *Civilization of the Renaissance*, 295. See also 312–13 (asserting that "classical antiquity . . . became an ideal of life, [and] ancient speculation and skepticism obtained in many cases a complete mastery over the mind of Italians").

27. Burckhardt, *Civilization of the Renaissance*, 319.

28. Burckhardt, *Civilization of the Renaissance*, 312.

29. Burckhardt, *Civilization of the Renaissance*, 309. See also 322 ("Nor could they treat of Christianity without paganizing it").

30. Burckhardt, *Civilization of the Renaissance*, 323–44.

31. Burckhardt, *Civilization of the Renaissance*, 138; Nauert, *Humanism*, 29, 77; Johnson, *The Renaissance*, 31.

Christians.[32] Indeed, they were seeking to recover not only the pagan past but also the purity of the Christian past, which they believed to have been cluttered and corrupted during the darkness of the Middle Ages.[33] "The inherent and general irreligiosity of Renaissance humanism is a creation of nineteenth-century historians," Nauert argues, "both secular liberals (who approved) and conservative Catholics (who were aghast), but not of the Renaissance itself."[34]

There is surely material in the record to support this interpretation as well. After all, Christian themes are as pervasive as pagan ones in Renaissance writing and art, maybe more so. Alongside the exuberant paintings of Venus, Bacchus, Cupid, and Apollo, there are also countless more pious Madonnas, Pauls, Peters, and Jeromes—not to mention, of course, numerous paintings and sculptures of Jesus lying in the manger, later ministering, dying, reviving, ascending, and reigning as the triumphant lord and judge of the world. There is the *Last Supper* of Leonardo, and Michelangelo's celestial ceiling in the Sistine Chapel (which, to be sure, also features a few sibyls peeking in around the edges). And it may be surprising—or, to some, disappointing—to learn that artistic geniuses like Botticelli and Michelangelo, as well as avant-garde Renaissance scholars like Ficino and Pico della Mirandola, were all friends, admirers, and even at times disciples of Savonarola, the apocalyptic Dominican who mesmerized the cultured citizens of Florence with his fire-and-brimstone preaching and led the city in bonfires of books and other worldly vanities.[35]

Burckhardt, though stressing the loss of faith in reaction to corruption in the church, acknowledged the age's "fanatical devotion to relics"[36] and the ongoing "need felt for the sacraments as something indispensable."[37] He acknowledged as well the "epidemics of revivalism, which few even among the scoffers and the sceptics were able to withstand."[38] Of Alfonso, King of Naples, Burckhardt remarked on "how strangely Christian and pagan sentiment . . . blended in his heart!"[39] The same might be said of many a Renaissance artist, thinker, or politician.

32. Nauert, *Humanism*, 64–70.
33. Nauert, *Humanism*, 153–63.
34. Nauert, *Humanism*, 64.
35. See Strathern, *Death in Florence*, 100, 106, 134, 147, 149.
36. Burckhardt, *Civilization of the Renaissance*, 307.
37. Burckhardt, *Civilization of the Renaissance*, 306.
38. Burckhardt, *Civilization of the Renaissance*, 310.
39. Burckhardt, *Civilization of the Renaissance*, 149.

So it should not be so surprising to learn, for example, that Botticelli could revel in pagan imagery for a time and then move back to more sober Christian themes.[40] Or that Pico della Mirandola, after writing daring and learned humanistic works that were condemned by the church as heretical, would later seriously consider giving up his villa and his concubine with the aim of becoming a monk and, like Saint Francis, making a barefoot pilgrimage through the towns of Italy (100, 209). (Unlike Francis and Augustine, who had struggled with similar temptations and aims, Pico never quite mustered up the faith or the will to act on this resolve.)

Lorenzo de Medici ("the Magnificent"), de facto ruler of Florence, might "involve himself in the affairs of Venus to an astonishing degree" (as Machiavelli put it), with both women and men (4, 84). He might write clever, bawdy ballads (37); conspire against the preacher Savonarola; and energetically promote pagan productions in Florentine art and writing. But then he would turn to composing religious verse, and worry that perhaps he had doomed both his soul and his city through excessive worldliness (93, 105). And on his deathbed he would call in his nemesis, Savonarola, and plead with the fanatical priest to take his confession and absolve him of his sins (4–10, 124–25). (The priest complied.)

So then, was Botticelli a Christian or a pagan? What about Pico? Lorenzo? There is no way for us—and probably there was no way for *them*—to be certain. Burckhardt offered his interpretations, as others have done, but he acknowledged that the matter is inherently conjectural, and he aptly concluded: "The movements of the human spirit, its sudden flashes, its expansions and its pauses, must forever remain a mystery to our eyes."[41] Was the Renaissance itself pagan or Christian? Perhaps the most accurate answer would be . . . yes.

The historian Paul Johnson thus discerns in the Renaissance "the first great cultural war in European history."[42] In a similar vein, Paul Strathern suggests in a recent study that the conflict in Florence between the radically spiritual Savonarola and the exquisitely worldly (but also deeply pious) Lorenzo the Magnificent was in reality "a struggle for the soul" of Florence. Lorenzo died in 1492; Savonarola survived and flourished as a leader in

---

40. Strathern, *Death in Florence*, 147. Hereafter, page references from this work will be given in parentheses in the text.

41. Burckhardt, *Civilization of the Renaissance*, 291. Cf. Johnson, *The Renaissance*, 32 (observing that "these masters of the fourteenth and fifteenth centuries waxed and waned in the intensity of their religious passions").

42. Johnson, *The Renaissance*, 55.

Florence—for a few years anyway, until political fortunes shifted and he was condemned and burned in the Piazza della Signoria. (Thousands of visitors walk over the spot almost every day as they enter the renowned Uffizi gallery to view the Florentine masterpieces—some pagan and some Christian.) And so the "struggle for the soul" raged on.

And on. And on. Strathern observes that the conflict that unfolded in Renaissance Florence "has continued to reverberate down the centuries—first in Europe, then in America, and now finally through the world the struggle continues. It is nothing less than the fight for the soul of humanity."[43] At least officially, we might say, Christianity maintained its ascendant position; underneath that official Christian canopy the eternal struggle persisted—in society, in the souls of Lorenzo and Botticelli and their contemporaries, and in the hearts and minds of their descendants.

The Indictment of Christianity. A yearning or at least admiration for the pagan past is evident not only in poetry and the visual arts, but also in the historical work of Edward Gibbon, Ramsay MacMullen, and many others. But this work also exhibits a different and darker though even more familiar way in which paganism has survived its ostensible defeat by Christianity. In addition to happy, exuberant, wistful recollections of the "merry dance of paganism" (as Heine put it) that had been repressed, there has also lingered in the Western memory a deep and persistent resentment—sometimes a hatred—of the institution that repressed it: Christianity.

A fair and comprehensive assessment of the effects of biblical religion on Western civilization would surely recognize both negative and positive contributions. On the negative side, as Jan Assmann and others have indicated, Judaism and Christianity introduced a new kind of intolerance into the world. Careful in his judgments, Assmann does not fall into the familiar simplistic depiction of tolerant paganism and intolerant Christianity. Pagan religion, he says, could support violence and oppression. And paganism de-

---

43. Strathern, *Death in Florence*, 10. The Renaissance, with its open celebration of paganism mixed with Christian devotion, is sometimes said to have come to an end with the Counter-Reformation's attempt to rebut the Protestant challenge with a more puritanical Catholicism. And yet the fondness for the pagan past hardly disappeared. It is spectacularly manifest, in the baroque period, in the exquisite Bernini sculptures of Apollo and Daphnae, of the rape of Proserpina, of Aeneas carrying his father and leading his son from Troy. Or in that sculptor's Oceanus and tritons spouting forth in the Trevi Fountain. Or in Rubens's numerous representations of scenes from mythology. Or in hundreds of other post-Renaissance paintings and sculptures.

serves no credit for tolerance: insofar as pagan religions were largely unconcerned about truth, they had no cause or opportunity to manifest tolerance: there was nothing they needed to tolerate.[44] Even so, Assmann thinks it must be acknowledged that Judaism and Christianity, with their more exclusive and ambitious concerns and claims about truth, introduced a new form of intolerance into the world.[45] "The world of the primary [polytheistic] religions . . . was filled with violence and aggression in the most diverse forms, and many of these forms were domesticated, civilized, or even eliminated by the monotheistic religions as they rose to power. . . . Yet neither can it be denied that these religions simultaneously brought a new form of hatred into the world: hatred for pagans, heretics, idolaters and their temples, rites, and gods."[46]

The depiction of Christianity in particular as intolerant, usually in cruder and less discriminating terms, is pervasive in Western culture. The theme was aggressively promoted in the eighteenth century by Enlightenment thinkers like David Hume and Edward Gibbon, and it is emphasized perhaps even more vehemently by contemporary historians including Ramsey MacMullen, Charles Freeman, and Jonathan Kirsch[47] (not to mention in more popular treatments by authors like Dan Brown). Oxford historian Averil Cameron observes that

> ancient historians have customarily been wary of committed writing on early Christianity, of the "hidden agenda"; ironically, however, it has often been the practice to write in academic books about the period of the Christianization of the Roman Empire from an opposite but equally committed point of view. Whether viewed from the rationalist or the overtly Marxist perspective, the advance of Christianity is seen as bad in itself. . . . It is surprisingly hard to escape from the pervasive association of Christianity with ideas of "decline," "authoritarianism," and "irrationality," which tend to be expressed in words such as "gloom" or "twilight." From a deep-seated habit of privileging

44. Jan Assmann, *The Price of Monotheism*, trans. Robert Savage (Stanford: Stanford University Press, 2010), 18.

45. Assmann, *The Price of Monotheism*, 20.

46. Assmann, *The Price of Monotheism*, 16.

47. MacMullen, *Christianity and Paganism in the Fourth to Eighth Centuries*; Charles Freeman, *AD 381: Heretics, Pagans, and the Dawn of the Christian State* (New York: Overlook Press, 2008); Jonathan Kirsch, *God against the Gods: The History of the War between Monotheism and Polytheism* (New York: Penguin, 2004).

the classical, Christianity is relegated to the realm of the irrational, that which we do not ourselves care to accept.[48]

A closely associated indictment emphasizes how Christianity has been and is sexually repressive:[49] it spoiled and crushed the "sexual paradise,"[50] as Norman Cantor puts it, of the Roman Empire. We have already seen this complaint in Kyle Harper's lament concerning the change wrought by Justinian's implementation of Christian sexual ethics. "Gone is the warm eroticism of the Pompeian fresco, vanished is the charmed sensuality of the Greek romance."[51] Instead we find only "the haze of ruin and violent puritanism."[52]

These accusations have their historical bases. There were of course the Crusades, and the inquisitions (and one critical reader urges that these should be mentioned more frequently and underscored in these pages). On the positive side, however, a fair assessment would likely credit Christianity with helping to bring about many of the features of modern civilization that are most valued—including respect for the dignity of the individual,[53] human rights,[54] the commitment to equality,[55] and concern for the poor.[56]

48. Averil Cameron, *Christianity and the Rhetoric of Empire: The Development of Christian Discourse* (Berkeley: University of California Press, 1991), 25–26.

49. The theme is pervasive in Geoffrey R. Stone, *Sex and the Constitution* (London: Norton, 2017).

50. Norman F. Cantor, *Antiquity: From the Birth of Sumerian Civilization to the Fall of the Roman Empire* (New York: HarperCollins, 2003), 29.

51. Kyle Harper, *From Shame to Sin: The Christian Transformation of Sexual Morality in Late Antiquity* (Cambridge, MA: Harvard University Press, 2013), 14–15.

52. Harper, *From Shame to Sin*, 1.

53. Cf. Sarah Ruden, *Paul among the People: The Apostle Reinterpreted and Reimagined in His Own Time* (New York: Random House, 2010), xix: "More than anyone else, Paul created the Western individual human being, unconditionally precious to God and therefore entitled to the consideration of other human beings. There is no sign that Paul intended all the social change that gradually (and sometimes traumatically) resulted, the development of the rights and freedoms that characterize the West. . . . But broad social change did follow inevitably from the idea he spread: that God's love was sublime and infinite, yet immediately knowable to everyone. No other intellect contributed as much to making us who we are."

54. See Luc Ferry, *A Brief History of Thought: A Philosophical Guide to Living*, trans. Theo Cuffe (New York: HarperCollins, 2011), 60. See generally Michael J. Perry, *The Idea of Human Rights* (New York: Oxford University Press, 1998), 11–41 (arguing that human rights are based on a religious foundation).

55. See, e.g., Jeremy Waldron, *God, Locke, and Equality: Christian Foundations of John Locke's Political Thought* (Cambridge: Cambridge University Press, 2002).

56. See, e.g., Robin Lane Fox, *Augustine: Conversions to Confessions* (New York: Basic Books, 2015), 21: "Where [the pagan thinker and orator] Libanius represented people 'hap-

These ideas and ideals, foreign to ancient paganism, reflect the biblical claims that humans are made "in the image of God," that God has infinite concern or love for these creatures or children (even "the least among them"),[57] and that God gave himself for human beings.

Thus, while declaring that modern science has rendered the Christian worldview untenable,[58] the French philosopher Luc Ferry explains that by contrast to "the Greek world [which] was fundamentally an aristocratic world . . . founded on slavery," Christianity "introduce[d] the notion that humanity was fundamentally identical, that men were equal in dignity—an unprecedented idea at the time, and one to which our world owes its entire democratic inheritance."[59]

In his history of secularism, likewise, Graeme Smith asserts that "ideas of individual human worth and dignity, shared public reason, the progress of human society through history, and the ability of humanity to investigate its world, can all be traced to Christian theological sources."[60]

This part of the Christian or Judeo-Christian legacy is often overlooked or downplayed, however, especially among more educated critics, in favor of an emphasis on Christianity's ostensible intolerance and repressiveness. In this vein, University of Pennsylvania sociology professor Ross Koppel remarks that "on a macro level, the net effects of religion and faith are . . . a few thousand years of horrible wars, genocide, slavery's ideology, sexual exploitation, torture, devaluing others as not human, terrorism, and organized hatred."[61] From a detached perspective, Koppel's assessment of "*net effects*" may seem grotesquely distorted, to the point of being grimly comical, but it faithfully reflects (and is made possible by) a proclivity on the part of many in the intelligentsia to remember only the negative contributions of transcendent religiosity while taking the positive contributions for granted.

And in a sense, this tendency to accuse or blame is predictable; it is, arguably, simply the reverse side of the more positive recollections of pa-

---

pily' starving, John [Chrysostom] saw the very image of Christ present among the ranks of Antioch's poor. He was present there, appealing for much-needed charity, as John's sermons emphasized. . . . At least a fifth of [Augustine's] sermons characterize the plight of the poor in similarly bleak terms and contain encouragement to give them alms."

57. Matt. 25:40.

58. Ferry, *Brief History of Thought*, 144–45, 263.

59. Ferry, *Brief History of Thought*, 72. See also 71–78.

60. Graeme Smith, *A Short History of Secularism* (London: I. B. Tauris, 2008), 15.

61. Cf. Ross Koppel, "Public Policy in Pursuit of Private Happiness," *Contemporary Sociology* 41 (2012): 49–52.

ganism considered a few pages ago. If classical Rome was a "golden age," as Gibbon contended,[62] and if classical paganism was joyous, exuberant, beautiful, and inclusive, then it is natural enough to feel a profound resentment toward the force that suppressed that splendid world—namely, Christianity—and to attribute the opposite qualities to that historical force.

This negative and accusatory inference from the positive evaluation of paganism became conspicuous in the period we call "the Enlightenment." Consequently, in his admired and admiring history of the movement, Peter Gay interprets the Enlightenment as "the rise of modern paganism."[63] And how exactly were the Enlightenment thinkers "pagan"? Primarily, in Gay's telling, in their forceful criticism and rejection of Christianity. "The most militant battle cry of the Enlightenment," Gay explains, "*ecrasz l'infame*, was directed against Christianity itself, against Christian dogma in all its forms, Christian institutions, Christian ethics, and the Christian view of man."[64] The Enlightenment amounted to a "great campaign against Christianity."[65]

This hostility to Christianity was conspicuous both in the movement's most celebrated figure and in its leading English-speaking representative. Of Voltaire, Gay explains that

> the torrent of pamphlets that poured out . . . in the last sixteen years of Voltaire's life reveals a distaste for Christianity amounting almost to an obsession. Interpreters who restrict *l'infame* to intolerance or fanaticism or Roman Catholicism shrink from a conclusion that Voltaire himself drew innumerable times, in these frenetic years: "Every sensible man, every honorable man, must hold the Christian sect in horror." This is the central message of Voltaire's last and most intensive campaign: he repeats it with endless variations, with blasphemies, playful absurdities, and sometimes obscenities. Nothing was safe: the Trinity, the chastity of the Virgin Mary, the body and blood of Christ in the Mass, all are cruelly lampooned.[66]

62. See above, 50–59.
63. Peter Gay, *The Enlightenment: An Interpretation; The Rise of Modern Paganism* (New York: Norton, 1966).
64. Gay, *The Enlightenment*, 59.
65. Gay, *The Enlightenment*, 296.
66. Gay, *The Enlightenment*, 391.

Gay perceives a similar if more subdued agenda in David Hume, "the complete modern pagan."[67] In his work on religion, Hume compared pagan polytheism and Christian monotheism, giving distinctly higher marks to the former. Polytheism is intrinsically "sociable," Hume argued, while monotheistic religions such as Judaism and Christianity are inherently dogmatic and intolerant. Such intolerance was manifest in "the efforts of priest and bigots" as institutionalized in "the Inquisition and persecutions of Rome and Madrid"—institutions that take "fatal vengeance" on "virtue, knowledge, love of liberty," and thereby "leave the society in the most shameful ignorance, corruption, and bondage."[68] The dying Hume lamented that he had not been more successful in freeing his countrymen from "the Christian superstition," and he worried that the English were "relapsing into the deepest Stupidity, Christianity & Ignorance."[69]

So successful were the Enlightenment thinkers in associating Christianity with ignorance, stupidity, and intolerance that the association, subtly or aggressively reinforced by later thinkers like Marx, Neitzsche, and Mill, and by journalists like H. L. Mencken (who was, as a recent history recalls, "implacably hostile to anything that might reflect favorably on Christian faith"),[70] has become almost an axiom, in many literary or intellectual circles at least. Later authors and polemicists (like Professor Koppel) have been able to confidently rely on that axiom largely free of risk or charge, so to speak.[71] Rodney Stark identifies a number of "notorious falsehoods" about Catholic history in particular that "are so mutually reinforcing and deeply embedded in our common culture that it seems impossible for them not to be true."[72] Writers and intellectuals can sound this sort of anti-Christian theme, thereby signaling their sophistication and their sympathy for freedom, tolerance, and "reason," without fear of being seriously challenged by their peers. Indeed, they can reiterate the venerable theme—and *have been* reiterating it—over

67. Gay, *The Enlightenment*, 401.

68. David Hume, *The Natural History of Religion*, ed. H. E. Root (Stanford: Stanford University Press, [1757] 1956), 51.

69. Gay, *The Enlightenment*, 403.

70. Mark Noll, foreword to *Damning Words: The Life and Religious Times of H. L. Mencken*, by D. G. Hart (Grand Rapids: Eerdmans, 2016), x.

71. For a survey of the anti-Christian theme in a number of important twentieth-century English authors, see Maurice Cowling, *Religion and Public Doctrine in Modern England*, vol. 2, *Assaults* (Cambridge: Cambridge University Press, 1985), 186–283.

72. Rodney Stark, *Bearing False Witness: Debunking Centuries of Anti-Catholic History* (West Conshohocken, PA: Templeton Press, 2016), 6.

and over, for decades and even centuries, and in doing so, ironically, can still somehow suppose themselves to be exhibiting a kind of avant-garde courage and independence of mind.[73]

Still, we might ask: Is hostility to Christianity enough to make one a "pagan," as Gay implies? Our Enlightened friend Edward Gibbon would likely have dissented. Gibbon deprecated Christianity, as we have seen, but he was equally ready to object to the "superstition" that he perceived in pagan religion.[74] To qualify as "pagan," we might think, at least as we have been using the term, an opponent of Christianity would also need to exhibit an orientation toward a more immanent religiosity.

Some Enlightenment figures arguably did demonstrate such an orientation, and there was, as David Sorkin has shown, a strong religious streak in the Enlightenment.[75] Gay acknowledges that at times the philosophes felt a sense of "awe before Power or even the grand regularity of nature" or "were animated by what Freud has called the 'oceanic feeling'—that sense of oneness with the universe that is the ground of so much poetic religious feeling." And yet the Enlightenment thinkers "subdued or excised" such feelings, which were "marginal to their thought."[76] We can accordingly defer the search for an orientation of immanent religiosity until we come to more contemporary thinkers in whom (as we will see in chapter 9) that orientation is more overt and unapologetic.

The Pagan Orientation

Our discussion has suggested that despite its official and ostensible defeat by Christianity in late antiquity, paganism persisted in a variety of ways—in the incidents or features of paganism that survived or were incorporated into Christian culture, in the nostalgia for and the effort to recover pagan civilization manifest in the Renaissance and later, and in the ongoing, profound resentment against Christianity harbored especially in the more educated and enlightened classes. These are all ways in which it might be said that

---

73. See, e.g., Stone, *Sex and the Constitution*.

74. See, e.g., Gibbon, *History of the Decline*, 1:498–99.

75. David Sorkin, *The Religious Enlightenment: Protestants, Jews, and Catholics from London to Vienna* (Princeton: Princeton University Press, 2008). Sorkin argues that "the religious Enlightenment . . . may have had more influential adherents and exerted more power in its day than either the moderate or the [antireligious] radical version of the Enlightenment" (21).

76. Gay, *The Enlightenment*, 122.

classical paganism—the paganism of ancient Greece and Rome—continued to resonate after its supposed suppression by Christianity.

Less conspicuous but even more important, though, is the persistence, or perhaps the perpetual recurrence, of what we earlier described as the pagan orientation, or the commitment to the immanent sacred. This is the orientation that beatifies and sacralizes the goods of this world—that holds that "the sacred" exists, and that it exists in *this* world and *this* life. In this sense, it might be said that paganism persisted and would likely persist even if all memory of the classical past could be blotted out (as perhaps it may be, in some sectors of the population anyway, as classics departments close and as fewer students read Homer, Virgil, Ovid, or Cicero—or Gibbon).[77]

Indeed, it might plausibly be argued that paganism is the natural condition of humanity. From the moment of our birth until the hour of our death, after all, we see and hear and feel and act within *this* world. This is the world that we know directly and personally—the world we can be sure of. Conversely, we are consigned to rely on inference or intimation or faith to discern anything beyond this world. So we will naturally tend to find meaning and sublimity within this world—the one we know and inhabit. Paganism in this existential sense may draw sustenance from ancient precedent, but even without that support, it will naturally arise on its own. And Christianity could not reasonably expect to eradicate that natural orientation.

Indeed, it hardly wanted to. As discussed in earlier chapters, the Christian position has never been to deny the goodness of this world, but only to insist that it is not the ultimate good, and that its goodness derives from a more transcendent source. A Christianity that somehow managed to extinguish the sense of the goodness and sublimity of the world would have betrayed its mission and fallen into a sort of gnostic heresy. The more delicate aim for Christians, rather, has been to retain that sense of sublimity, even to intensify it, while bringing it under the jurisdiction of a higher, transcendent good—namely, God. That is a task that by its nature never has been and probably never could be accomplished once and for all—in a society, and perhaps even in any given individual.

Indeed, Christian teachers perhaps more than anyone else have insisted on the point. For centuries now, Christian leaders have implored followers to come to church to be reminded of the faith to which they purported or

---

77. Cf. Nauert, *Humanism*, 8 (referring regretfully to "our own era, which has cast aside most of its classical heritage"). See also Anthony Grafton et al., *The Classical Tradition* (Cambridge, MA: Belknap Press of Harvard University Press, 2010), ix (lamenting that "the easy familiarity with the classical tradition that used to be the identifying mark of those who had benefited from a civilized, and civilizing, education has become increasingly rare").

attempted to commit themselves at baptism or confirmation or confession. A central feature of such services is the homily, and a persistent theme of such sermonizing has been the fallenness of humanity—its immersion in the gods and goods of this world—and hence the desperate need for regeneration that will orient (and reorient, and *reorient*) humans to their true good. Sometimes the denunciations have been sharp and shrill. Savonarola has already been mentioned; others will think of Jonathan Edwards convicting his wailing parishioners of being "sinners in the hands of an angry God."[78] Sometimes the reminders have been more gentle and encouraging. Either way, the propensity of most people, Christian or otherwise, to become mired in idolatry toward the goods of this world has been a prevalent Christian theme. The theme amounts to an admission of the ongoing power of the orientation we are here describing as "paganism."

The Perpetual Dominance of Paganism?

We began this chapter by noticing the common view that holds that for better or worse, paganism was eliminated in late antiquity by the triumph of Christianity. Aiming to challenge this view, our discussion may seem to have veered to the opposite conclusion: despite its political defeats, it was in fact paganism that remained the dominant cultural position. Christianity has been little more than a veneer covering over a mainly pagan world. It has been a sort of "sacred canopy"[79] enclosing a quotidian reality that is some combination of pagan and secular.

So, is this reverse judgment correct? Yes and no. For reasons we have discussed, it is plausible to say that paganism is the natural condition of humankind. And an up-close look at actual, daily life in virtually any place or period, under the ostensible jurisdiction of Christendom or elsewhere, will reveal countless acts and attitudes—of violence, greed, lust, pride—that depart drastically from the Christian ideal.

Still, before we reclassify the Western world as pagan, two qualifications are imperative. Or maybe three. The first qualification we have already noted: for most periods in the West, and arguably for most individuals, the conflict

78. The famous sermon has been repeatedly reprinted. See Jonathan Edwards, *Representative Selections*, ed. Clarence H. Faust and Thomas H. Johnson (New York: Hill and Wang, 1935), 155–72.

79. Cf. Peter L. Berger, *The Sacred Canopy: Elements of a Sociological Theory of Religion* (New York: Random House, [1967] 1990).

between a transcendent orientation and a more immanent orientation to the goods of this world has constituted an ongoing struggle. Thus, most periods and most people have not been simply pagan or simply Christian; rather, they have wavered and wandered between the two.

Second, even while falling far short of compliance with Christian teachings, governments and individuals in the West, at least from late antiquity through the modern period, have over and over acknowledged Christian precepts, doctrines, and rites as a sort of recognized regulative ideal and dominant authority. That acknowledgment has been recurrently expressed in both positive and negative forms.

The positive expressions are pervasive and conspicuous, if we are inclined to notice them. So we see Christian religion enlisted in the consecration of kings and emperors. And of the other important events that constitute and define human life—births, marriages, deaths. We have already noticed how the spectacularly worldly Lorenzo the Magnificent calls in his longtime nemesis, Savonarola, to take his deathbed confession. We see the acknowledgment of Christian authority in the thousands upon thousands of paintings of Jesus, the Virgin, and the saints, by artists celebrated or obscure, adorning the churches, some majestic and some humble, that shape the skyscapes of thousands upon thousands of towns and cities through Europe and America. It is not uncommon for such paintings to feature a depiction of the patron or sponsor—most likely some noble or merchant who, after a life of acquisitiveness and strife and perhaps occasional or regular debauchery, wants nonetheless to be portrayed and remembered as a tiny, submissive figure kneeling before the Virgin and the infant Lord.

The acknowledgment of Christianity as an authority is evident in the political rhetoric of the medieval period in which, even as kings battle the church, they defer to and enlist Scripture and Christianity in their own cause.[80] It is evident as well, though more implicitly and indirectly, in modern political rhetoric that invokes themes that would have had no appeal to ancient pagans, and that are part of the Christian legacy. David Bentley Hart observes:

> Even the most ardent secularists among us generally cling to notions of human rights, economic and social justice, providence for

80. See William Chester Jordan, *Europe in the High Middle Ages* (London: Penguin, 2001), 85-87; Brian Tierney, *The Crisis of Church and State, 1050-1300* (Toronto: University of Toronto Press, 1964); Walter Ullmann, *Principles of Government and Politics in the Middle Ages* (New York: Routledge, [1961] 2010), 57-114.

the indigent, legal equality, or basic human dignity that pre-Christian Western culture would have found not so much foolish as unintelligible. It is simply the case that we distant children of the pagans would not be able to believe in any of these things—they would never have occurred to us—had our ancestors not once believed that God is love, that charity is the foundation of all virtues, that all of us are equal before the eyes of God, that to fail to feed the hungry or care for the suffering is to sin against Christ, and that Christ laid down his life for the least of his brethren.[81]

To be sure, there are good grounds to suspect hypocrisy in many of these outward displays of Christian religiosity by princes, merchants, and even popes and priests, whose lives reflect not piety but rather a strong proclivity to prefer the goods of the world over the supposedly higher blessings promised by Christianity.[82] And yet that hypocrisy confirms rather than discredits the proposition offered here—namely, that the authority of Christianity as a regulative ideal has been acknowledged and accepted through much of Western history. A man may be primarily and essentially a pagan and yet aspire to be Christian; his actual behavior will thus look hypocritical relative to his (sincere) aspirations. Or even if he has no such aspirations and puts on a show of religiosity only as a pretense for the public or for posterity, he thereby acknowledges at least the public authority of the Christian ideal.

More generally, the acknowledgment of Christianity as an ideal or a standard is powerfully if inadvertently apparent even in the familiar accusations made by Christianity's critics, as discussed earlier. The most familiar criticisms, after all, essentially accuse Christianity of failing to live up to its own ideals and commitments—to ideals and commitments that the critics themselves at least implicitly take as authoritative but that for the most part would not even have been embraced as such by ancient pagans.

Thus, Christian princes and priests are accused of supporting violence and warfare against perceived opponents; the Crusades and the inquisitions are the most commonly invoked instances. But in the Roman world, this militant policy toward opponents would hardly have been perceived as a failing at all. On the contrary, the Romans unashamedly celebrated their

81. David Bentley Hart, *Atheist Delusions: The Christian Revolution and Its Fashionable Enemies* (New Haven: Yale University Press, 2009), 32–33.
82. The criticism is enthusiastically presented in David Niose, *Nonbeliever Nation: The Rise of Secular Americans* (London: St. Martin's Press, 2010), 37–42.

military conquests with spectacular processions (or "triumphs") in which the conquerors were glorified and the defeated paraded in humiliation before respectively cheering and jeering Roman crowds.[83] Or Roman conquests were memorialized for posterity in monuments such as Trajan's Column or the Arch of Titus, proudly depicting in enduring marble for all to see the slaughter and humiliation of the Dacians or the Jews. In indicting Christianity for its violence, critics thus embrace a Christian standard and deploy it against Christianity.

Or Christianity is criticized for accepting slavery, or for leaving classes of serfs or women in an abject and oppressed condition. The criticisms may be cogent enough—again, though, *under Christian standards*. Under pagan customs and views, by contrast, these social inequalities would hardly have been seen as faults at all.[84]

For centuries, in short, Christianity has been fiercely and often cogently criticized; such criticism has intensified and become more respectable (or hackneyed) since the Enlightenment. But the criticisms themselves have typically traded on Christian values, principles, and aspirations. They have thus acknowledged, perhaps inadvertently, the authority of Christianity as an ideal. In that respect, it continues to seem apt to describe Western societies, as T. S. Eliot did, as (at least latently) Christian.

The Secular Alternative?

We have noted two responses to the proposition that despite their Christian veneer, Western societies have all along been more pagan than Christian. The first response suggested that the conflict between Christianity and paganism, or between transcendent and immanent religiosity, has all along been a struggle, both within societies and within individuals; so univocal descriptions of any society, or even any person, as simply "Christian" or "pagan" are doomed to be misleading. The second response suggested that despite their rampant paganism on the level of actual or daily practice, at least through much of Western history most people and societies nonetheless have recognized Christianity, consciously or not, as a sort of authority or ideal. Even to the extent that Christianity has been more a veneer than a deep reality, the veneer has been important in its own right, because it has

---

83. See Greg Woolf, *Rome: An Empire's Story* (New York: Oxford University Press, 2012), 72.

84. Woolf, *Rome*, 82–93.

meant that Christianity has persisted as a sort of ideal for organizing and evaluating culture and society.

But there may be a third objection, which at least from a modern perspective might seem even more obvious and powerful. Our discussion may seem to have proceeded on the assumption that Christianity and paganism, or transcendent and immanent religiosity, are the only or at least the salient alternatives. On that assumption, if despite their Christian pretensions a person or a society behave and believe in manifestly un-Christian ways, it would seem to follow that they are in reality pagan. But this inference ignores the possibility of other alternatives. And from a modern perspective, one such alternative may seem overwhelmingly obvious—namely, secularism.

So if a person is not Christian, or not *truly* Christian (or Jewish, or Muslim, or something else), he or she is not necessarily "pagan." It seems far more likely—today, at least—that the person is not religious at all, but rather "secular." That at least is surely how most people today who do not identify with any traditional religion would describe themselves. And so for a person or a society, it seems, the salient choice today is not between transcendent and immanent religion, but rather between being religious and not being religious. In other words, between being religious and being "secular." And in fact, most Western societies have chosen the latter alternative: they have become "secular."

So goes a familiar story, at least, which is no doubt true to a significant extent. And yet it will turn out that secularism is also more complex than has often been supposed. Secularism comes in various forms, and in at least one of its influential forms it has functioned as a sort of cover for a resurgence of paganism—of Eliot's "modern paganism." We will consider how this has happened in the next chapter.

CHAPTER 9

Secularism and Paganism

Venerable antagonisms can be rendered obsolete by a powerful new contender. In the early Middle Ages, struggles in the eastern empire between Persians and Byzantines were made moot by the arrival of militant Islam. In the mid-twentieth century, long-standing jealousies among nations of Western Europe came to be overshadowed by the emergence of a menacing Soviet Union. In sports, a legendary rivalry between Bird's Celtics and Magic's Lakers was rendered a memory with the ascendancy of Jordan's Bulls.

So it was supposed to be with the old struggles of the classical world between Christianity and paganism. Christianity is thought to have prevailed, at least officially and politically, in the fourth or fifth or maybe sixth century. As the preceding chapter explained, paganism was not so much eradicated as driven underground—and just barely and occasionally underground; so the old conflict continued to smolder just beneath the political and cultural surface. Then a new force came onto the scene—secularism. And the classical Christian-pagan antagonism was displaced, except as a remote recollection. In its place, we have modern secular society—which, as Charles Taylor observes, is a novel phenomenon unlike "anything else in human history"[1]— with its own distinctive promises, problems, and challenges.

So goes a familiar story. It is a story that most major thinkers over the past century or so have told and retold, or pretold, in one version or another,[2]

---

1. Charles Taylor, *A Secular Age* (Cambridge, MA: Harvard University Press, 2007), 1.

2. Jose Casanova explains: "In one form or another, with the possible exception of Alexis de Tocqueville, Vilfredo Pareto, and William James, the thesis of secularization was shared by all the founding fathers: from Karl Marx to John Stuart Mill, from Auguste Comte to Herbert Spencer, from E. B. Tylor to James Frazer, from Ferdinand Toennies to Georg Simmel, from Emile Durkheim to Max Weber, from Wilhelm Wundt to Sigmund Freud, from Lester Ward

and a story that has much to recommend it—on the surface, at least. But our actual history has turned out to be more complicated, and more confounding, than the standard story contemplates. In this chapter we will need to consider some of the complications.

More specifically, we will see that the old conflict between paganism and Christianity, or between immanent and transcendent religiosities, is not defunct after all; on the contrary, the opposition is alive and well. Christianity has not followed script and quietly faded away. Not yet, at least. Neither have other forms of transcendent religiosity, such as orthodox Judaism—not to mention Islam. That much is obvious, and widely recognized. What is less obvious is that rather than disappearing, immanent religiosity—or paganism, as we have called it—has (like Proteus) merely altered its forms and manifestations.[3]

And the old rivalry in the West between paganism and Christianity, or between immanent and transcendent religiosities, shows signs of becoming reinvigorated. As James O'Donnell observes, "The ancient ways of thinking and speaking about religion remain powerful even among those of us who think we share nothing in common with those backward pagans."[4]

And to make matters more interesting, or at least more confusing, all of this is happening behind a facade of secularism. A facade is of course not merely an illusion; it is a real and essential part of the building. It gives character to the building. For those who merely pass by, or who pause but don't bother to enter, it *is* the building. And yet in reality the facade is only the outward semblance of a much larger edifice, serving to hide from

---

to William G. Sumner, from Robert Park to George H. Mead. Indeed, the consensus was such that not only did the theory remain uncontested but apparently it was not even necessary to test it, since everybody took it for granted." Jose Casanova, *Public Religion in the Modern World* (Chicago: University of Chicago Press, 1994), 17. See also David Martin, *On Secularization: Toward a Revised General Theory* (New York: Routledge, 2005), 8–9 (noting "the ubiquity of secularization stories, and the varied ways they combine prescription and description").

3. Paganism is hardly unique in this respect; Christianity is also very different than it was in late antiquity. See Peter Brown, *The Body and Society: Men, Women, and Sexual Renunciation in Early Christianity*, 2nd ed. (New York: Columbia University Press, 2008), xvii (remarking that "the Christianity of the High and Late Middle Ages—to say nothing of the Christianity of our own times—is separated from the Christianity of the Roman world by a chasm almost as vast as that which still appears to separate us from the moral horizons of a Mediterranean Islamic country"). The distinction is that there is a major modern constituency that *calls itself* "Christianity" but no major modern constituency that calls itself "paganism."

4. James J. O'Donnell, *Pagans: The End of Traditional Religion and the Rise of Christianity* (New York: HarperCollins, 2015), 66.

view the inner chambers where people actually live and work and love—
and squabble, and sometimes assail each other. Like an old Roman church
with a modern facade covering an inner structure that has endured since
antiquity, the contemporary period—the one in which *we* live—is one of
a conspicuous secularism covering an ongoing conflict that traces back to
the ancient world.

Secularization: A Synopsis in Two Episodes

Standard tellings of the story of secularization tend to emphasize two main
developments or episodes that culminated (or at least were supposed to
culminate) in two different types or dimensions of secularism. One episode
focuses on political and legal developments that have produced a *political*
secularism. The other episode features more philosophical developments—
the initially epistemic and by derivation ontological developments often
described as "naturalism"—that have produced, at least in some quarters, a
more *comprehensive* or philosophical secularism.[5]

The political episode recounts how the chaos following the collapse of
an overarching Christendom in the sixteenth and seventeenth centuries led
to a series of destructive "wars of religion": the relatively small-scale Schmal-
kaldic War of 1546 and 1547 between Catholics and Protestants within the
Holy Roman Empire, the larger and longer French wars of religion (including the legendary and horrific Saint Bartholomew's Day massacres) in the
latter decades of the sixteenth century, the even more devastating Thirty
Years' War on the Continent between 1618 and 1648, the English Civil War
of the mid-seventeenth century. Through decades of violence and political
disintegration, it gradually became apparent that the project of resettling
society and government on the medieval foundation of official Christianity
was not a viable one; this realization in turn fostered a consensus that in a
religiously pluralistic world, governments could best maintain peace and
stability by staying out of the religious realm—by confining themselves to
the domain of the "secular."[6]

---

5. The parallel here to Rawls's well-known distinction between political and comprehensive liberalism is intended.

6. See generally Mark Lilla, *The Stillborn God: Religion, Politics, and the Modern West*
(New York: Vintage Books, 2007). See also Charles Taylor, "Modes of Secularism," in *Secularism and Its Critics*, ed. Rajeev Bhargava (New York: Oxford University Press, 1998), 32 ("The
origin point of modern Western secularism was the wars of religion; or rather, the search

To be sure, the preceding paragraph reflects a good deal of historical consolidation, simplification, and perhaps distortion. In fact, the wars of religion did not immediately lead to the embrace of public secularism; on the contrary, the Peace of Westphalia that ended the Thirty Years' War ratified the principle of *cuius regio eius religio* (the religion of the prince shall be the religion of the realm), thereby initiating the era of the confessional state.[7] Indeed, it is difficult to say just when the idea of governmental secularism as the preferred remedy for religious diversity came to be adopted. One might argue that this is a relatively recent and still contestable idea that we (or at least some among us) now cling to and project back onto history, thereby attempting to claim whatever measure of legitimacy or inevitability history can bestow.[8]

But however meandering the historical path may have been, the idea is widely held today, at least in politically and culturally influential circles. "There is a broad consensus," Jocelyn Maclure and Charles Taylor approvingly report, "that 'secularism' is an essential component of any liberal democracy composed of citizens who adhere to a plurality of conceptions of the world and of the good."[9] This consensus is reflected in current American constitutional law, which purports to require that government act only for "secular purposes" and that government remain detached from and "neutral" with respect to religion.[10]

The political dimension of secularism does not in itself require the disappearance of religious faith or practice, but merely assigns religion to the private domain (where, at least according to some accounts, it is likely to flourish better anyway than it would if implicated and corrupted in the public sphere).[11] By contrast, the other and more philosophical movement is more ambitious, predicting and prescribing a general decline of religion.

---

in battle-fatigue and horror for a way out of them"); Wolfhart Pannenberg, *Christianity in a Secularized World* (New York: Crossroad, 1989), 11–14, 18.

7. See Craig Calhoun, "Secularism, Citizenship, and the Public Sphere," in *Rethinking Secularism*, ed. Craig Calhoun et al. (New York: Oxford University Press, 2011), 75, 80 ("What issued from the Peace of Westphalia was not a Europe without religion but a Europe of mostly confessional states").

8. See Jocelyn Maclure and Charles Taylor, *Secularism and Freedom of Conscience*, trans. Jane Marie Todd (Cambridge, MA: Harvard University Press, 2011), 17 (asserting that the secularist conception that they advocate, and that they perceive to enjoy a global consensus in liberal democratic societies, "has appeared only recently in history"). See generally Steven D. Smith, "The Plight of the Secular Paradigm," *Notre Dame Law Review* 88 (2013): 1409.

9. Maclure and Taylor, *Secularism and Freedom*, 2.

10. Lemon v. Kurtzman, 403 U.S. 602, 612–13 (1971).

11. See Andrew Koppelman, *Defending American Religious Neutrality* (Cambridge, MA: Harvard University Press, 2013), 46–77.

The central episode in this development is the emergence of modern science, which teaches us to see the world in different and less religious ways.[12] Science operates on the basis of naturalistic premises; what the universe consists of is the sort of material or natural, empirically observable stuff susceptible to scientific investigation.[13] This view is secular because it excludes—at least for the purposes of scientific studies and explanations—nonnatural or religious entities (like spirit, or God) and nonempirical or religious methods of knowing (like revelation). And the fact that science (in contrast to older disciplines like philosophy or theology) has made spectacular progress in understanding and reshaping the world has naturally led to a kind of science envy in other fields, and thus to an aspiration to be like science; this aspiration has sustained a pervasive naturalism—and hence secularism—at least within the academy.[14]

To be sure, even among self-identifying "naturalists," debates flourish over what "nature" includes, what "science" is, and whether science should be deemed the exclusive method for knowing the world.[15] More-

12. See Graeme Smith, *A Short History of Secularism* (London: I. B. Tauris, 2008), 20–41.

13. In this vein, the philosopher John Searle describes the "picture of reality" that he says is mandatory for educated people in the twentieth and twenty-first centuries: "The world consists entirely of entities that we find it convenient, though not entirely accurate, to describe as particles. These particles exist in fields of force, and are organized into systems. The boundaries of systems are set by causal relations. Examples of systems are mountains, planets, H_2O molecules, rivers, crystals, and babies. Some of these systems are living systems; and on our little earth, the living systems contain a lot of carbon-based molecules, and make a very heavy use of hydrogen, nitrogen, and oxygen. Types of living systems evolve through natural selection, and some of them have evolved certain sorts of cellular structures, specifically, nervous systems capable of causing and sustaining consciousness. Consciousness is a biological, and therefore physical, though of course also mental feature of certain higher-level nervous systems, such as human brains and a large number of different types of animal brains." John R. Searle, *The Construction of Social Reality* (New York: Free Press, 1995), 6.

14. With respect to philosophy, for example, Hilary Putnam explains that "philosophers announce in one or another conspicuous place in their essays and books that they are 'naturalists' and that the view or account being defended is a 'naturalist' one; this announcement, in its placing and emphasis, resembles the placing of the announcement in articles written in Stalin's Soviet Union that a view was in agreement with Comrade Stalin's; as in the case of the latter announcement, it is supposed to be clear that any view that is not 'naturalist' (not in agreement with Comrade Stalin's) is anathema, and could not possibly be correct." Hilary Putnam, "The Content and Appeal of 'Naturalism,'" in *Naturalism in Question*, ed. Mario de Caro and David MacArthur (Cambridge, MA: Harvard University Press, 2004), 59.

15. For a helpful survey of divergent views on these questions among professing "naturalists," see Mario de Caro and David MacArthur, "Introduction: The Nature of Naturalism," in de Caro and MacArthur, *Naturalism in Question*, 1–20.

over, scientists sometimes describe theirs as a "*methodological* naturalism": the approach employs naturalistic assumptions for the working purposes of the scientific enterprise but remains agnostic about whether there are realities beyond the natural world. Consequently, following the example of the illustrious Isaac Newton, scientists may be devoutly religious when off duty, so to speak. Even so, the conspicuous successes of science can lead its devotees to suppose that other, nonscientific views of the world are inferior, primitive, not to be trusted. "Science is the measure of all things": so intones a revealing slogan.[16]

In this spirit, after perceptive and sympathetic depictions of the classical Greek and Christian worldviews, the philosopher Luc Ferry pronounces that science has rendered these views unavailable. "Neither the ancient model nor the Christian model remain credible for anyone of a critical and informed disposition."[17] Scientists themselves sometimes make similar assertions.[18]

Though severable, the different aspects of the secularization story are nicely complementary. Political secularism will seem more solid if it is taken not merely as a political strategy but as a reflection of the way reality actually is. And comprehensive or philosophical secularism will be all the more compelling if it can plausibly claim to be not only true but also good, or conducive to good order and political peace. Not surprisingly, therefore, in their real-world manifestations, political and comprehensive secularism often come intertwined.[19] Joined, they can seem almost irresistible; hence the near universal predictions among eminent social theorists, noted earlier, that the modern world was destined to become increasingly "secular."

Even so, the two dimensions of secularism can be taken and appreciated separately. It is entirely possible to endorse political secularism without embracing a more comprehensive secularism[20] (and perhaps, at least in principle, vice versa).[21] And of the two versions, the philosophical or

16. Wilfrid Sellars, *Science, Perception, and Reality* (Atascadero, CA: Ridgeview, 1963), 173.

17. Luc Ferry, *A Brief History of Thought: A Philosophical Guide to Living*, trans. Theo Cuffe (New York: HarperCollins, 2011), 97.

18. In this vein, physicist Steven Weinberg confidently declares that "the more the universe seems comprehensible, the more it also seems pointless." Steven Weinberg, *The First Three Minutes: A Modern View of the Origin of the Universe* (New York: Basic Books, 1977), 154.

19. See, e.g., David Niose, *Nonbeliever Nation: The Rise of Secular Americans* (London: St. Martin's Press, 2010).

20. See, e.g., Jacques Berlinerblau, *How to Be Secular: A Call to Arms for Religious Freedom* (New York: Houghton Mifflin Harcourt, 2012), 53–68; Darryl Hart, *A Secular Faith: Why Christianity Favors the Separation of Church and State* (Chicago: Ivan R. Dee, 2006).

21. One can, in other words, hold an utterly naturalistic worldview and yet think that

comprehensive secularism is more far-reaching in its implications—and (for some) more unsettling.

The Abolition of the Sacred

The comprehensive secularization associated with a scientific or naturalistic worldview implies, as Max Weber put it, the "disenchantment of the world."[22] Science and secularism can thus be viewed as completing a process that Christianity set in motion. The classical world was "enchanted"; it was full of gods. Every hill, every valley, every stream or lake had its proper deity. Though capable of jealousy and vengefulness, these deities could also be quite alluring—like the nubile nymphs who inhabited woods and rivers (and who gave their name to the term "nymphomania"), or like the comely Calypso who on her island of Ogygia hosted the forlorn wayfarer Odysseus and consoled him with seductive singing as a prelude to more intimate amenities. Then Judaism and later Christianity came and banished all these fearsome or delightsome gods in favor of the one true God—a stern and lofty sovereign, alas, who was incorporeal and metaphysically detached from time and space. So the world itself—the knowable world, the world we humans actually live in—became less immediately charged with divinity. The naturalism of modern comprehensive secularism in turn dissolves that far-off God as well, leaving the cosmos bereft of sacredness and enchantment altogether.

This view of the world suggests a different kind of existential orientation. In previous chapters we considered two such orientations. One, associated with paganism, is an immanently religious orientation that affirms the reality of the sacred but locates that sanctity within nature, or within life in this world. The other, associated with Christianity, asserts a transcendent sanctity that, while entering into the world, ultimately lies beyond nature. By contrast to these orientations, the modern secularism associated with scientific naturalism denies the existence of the sacred altogether. The modern conception is ontologically egalitarian, so to speak; in a universe consisting of matter and energy and nothing else, there is no space or category for a

"religion" serves a valuable and necessary social function. See, e.g., John Gray, *Black Mass: Apocalyptic Religion and the Death of Utopia* (New York: Penguin, 2011), 207–9.

22. See, e.g., *From Max Weber: Essays in Sociology*, ed. and trans. H. H. Gerth and C. Wright Mills (New York: Oxford University Press, 1946), 155 ("The fate of our times is characterized by rationalization and intellectualization and, above all, by the 'disenchantment of the world'").

different order of being (or *beyond* being) corresponding to either Christian or pagan descriptions of "the holy," or "the sacred." There are only different, more or less complex arrangements or systems of matter.[23]

So a man is more complex than an amoeba, and is capable of functions that an amoeba cannot perform: an amoeba cannot write a philosophical treatise or play a violin concerto. But in terms of their basic substance, both boil down to the same common elements—the same kinds of molecules, just more or fewer of them, and differently arranged. And of each we can say that "it is what it is": neither man nor amoeba has some sort of "purpose" or telos that transcends its temporary material existence. In this vein, biologist E. O. Wilson observes that "no species, ours included, possesses a purpose beyond the imperatives created by its genetic history. Species may have vast potential for material and mental progress but they lack any immanent purpose or guidance from agents beyond their immediate environment."[24]

A poignant, quietly heroic (or perhaps mock heroic) statement of this brave new spiritually desolate condition comes from the philosopher Bertrand Russell:

> That man is the product of causes which had no prevision of the end they were achieving; that his origin, his growth, his hopes and fears, his loves and his beliefs, are but the outcome of accidental collocations of atoms; that no fire, no heroism, no intensity of thought and feeling, can preserve an individual life beyond the grave; that all the labors of the ages, all the devotion, all the inspiration, all the noonday brightness of human genius, are destined to extinction in the vast death of the solar system, and that the whole temple of man's achievement must inevitably be buried beneath the debris of a universe in ruins—all these things, if not quite beyond dispute, are yet so nearly certain that no philosophy which rejects them can hope to stand. Only within the scaffolding of these truths, only on the firm foundation of unyielding despair, can the soul's habitation henceforth be safely built.[25]

23. For a sustained critical exploration of this worldview, see Joseph Vining, *From Newton's Sleep* (Princeton: Princeton University Press, 1995).

24. Edward O. Wilson, "On Human Nature," in *The Study of Human Nature: A Reader*, ed. Leslie Stevenson, 2nd ed. (New York: Oxford University Press, 2000), 271, 272.

25. Bertrand Russell, "A Free Man's Worship," in *Why I Am Not a Christian* (New York: Simon and Schuster, 1957), 104, 107.

Is the Disenchanted World Fit for Humans?

As this picture began to emerge in the course of secularization, a question was often raised along with it: Can human beings actually live under the apprehension of such a forbiddingly empty, intrinsically meaningless world? Writing in the aftermath of World War II, the Princeton philosopher Walter Stace was doubtful. Science, he said, had given us "a new imaginative picture of the world. The world, according to this new picture, is purposeless, senseless, meaningless. Nature is nothing but matter in motion."[26] This new worldview, Stace thought, "though silent and unnoticed, was the greatest revolution in human history, far outweighing in importance any of the political revolutions whose thunder has reverberated through the world."[27] That was because "if the scheme of things is purposeless and meaningless, then the life of man is purposeless and meaningless too. Everything is futile, all effort is in the end worthless."[28]

From out of this Qoheleth-like, "all is vanity" despair, Stace nonetheless mustered up the faint hope that "philosophers and intellectuals generally . . . [might] discover a genuine secular basis for morals."[29] And indeed, both well before and since Stace, "philosophers and intellectuals generally" had and have devoted themselves to this project. So, how have they fared?

One common approach, usually described as utilitarian or consequentialist, sees morality in instrumentalist terms as the business of prescribing how life should be lived so as to satisfy human desires or preferences as fully and efficiently as possible. As discussed in chapter 2, this kind of morality is taken as axiomatic in disciplines like economics and rational choice theory that are based on the "interest-seeking" conception of the person. And indeed, an interest-satisfying or preference-fulfilling consequentialism does seem to be the normative posture most congruent with the disenchanted world of philosophical naturalism. Humans exist—the product of a long evolutionary process—and they have desires and preferences: these, it seems, are natural, empirically observable facts. Some actions or policies will satisfy these desires or preferences more fully or more efficiently than others; this also is a matter subject to empirical study (even if the questions are often complex and the answers contested). Thus,

---

26. W. T. Stace, "Man against Darkness," in *Man against Darkness and Other Essays* (Pittsburgh: University of Pittsburgh Press, 1967), 6–7.

27. Stace, "Man against Darkness," 6.

28. Stace, "Man against Darkness," 7.

29. Stace, "Man against Darkness," 11.

an interest-oriented instrumentalism seems the natural and prescribed posture within a naturalistic worldview.

But the consequentialist, instrumentalist approach also generates familiar objections. It has seemed to many that however legitimate it may be in its own right, the enlightened pursuit of self-interest or the satisfaction of desires is just not what we understand morality or ethics to be about.[30] And if the goal of morality is nothing more lofty than the satisfaction of desires, why should anyone ever care about the good of others, except in a self-serving, *quid pro quo* way? What is the warrant for generosity, altruism, self-sacrifice? For heroism? For love?

The utilitarian David Hume tried to address such challenges by postulating a human quality of sympathy; we happen to be constituted so that we actually *do* care about our fellows,[31] and so we help them because our own happiness is connected to theirs. Well, maybe, sometimes anyway—but there is surely a good deal in observable human behavior to cast doubt on Hume's happy and highly convenient anthropology. For a man reputed to be the consummate hardened skeptic, Hume seems remarkably sanguine on this point. And it is hard to know what exactly to say to the idiosyncratic person who introspects and finds no such sympathy or fellow feeling in himself. Why should *that* person avoid trampling on others if he can profit thereby? The sociopath, it seems, or the egoist is not inherently either more or less intrinsically praiseworthy than the philanthropist or the saint; these are just people who happen to be constituted with different desires and interests.

Consequentialists have rebuttals to these objections,[32] of course; we cannot and need not review the debates here. Those who find the rebuttals unpersuasive will look elsewhere for an account of morality. And perhaps the other most influential effort to ground morality on assumptions of secular rationality lies in the Kantian approach, resting on a declared "categorical imperative" to act only on maxims or principles that we can will to

30. See Nancy Ann Davis, "Contemporary Deontology," in *A Companion to Ethics*, ed. Peter Singer (Oxford: Blackwell, 1991), 205.

31. David Hume, "An Enquiry concerning the Principles of Morals," in *Enquiries concerning Human Understanding and concerning the Principles of Morals*, ed. L. A. Selby-Bigge, 3rd ed. (New York: Oxford University Press, 1975), 167, 212–84.

32. See Philip Pettit, "Consequentialism," in Singer, *A Companion to Ethics*, 230. For my part, I have tried to suggest a religiously grounded answer to some of the major objections to consequentialism. See Steven D. Smith, "Is God Irrelevant?" *Boston University Law Review* 94 (2014): 1339.

be universal laws.[33] The imperative is thought to arise out of our nature as rational beings.

But again, doubts arise. If you can improve your personal situation by acting on self-serving considerations, *why* should you refrain just because you wouldn't want everyone else to act on the same considerations? ("Because you would be acting against reason," says the Kantian—"performatively contradicting yourself." "No problem," say you; "that doesn't bother me." "But then you would not have the purity and freedom of a wholly rational agent." "Like I said, Immanuel, it doesn't bother me.") And in any case, if like Kant you happen to be queasy about performative self-contradiction, then with just a little ingenuity you should be able to formulate a universalizable maxim for anything you're inclined to do. ("Take what you want if you're confident you won't get caught and are tough enough to protect your own stuff." "Always act in the way most beneficial to [fill in your own name here].")

Perhaps you'll be told: "Your maxim can't include proper nouns, especially including your own name." But why not? Where's the logical inconsistency in using proper nouns? Someone may say: "Because that kind of maxim wouldn't be a *moral* one"; but to say that would be to beg the question. Suppose, though, that some Kantian pounds the table and insists on the prohibition. Well, you can get around it through the same tactic of generic individuation legislators sometimes use to avoid constitutional prohibitions on "special legislation." If the New York legislature can't enact a law specifically for New York City, it can pass one covering "any city with a population of over eight million," or whatever. With a little ingenuity, I can do the same thing with my moral maxims; so can you.

The part of Kant that seems most promising, and that moralists perhaps most rely on, is his injunction that we should always treat people as *ends* rather than as *means*.[34] This edifying prescription seems to supply more substantive moral content than does a formalistic command to avoid contradicting oneself. But once again, *why* must we do this—treat everyone as ends? Why, on naturalistic assumptions, that is? It seems difficult or impossible to derive the injunction from the basic categorical imperative, even if we accept that imperative: without logically contradicting yourself, you can adopt (and can enthusiastically will to be universal law) the maxim that "[Fill

33. Immanuel Kant, *Groundwork of the Metaphysic of Morals*, trans. H. J. Paton (New York: Harper and Row, 1964), 82–84.

34. Kant, *Groundwork of the Metaphysic*, 100–102.

in your name] is to be treated as an *end*, and everyone else is to be treated as a *means*." What you perhaps cannot consistently do is assert in an exclusive way that "I *deserve* to be treated as an end" or "I *have a right* to be treated as an end"—because any grounds of desert or worthiness you might offer for yourself (self-consciousness? rationality? linguistic capabilities? a capacity for free choice? a capacity to formulate a life plan?) would apply to other humans as well. But then, why would you need or want to formulate your maxim in this more vulnerable way anyway?

From a detached perspective, such claims ("Beings with rationality and a capacity for free choice have intrinsic worth and hence are to be treated as ends not means") look like frail attempts to salvage or smuggle back something from the more meaning-laden, consecrated world—namely, the sacred—that the naturalistic, disenchanted world is supposed to have eliminated. Without some such tacit smuggling operation, the move from "James has the capacity to formulate a life plan" to "James is intrinsically valuable and entitled to respect" looks like a stark non sequitur. Looked at from the outside, those who invoke Kantian ethics thus seem intent on recovering something like the Judeo-Christian idea that every person is sacred—or of infinite worth, or possessed of intrinsic dignity—because made by and in the image of God.

But on purely naturalistic premises, this appeal would seem to be unavailable. Human beings are rather highly complex systems of interacting molecules formed through aeons of blind natural selection. "Straw dogs," as John Gray affirms.[35] Or, as Stephen Hawking explains, "The human race is just a chemical scum on a moderate-sized planet."[36]

So both the consequentialist and Kantian strategies seem less than compelling. It is impossible, of course, decisively to dispose of several centuries of moral philosophizing, or of a system as intricate and sophisticated as Kant's, in a few paragraphs. (It may also seem presumptuous, and irreverent, to treat so summarily and casually positions that earnest philosophers have pondered and pontificated on for many decades now.) We need not pretend to anything conclusive here, though; it is sufficient to say that philosophers have tried to provide a secular basis for ethics, but whether they have succeeded is questionable.[37]

35. John Gray, *Straw Dogs* (New York: Farrar, Straus and Giroux, 2002).

36. Quoted in Paul Davies, *Cosmic Jackpot: Why Our Universe Is Just Right for Life* (New York: Penguin, 2007), 222.

37. For a classic treatment of the issue leading to a negative verdict, see Alasdair Mac-Intyre, *After Virtue: A Study in Moral Theory*, 3rd ed. (Notre Dame: University of Notre Dame

Suppose for the sake of argument, though, that the secular arguments *have* succeeded—succeeded, that is, in supplying a secular basis for ethics, or "morality." Would that be enough to make the world a commodious abode for humans? How can "morality," often perceived mostly as a source of irksome restrictions, instead affirmatively make life worth living? We saw in chapter 2 that thinkers like Viktor Frankl and Susan Wolf argue that what people ultimately need is neither the satisfaction of their "interests" nor mere "morality," but rather something those thinkers describe as "meaning." And meaning, as Wolf argues, requires *objective value*—something she admits philosophers have had difficulty explaining.[38] Even a successful version of "secular morality," though imposing *duties*, might not supply such *meaning*; it might leave human life more morally respectable, perhaps, but also more restricted—and still empty and pointless.

So then, what to do? One alternative would be to accept the truth, bleak though it may be—to build on Russell's "firm foundation of unyielding despair"—and thus perhaps to live out our days in this disenchanted and purposeless world in (as Stace recommended) "quiet content, accepting resignedly what cannot be helped, not expecting the impossible, and being thankful for small mercies."[39] There is venerable precedent in antiquity for this course of quietist resignation, in the Epicurean way of life.[40] Or, if we find this deflationary approach to life insufficiently fulfilling, we might instead embrace the necessity of fictions or illusions that offer direction and value to our lives, even though, upon reflection (from which we would be prudent to abstain), these would have to be regarded as merely illusory.[41] There is not *really* any point to our lives, but it is pleasant to pretend otherwise.

From a different perspective, though, all this gloominess will seem puzzling, and gratuitous. That is because nothing in science requires us to accept the picture of a purposeless, meaningless, disenchanted cosmos described

---

Press, 2007). For a more popular essay to similar effect, see Arthur A. Leff, "Unspeakable Ethics, Unnatural Law," *Duke Law Journal* 1979, no. 6 (1979): 1229.

38. See above, 23.

39. Stace, "Man against Darkness," 16–17.

40. See A. A. Long, *Hellenistic Philosophy: Stoics, Epicureans, Sceptics*, 2nd ed. (Berkeley: University of California Press, 1986), 14–21. For a recent popular book advocating this Epicurean approach to life, see Stephen Greenblatt, *The Swerve: How the World Became Modern* (New York: Norton, 2011).

41. In this vein, see Richard Joyce, *The Myth of Morality* (Cambridge: Cambridge University Press, 2001).

(sometimes, it almost seems, with a kind of smug bravado, or sometimes with a heavy touch of indulgent self-pity) by scientists like Wilson or philosophers like Russell. Conversely, much in human experience contradicts and subverts that picture.

Or at least, so many believe. In this respect, it is clear that the predictions of religion's decline spawned by the secularization story have turned out to be embarrassingly mistaken, or at least grossly premature. The embarrassment is apparent in two phenomena, one quite obvious and the other less so.

The obvious phenomenon is the persistence of traditional, transcendent religion. The less obvious development is the reappearance in surprising cultural quarters of immanent religion—or of what might be described as modern paganism.

The Persistence of Transcendent Religion

Writing in 1968, the sociologist Peter Berger expressed a common view in predicting that "by the 21st century, religious believers are likely to be found only in small sects, huddled together to resist a world-wide secular culture."[42] By century's end, though, it had become apparent that Berger and like-minded thinkers were badly off base, at least in their projections. Religion had not withered away; indeed, it showed no sign of receding (although there were indications of some migration).

Berger admitted as much. "The assumption that we live in a secularized world is false," he later declared. "The world today, with [the] exceptions [of Europe and of 'an international subculture composed of people with Western-type higher education'], is as furiously religious as it ever was, and in some places more so than ever. This means that a whole body of literature by historians and social scientists loosely labeled 'secularization theory' is essentially mistaken."[43]

In a similar vein, in a recent book called *God's Century*, three political scientists argue that religion continues to be a powerful force in politics worldwide and is likely to remain so in coming decades. Indeed, both religion and religious influence on politics have actually grown stronger over

42. Peter Berger, "A Bleak Outlook Is Seen for Religion," *New York Times*, February 25, 1968, 3.

43. Peter L. Berger, "The Desecularization of the World: A Global Overview," in *The Desecularization of the World*, ed. Peter L. Berger (Washington, DC: Ethics and Public Policy Center; Grand Rapids: Eerdmans, 1999), 1, 2, 9, 10.

the last several decades.[44] Canadian political scientist Ran Hirschl reports resignedly that "approximately half of the world's population, perhaps more, now lives in polities where religion not only has remained public but also has been playing a key role in political and constitutional life."[45]

Ardent secularists may deplore this development, depicting traditional religion as backward-looking and ignorant or contemptuous of science. The depiction fits some believers but not others. There is, to be sure, a substantial "fundamentalist" constituency in America and elsewhere that rejects the theory of evolution, for example.[46] But there are also many other believers, including devout scientists, who see science and religious belief as complementary, not conflicting.[47]

In this vein, Rabbi Jonathan Sacks argues that science and religion constitute "the great partnership." Science, Sacks asserts, is "one of the two greatest achievements of the human mind."[48] But science has no competence to adjudicate between an account that denies any cosmic meaning and one that discerns meaning in life and the universe; both accounts are equally consistent with the facts and truths cognizable by science.[49] "The first story says there is no why. The second says there is," Sacks observes. "The science is the same in both stories. The difference lies in how far we are willing to push the question, 'Why?'"[50]

Scientist-theologian Alister McGrath elaborates on the point:

> My Oxford colleague John Lennox, who is a mathematician and philosopher of science, uses a neat illustration to make this point.

---

44. Monica Duffy Toft, Daniel Philpott, and Timothy Samuel Shah, *God's Century: Resurgent Religion and Global Politics* (New York: Norton, 2011). With respect to religion itself, the authors explain that "contrary to . . . predictions, the portion of the world population adhering to Catholic Christianity, Protestant Christianity, Islam, and Hinduism jumped from 50 percent in 1900 to 64 percent in 2000" (2). Moreover, "a dramatic and worldwide increase in the political influence of religion has occurred in roughly the past forty years" (9 [emphasis deleted]).

45. Ran Hirschl, *Constitutional Theocracy* (Cambridge, MA: Harvard University Press, 2010), 47.

46. See, e.g., Edward J. Larson, *Summer of the Gods: The Scopes Trial and America's Continuing Debate over Science and Religion* (New York: Basic Books, 1997), 264–65.

47. See Edward J. Larson, *Evolution: The Remarkable History of a Scientific Theory* (New York: Random House, 2004), 284–85.

48. Larson, *Evolution*, 292.

49. Larson, *Evolution*, 20–25.

50. Jonathan Sacks, *The Great Partnership: Science, Religion, and the Search for Meaning* (New York: Schocken, 2011), 24.

Imagine a cake being subjected to scientific analysis, leading to an exhaustive discussion of its chemical composition and of the physical forces which hold it together. Does this tell us that the cake was baked to celebrate a birthday? And is this inconsistent with the scientific analysis? Of course not. Science and theology ask different questions: in the case of science, the question concerns how things happen: by what process? In the case of theology, the question is why things happen: to what purpose?[51]

So traditional, transcendent religion can be either suspicious of or friendly to science. Either way, it seems unlikely that traditional religion will wither away in the foreseeable future, as theorists like Berger once predicted.

To be sure, traditional religion and Christianity in particular appear to flourish more in some parts of the world—Africa, Latin America, the United States, perhaps China (against strenuous governmental opposition)[52]—than in regions such as Europe.[53] Moreover, in the United States, recent surveys report a rise in the percentage of "nones"—people who on surveys of religiosity mark the box "None."[54] And yet, even the increase in self-declared unbelievers may not reflect any actual decline in religiosity. That is because, as we will see, even those who declare themselves free of any religion often openly acknowledge beliefs and commitments reflective of spirituality and a commitment to the sacred. This development is manifest in the career of the most influential (and thoroughly secular) English-speaking legal scholar and philosopher of recent decades, Ronald Dworkin.

Ronald Dworkin's Search for the Sacred

Though a consummately secular thinker, from his earliest writings Dworkin resisted the pervasively instrumentalist and interest-calculating character of modern legal thought. He championed "rights"—rights understood as "trumps" or categorical constraints on laws or governmental actions based

51. Alister McGrath, *Surprised by Meaning: Science, Faith, and How We Make Sense of Things* (Louisville: Westminster John Knox, 2011), 43.

52. See Yu Jie, "China's Christian Future," *First Things*, August 2016, https://www.first things.com/article/2016/08/chinas-christian-future.

53. See Philip Jenkins, *The Next Christendom: The Coming of Global Christianity*, 3rd ed. (New York: Oxford University Press, 2011).

54. See below, 242–43.

on instrumentalist policies.[55] He criticized law-and-economics.[56] He advocated a form of legal interpretation in which laws would be construed not to further either the subjective intentions of their enactors or the utilitarian aims of present-day policy makers; rather, laws would be interpreted in accordance with the best available moral philosophy.[57]

But in a secular, naturalistic world, where were these rights and categorical constraints and moral imperatives supposed to come from? Dworkin's distinguished career can be seen as a long struggle with the question.

Thus, in one early essay, he appeared to embrace a kind of refined moral conventionalism.[58] Although our moral commitments are conventional in character, Dworkin argued, we should be ruled not by shallow or unscrutinized conventions, but rather by conventions that we have carefully reflected on.[59] But this seemed a vulnerable position. If our morality is grounded merely in conventions, why does it matter whether we carefully examine those conventions? What would we examine them *for*, exactly?

For consistency, Dworkin said, among other desiderata.[60] But why? If we supposed there is some underlying moral truth against which conventions might be adjudged true or false, then it might matter whether our moral conventions are consistent, because under the so-called law of noncontradiction, internal inconsistency would be an indication of error (just as it is for scientific or mathematical propositions). But if morality is merely conventional, and if there is no objective or external standard against which conventions can be judged, then what difference does it make if we have one set of moral conventions for tall people and a different set for short people, or one set of conventions for Mondays and Wednesdays and a different set for Tuesdays and Thursdays? If my habit is to eat tacos on Tuesdays, pizza on Wednesdays, and kabobs on Thursdays, no one criticizes me for inconsistency. "It's what I (like to) do" is sufficient warrant—indeed, the only kind of warrant that might be pertinent. The same should be true for morality—if morality is merely conventional, that is.

55. Ronald Dworkin, *Taking Rights Seriously* (Cambridge, MA: Harvard University Press, 1977).

56. See Ronald Dworkin, *A Matter of Principle* (New York: Clarendon, 1985), 237–89.

57. Ronald Dworkin, *Law's Empire* (Cambridge, MA: Belknap Press of Harvard University Press, 1986).

58. Ronald Dworkin, "Liberty and Moralism," in *Taking Rights Seriously*, 240.

59. Dworkin, *Taking Rights Seriously*, 248–53. The chapter reprinted an article that had been originally published in 1966.

60. Dworkin, *Taking Rights Seriously*, 251.

Something more than conventions seemed to be needed. In a later essay, Dworkin tried to use utilitarianism against itself, or against the unchecked implementation of policies calculated to further utilitarian preferences, by arguing that some kinds of legal restrictions that he disfavored (such as laws regulating pornography) violated the utilitarian premise that everyone's utility should be counted equally.[61] This argument was clever but, as critics persuasively objected, demonstrably flawed.[62] While not conceding the point, in a later essay Dworkin moved on to what he at least *called* moral realism.[63] There are objectively right answers to moral questions, he asserted; slavery is and always was wrong, whether or not it was conventional, and whether or not people believed it was wrong.

In the same essay, however, while declaring that morality was "objective," Dworkin also insisted that it was not actually any sort of *object*: morality is not part of "the fabric of the universe."[64] This stance left some readers (or at least one) feeling puzzled, and disgruntled. If morality is not part of "the fabric of the universe," in what sense is morality real, or "objective," at all?

At about the same time, in an exploration of life-and-death issues such as abortion and euthanasia, Dworkin invoked the idea of "the sacred."[65] Insisting that the "sacred" need not be a religious concept, Dworkin emphasized a distinction between "sacred" or "inviolable" values and merely "instrumental" values.[66] In fastening onto the idea of the "sacred," it seemed that Dworkin had perhaps at last found the sort of idea he had needed all along in his effort to resist instrumentalism and to defend categorical constraints on merely utilitarian laws and policies.

And yet Dworkin's explication of "the sacred" seemed both half-baked and (confessedly) halfhearted. Once detached from its religious moorings, what does "sacred" even mean? Dworkin proposed that we regard some things as "sacred" or "inviolable" because they are the results of a long pro-

---

61. See Ronald Dworkin, "Do We Have a Right to Pornography?" in *A Matter of Principle*, 335.

62. John Hart Ely, "Professor Dworkin's External/Personal Preference Distinction," *Duke Law Journal* 1983 (1983): 959; H. L. A. Hart, "Between Utility and Rights," *Columbia Law Review* 79 (1980): 828.

63. Ronald Dworkin, "Objectivity and Truth: You'd Better Believe It," *Philosophy and Public Affairs Journal* 25 (1996): 87.

64. Dworkin, "Objectivity and Truth," 90, 99, 105.

65. Ronald Dworkin, *Life's Dominion: An Argument about Abortion, Euthanasia, and Individual Freedom* (New York: Vintage Books, 1993), 25, 68–101.

66. Dworkin, *Life's Dominion*, 25, 71–78.

cess we respect, such as artistic creation or natural evolution. We consider a great painting "sacred" because the artist put a lot of time and effort and genius into painting it. And we regret the loss of a species of plant or animal because it was the product of aeons of evolution, so the disappearance of the species would amount to "a waste of nature's investment."[67] But this seemed a curiously uncompelling explanation. Does our evaluation of a painting by Rembrandt really turn on how long he took to do it? If it turned out that da Vinci dashed off the *Mona Lisa* in a week (as Bernini is supposed to have done with his remarkable sculpture of Pope Innocent X), would we demote it from the category of masterpiece?[68]

Faced with this and other objections, Dworkin didn't attempt actually to defend his "process" and "loss of investment" account of the "sacred." Instead, he claimed merely to be describing intuitions many people in fact have (while at the same time purporting to be giving a revised and better account of beliefs that, as he acknowledged, people typically do *not* articulate in these terms). And having attributed these reworked intuitions to people, Dworkin expressed his own doubts about whether the ostensible intuitions are ultimately rational or justifiable at all. "It is not my present purpose," he explained, "to recommend or defend any of these widespread convictions about art and nature, in either their religious or secular form. Perhaps they are all, as some skeptics insist, inconsistent superstitions."[69]

Dworkin's convoluted discussion thus amounted to a halting effort to support his anti-instrumentalist commitments by tapping into an essentially religious notion—the "sacred"—even though he was at that point both unwilling to own the premises that gave the notion its significance and by his own admission unable to provide any persuasive defense of the concept.

And so in his last, posthumously published book, Dworkin explicitly embraced "religion"—albeit "religious atheism," as he called it.[70]

---

67. Dworkin, *Life's Dominion*, 79.

68. Dworkin's "process" explanation was the more suspect because, as he conceded, only some processes seem to elicit this reaction from us. "We do not treat everything produced by a long natural process—coal or petroleum deposits, for example—as inviolable," Dworkin acknowledged, "and many of us have no compunction about cutting down trees to clear space for a house or slaughtering complex mammals like cows for food." Dworkin, *Life's Dominion*, 80. So then, why would we regard the products of some long processes as "sacred" or "inviolable" *because of the process* and the products of other long processes as totally exploitable and expendable?

69. Dworkin, *Life's Dominion*, 81.

70. Ronald Dworkin, *Religion without God* (Cambridge, MA: Harvard University Press, 2013), 1. Hereafter, page references from this work will be given in parentheses in the text.

Religion, Dworkin now argued, need not include belief in God or gods. Rather, what he called the "religious attitude" rests on two beliefs or judgments. The first is that "human life has objective meaning or purpose." The second is that "what we call 'nature'—the universe as a whole and in all its parts—is not just a matter of fact but is itself sublime: something of intrinsic value and wonder" (10). These are judgments of "value," Dworkin explained, and they have an essential emotional component (10, 19–20).

But the judgments are not *merely* subjective or emotive reactions: they are a response to and a recognition of actual realities in the universe (6, 20–21). With that clarification, Dworkin maintained that we should "take these two [values]—life's intrinsic meaning and nature's intrinsic beauty—as paradigms of a fully religious attitude to life" (11). And the religious attitude serves to restore to us something that Weber and theorists of science and naturalism had pronounced forever lost—namely, "enchantment" (11).

As it happens, the two commitments identified by Dworkin correspond almost exactly to the two-themed account of religion we considered in chapter 2. One theme, associated with thinkers like Victor Frankl and Jonathan Sacks, sees religion as an affirmative response to the pervasive human desire or need for "meaning": this is the first of Dworkin's elements of religion. The other theme, articulated by Mircea Eliade, Rudolf Otto, and Abraham Heschel, understands religion as the product of the human encounter with the "holy," or the "sacred." Much like Otto, Dworkin described religious experience as "numinous"; much like Heschel, Dworkin used terms like "sublime," "awe," and "wonder" to convey the religious attitude (2–3, 10).[71] Also like Otto, Heschel, and Sacks, moreover, Dworkin insisted that these judgments and emotions are not merely subjective; they reflect the discernment of something in the universe that is objectively real, even though it eludes the more naturalistic devices of the scientists.

Unlike for those thinkers, however, for Dworkin that "something" real was not anything lying beyond or behind the perceived sublimity—not any God or gods. Rather, the sublimity is a property or aspect of nature itself, including the part of nature that is human life. In this sense, Dworkin's religion would seem to be of the immanent variety. The sublime, or the sacred, is within and part of life and of nature, not something beyond or outside of them.[72]

71. See also Dworkin, *Religion without God*, 24 ("The religious person perceives the universe as 'something of intrinsic wonder and beauty'").

72. To be sure, on this point Dworkin gave mixed signals. At one early point in the book

The immanent quality of Dworkin's religion is perhaps most clearly apparent in his admiring discussions of Spinoza and Einstein, whose philosophies he offered as representative of the kind of "religious atheism" he himself advocated. Spinoza, he conceded, talked incessantly about God. But "Spinoza's God is not an intelligence who stands outside everything and who, through the force of its will, has created the universe and the physical laws that govern it. His God is just the complete set of physical laws *considered under a different aspect*" (38–39 [emphasis added]). Under what aspect? Here Dworkin invoked Einstein, who also endorsed Spinoza's deity. And what was Einstein's understanding of that deity? Einstein "did not believe in a personal god," Dworkin explained, "but he did 'worship' nature. He regarded it with awe and thought that he and other scientists should be humble before its beauty and mystery" (40).

That is the sort of immanent "religious atheism" that Dworkin ultimately preached. It is the last answer he managed to give to his long search for something with a categorical quality that could stand against the pervasive instrumentalism of the modern world—for something "inviolable" or "sacred"—that could bring "enchantment" back into the world (6, 11–12).

From Disenchantment to Reenchantment

Whether Dworkin had in fact found what he needed is questionable, to be sure. Though he asserted that the sublimity of the world is "beyond nature," he offered no ontological account of just what that something "beyond na-

---

he appeared to endorse "the supernatural," or "something beyond nature," or "some transcendental and objective value [that] permeates the universe" (Dworkin, *Religion without God*, 6). And he insisted on distinguishing his view from "naturalism." E.g., p. 13 ("The religious attitude rejects all forms of naturalism"). But elsewhere, as we have seen, Dworkin said that the religious judgment holds that "what we call '*nature*'—*the universe as a whole and in all its parts*—is not just a matter of fact but is *itself* sublime: something of *intrinsic value and wonder*" (10 [emphasis added]). Dworkin also deliberately and laboriously distinguished the realm of "value" from the realm of "science" (22–29), or describable facts (a realm that for Dworkin included claims about God, who if he existed would be "a very exotic kind of scientific fact"). Religion, Dworkin emphasized, belongs in the realm of value, not of describable facts. This is surely a puzzling conjunction of propositions: namely, that the sublime is objectively real but that it does not belong to the realm of facts. Still, if the question is raised whether Dworkin located the sublime within or outside of nature, it seems that the better answer would be "*within* nature." The sublime would seem to be an aspect or feature or dimension of the world, albeit one that transcends the sorts of "matters of fact" that naturalistic science studies (23).

237

ture" could be, or of how it would relate to or emerge out of other, more purely naturalistic realities. It is as if someone were to describe the universe and its contents as having the naturalistic properties of, say, mass, temporal duration, motion, physical attraction and repulsion . . . oh, yes, and also of "sublimity." Plus "objective value." There is something incongruous in these add-ons. Dworkin's "religion without god" seems a sort of *ipse dixit*, "*(non) deus ex machina*" solution to the challenges of meaninglessness and morality in a naturalistic world.

We will return to the point. For now, the important observation is that Dworkin's odyssey—from moral conventionalism to a doctored utilitarianism to moral realism all the way across to the "enchantment" of "religion without god"—reflects a pattern discernible in other thinkers as well, and perhaps in elite secular culture generally. At stage one, thinkers look back, wistfully perhaps, on the "enchanted" world of antiquity and pronounce that world, alas, irretrievably lost: science has rendered it unavailable to moderns with any critical capacity. The first reaction to this loss is to announce the disenchantment and meaninglessness of the world. The announcement may be offered with resigned despair (as with Stace), or perhaps (as with Russell) with the darkly heroic satisfaction of Homeric warriors who are all the more noble because they fight courageously on without ultimate hope, knowing that they must soon and inexorably die and that will be the end of everything. And then, upon reflection, secular thinkers declare that we *can* have ethics or morality after all; indeed, we can place ethics upon an even more solid secular foundation.[73] And upon further thought, they announce the glad tidings that the secular, naturalistic world is not as empty of enchantment or objective value as had been supposed. It turns out that amidst the "nothing but matter in motion," as Stace put it, there is also, somehow . . . beauty, value, goodness. Enchantment. The sacred.

Nor are these merely subjective emotions; they are objectively real. Why had we somehow supposed that they had been lost? What was the reason for all our existential angst? Why were we, or in any case our parents, so taken with Sartre and Camus and Samuel Beckett? What could we, or they, have been thinking?

73. See, e.g., Martha C. Nussbaum, "Skepticism about Practical Reason in Literature and the Law," *Harvard Law Review* 107 (1994): 740 ("If we really think of the hope of a transcendent ground as uninteresting or irrelevant to human ethics, as we should, then the news of its collapse will not change the way we think and act. It will just let us get on with the business of reasoning in which we were already engaged").

Dworkin is hardly a lone traveler along this spiritual path to meaning and reenchantment. We might consider two more recent and notable representatives of this rediscovery of enchantment, or of the sacred. Both are secular, atheistic, scientific. But both discern something—something real—that overflows the normal terms and categories of mundane science.

Sam Harris, the truculently atheistic author of *The End of Faith* and other similar works, in a more recent book reports on a personal, drug-induced experience of a "state of being" in which "love, compassion, and joy in the joy of others extended without limit."[74] This and similar mystical or meditative experiences, both his own and others', lead Harris to observe that "there is more to understanding the human condition than science and secular culture generally admit."[75] While adamantly eschewing the label of "religion," and while purporting to "remain true to the deepest principles of scientific skepticism," Harris uses terms such as "*spiritual, mystical, contemplative*, and *transcendent*" to describe this additional dimension (10, 7). "Millions of people," he observes, "have had experiences for which *spiritual* and *mystical* seem the only terms available" (11). In such experiences it "is quite possible to lose one's sense of being a separate self and to experience a kind of boundless, open awareness—to feel, in other words, at one with the cosmos" (43). And, as noted, this oneness carries with it "love, compassion, and joy" (5).

Harris does not postulate anything supernatural or metaphysically exotic as the source of such experiences; rather, he assumes that they are manifestations of an expanded human consciousness. The mystical experience "says a lot about the possibilities of human consciousness, but it says nothing about the universe at large" (43–44). Harris acknowledges that consciousness is a "mystery" and that "we know nothing about how consciousness comes into being" (51, 205); even so, treating mystical experience as merely an aspect of consciousness saves Harris from passing into the (for him) dreaded category of "religion." With an unwaveringly confident bellicosity, he thus continues to insist that "the world's religions [are] mere intellectual ruins" (5). (Except maybe, it seems, for Buddhism [21–31].)

Whether Harris should be admitted as an acolyte of Dworkin's atheistic religion is debatable. He shuns the *term* "religion." And his claim that tran-

---

74. Sam Harris, *Waking Up: A Guide to Spirituality without Religion* (New York: Simon and Schuster, 2014), 5.

75. Harris, *Waking Up*, 6. See also 202 ("Spirituality remains the great hole in secularism, humanism, rationalism, atheism, and all the other defensive postures that reasonable men and women strike in the presence of unreasonable faith"). Hereafter, page references from this work will be given in parentheses in the text.

scendence is within consciousness, not part of "the universe at large," might disqualify him. But then again, maybe not. After all, while insisting that objective beauty and value are real, not merely subjective, Dworkin himself is less than clear about *where* in the universe these blessed qualities reside. Why couldn't they reside in the human consciousness? And then there is Harris's admiration for Buddhism. In its substance, Harris's view seems to be kin to the same general family as Dworkin's.

In this respect, the recent spiritual autobiography of another admired atheist and writer, Barbara Ehrenreich, presents an even sharper instance. While describing herself as "a rationalist, an atheist, a scientist by training," Ehrenreich recounts how, as a teenager, she set as a "goal for life . . . to find out why. What is the point of our brief existence?"[76] Later, as she pursued a career in science, the naturalistic worldview she learned and accepted did not negate but rather underscored the *why* question. "Why was there anything at all? Why interrupt the perfection of universal Nothing with the momentary clutter and confusion of Something?" (85).

She was debarred from looking to conventional religion for answers. "I was born to atheism and raised in it, by people who had derived their own atheism from a proud tradition of working-class rejection of authority in all its forms, whether vested in bosses or priests, gods or demons. This is what defined my people, my tribe: We did not *believe*" (3).

While dutifully maintaining this atheistic heritage throughout her life, Ehrenreich recalls having had brief quasi-mystical experiences as a teenager (47–53) in which it seemed as if "another universe, intimately superimposed on our own, normally invisible, but every so often, where the dividing membrane had worn thin, [was] shining through into our own" (52). These culminated in a shattering and transforming experience, or "epiphany" (127), when Ehrenreich was walking in the early dawn in Lone Pine, California. While cautioning that the experience was ineffable, beyond "the jurisdiction of language," she nonetheless struggles to convey the sense of it: "The world flamed into life. How else to describe it? There were no visions, no prophetic voices or visits by totemic animals, just this blazing everywhere. Something poured into me and I poured out into it. This was not the passive beatific merger with 'the All,' as promised by the Eastern mystics. It was a furious encounter with a living substance that was coming at me through all things

---

76. Barbara Ehrenreich, *Living with a Wild God: A Nonbeliever's Search for the Truth about Everything* (New York: Twelve, 2014), xx, 1. Hereafter, page references from this work will be given in parentheses in the text.

at once, and one reason for the terrible wordlessness of the experience is that you cannot observe fire really closely without becoming part of it" (116).

A quest to discern the meaning of this "epiphany" has occupied much of the rest of Ehrenreich's life. Shortly after the experience she remarked to a friend, "I saw God"—but then hastened to recant, explaining that "I was only kidding, that I was as firm in my atheism as ever" (116). In subsequent decades, immersed in graduate study, in writing, in political activism, and in raising two children, Ehrenreich sometimes lost sight of the *why* question, but the quest revived at a later stage, reinforced by later mystical experiences. Her last chapter speculates on various ways of conceiving of what she can only describe as "the Presence" or "the Other" (216, 221), and reflects on ways in which science itself seems to be overcoming "the collective solipsism our species has embraced for the last few centuries in the name of modernity and rationality, a worldview in which there exists no consciousness or agency other than our own" (234).

The Ranks of the Immanently Religious

Of these three cases, Ehrenreich's is the most dramatic—and probably the least typical (though she observes that "almost half of Americans report having had a 'mystical experience'").[77] Dworkin, for example, though he talked of sublimity and the sacred, reported no experience similar to Ehrenreich's Lone Pine epiphany.

He did suggest, however, very plausibly, that his sort of less spectacular "religion without God" is widely shared. Not by everyone; perhaps unfairly,[78] Dworkin classified Richard Dawkins, the prominent scientist-writer who crusades against religion and for evolution, as a nonreligious naturalist. Dawkins comes in for repeated criticism in Dworkin's book.[79] But Dawkins is the exception.

> Many millions of people who count themselves as atheists have convictions and experiences similar to and just as profound as those that believers count as religious. They say that though they do not believe

77. Ehrenreich, *Living*, 216.

78. Dawkins at least sometimes seems to endorse the same Einsteinian sense of the mystery and beauty of the world that is central to Dworkin's "religion." Richard Dawkins, *The God Delusion* (New York: Houghton Mifflin, 2008), 40.

79. Dworkin, *Religion without God*, 5, 42–43.

in a "personal" god, they nevertheless believe in a "force" in the universe "greater than we are." They feel an inescapable responsibility to live their lives well, with due respect for the lives of others; they take pride in a life they think well lived and suffer sometimes inconsolable regret at a life they think, in retrospect, wasted. They find the Grand Canyon not just arresting but breathtakingly and eerily beautiful. They are not simply interested in the latest discoveries about vast space but enthralled by them. These are not, for them, just a matter of immediate sensuous and otherwise inexplicable response. They express a conviction that the force and wonder they sense are real, just as real as planets and pain, that moral truth and natural wonder do not simply evoke awe but call for it.[80]

These are judgments, emotions, and convictions, Dworkins suggested, that cannot be fully accounted for and credited—as opposed to being "explained away"—by the "just the facts, ma'am" naturalism espoused by thinkers like Dawkins. Insofar as many or most people have such judgments, emotions, and convictions and do not attempt to dismiss them or explain them away, Dworkin suggested, these people are harboring and acting on a view that is "religious."

So, how large might this congregation of the immanently religious be? As noted, Dworkin himself claimed for his fellowship "many millions of people who count themselves as atheists." Perhaps he was exaggerating. And yet there is reason to suspect just the opposite. Recent research by the Pew Foundation suggests that between 2007 and 2014, the percentage of self-described atheists who reported feeling a sense of awe or wonder about the universe increased, from 37 to 54 percent; for self-identifying agnostics the increase went from 48 to 55 percent.[81] Beyond the group of atheists and agnostics, Dworkin's description might fit the growing fold of people who describe themselves as "spiritual but not religious."[82] It might fit as well the proportionally small but swelling portion of Americans who are classified as "nones."[83] Some of these people may be reductionist naturalists after the

80. Dworkin, *Religion without God*, 2–3.

81. See David Masci and Michael Lipka, "Americans May Be Getting Less Religious, but Feelings of Spirituality Are on the Rise," Pew Research Center, January 21, 2016, http://www .pewresearch.org/fact-tank/2016/01/21/americans-spirituality.

82. See Masci and Lipka, "Americans May Be Getting Less Religious, but Feelings of Spirituality Are on the Rise."

83. See Michael Lipka, "A Closer Look at America's Rapidly Growing Religious 'Nones,'"

manner of Dworkin's Dawkins. But it seems that many, while skeptical about God and suspicious of "religion" in its more conventional sense, would share the kinds of judgments about beauty and the moral seriousness described by Dworkin.[84]

By expanding "religion" beyond conventional theism,[85] Dworkin delineated a category that might well encompass such people—even if (like Harris) they still recoil from the *term* "religion." Indeed, even many who describe themselves as belonging to more traditional religions—to Christianity, in particular—might more accurately belong in the camp of the immanently religious. This contingent might well include the vast ranks of the religiously tepid—people who for reasons of habit or family tradition may self-identify as "Catholic" or "Methodist" or whatever, and who have experiences of beauty and value as Dworkin described, but who exhibit no live commitment to a transcendent deity. And even active churchgoers may recite the ancient Christian creeds and yet maintain a faith in something more immanent than transcendent. Martin Gardner observes that "today, you will have a difficult time discovering what any prominent Christian actually believes."[86] And he adds, with evident irritation: "Millions of Catholics and Protestants around the world now attend liberal churches where they listen to music and Laodicean sermons, and (if Protestant) sing tuneless Laodicean hymns. They may even stand and recite the Apostles' Creed out of force of habit and not believe a word of it. If a pastor or priest dared to preach a sermon on, say, whether Jesus' corpse was actually revivified, the congregation would quickly find a way to get rid of him."[87]

Pew Research Center, May 13, 2015, http://www.pewresearch.org/fact-tank/2015/05/13/a-closer-look-at-americas-rapidly-growing-religious-nones.

84. Among Americans who say their religion is "nothing in particular," 48 percent reported regularly feeling a sense of awe or wonder at the universe. See Masci and Lipka, "Americans May Be Getting Less Religious, but Feelings of Spirituality Are on the Rise."

85. Indeed, self-adopted labels such as "atheist" can be quite unilluminating or misleading with respect to people's actual beliefs. For example, Pew research reveals that although about 9 percent of Americans say they do not believe in God, only about 3 percent describe themselves as "atheists," but of those who do so self-describe, about 8 percent say they believe in God or a universal spirit. See Michael Lipka, "7 Facts about Atheists," Pew Research Center, November 5, 2015, http://www.pewresearch.org/fact-tank/2015/11/05/7-facts-about-atheists/.

86. Martin Gardner, introduction to *The Ball and the Cross*, by G. K. Chesterton (New York: Dover, 1995), vi.

87. Gardner, introduction to *The Ball and the Cross*, vii. Cf. Frank Viola and George Barna, *Pagan Christianity? Exploring the Roots of Our Church Practices* (Carol Stream, IL: Tyndale House, 2002) (arguing that a great deal in modern Christian practice and worship is

So in the end, there is no way to count. Still, it seems most likely that the church of the immanently religious is, to borrow from the eminent poetic pagan Walt Whitman, "large; [it] contain[s] multitudes."[88]

Paganism Triumphant?

Insofar as this sort of religiosity, held by "many millions of people" (as Dworkin asserted), is a belief in an immanent sacred, it could aptly be described as a kind of "modern paganism," as T. S. Eliot claimed.

To recall the distinctions presented in chapter 4, this would of course not be "mythical paganism." There are, to be sure, people who actually *call themselves* "pagans" and who purport to worship nature deities.[89] And the shelves of bookstores are stocked with books about the occult or the paranormal; movies on such subjects—and about superheroes who resemble and are occasionally named for pagan deities—likewise proliferate. But these are not the socially salient and politically and culturally influential movements we are considering here. No one today (or almost no one) is claiming that Zeus, Athena, Apollo, and company are still hanging out on Mount Olympus and from time to time officiously intruding themselves into the affairs of mortals.

In that respect, though, modern paganism is not so very different from the ancient paganism of the educated classes, who likewise regarded the myths as "lying fables" and often viewed the gods as symbols of a spiritual reality.[90] Primarily, "modern paganism" would be a modern variation on the kind of immanent religiosity or "philosophical paganism" expounded by the character Balbus in Cicero's dialogue on the gods (and by Cicero himself, at least according to his own profession).[91]

---

more pagan than authentically Christian). Viola and Barna define "pagan" rather loosely as indicating "those practices and principles that are not Christian or biblical in origin" (xxxv).

88. Walt Whitman, "Song of Myself," Modern American Poetry, accessed July 13, 2017, http://www.english.illinois.edu/maps/poets/s_z/whitman/song.htm.

89. For a discussion of modern movements that call themselves "pagan," see Owen Davies, *Paganism: A Very Short Introduction* (Oxford: Oxford University Press, 2011), 106–22. Several readers suggested to me that paganism so-called has been making a comeback in Scandinavia in recent years. See, e.g., "Enormous Increase in Pagan Ásatrú Religion," *Iceland Monitor*, March 28, 2017, http://icelandmonitor.mbl.is/news/culture_and_living/2017/03/28/enormous_increase_in_pagan_asatru_religion_in_icela.

90. See above, 88–93.

91. See above, 90–94.

Barbara Ehrenreich provides explicit if perhaps idiosyncratic evidence for this interpretation. Though a professing atheist from childhood to the present, Ehrenreich "realized that the theism I rejected was actually only monotheism, or the particular version of it represented by Christianity, Judaism, and Islam, in which the 'one God' or 'one true God' is not only singular but perfect." Conversely, "amoral gods, polytheistic gods, animal gods—these were all fine with me, if only because they seemed to make no promises and demand no belief."[92] But she does not positively assert the existence of these sorts of deities either. The meaning of her Lone Pine and later epiphanies, as she has come to interpret them, points not to traditional religion but rather to "a world that glowed and pulsed with life through all its countless manifestations, where God or gods or at least a living Presence flamed out from every object."[93] To a modern paganism, once again, that is not so different from the ancient philosophical paganism of the educated classes.

For Dworkin, in short, and for Ehrenreich, and for the millions of "nones," and for the millions more who consider themselves "spiritual," and for the additional millions who report an identification with some traditional denomination but without exhibiting any active belief in a transcendent deity, "religion" (a term they may embrace or may eschew) denotes a world reenchanted with intrinsic meaning and beauty, in the way the world was enchanted before the coming of Christianity. *Not* a world under the stern judgment of the biblical God. Could there be a more apt, succinct description of this position, or this spiritual orientation, than "modern paganism"?

So understood, paganism is hardly a marginal or exotic phenomenon; on the contrary, it arguably surrounds us. At least as a cultural matter, we might say that in it we live and move and have our being.[94]

In this vein, in a book called *Full Circle: How the Classical World Came Back to Us*, Ferdinand Mount argues that "often without our being aware of it, the ways in which we live our rich and varied lives correspond, almost eerily so, to the ways in which the Greeks and Romans lived theirs."[95] It is not just that we *owe* much to the Greeks and Romans; rather, "in so many ways, large and small, trivial and profound, we *are* them, and they are us."[96] Mount acknowledges that his claim runs contrary to "the ideology of moder-

92. Ehrenreich, *Living*, 213.
93. Ehrenreich, *Living*, 215.
94. Cf. Acts 17:28.
95. Ferdinand Mount, *Full Circle: How the Classical World Came Back to Us* (New York: Simon and Schuster, 2010), 1.
96. Mount, *Full Circle*, 3.

nity . . . that we are moving forward and that we are going somewhere new."[97] Nonetheless, he argues, in a series of comparative chapters, that modern society is closer in its assumptions, values, and practices to classical culture than to the intervening Christian culture in a whole variety of areas: science, art, politics, sexuality (where he discerns a "Neo Pagan yearning for a return to the easy, down-to-earth sexual life of the ancient world"),[98] culinary arts, hygiene, and appreciation of the physical body.

And religion. Modern Western societies, Mount contends, closely resemble second-century Rome in its religious propensities—in the smorgasbord of religious options[99] covering over an underlying and immanent spirituality that he labels the "new pantheism." In what might be taken as a one-sentence preview of Dworkin's Einstein Lectures, Mount describes this prevalent faith as one that "sheds an equal radiance over the whole earth and every creature on it, the sort of reverence and admiration for the structure of the universe as revealed by science which have become especially associated with the godlike figure of Albert Einstein."[100]

So it seems that immanent religiosity—modern paganism—is all around us. And where exactly is the sacred located for "modern paganism"? Here there can be no single or uniform answer. Just as classical paganism sponsored countless diverse cults, all fitting comfortably under the broad canopy of immanent religion or "paganism," so also modern paganism takes various forms.[101] For someone like Barbara Ehrenreich, the Other or the Presence

---

97. Mount, *Full Circle*, 6. See also 6 ("We are now hard-wired to expect history to deliver progress, flawed progress marred by horrors usually of our own making, but progress nonetheless").

98. Mount, *Full Circle*, 96.

99. Mount, *Full Circle*, 441:

By the time of the Antonine emperors in the second century AD—that period which Gibbon regarded as the summit of human felicity—Rome was a ferment of religious choice. You could believe in anything or nothing. You could put your trust in astrologers, snake-charmers, prophets and diviners and magicians; you could take your pick between half a dozen creation myths and several varieties of resurrection. Or if you belonged to the educated elite, you could read the poetry of Lucretius and subscribe to a strictly materialist description of the universe.

In short, this is a time when anything goes and the weirdest, most frenzied creations of the human mind jostle with the most beautiful visions, the most inspiring spiritual challenges and the most challenging lines of scientific inquiry. It is hard to think of any period quite like it, before or since—until our own time.

100. Mount, *Full Circle*, 204–5.

101. Writing critically as a Christian theologian, William Cavanaugh asserts that "what

glows through the world in "all its countless manifestations." This would appear to be a modern variation on Balbus's declaration that "the universe is god."[102] Others—environmentalists, for example—locate the sacred in "nature," or in parts of nature: Dworkin gives as an example the Grand Canyon.[103] Some observers perceive in modern progressivism a tendency to exalt or sacralize the state.[104] Still others attach a sacred quality to the individual person. Thus, in discerning "a reemergence of the pagan elements of Western civilization," the distinguished Protestant theologians Carl Braaten and Robert Jenson identify this "neopaganism" with "modern variations of the ancient belief of pre-Christian mystery religions that a divine spark or seed is innate in the individual human soul."[105]

More generally, Terry Eagleton observes that "the history of the modern age is among other things the search for a viceroy for God. Reason, Nature, *Geist*, culture, art, the sublime, the nation, the state, science, humanity, Being, Society, the Other, desire, the life force and personal relations: all of these have acted from time to time as forms of displaced divinity." Eagleton adds that "suitably degutted of its dogma, [religiosity] is then easily wedded with secular modes of thought, and as such can fill ideological gaps and offer spiritual solutions more persuasive than orthodox religion can."[106]

Ross Douthat argues that in America, Christian orthodoxy has increasingly given ground to new movements that Douthat regards as Christian heresies but that might be classified with what I am here calling "modern paganism." Perhaps the most pervasive and influential of Douthat's heresies, especially among cultural elites, is what he calls the "God Within" philosophy, which holds that "somewhere within us all, there does exist a supreme self who is eternally at peace. That supreme Self is our true identity universal and divine." And a person's highest duty is to "honor the divinity that resides

---

remains when humans attempt to clear a space of God's presence is not a disenchanted world but a world full of idols." William T. Cavanaugh, *Migrations of the Holy: God, State, and the Political Meaning of the Church* (Grand Rapids: Eerdmans, 2011), 120.

102. See above, 91.

103. Dworkin, *Religion without God*, 2–3.

104. See especially Benjamin Wiker, *Worshipping the State: How Liberalism Became Our State Religion* (Washington, DC: Regnery, 2013). See also Cavanaugh, *Migrations of the Holy*, 117 (observing that "the nation in Western civilization in many ways replaces the church").

105. Carl E. Braaten and Robert W. Jenson, preface to *Either/Or: The Gospel or Neopaganism*, ed. Carl E. Braaten and Robert W. Jenson (Grand Rapids: Eerdmans, 1995), 14, 7.

106. Terry Eagleton, *Culture and the Death of God* (New Haven: Yale University Press, 2014), 44.

within me."[107] This view seems almost identical to the "neopaganism" discerned by Braaten and Jenson.

The Orthodox and The Pagan

Douthat, however, writes in defense of Christian orthodoxy, as do others. That is an important fact, not to be overlooked. Within the last few pages, it may appear that paganism has gone from being something long since extinct, to an exotic and marginal phenomenon, to the triumphant and almost universal condition of our time. But that conclusion overcorrects. Although immanent religion or "modern paganism" seems to be increasing and growing more conspicuous in the modern world, it has surely not wholly displaced transcendent religion, such as traditional Christianity. There are presumably still many and perhaps millions of believers in transcendent religion—orthodox Christians, devout Jews and Muslims.

For reasons already discussed, there is no way to take an accurate census of pagans and Christians (and devout Jews, etc.). In this context, self-identifications—even sincere ones—are far from reliable. As when Eliot lectured, it is still true that "the great majority of people are neither one thing nor the other, but are living in a no man's land."[108] And a person may be partly Christian and partly pagan, more Christian one day, more pagan the next.

And yet the provocations of the "culture wars" make it harder than it once was to remain neutral or undecided. The old opposition—between Christians and pagans or, more broadly, between transcendent and immanent religious orientations—is once again alive and well and, after many centuries, increasingly out in the open; and more and more people are forced to take a side. We will return to the point in the next chapters.

First, though, we need to conclude by revisiting this chapter's initial theme, from which we may seem to have wandered—namely, secularism.

107. Ross Douthat, *Bad Religion: How We Became a Nation of Heretics* (New York: Free Press, 2012), 215.

108. T. S. Eliot, "The Idea of a Christian Society," in *Christianity and Culture* (New York: Harcourt/Harvest, 1948), 39.

Trisecting the Secular

As we saw earlier, most of the major thinkers over the past couple of centuries had predicted that the modern world would become secular, in the sense of "not religious." Those prophecies seem not to have been fulfilled. On the contrary, as we have seen, traditional religion remains vigorous, and a new and more immanent religiosity—a "religion without God," as Ronald Dworkin puts it—seems to be emerging even in quite unlikely cultural neighborhoods. So, is the upshot that secularization is a myth—that it has not happened and is not going to happen?

Not exactly. But as theorists increasingly recognize, the concept of "the secular" turns out to be more complicated than is sometimes supposed; any simple equation of "secular" with "not religious" is dubious.[109] Some scholars maintain that instead of referring to "secularism," we need to start talking of "secularisms," in the plural.[110] The eminent historian of American religion Martin Marty has begun using the term "religio-secular."[111] For some, the need to rethink the meaning of "secular" is underscored by a case like India's, where the constitution (unlike that of the United States) explicitly provides that government must be "secular" but both culture and politics are pervasively religious.[112]

At least for some purposes, it seems, if we are not going to simply renounce the idea of secularization, then we need "secular" to mean something other than "not religious." But *can* "secular" be severed from "not religious" without becoming mere double-talk, or gobbledygook?

---

109. See Rajeev Bhargava, "Rehabilitating Secularism," in Calhoun, *Rethinking Secularism*, 92. Acknowledging these difficulties and complications, even as he advocates its renewal, Rajeev Bhargava observes that "only someone with blinkered vision would deny the crisis of secularism." See also Jose Casanova, "The Secular, Secularizations, Secularisms," in Calhoun, *Rethinking Secularism*, 54, 63: "For example, American, French, Turkish, Indian, and Chinese secularisms, to name only some paradigmatic and distinctive modes of drawing boundaries between the religious and the secular, represent not only very different patterns of separation of the secular state and religion but also very different models of state regulation and management of religion and of religious pluralism in society."

110. This theme runs through many of the essays in *Rethinking Secularism*. See especially Alfred Stepan, "The Multiple Secularisms of Modern Democratic and Non-Democratic Regimes," in Calhoun, *Rethinking Secularism*, 114. See also Michael Warner et al., eds., *Varieties of Secularism in a Secular Age* (Cambridge, MA: Harvard University Press, 2013).

111. See, e.g., Martin Marty, "Religio-Secular . . . Again," University of Chicago Divinity School, Martin Marty Center for the Public Understanding of Religion, April 24, 2017, https://divinity.uchicago.edu/sightings/religio-secular-again.

112. See Bhargava, "Rehabilitating Secularism."

Perhaps surprisingly, consideration of the term's history suggests that the severance is not only possible but easier than one might suppose; it is more a recovery than a renunciation of the term's core meaning. The term "secular" traces back to the Latin word *saeculum*, meaning "generation" or "age"; the general original sense of the term is something like "of this age" or "of this world."[113] Pagan religion and pagan deities, as we have seen, *were* of this world. So, as we saw in chapters 3, 4, and 5, paganism might accurately be described as a thoroughly and intrinsically secular species of religiosity[114]—even though in paganism the adjective "secular" might seem otiose (like "wet rain" or "cold ice").

The term began to offer a genuine and useful distinction with the rise of Christianity, in which the difference between this world and the next, or between the temporal and the eternal, was crucial.[115] "Secular" now served to distinguish *this world*—the here and now, the "secular" domain—from the next life, or from eternity. The secular domain was still *not* "not religious"; rather, as Nomi Stolzenberg explains, it constituted "a specialized area of God's domain."[116] This sense of the term is perhaps most clearly reflected in the common distinction between the "secular clergy" and the "regular clergy": the label "secular" clergy refers not to priests who have lost their faith or renounced religion, but rather to priests who perform their religious work *in the world*—in a parish—as opposed to priests who retreat from the world to the rule (or *regula*) of a monastery.

Thus, even before modern secularism came onto the scene, two versions of the "secular" were already discernible. The most conspicuous was the Christian version, but we might also refer to the "pagan secular." In both its Christian and pagan versions, "secular" emphatically did *not* mean "not religious."

113. "Secular," English Oxford Living Dictionaries, accessed July 13, 2017, http://www.oxforddictionaries.com/us/definition/american_english/secular.

114. Cf. Paul Veyne, *When Our World Became Christian: 312–394*, trans. Janet Lloyd (Cambridge: Polity Press, 2010), 135 (asserting that "paganism . . . was such a lightweight religion as to constitute a very model of secularity").

115. Charles Taylor thus explains that the concept of the secular became important in Christian discourse in describing "profane time, the time of ordinary historical succession which the human race lives through between the Fall and the Parousia [or second coming of Christ]." Charles Taylor, "Modes of Secularism," in *Secularism and Its Critics*, ed. Rajeev Bhargava (New York: Oxford University Press, 1998), 32. For Taylor's more detailed explanation of the relation of spiritual and secular time in premodern sensibilities, see Charles Taylor, *A Secular Age* (Cambridge, MA: Harvard University Press, 2007), 54–59.

116. Nomi Stolzenberg, "The Profanity of Law," in *Law and the Sacred*, ed. Austin Sarat (Stanford: Stanford University Press, 2007), 51.

Then, in early modernity, usage changed; "secular" came to acquire its more standard contemporary meaning of "not religious."[117] "Modern secularism," Stolzenberg observes, is "reductive." It "eliminates the tension between [the profane and the sacred] by simply preserving one and discarding the other."[118] This newer conception seems most resonant with the naturalistic worldview associated with modern science, as we have discussed. We might describe this as the "positivistic" conception of the secular, in contrast to the Christian and pagan versions. And it was this positivistic or "not religious" kind of secularism that was ostensibly foreordained to dominate modern thought and culture.

In sum, history has handed down to us three broad categories or families of "the secular." There is the *pagan secular*, in which heavy if not exclusive emphasis is placed on this world and this life, but this world and this life (or at least some parts or aspects of this world or this life) are viewed as having a sacred quality. Then there is the *Christian secular*, in which this temporal world and this life are a "specialized area of God's domain." As such, this life has value—indeed, immense value—because it is a (subordinate) piece of the larger domain of eternity. Finally, there is the distinctively modern *positivistic secular* reflected in the naturalistic worldview associated with modern science. This is the "not religious" and "disenchanted" world of Weber, Russell, Stace, and company. These three versions of the secular correspond to the three existential orientations we have considered earlier.

Each of these secular possibilities—and each of these existential orientations—remains available to people today, and each has its adherents. Perhaps ironically, however, positivistic secularism seems to be the official version, so to speak, and yet in reality to have the smallest constituency and the least political influence. Its official status is manifest in the fact, as noted, that "secular" is today typically taken to *mean* "not religious," and it is only the positivistic secularism that does not recognize "the sacred" and hence is genuinely not religious (in a conventional sense, and also as we have conceived of religion in chapter 2). But although there is no way to take an accurate head count, the positivistic version of secularism probably has the fewest real adherents. Most people, even including thoroughly worldly mem-

---

117. Cf. John Ayto, *Dictionary of Word Origins: Histories of More Than 8,000 English-Language Words* (New York: Arcade, 1990), 465: "**secular** Latin *saeculum*, a word of uncertain origin, meant 'generation, age.' It was used in early Christian texts for the 'temporal world' (as opposed to the 'spiritual world'). . . . The more familiar modern English meaning 'non-religious' emerged in the 16th century."

118. Stolzenberg, "The Profanity of Law," 35.

bers of the cultural elite like Dworkin, are probably *not* simply secular *in the positivistic sense*. They believe in science, to be sure, but they also embrace commitments and endorse values that are not reducible to the materialistic or naturalistic terms and entities that science studies.

As a test question, we might ask people today whether they think it is acceptable and desirable to use human beings—perhaps old or disabled ones—as mere material subjects for scientific research, as was done in Nazi Germany. Or whether it is acceptable to resolve social and political conflicts by simply exterminating particularly troublesome ethnic groups or human populations where this can be done without undue cost or difficulty. Nearly everyone will recoil with indignation from these questions, and will protest that such measures are impermissible and indeed monstrous. We may *say*, with Stephen Hawking, that "the human race is just a chemical scum on a moderate-sized planet."[119] We may even concede the logic, on purely scientific grounds, of Nobel Prize–winning molecular biologist Jacques Monod's dismissal of Western liberal humanism as "a disgusting farrago of Judeo-Christian religiosity, scientistic progressism, belief in the 'natural rights' of man and utilitarian pragmatism."[120] And yet most people today seem utterly unwilling to embrace the normative implications of those deflationary views.[121]

Luc Ferry makes the point with a different example. "I am sure," Ferry says, "that if you witnessed the lynching of somebody because of the colour of his skin, or on account of his religion, you would do what was in your power to help him, even if to do so was dangerous. And if you were to lack the courage, . . . you would nevertheless admit to yourself that, morally this is what ought to happen. And if the person being attacked was someone you love, then you would probably take enormous risks to save him or her."[122] In this taking of enormous risks, Ferry continues, there is a willingness to sacrifice. "Sacrifice, which returns us to the notion of a value regarded as *sacred* (both from the Latin 'sacer'), paradoxically retains, even for the committed materialist, an aspect which can almost be described as religious." More specifically, we see in this commitment "a *making sacred of the human*."[123]

119. Quoted in Paul Davies, *Cosmic Jackpot*, 222.

120. Quoted in Joseph Vining, *The Song Sparrow and the Child: Claims of Science and Humanity* (Notre Dame: University of Notre Dame Press, 2004), 50.

121. For a searching exploration of this conflict, see Vining, *From Newton's Sleep*.

122. Ferry, *Brief History of Thought*, 243.

123. Ferry, *Brief History of Thought*, 244, 245.

Perhaps there are exceptions—the playwright George Bernard Shaw, for example. "Throughout his life," John Gray reports, "the great playwright argued in favour of mass extermination as an alternative to imprisonment. It was better to kill the socially useless, he urged, than to waste public money locking them up."[124] But if this was indeed Shaw's position, nearly all of us would react to it with horror—because, we would say, human life is "sacred," or "inviolable," or "infinitely precious," or something of that sort. Insofar as we insist on some such proposition, we depart from the positivistic secular in favor of something else—perhaps the transcendent secularism of traditional Christianity or Judaism, or perhaps the more immanent sacredness of modern paganism.

In sum, positivistic or naturalistic secularism may be appropriate to our scientific enterprises. But in the realm of moral and political discourse, it has a more complicated and less exclusive role. People do have their "interests," and the use of science in the instrumentalist effort to satisfy those interests is perfectly appropriate. Economists, practitioners of the "dismal science," are not evil; on the contrary, they perform a function that is valuable and necessary. And yet the near universal and categorical condemnations of genocide, and the widespread assertions of human rights said to grow out of some quality of intrinsic "human dignity," suggest that most people and most governments today also have a continuing commitment to the sacred in some form. Perhaps to the transcendental sacred of Christianity and associated faiths. Or perhaps to the immanent sacred of "modern paganism."

Under Cover of Secularism

And so we return to the metaphor proposed at the beginning of this chapter—of secularism as a facade. Descriptions of the modern world as "secular" are, it seems, accurate and at the same time profoundly unilluminating, even obfuscating.

Thus, politics today concerns itself with *this* world, not the next world (if there is a next world). Even the most ardent activists on the "religious right" do not defend favored policies on the ground that these will send more people to heaven.[125] And today's pervasively consumerist culture immerses

124. See Gray, *Straw Dogs*, 94.

125. For discussion, see Steven D. Smith, "The Constitution and the Goods of Religion," in *Dimensions of Goodness*, ed. Vittorio Hösle (Newcastle, UK: Cambridge Scholars, 2013), 328–33.

us in the here and now; it does not defer gratification to—or seem to put much stock in—the life to come. So the political world today, and much of the cultural world as well, are thoroughly "secular" in the *older* sense of "concerned with this world."

But modern life—modern political life in particular—is *not* "secular" in the *modern* sense of "not religious." Nearly everyone continues to attach "sacred" status to something or other—if not to God and the angels, then to nature, or to the human person (or at least to *some* human persons at some stages of development), or to the state, or to some sacralized conception of the course of history, or to something else. The political and cultural struggles of our time grow out of these competing sanctities. "Modern politics is a chapter in the history of religion," the political philosopher John Gray observes; as an agnostic and secularist in the positivistic sense, he offers the observation with a sigh.[126]

To be sure, insofar as the pertinent categories presented to us by modern culture are still "religion" and the "secular," and insofar as the "secular" is deemed more respectable for the political and philosophical reasons suggested at the outset of this chapter, many educated people will still classify themselves as "secular"—and hence, by implication, "not religious." Their commitments to the sacred will be largely inarticulate and ad hoc. They may stand zealously and righteously on their commitments to human rights or equality or the environment, but they will not acknowledge that these commitments are a form of "religion," or of an intuition of the sacred.

Often they will still struggle to present their positions in terms of "interests." The reason we must sacrifice urgently and presently needed energy and jobs to preserve some obscure and minuscule species, such as the snail darter, they may say, is that the species just might turn out at some future date to have some unforeseeable medicinal value;[127] this remote possibility, which on its own terms would convince no one to sacrifice significant present interests, serves to give positivistic respectability to a more obscure judgment about the sanctity of a species.

Some decades ago, G. K. Chesterton observed that in many such controversies, what we see is "a fight of creeds masquerading as policies." And he noted that "we have contrived to invent a new kind of hypocrite. The old hypocrite . . . was a man whose aims were really worldly and practical, while he pretended that they were religious. The new hypocrite is one

126. Gray, *Black Mass*, 1.
127. John Copeland Nagle, "Playing Noah," *Minnesota Law Review* 82 (1998): 1171, 1208.

whose aims are really religious, while he pretends that they are worldly and practical."[128]

Comfortable descriptions of our world and our age as "secular" thus work to make us opaque to ourselves. Ronald Dworkin was among the more articulate philosophers of our time, and his identification of the pervasive religiosity lying beneath the surface of ostensibly positivistic secularism was a contribution we can appreciate. But Dworkin also recognized that although millions of people in fact adhere to something like his immanent religion, most of them would not think—or, probably, consent—to describe themselves in this way. They are, Dworkin implied, religious without knowing it. Theologians like Karl Rahner argued, controversially, that many devotees of non-Christian religions are in reality "anonymous Christians";[129] Dworkin showed that many self-proclaimed secularists are in fact "anonymous religionists." Or, most likely, "anonymous pagans."

One consequence of this situation is that on surveys of religiosity, these people—these immanent religionists—will check the box for "none," or perhaps the box for "agnostic." Or, sometimes, for "Catholic" or "Jewish," even though these reports reveal next to nothing about what the respondents *really* believe and about what they *really* hold sacred. Nor is it just the surveys that are insufficient; the modern conceptual scheme, still in thrall to an ostensibly inevitable positivistic secularism, may not offer the immanently devout the conceptual resources to describe *even to themselves* what they really believe and hold sacred.

Pundits and scholars and social scientists will accordingly continue to describe the social and political world and its movements in terms of "religious" versus "secular," even though these categories do more to conceal than to reveal the real motivations and values of the relevant actors. And thus, as T. S. Eliot suggested in the essay that provoked and gives shape to this book, "the current terms in which we describe our society . . . only operate to deceive and stupefy us."[130]

Modern paganism, in sum, is alive and even pervasive—but mostly inarticulate, and concealed (even from itself). We cannot count on it openly to declare itself; we can only attempt to discern its influence, its manifestations,

128. G. K. Chesterton, *What's Wrong with the World* (Lexington, KY: CreateSpace, [1910] 2016), 15.

129. See Jacques Dupuis, SJ, *Toward a Christian Theology of Religious Pluralism* (New York: Orbis, 1997), 143–49.

130. Eliot, "The Idea of a Christian Society," 6–7.

and its occasional self-expressions. The next two chapters will attempt such discernment with respect to the contemporary "culture wars."

Postscript

After this book had been submitted for publication, Anthony Kronman, the eminent legal scholar and former Yale Law School dean (and, as it happens, my former teacher in, of all things, Uniform Commercial Code), published his massive *Confessions of a Born-Again Pagan*.[131] Running to over eleven hundred pages, the book is an intensive spiritual-philosophical reexamination of Western thought from Aristotle through Augustine through Spinoza and up to more modern thinkers including Nietzsche and Heidegger. And that reexamination culminates, as the title indicates, in a philosophy or orientation toward life that Kronman describes as "pagan"—a term Kronman understands in much the same sense of immanent religiosity proposed here.

As the title also suggests, Kronman's book seems calculated to be a sort of sequel/counter to Augustine's famous *Confessions*. Just as that book narrated the saint's conversion from paganism to Christianity, Kronman criticizes Christianity and its influences and (in an early chapter) describes his own more contemporary conversion—not from Christianity but rather from Marxism back to paganism. If Augustine's spiritual autobiography was reflective of the Christian revolution of the period in which that book was written, Kronman's tome reflects the contemporary movement to throw off the effects of that revolution and recapture something like the classical or "pagan" orientation that preceded it.

Given the book's length and depth, and considering that my own book had effectively been completed before his was published, it has seemed prudent to resist the temptation to incorporate or respond to Kronman's *Confessions* in any serious way here. The book represents a major intellectual achievement that deserves close and deliberate study and reflection, not hasty reaction. It seems not amiss, though, to observe that the book provides weighty evidence for the central argument of this chapter.

When this chapter was being written, Kronman's book was unavailable; I accordingly used Dworkin's *Religion without God* as "Exhibit A" evidencing the development of "modern paganism." But Kronman's book might have

---

131. Anthony T. Kronman, *Confessions of a Born-Again Pagan* (New Haven: Yale University Press, 2016).

served even better. Like Dworkin, Kronman finds the theism of Christianity and Judaism impossible to accept but thinks a more immanent religiosity is defensible, and attractive. Also like Dworkin, he offers Spinoza as the seminal theorist or exponent of a more immanent faith that is the appropriate modern alternative to Christian and Jewish theism. Kronman's argument is more extensively developed. And, perhaps most conveniently, Kronman actually recognizes his position as "pagan," and openly calls it that.

Without pretending to offer any full-scale analysis or critique, therefore, I offer Kronman's book as a further and substantial piece of evidence supporting the interpretation advanced here.

CHAPTER 10

Counterrevolution, Part I:
Symbols, Sex, and the Constitution

Rome, we saw in chapter 3, was the city of the gods—a city whose might, opulence, and splendor were sustained and consecrated by the worship of the pagan gods. That religion could embrace numerous and sundry cults and deities—by in effect absorbing or annexing them. But it could not embrace the Jerusalem-based faiths, Judaism and Christianity, which (as we saw in chapter 5) represented a radically new, different, and unassimilable form of religiosity—one devoted to a single *transcendent* deity rather than to a sprawling pantheon of *immanent* deities. Thus, as Christianity began to grow in the empire, Roman authorities correctly perceived the new faith as subversive (despite sincere protestations of loyalty by Christians like Tertullian) and as threatening. The authorities responded to that threat by episodically persecuting Christianity and, in the "Great Persecution" at the beginning of the fourth century, attempting to eradicate it.

The attempt failed, and so the fourth century witnessed an epic, back-and-forth cultural and political and sometimes military struggle between Christianity and paganism for mastery within the city. (We can see this in hindsight, although contemporaries often could not perceive the nature of that struggle.) By century's end, Christianity had prevailed—in the *political* struggle, that is. Christianity's political dominance persisted in the ensuing centuries; observers like T. S. Eliot could accordingly describe the nations that arose after the decline of Rome as "Christian societies," even though the practical substance of those societies sometimes, or rather always, fell dismally short of Christian ideals.

And yet paganism was hardly eliminated; rather, it continued to exist just beneath the surface, and often hidden in plain sight, in the variety of ways we considered in chapter 8. One mode of continued existence was in the Western historical imagination. A persistent and recurring regret for the loss of the "merry dance of paganism," together with resentment of the oppressive force that had ostensibly turned out the lights on that "merry dance"—namely, Christianity—inspired countless theories, books, tracts, poems, works of art, secular sermons, and fulminations of all sorts. And in recent times, immanent religiosity or "modern paganism" in a variety of forms—we have taken Ronald Dworkin's "religion without god" as a cogent manifestation—has begun to reassert itself openly and unashamedly.

In these circumstances, it should hardly be surprising—it might well be inevitable—that paganism would at some point challenge the increasingly tattered and threadbare canopy of Christianity. It would be unsurprising, in other words, if paganism might attempt to reclaim the city that Christianity wrested away from it centuries ago.

And in fact, that is what has happened. The latter part of the twentieth century and the beginning of the twenty-first have witnessed a renewal of the fourth-century struggle between Christianity and paganism—a struggle seeking to reverse the "revolution" that Christianity achieved in late antiquity. As with the ancient struggle, the modern one may become clearer as the years pass and give us a more detached perspective. But even now the struggle is discernible, if we are willing to see it.

This at least is one way—and, I will suggest in this chapter, a perspicuous way—of understanding the salient cultural, legal, and political conflicts of our times. This interpretation, like all interpretations, is to some extent an artificial imposition upon a complex and messy reality. Modern pagans, like ancient ones, typically do not label themselves or conceive of themselves as "pagans." (Although sometimes they do—Anthony Kronman, for example.)[1] More generally, as we saw in the last chapter, self-identification—whether by pagans or by putative Christians, putative atheists, putative "nones," or people who deem themselves "spiritual but not religious"—is in this context profoundly unilluminating and unreliable. And people often slide unawares between one category and another, and back again, and again. Ours is a situation in which, as Matthew Arnold put it, "ignorant armies clash by night"[2]—on a whole variety of levels and issues. The interpretation of our period as one in which the fourth-century struggle between Christianity and

---

1. See Anthony T. Kronman, *Confessions of a Born-Again Pagan* (New Haven: Yale University Press, 2016).

2. Matthew Arnold, "Dover Beach," Poetry Foundation, accessed July 13, 2017, https://www.poetryfoundation.org/poems/43588/dover-beach.

paganism is being reenacted will nonetheless be useful just to the extent that it provides illumination into our profoundly confused and confusing times.

One caveat: although a parallel struggle is arguably occurring through much of the Western world (and perhaps beyond), the precise political and legal developments will be different from place to place. For reasons both of scope and limited competence, the following discussion will focus on developments in the United States. Readers with more intimate knowledge of other regions and countries will judge to what extent similar developments are discernible in other places.

How We Got Here: From Civic Religion to Culture Wars

In 1892, in a case aptly or perhaps portentously entitled *Holy Trinity Church v. United States*, the Supreme Court declared that "this is a Christian nation."[3] A century later, the Court's declaration would be seen by many as an embarrassment,[4] comparable in its offensiveness to the Court's approval four years later of the "separate but equal" doctrine that effectively put an official imprimatur on the segregationist "Jim Crow" position.[5] At the time it was uttered, however, the Court's statement in *Holy Trinity Church* would likely have seemed to most Americans little more than an obvious truism. The nation was not *officially* Christian, of course, in the way that, say, England was officially Anglican, but it was pervasively if sometimes amorphously Christian in its culture and substance.[6]

Thus, the Court supported its "Christian nation" interpretation with a lengthy recitation of an array of laws and "organic utterances" going all the way back to Columbus.[7] And indeed, more recent studies by scholar after scholar have vindicated the Court's interpretation, showing how pervasive

3. Holy Trinity Church v. United States, 143 U.S. 457, 470 (1892).

4. See, e.g., Adrian Vermeule, "Legislative History and the Limits of Judicial Competence: The Untold Story of Holy Trinity Church," *Stanford Law Review* 50 (1998): 1844 (describing the case as "notorious in the distinct context of debates about religious liberty").

5. Plessy v. Ferguson, 163 U.S. 537 (1896).

6. See John Fea, *Was America Founded as a Christian Nation? A Historical Introduction* (Louisville: Westminster John Knox, 2011), 21 ("Between 1789 and 1865 Americans—North and South, Union and Confederate—understood themselves to be citizens of a Christian nation. . . . Despite the religious skepticism of many of the founders, evangelical Protestantism . . . defined the culture").

7. *Holy Trinity Church*, 143 U.S. at 471.

Christian or biblical assumptions were in public and political discourse during the colonizing and founding periods and continuing through the nineteenth century.[8] Sometimes the scholars report this situation critically, even bitterly;[9] nonetheless, the basic fact is well attested.

In this vein, the sociologist Robert Bellah's influential scholarship described a prevalent public philosophy or national self-understanding that he called "civil religion." "By civil religion," he explained, "I refer to that religious dimension, found I think in the life of every people, through which it interprets its historical experience in the light of *transcendent reality*."[10] Citing the appeals to deity in the Declaration of Independence, Bellah argued that "it is significant that the reference to a suprapolitical sovereignty, to a God who stands above the nation and whose ends are standards by which to judge the nation and indeed only in terms of which the nation's existence is justified, becomes a permanent feature of American political life ever after."[11]

American civil religion, Bellah showed, was a species of Christianity, or at least a biblically based form of public religion.[12] "[Americans] saw themselves as being a 'people' in the classical and biblical sense of the word."[13] Like other faiths, American civil religion had its sacred texts (the Declaration of Independence, the Constitution), its prophets (Washington, Jefferson, Lincoln), its martyrs (Lincoln, later Martin Luther King Jr.), its theologians (Lincoln again),[14] its holy days (Independence Day,

8. The sources and studies are so numerous that citation of any particular study is largely arbitrary. For examples, see Mark A. Noll, *America's God: From Jonathan Edwards to Abraham Lincoln* (New York: Oxford University Press, 2002); Michael Novak, *On Two Wings: Humble Faith and Common Sense at the American Founding* (San Francisco: Encounter Books, 2003). Frank Lambert explains that "despite sectarian differences, the thirteen states were overwhelmingly Protestant, and Protestantism provided the moral foundation for society. In their ardent belief that they were God's chosen people, Americans interpreted history through a moral lens: good times pointed to divine blessing; bad times indicated divine disapproval" (Frank Lambert, *Religion in American Politics* [Princeton: Princeton University Press, 2008], 19–20).

9. See, e.g., David Sehat, *The Myth of American Religious Freedom* (New York: Oxford University Press, 2011).

10. Robert N. Bellah, *The Broken Covenant: American Civil Religion in Time of Trial* (Chicago: University of Chicago Press, 1975), 3 (emphasis added).

11. Bellah, *The Broken Covenant*, 174.

12. Bellah, *The Broken Covenant*, 168 (suggesting that "the American republic, which has neither an established church nor a classic civil religion, is, after all, a Christian republic, or I should say a biblical republic, in which biblical religion is indeed the civil religion").

13. Bellah, *The Broken Covenant*, 2.

14. See Bellah, *The Broken Covenant*, 179 (describing Lincoln as "our greatest, perhaps our only, civil theologian").

Memorial Day, Veterans Day), its rituals (presidential inaugurations, State of the Union addresses, Fourth of July parades and fireworks). This situation continued into the 1960s, when Bellah began writing on the subject. "Biblical imagery provided the basic framework for imaginative thought in America up until quite recent times and unconsciously, its control is still formidable."[15]

To be sure, in the first half of the twentieth century, the religious landscape had become more complicated. The hegemony of the "nonsectarian" ecumenical Protestantism of the nineteenth century was broken.[16] Even so, by the 1950s, public religiosity remained strong, and conspicuous. This was the era of "piety on the Potomac," joined in by all branches of government. President Eisenhower repeatedly endorsed the importance of religion to the American way of life.[17] Borrowing from Lincoln's Gettysburg Address, Congress added the words "under God" to the Pledge of Allegiance and ratified the national motto (already announced many decades earlier in the national anthem): In God We Trust.[18] And the Supreme Court declared, not that we are a "Christian nation," as it had said in 1892, but rather and more ecumenically that "we are a religious people whose institutions presuppose a Supreme Being."[19]

15. Bellah, *The Broken Covenant*, 12.

16. For discussions of this change, see, e.g., Andrew Koppelman, *Defending American Religious Neutrality* (Cambridge, MA: Harvard University Press, 2013), 28–42; Kevin M. Schultz, *Tri-Faith America: How Catholics and Jews Held Postwar America to Its Protestant Promise* (New York: Oxford University Press, 2011). On nineteenth-century "nonsectarianism," see Noah Feldman, *Divided by God: America's Church-State Problem—and What We Should Do about It* (New York: Farrar, Straus and Giroux, 2005), 61–62, 109.

17. For a somewhat disdainful contemporary account, see William Lee Miller, *Piety along the Potomac: Notes on Politics and Morals in the '50s* (New York: Houghton Mifflin, 1964). See p. 41 (report dated August 17, 1954): "The manifestations of religion in Washington have become pretty thick. We have had opening prayers, Bible breakfasts, special church services, prayer groups, a 'Back to God' crusade, and campaign speeches on 'spiritual values'; now we have added a postage stamp, a proposed Constitutional amendment, and a change in the Pledge of Allegiance. The Pledge, which has served well enough in times more pious than ours, has now had its rhythm upset but its anti-Communist spirituality improved by the insertion of the phrase 'under God.' The Postmaster General has held a dedications ceremony, at which the President and the Secretary of State explained about spiritual values and such, to launch a new red, white, and blue eight-cent stamp bearing the motto 'In God We Trust.' A bill has been introduced directing the post office to cancel mail with the slogan 'Pray for Peace.'"

18. "History of 'In God We Trust,'" U.S. Department of the Treasury, last updated March 8, 2011, https://www.treasury.gov/about/education/Pages/in-god-we-trust.aspx.

19. Zorach v. Clauson, 343 U.S. 306, 312 (1952).

Moreover, the public religiosity was still discernibly biblical in nature. Will Herberg wrote his classic *Protestant-Catholic-Jew*, elaborating on "the conception of the three 'communions'—Protestantism, Catholicism, Judaism—as three diverse, but equally legitimate, equally American, expressions of an over-all American religion."[20] Significantly, all three supporting "communions" were grounded in the Bible. Or, in other words, in a transcendent religiosity.

From the beginning, the ongoing existence of a general rough consensus about an increasingly inclusive civil religion emphatically did not mean that American culture and politics were happily harmonious; any such suggestion would of course be preposterous. To name just the most obvious and horrific counterexample, there was the enormity of slavery, leading to the unfathomable agonies of the Civil War. And yet, paradoxical or shameful as the fact may be, even that catastrophic conflict was fought out, explained, and rationalized, on both sides, largely under the encompassing canopy of the biblical civil religion.[21] As Lincoln recalled in his Second Inaugural Address, surely the most profound public reflection ever offered by an American political leader, Americans had fought over slavery, but they had "read the same Bible and prayed to the same God." Their common commitment to the same Bible and the same God was the premise on which Lincoln could interpret the war for the nation as a working out of divine justice, and on which he could issue his celebrated call for reconciliation: "With malice toward none, with charity for all . . ."

Bellah believed that although the American civil religion had endured and developed through most of the nation's history, it was in the process of disintegrating by the late 1960s and early 1970s. The civil religion had become "an empty and broken shell."[22] "We have lost our sense of direction."[23]

So then, what would follow the dissolution of this guiding narrative? The answer was in effect announced by another prominent sociologist, James Davison Hunter, in a 1991 book called *Culture Wars*. Hunter found that across a surprising variety of issues ranging from education to family to media to law and politics, Americans were increasingly coalescing into two broad and contending camps, which he labeled "orthodox" and "progres-

---

20. Will Herberg, *Protestant-Catholic-Jew: An Essay in American Religious Sociology* (Chicago: University of Chicago Press, [1955] 1983), 87.

21. See Noll, *America's God*, 367–438.

22. Bellah, *The Broken Covenant*, 142.

23. Bellah, *The Broken Covenant*, 153. See also 162 ("The present spiritual condition of America is not very cheering").

sive."[24] The former maintained continuity with the old, biblically oriented civil religion, while the latter challenged it.[25]

Consequently, the earlier situation in which Americans might disagree fiercely and even violently over issues like slavery but still be united under a common commitment to "the same Bible" and "the same God" emphatically no longer obtained; on the contrary, the authority of the Bible and the relevance of God were major points of disagreement. Though living side by side as Americans, orthodox and progressive citizens held to moral conceptions so different that each effectively inhabited "a separate and competing moral galaxy."[26]

Critics objected that Hunter had exaggerated the cultural divisions and that the polar positions he described were occupied mostly by activists, not ordinary Americans. To be fair, Hunter himself had explained that the major disagreements were mostly among "elites."[27] Even so, the critics may have had a point. The early 1990s seem at least in retrospect and by comparison to the present a relatively placid time in which Congress and president could join in near unanimity in passing a law giving strong protection to religious freedom—more on that in the next chapter—and in which the inflammatory issue of same-sex marriage was barely visible on the political horizon. But if Hunter overstated his case *then*, it seems that his assessment is cogent *now*: in the two and a half decades since his book was published,[28] political and cultural polarization has increased dramatically.[29] Thus, Hunter's diagnosis seems even more apt today than when it was first offered.

Three features emphasized by Hunter are especially pertinent to our inquiry. First, Hunter explained that the different cultural orientations represented more than differences of opinion on private matters. Rather, the competing sides in the culture wars pressed conflicting visions of "how we are to live our life together."[30] Each side was struggling to "define Amer-

24. James Davison Hunter, *Culture Wars: The Struggle to Define America* (New York: Basic Books, 1991), 43–44.

25. See Hunter, *Culture Wars*, 120–25.

26. Hunter, *Culture Wars*, 128.

27. Hunter, *Culture Wars*, 59.

28. For an update and debate, see James Davison Hunter and Alan Wolfe, *Is There a Culture War? A Dialogue on Values and American Public Life* (Washington, DC: Brookings Institution Press, 2007).

29. See, e.g., "Political Polarization in the American Public," Pew Research Center, June 12, 2014, http://www.people-press.org/2014/06/12/political-polarization-in-the-american-public.

30. Hunter, *Culture Wars*, 50–51.

ica," as Hunter's subtitle put it. So the culture war was and is a struggle for "domination"[31]—for control of the cultural and political community and the self-conception by which the community constitutes and governs itself.[32]

A second feature of the conflict follows directly from the first. Thus, Hunter explained that in the struggle to define America, symbols and discourse are crucial.[33] Consequently, each side "struggles to *monopolize the symbols of legitimacy.*"[34]

In this vein, we might say that the cultural combatants have intuitively understood the main claim of an admired academic study—we noted it already in considering the struggle in ancient Rome over symbols[35]—which persuasively contends that political communities are "imagined."[36] What transforms a collection of people into a "community," in other words, rather than merely an assortment of disparate individuals and groups buzzing around and bouncing off each other, is not simply the empirical fact of geographic proximity. Communities are not physical objects; they are conjured up and consolidated, rather, in people's imaginations—in their minds and souls. People constitute a community because, often for complex and elusive reasons, they think of themselves, or *imagine themselves*, as a community. And the imaginings that create a community arise around and in response to—and express and maintain themselves in—symbols and discourse; public symbols *express* the character of the community, but even more importantly, they help to *constitute* that character. And so, not surprisingly, the culture wars have been in large measure a struggle to control public symbols.

31. Hunter, *Culture Wars*, 52.

32. When the conflict is described as one for "domination," of course, neither side may seem especially attractive. Americans, with their historic commitment to liberty, are unlikely to sympathize with a party that strives for "domination." Advocates on both sides take advantage of this fact. In this vein, Martha Nussbaum accuses the Religious Right of wanting to "lord it over" their fellow citizens; Martha C. Nussbaum, *Liberty of Conscience: In Defense of America's Tradition of Religious Equality* (New York: Basic Books, 2009), 8, 28, while Jonah Goldberg describes the progressive agenda as one of "liberal fascism"; Jonah Goldberg, *Liberal Fascism* (New York: Doubleday, 2009). It should be remembered, though, that in a culture war, as in other kinds of war, the likely alternative to *dominating* is *being dominated*. We may be more sympathetic if we recognize that both sides are struggling to avoid being dominated, culturally and politically.

33. Hunter, *Culture Wars*, 58.

34. Hunter, *Culture Wars*, 147.

35. See above, 172–76.

36. Benedict Anderson, *Imagined Communities* (London: Verso, 2006).

A third crucial insight in Hunter's study was that the contemporary culture wars revolve around religion. "The struggle for power . . . is in large part a struggle between competing truth claims, claims which by their very nature are 'religious' in character if not in content."[37] But the important religious differences today are not those that mattered in early modern and even relatively recent history. In centuries past, "wars of religion" had pitted Catholics against Protestants, and sometimes Protestants against other Protestants. By contrast, current cultural alignments and coalitions cut across denominational fault lines.[38] In place of the older, denominational disagreements, Hunter now saw the opposing coalitions as manifestations of competing "moral visions" or competing views of "moral authority"[39]—competing visions with their respective and competing religious groundings.

Thus, the "orthodox" coalition was united by a commitment to "an external, definable, and *transcendent* source of authority." In this view, "moral and spiritual truths have a supernatural origin beyond . . . human experience."[40] By contrast, the "progressive" camp was composed of "secularists" and also of persons who, though counting themselves religious, looked more to "*inner-worldly* sources of moral authority."[41]

In short, the conflicting orientations—toward "transcendent" or conversely toward "inner-worldly" sources of moral authority—reflected, and reflect, the competing transcendent and immanent religiosities we have been discussing in this book. Each kind of religiosity is struggling to "define America." In that sense, the condition of contemporary America is comparable to that of fourth-century Rome, when Christianity and paganism, each with its powerful representatives (Theodosius and Julian, Ambrose and Symmachus), struggled for mastery within the city. In the remainder of this chapter we will look at three partly overlapping theaters of that struggle: symbols or expressions of public religiosity, public recognition and ratification of the norms of sexuality, and the Constitution itself.

In the first two of these arenas, the effort has been to remove elements that have borne a Christian or biblical character, leaving symbols or messages or sexual norms that are "secular" in the positivistic or immanently religious sense. With respect to the Constitution, by contrast, the dynamic has been somewhat different. From the outset, the framers of the Constitu-

37. Hunter, *Culture Wars*, 58.
38. Hunter, *Culture Wars*, 47, 86–88.
39. Hunter, *Culture Wars*, 48, 42.
40. Hunter, *Culture Wars*, 120.
41. Hunter, *Culture Wars*, 124.

tion consciously declined to use the document to endorse Christianity or biblical religion.[42] Rather, the document was designed to be a sort of meta-legal instrument, or a framework for governance, under which (subject to a few entrenched and more substantive commitments—to freedom of speech, for example) the states and the nation could pursue and express whatever policies or principles "we the people" might embrace. To be sure, particular restrictions, such as those of the First Amendment's religion clauses, might reflect Christian or biblical assumptions; we will say more on that subject in the following chapter. But the document itself—and the overall framework it created—were agnostic in matters of religion; they were compatible with a Christian nation, a pagan nation, a pluralistic nation, or a nation mostly devoid of religious convictions and commitments.

In recent decades, however, activists and lawyers in the "progressive" camp have worked—with considerable success—to reconceive and reconstruct the Constitution as an instrument that can be used to resist and invalidate the earlier civil religion and its manifestations. In this context, therefore, the struggle has not been to transform a Christian element into a pagan one, but rather to capture what had previously been a more neutral framework or arrangement for governance and turn it to the cause of secularism or immanent religion. This development is especially portentous because, insofar as it has succeeded, it has transformed a revered and previously inclusive authoritative artifact—the Constitution—into a partisan weapon, and has thereby undermined the ability of that authority to hold together a community increasingly divided between "orthodox" and "progressive" constituencies.

The Struggle over Public Religious Symbols

Symbols, once again, are expressive but also constitutive of community. Thus, in fourth-century Rome, as we saw in chapter 7, the struggle for control between paganism and Christianity was in large part a struggle over symbols. The Altar of Victory intermittently placed outside the Senate House in Rome was symptomatic of but also to a degree constitutive of the community; hence the back-and-forth conflict over the shrine. The altar had been preserved under the pagan emperors, and had manifested the com-

---

42. The point is developed in Isaac Kramnick and L. Laurence Moore, *The Godless Constitution: A Moral Defense of the Secular State* (New York: Norton, 2005), 150–206.

munity's dedication to pagan religion. With the ascendancy of Christianity under Constantius, the altar had been removed, but it was returned to its place during the short-lived pagan revival of the emperor Julian. Then, under Gratian, it was again removed, and the eloquent pleas of the pagan senator Symmachus were rejected by the Christian emperors. In a similar way, the erection of impressive Christian churches and their domination of city skylines, accompanied by the closure and sometimes the destruction of the pagan temples, helped to signal and solidify the political supremacy of Christianity.[43]

In the American republic, likewise, from the founders to the present, statesmen and citizens have appreciated the significance of public symbols. Through much of the nation's history, central symbols have been biblical in character. Thus, in the first committee to craft a seal for the new nation, Benjamin Franklin favored an image of Moses standing on the shore of the Red Sea, while Thomas Jefferson proposed a depiction of the children of Israel in the wilderness being led by a cloud by day and a pillar of fire by night. (John Adams favored a more pagan symbol—a picture of Hercules.) The Continental Congress deliberated with some care, and ended up approving a symbol containing the "Eye of Providence" that stares at us from above on every dollar bill.[44] And of course the national motto (In God We Trust), though not formally approved by Congress until the 1950s, traces back to the proclamation in "The Star-Spangled Banner": "And this be our motto, in God is our trust."

It should hardly be surprising, therefore, that as immanent religion has risen to challenge the dominance of Christian or transcendent religiosity, the dominance of transcendent public religious symbols would be increasingly resented and resisted. And that is what has happened.

The Shift to Symbolism. A principal instrument through which this resistance has worked has been the nonestablishment clause of the First Amendment ("Congress shall make no law respecting an establishment of religion . . ."). For almost four decades after the United States Supreme Court began in the 1940s to interpret and impose that clause in a serious way, most of the major controversies involved disputes over money and material resources. The big majority of cases decided by the Court involved public as-

---

43. Peter Brown, *Power and Persuasion in Late Antiquity: Towards a Christian Empire* (Madison: University of Wisconsin Press, 1992), 120–21.

44. "Portraits & Designs," U.S. Department of the Treasury, last updated December 1, 2015, https://www.treasury.gov/resource-center/faqs/Currency/Pages/edu_faq_currency_por traits.aspx; see also Derek H. Davis, *Religion and the Continental Congress, 1774–1789* (New York: Oxford University Press, 2000), 138–40.

sistance in various forms to religious schools.[45] Tax exemptions for religious institutions were another subject of controversy.[46] While not disappearing, these subjects, since the mid-1980s, seem to have receded in prominence, and a different set of controversies has taken center stage—namely, conflicts over public religious symbols.

Litigants and other advocates accordingly do never-ending battle, it seems, over publicly sponsored Christmas displays, public slogans (the national motto, In God We Trust; the words "under God" in the Pledge of Allegiance), Ten Commandments monuments, legislative prayer, crosses officially erected as war memorials on public property, the inclusion of the words "so help me God" in the presidential oath of inauguration, and the like.[47] Perhaps as cause or perhaps as effect of this newly intensified concern with symbols, the constitutional doctrine announced by the Supreme Court has also shifted its focus. Thus, beginning in the mid-1980s, the Court explicitly began to articulate doctrine in terms of a constitutional prohibition on public messages of "endorsement" of religion.[48]

To be sure, this interest in symbols and messages was not a wholly novel development. Cases and commentators had raised issues about, say, public nativity scenes before the 1980s, even though constitutional doctrine was not yet explicitly formulated to address such issues.[49] And the Supreme Court's immensely controversial school prayer decisions in the early 1960s[50] were

45. See, e.g., Everson v. Board of Education, 330 U.S. 1 (1947); Lemon v. Kurtzman, 403 U.S. 602 (1971); Committee for Public Education & Religious Liberty v. Nyquist, 413 U.S. 756 (1973); School District of City of Grand Rapids v. Ball, 473 U.S. 373, 373 (1985) *overruled by* Agostini v. Felton, 521 U.S. 203 (1997).

46. See Texas Monthly, Inc. v. Bullock, 489 U.S. 1 (1989); Walz v. Tax Commission, 397 U.S. 664 (1970).

47. See, e.g., Lynch v. Donnelly, 465 U.S. 668 (1984); Allegheny County v. ACLU, 492 U.S. 573 (1989); Van Orden v. Perry, 545 U.S. 677 (2005); McCreary County v. ACLU of Kentucky, 545 U.S. 844 (2005); Aronow v. United States, 432 F.2d 242 (9th Cir. 1970); Gaylor v. United States, 74 F.3d 214 (10th Cir. 1996); Newdow v. Lefevre, 598 F.3d 638, 640 (9th Cir. 2010); Newdow v. Peterson, 753 F.3d 105, 106 (2d Cir. 2014); O'Hair v. Murray, 588 F.2d 1144 (5th Cir. 1979); Town of Greece v. Galloway, 572 U.S. ___ (2014); Elk Grove School Dist. v. Newdow, 542 U.S. 1, 35 (2004); Trunk v. City of San Diego, 629 F.3d 1099, 1118 (9th Cir. 2011); Newdow v. Roberts, 603 F.3d 1002 (D.C. Cir. 2010).

48. See *Allegheny County*, 492 U.S. 573; *Lynch*, 465 U.S. 668.

49. See, e.g., Allen v. Morton, 495 F.2d 65 (D.C. Cir. 1973); Citizens Concerned for Separation of Church & State v. City & County of Denver, 481 F. Supp. 522, 532 (D. Colo. 1979); Conrad v. City & County of Denver, 656 P.2d 662 (Colo. 1982).

50. Abington School District v. Schempp, 374 U.S. 203 (1963); Engel v. Vitale, 370 U.S. 421 (1962).

provocative in part or mostly because of what the rejection of school prayer symbolized. After all, a brief, theologically thin prayer recited in class or over the loudspeaker at the beginning of the school day probably did little, as critics pointed out, to instill genuine piety in students. Conversely, one might think that in a school setting in which students are routinely compelled to listen to a great deal that many of them may find disagreeable or boring, sitting or fidgeting in silence during a brief rote prayer should have inflicted no great damage on dissenting students.[51] Or at least such exercises just *in themselves* wrought no great good, or great harm. And yet these exercises, conducted daily in the public institutions understood to be entrusted with the formation of citizens, arguably had a powerful even if partly unspoken effect in signaling the community's official commitment to biblical "higher authority" premises. Indeed, whatever psychological damage the prayers did inflict was no doubt caused by and inseparable from this signaling.

The Importance of Symbols. Although symbolism had not been absent from establishment clause jurisprudence, beginning in the 1980s the shift to an emphasis on symbols became manifest, as noted, both in the number and notoriety of the cases and in the Court's explicit reformulation of the doctrine to address the issue of symbolism or "endorsement." From a pragmatic or "interest"-oriented perspective, this reorientation could seem surprising, and regrettable. With reference to controversies over crosses, crèches, and monuments, Adam Samaha asks sarcastically: "The question is whether anyone, especially courts, should care about the way government is decorated."[52] Wouldn't the Court's and the litigants' scarce resources—and the public's scanty attention—be better spent on matters that actually affect people in coercive or material ways?

Suppose, for example, that as part of its annual Christmas display, your city of residence puts up in a prominent downtown space a nativity scene, complete with Mary, Joseph, shepherds, angels, wise men, and, of course, the baby Jesus. Possibly among other objectives, some perhaps more spiritual in nature, the display presumably seeks to promote a celebratory or festive spirit; it may also serve as a stimulus to local commerce. Cheerfulness, commerce: these are good things. So even if you do not happen to be

51. Cf. Frederick Mark Gedicks, "The Ironic State of Religious Liberty in America," *Mercer Law Review* 46 (1995): 1158 (commenting on the "theologically vacuous nature of most organized public school prayers").

52. Adam Samaha, "Endorsement Retires: From Religious Symbolism to Anti-Sorting Principles," *Supreme Court Review* 2005, no. 1 (2005): 143. However, Samaha goes on to argue that the courts *should* care about public symbols.

a Christian, why should you object? What is the harm? No one says you have to *believe in* the angels, the Virgin, or Christianity, or even to *pretend* to believe in them. No one says you have to look at the display at all. Why not save your indignation and your litigating zeal for measures (like school voucher programs or tax exemptions for churches) that actually take dollars out of people's pockets?[53]

Of course, the question can be—and often is—turned around. Suppose you are a pious Christian, and a court orders your town to take down its nativity scene. You can still put up a devout display in your own front yard or on the grounds of your local church. So, why should it matter that the display is no longer located on public property?

And yet it is perfectly clear that people *do* care, sometimes intensely, not only about symbols but, more pertinently, about the sponsorship of such symbols. If we criticize this attitude as frivolous or irrational, moreover, we may logically be forced to condemn as frivolous or irrational our own founders (who, as we have seen, gave careful consideration to selecting the public symbols of the new nation), and the marines who fought heroically to raise the flag at Iwo Jima, and all the songwriters (from Francis Scott Key to Lee Greenwood) who have composed patriotic anthems, and the presidents from Washington on who have been carefully attentive to the symbols and messages associated with their inaugurations into the office of president.

The fact is, as Justice Holmes asserted, "we live by symbols."[54] Max Lerner quoted Holmes, cited Freud, and elaborated: "Like children and neurotics man as a political animal lives in . . . a dream-world of symbols in which the shadows loom far larger than the realities they represent."[55] More specifically, as noted, our political communities are not physical facts; they are constructed, or "imagined."[56] And the imagination that constructs and maintains community arises from and around symbols—around symbols that are understood to be publicly sponsored, and thus to be expressive and constitutive not just of particular private speakers or groups, but of the community.

---

53. Thus, while strongly urging a more committed embrace of public secularism, Jacques Berlinerblau criticizes "the obsession [of some secularists] with religious icons in public spaces," and he reiterates Madison's admonition not to waste time on "unessential points." Jacques Berlinerblau, *How to Be Secular: A Call to Arms for Religious Freedom* (New York: Houghton Mifflin Harcourt, 2012), 51.

54. Oliver Wendell Holmes Jr., *The Collected Legal Papers* (New York: Dover, 2007), 270.

55. Max Lerner, "Constitution and Court as Symbols," *Yale Law Journal* 46 (1937): 1290.

56. See above, 174.

So it is neither surprising nor irrational that citizens care, deeply at times, about what symbols are adopted to constitute and represent their community (just as ancient pagans and Christians cared not just about the sacrifices to the gods but about the *public* sponsorship of the sacrifices).[57] In this sense, arguments over symbols may be *more* consequential than disputes over mere allocations of dollars. Disputes over money affect our *interests*. But disputes over symbols amount to battles over *who we are*, or what kind of community we live in.

Justice Sandra Day O'Connor, the principal sponsor on the Supreme Court of the "no endorsement" doctrine, understood this point. The reason why government should not send messages endorsing or disapproving of religion, she explained, is that such messages cause some Americans to feel like "outsiders" or "lesser members of the political community."[58] Critics of the doctrine (like myself)[59] have sometimes ridiculed this rationale. Dissenters from a publicly endorsed religion are *not* treated as lesser members of the political community, the critics have argued:[60] unless we assume, in question-begging fashion, that there is a constitutional right not to be exposed to public messages inconsistent with one's faith or one's disbelief (which is, of course, precisely the question at issue), such dissenters are afforded exactly the same rights—freedom of speech, the right to vote, the right to counsel, and so forth—that other Americans enjoy.[61] Religious minorities or dissenters are full members of the community who (like most other citizens) sometimes happen to disagree with some things governments say.

Religious minorities may, to be sure, feel like political "outsiders" by virtue of their minority status, with the attendant political disadvantages and discomforts that minority status may sometimes entail. But in this sense, the reality is that the dissenters *are* outsiders, just as a host of other people are

57. See above, 174.

58. *Lynch*, 465 U.S. at 688 (O'Connor, J., concurring).

59. See, e.g., Jesse H. Choper, "The Endorsement Test: Its Status and Desirability," *Journal of Law and Politics* 18 (2002): 499; Steven D. Smith, "Symbols, Perceptions, and Doctrinal Illusions: Establishment Neutrality and the 'No Endorsement' Test," *Michigan Law Review* 86 (1987): 266.

60. See Smith, "Symbols, Perceptions," 305–9.

61. See Samaha, "Endorsement Retires," 143 ("Nobody is losing the right to vote, or speak, or receive tangible government benefits; nobody is formally compelled to attend or not attend religious ceremonies; nobody is taxed to pay for substantial material benefits to religious causes").

fully citizens but more or less permanent political "outsiders"—communists, monarchists, anarchists, theocrats, segregationists, Ayn Rand libertarians, . . . Republicans in the state of California. In this sense, "outsiders" (like the poor) will always be with us; no law, not even one as august as the Constitution, can provide a remedy for that sometimes painful reality.[62]

Moreover, the reality will sometimes be reflected in public messages and symbols. Government and its multitude of officials will inevitably make all manner of statements on all manner of controversial issues. Some citizens will care deeply about those issues and will resent official statements that contradict or disapprove of their views and values. Such is democracy in a pluralistic world. How is a religious dissenter any different in this respect than someone who is distressed about being outnumbered and sometimes outvoted in the democratic free-for-all?

But while these criticisms may be cogent enough in the analytical abstract, they arguably fail to reckon with the fact that, as studies by scholars like Bellah have shown, in America religion has been more central to—more constitutive of—the conception of political community than many other factors have been.[63] Hence, religious expressions by government do not merely take sides on potentially divisive political issues, as virtually anything government does or says may do. Within the American political tradition, rather, such expressions may serve not merely to endorse positions on controversial issues, but to define the *kind of community* this is.[64] And in this sense, as Justice O'Connor perceived but her critics sometimes did not, religious expressions may have a more fundamental alienating effect than other sorts of controversial public statements typically have.

Public religious symbols, in short, are not merely expressions of particular public policies; they help to constitute and define the community itself. A corollary is that the public discourse by which important political and legal decisions are made is shaped by the community's image or interpretation of

62. See Koppelman, *Defending American Religious Neutrality*, 47 ("It is not clear . . . how endorsement either threatens religious liberty or fails to respect diversity. Alienation is as inescapable a part of political life as division. In a democracy, somebody loses any vote and therefore feels like an outsider. Here, too, judicial intervention may simply make things worse"); Mark Tushnet, "The Constitution of Religion," *Connecticut Law Review* 18 (1986): 712 ("Nonadherents who believe they are excluded from the political community are merely expressing the disappointment felt by everyone who has lost a fair fight in the arena of politics").

63. See above, 261–63.

64. Cf. Samaha, "Endorsement Retires," 137 ("Religious messages . . . can also signal the community's character to non-members").

itself, which is in turn influenced by the symbols that are taken as expressive of the community.

Take one important recent example. In the major cases adjudicating the issue of same-sex marriage, judges, including justices of the Supreme Court, assumed that "religious" views about marriage could not count in the public justification of marriage laws.[65] Given the enormous religious divide on the issue—contemporary research by the Pew Foundation suggested that 85 percent of religiously unaffiliated Americans supported same-same marriage compared to only 35 percent of white evangelicals and 44 percent of black Protestants[66]—this threshold exclusion of reasons deemed "religious" was likely decisive. If the central views and values of one side are excluded from the start, the other side is likely to win the argument. And that is just what happened.[67]

But *why* were "religious" reasons inadmissible? The short and (for many) sufficient answer, so obvious that the judges did not bother even to articulate or defend it, was that the Constitution requires that government be "secular," thereby forbidding reliance on "religious" reasons. And this answer is no doubt correct if it is taken as a shorthand abbreviation for the fact that powerful constituencies in our country, including legal elites, have come to conceive of the political community as "secular" (in a conveniently ambiguous and mostly unarticulated sense) and have projected that conception back onto the Constitution. That is the sort of "imagined community" in which these Americans want to live, and suppose that they *do* (or at least have a right to) live.

It is also true, however,[68] that the First Amendment does not actually *say* (either explicitly or by persuasive implication) that government must

---

65. Obergefell v. Hodges, 135 S. Ct. 2584, 2607 (2015) ("Finally, it must be emphasized that religions, and those who adhere to religious doctrines, may continue to advocate with utmost, sincere conviction that, by divine precepts, same-sex marriage should not be condoned. . . . The Constitution, however, does not permit the State to bar same-sex couples from marriage on the same terms as accorded to couples of the opposite sex"); Varnum v. Brien, 763 N.W.2d 862, 904 (Iowa 2009) ("The County's silence reflects, we believe, its understanding [that religious sentiment] cannot, under our Iowa Constitution, be used to justify a ban on same-sex marriage").

66. "Changing Attitudes on Gay Marriage," Pew Research Center, June 26, 2017, http://www.pewforum.org/fact-sheet/changing-attitudes-on-gay-marriage.

67. The final decision, of course, was *Obergefell*, 576 U.S. __ , 135 S. Ct. 2584.

68. I have argued for the potentially contentious claims that follow at much greater length elsewhere. E.g., Steven D. Smith, *The Rise and Decline of American Religious Freedom* (Cambridge, MA: Harvard University Press, 2014). For a much condensed version, see Steven D. Smith, "Political Decisions Must Be 'Secular'? Since When?" Law and Liberty, July 31, 2014, http://www.libertylawsite.org/2014/07/31/political-decisions-must-be-secular-since-when.

be "secular," and that the Americans who drafted and enacted that amendment almost certainly did not understand it to have any such implication. Moreover, the modern secularist conception of the community goes strongly against the grain of a great deal in our political tradition, including perhaps the two most eloquent and powerful statements of the central meaning of that tradition—namely, the Declaration of Independence[69] and Lincoln's Second Inaugural Address. (Or, if you prefer, his Gettysburg Address, which is the source of the phrase "one nation, under God.") Efforts by modern luminaries like the vastly influential Harvard political philosopher John Rawls to square the contemporary secularist conception of American political community with Lincoln's majestic declamation are almost comical in their implausibility;[70] nothing but an adamantine determination to adhere to the secularist conception could render such arguments respectable. And even conceding that political decisions should be made on "secular" grounds, the concerns relevant to marriage that many churchgoing Americans found pertinent would likely have qualified as "secular" upon any sort of attentive analysis.[71]

The judges did not pause to notice any of these complications, of course. Rather, they dismissed "religious"-looking reasons peremptorily and automatically, evidently under a secularist conception of community that, without either specifying or defending it, they treated as axiomatic. That conception in turn was surely shaped and informed by, among other things, recent constitutional doctrine forbidding public religious symbols or messages.

The (Deceptive) Lines of Division. In sum, Americans on both sides of the cultural divide are not being merely petty or irrational when they care about, and fight over, public symbols. But how exactly are the battle lines in that fight drawn up?

On its face, the conflict has pitted supporters of "religious" symbols and expressions against proponents of a "secular" public square. So here, on first inspection anyway, a "religious versus secular" characterization of the culture wars may seem apt. And at least on a straightforward or conventional reading, the current constitutional doctrine prohibiting endorsements of

69. See George Fletcher, *Our Secret Constitution* (New York: Oxford University Press, 2001), 102.

70. See below, 356.

71. For further discussion, see Steven D. Smith, "Goods of Religion," in *Dimensions of Goodness*, ed. Vittorio Hösle (Newcastle, UK: Cambridge Scholars, 2013). See also Francis Beckwith, *Taking Rites Seriously: Law, Politics, and the Reasonableness of Faith* (New York: Cambridge University Press, 2015).

"religion" may seem to support this description: public expressions that are "religious" are forbidden, it seems, while public expressions that are "secular" are permissible.[72]

But we need to recall, from the previous chapter, the ambiguous or equivocal character of the term "secular," and also the distinction between the (familiar) transcendent conception and the (less familiar) immanent conception of "religion." Viewed in light of these distinctions, the current struggle over public symbols turns out to be more complicated than it initially appears. In prohibiting endorsements of "religion," the "no endorsement" doctrine *might* mean that government is forbidden to endorse *traditional or transcendent religion*. Conversely, "secular" expressions of more immanent religiosity might be permissible.

The Supreme Court has not explicitly articulated the doctrine in those terms, to be sure; but then, the modern Court has not offered any precise or even imprecise definitions of what either "secular" or "religion" means for constitutional purposes anyway. To many Westerners, "religion" connotes traditional, transcendent religion—the sort of thing conveyed in the Bible and the Qur'an and practiced by Christians, devout Jews, and Muslims.[73] It may well be that this is what the justices have implicitly had in mind when they have declared endorsements of "religion" to be impermissible.[74] Conversely, if religious expressions are at least susceptible of being interpreted in more immanent or this-worldly terms, perhaps the prohibition does not apply.

So, how would we go about determining whether the conventional "religion versus (undifferentiated) secular" interpretation of the Court's doctrine is correct, or whether instead the revised interpretation is more apt—the interpretation in which transcendent messages are excluded but messages of immanent sanctity are permitted? Well, we might begin by imagining that, as some scholars and litigants have urged,[75] *all* conventionally "religious"

72. See, e.g., *Allegheny County*, 492 U.S. 573.

73. See, e.g., Lambert, *Religion in American Politics*, 11 ("In this book religion is defined as a set of beliefs in a transcendent God, grounded in an authoritative sacred text, and expressed by a body of believers through the performance of certain rituals and adherence to a specific moral code").

74. Cf. Abner Greene, "Religious Freedom and (Other) Civil Liberties: Is There a Middle Ground?" *Harvard Law and Policy Review* 9 (2015): 161, 174 (arguing that Ronald Dworkin's conception of religion "is not a very good interpretation of religion in our constitutional culture" because "religion in America is primarily about theism, about faith in God and what follows from that").

75. See, e.g., Stephen B. Epstein, "Rethinking the Constitutionality of Ceremonial Deism," *Columbia Law Review* 96 (1996): 2083–2174.

public symbols and expressions—the words "under God" in the Pledge of Allegiance, the words "In God We Trust" in the national motto (and also the national anthem), legislative prayer, and so forth—were systematically eliminated or relegated to the private domain. That, after all, is what a straightforward application of the conventional "religion versus secular" interpretation would seem to dictate, at least in principle. The result of this drastic purge would *not* be to remove all symbols and patriotic expressions from public life. After all, no one argues that the national community cannot express itself—and define itself, and celebrate itself—in words and symbols. The national motto would be gone, for sure. But there would surely still be the (expurgated) Pledge of Allegiance, for example. And the (expurgated) national anthem. And of course, the flag.

So, should these remaining symbols and expressions be described as merely "secular"? Perhaps. And yet they would still seek to elicit the citizens' allegiance—to stir citizens' feelings of reverence and devotion. They would still have an important function—a *sacralizing* or consecrating function, in a more than metaphorical sense. And the Court has never suggested that there is anything impermissible or even suspect about *that* kind of this-worldly sacralization.

Consider two major cases decided by the Supreme Court just two weeks apart in 1989. In *Allegheny County v. American Civil Liberties Union*,[76] a majority of justices interpreted the First Amendment to prohibit a local government from sponsoring symbols that send a message endorsing religion. On that premise, the Court invalidated a county's sponsorship of a traditional Christmas crèche in a Pittsburgh courthouse.[77] By contrast, in *Texas v. Johnson*,[78] a decision invalidating a state prohibition on flag desecration, both the majority opinion by Justice William Brennan and a dissenting opinion by Chief Justice William Rehnquist acknowledged the sacralizing function performed by the American flag. Thus, Brennan acknowledged for the Court that the flag was "virtually sacred to our nation as a whole,"[79] but he contended that the way to "consecrate" the flag is not to prohibit its "desecration."[80] To "consecrate," of course, means to associate with the sa-

---

76. *Allegheny County*, 492 U.S. 573.

77. However, the Court found that a Jewish menorah standing next to a Christmas tree beside an entrance to the building had been acceptably secularized.

78. Texas v. Johnson, 491 U.S. 397 (1989).

79. *Johnson*, 491 U.S. at 418.

80. *Johnson*, 491 U.S. at 420. For his part, with the assistance of extensive quotations of patriotic poetry, Rehnquist expounded on the "almost mystical reverence" that the flag

cred: "desecration," conversely, is synonymous with "desacralization." And yet, neither the justices nor the commentators perceived any constitutional problem with the nation's sponsorship and promotion of what one scholar described as the "sacred flag."[81]

So then, why was the flag itself not subject to the ostensible constitutional prohibition on official public religiosity, insisted on contemporaneously in the *Allegheny County* case? Why did the issue not even occur to any of the justices in the case? The answer, it seems, is that *that sort* of sacralizing or religious message—a message, arguably, of *immanent*, not transcendent, sacralization—is not what the prohibition on endorsement contemplates.

So it seems that when the Court declares that public symbols must be "secular," it does not mean "secular" *in the positivistic sense.* Under the cover of the amorphous and ambiguous term "secular," the justices have implicitly embraced, wittingly or unwittingly, a conception of the political community formed in immanently religious terms.

In reality, of course, the Court has not eliminated even all conventionally religiously public symbols and messages. Thus, the Supreme Court and lower federal courts have invalidated a number of public religious expressions—including the Pittsburgh nativity scene, a cross, and some Ten Commandments monuments.[82] But judges have also approved a number of other apparently religious expressions, including the national motto (In God We Trust),[83] a Ten Commandments monument on the Texas state capitol grounds,[84] and the commencement of legislative or city council sessions with prayer.[85] The

---

elicits in many citizens (at 429 [Rehnquist, J., dissenting]). Justice John Paul Stevens arguably acknowledged the sacralizing function as well, albeit indirectly. Stephens argued that the American flag, unlike many other flags and many other symbols of nationhood, is much more than just a symbol, but he had difficulty explaining just how this was so. Destruction of the flag, he said, is offensive to patriotic Americans; this may be true, but the flag is hardly unique in this respect (at 436 [Stevens, J., dissenting]). Stephens's intuition that the flag is much more than a symbol might plausibly be understood as an inarticulate gesture toward its sacralizing function.

81. Sheldon Nahmod, "The Sacred Flag and the First Amendment," *Indiana Law Journal* 66 (1991): 511.

82. *Allegheny County*, 492 U.S. 573; *Trunk*, 629 F.3d at 1118; *McCreary County*, 545 U.S. 844.

83. See, e.g., *Aronow*, 432 F.2d 242; *Gaylor*, 74 F.3d 214; *Newdow v. Lefevre*, 598 F.3d at 640; *Newdow v. Peterson*, 753 F.3d at 106; *O'Hair*, 588 F.2d 1144.

84. *Van Orden*, 545 U.S. 677. Critics (and supporters) found this ruling especially puzzling insofar as on the same day the Court ruled invalid some displays containing the Ten Commandments in some Kentucky courthouses. *McCreary County*, 545 U.S. 844.

85. *Town of Greece*, 572 U.S. ___.

jurisprudence in this respect is notoriously confused; everyone admits this. Nonetheless, the revised interpretation may help make some sense—though probably not complete sense, alas—of that jurisprudence.

Thus, the closest thing to an official explanation for why some conventionally religious expressions remain permissible despite the ostensible constitutional prohibition on endorsements of religion asserts that the acceptable expressions have lost their religious significance (at least in the eyes of a "reasonable observer") and instead serve now to "solemniz[e] public occasions, [express] confidence in the future, and encourag[e] the appreciation of what is worthy in our society."[86] Justice O'Connor elaborated on this justification at some length in explaining why the words "under God" in the Pledge of Allegiance are not an impermissible endorsement of religion.[87] For their part, critics find this kind of explanation doubly infirm. In the first place, words like "under God" in the Pledge of Allegiance have *not* lost their religious meaning, even (or especially) to reasonable observers.[88] And even if we accept that such expressions serve mostly to "solemnize public occasions," for example, how is it that these particular words and expressions serve this solemnizing function? It is only because of their religious content, critics argue, that such expressions perform the laudable functions that the Court ascribes to them.[89]

These are powerful objections—at least under the conventional interpretation that understands the doctrine to prohibit *all* religious expressions and to permit only expressions that are secular *in the positivistic sense*. But on the alternative interpretation, the criticisms may be less cogent. If the doctrine prohibits transcendent public religiosity, in other words, but allows for immanent religiosity, then religious expressions that are at least susceptible of being interpreted in more immanent or this-worldly terms may not fall under the prohibition. Consistent with this understanding, the courts have seemed most opposed to more obviously sectarian religious expressions—

---

86. *Elk Grove School Dist.*, 542 U.S. at 35 (O'Connor, J., concurring).

87. *Elk Grove School Dist.*, 542 U.S. at 33–44 (O'Connor, J., concurring).

88. See, e.g., Douglas Laycock, "Theology Scholarships, the Pledge of Allegiance, and Religious Liberty: Avoiding the Extremes but Missing the Liberty," *Harvard Law Review* 118 (2004): 235 (observing that "this rationale is unconvincing both to serious nonbelievers and to serious believers"); Steven H. Shiffrin, "The Pluralistic Foundations of the Religion Clauses," *Cornell Law Review* 90 (2004): 70–71 ("I am sure that a pledge identifying the United States as subject to divine authority is asserting the existence and authority of the divine").

89. Caroline Mala Corbin, "Ceremonial Deism and the Reasonable Outsider," *UCLA Law Review* 57 (2010): 1589.

expressions clearly distinctive to Christianity, for example.[90] Conversely, more generic expressions that might be amenable to incorporation into an immanent religiosity seem to fare better in the courts.[91]

The term "God" presents a delicate case. Conventionally, the term "God" is associated with Christianity, Judaism, and biblical religion generally; the term would thus seem to have a transcendent referent. As we saw in the preceding chapter, therefore, Ronald Dworkin took care to insist that his own more immanent religiosity was a "religion *without God.*" And yet Dworkin also claimed for his fold of atheistic religiosity luminaries including Spinoza, Einstein, and the Protestant theologian Paul Tillich, even though all these figures talked approvingly of "God." They used the *word*, but in Dworkin's interpretation they did not mean the transcendent God, and instead were using the term in a more immanent sense.[92] And of course, the pagan deities of antiquity were immanent to this world and yet are routinely referred to as "gods." It seems, therefore, that the term "God" is capable of being taken in either a transcendent or an immanent sense. And, as in the Pledge of Allegiance case, the justices seem most comfortable with the expression when it is at least susceptible—to the hypothetical "reasonable observer"—of an immanent interpretation.[93]

This understanding of the prohibition might also help to make sense of scholarly pronouncements that otherwise seem quite baffling. At the time of the Pledge of Allegiance controversy, for example, distinguished commentators, including Columbia professor Kent Greenawalt and University of Chicago professor Martha Nussbaum, argued that the words "under God" in the Pledge of Allegiance clearly sent an unconstitutional message of endorsement; at the same time, these same scholars contended that the national motto, In God We Trust, should *not* be construed as sending any such forbidden message.[94] This juxtaposition of judgments seems curious:

90. See, e.g., *Allegheny County*, 492 U.S. 573 (invalidating Christmas crèche display); *Trunk*, 629 F.3d at 1118 (finding that a publicly displayed cross, despite its historical context, conveys a message of government endorsement of religion that violates the establishment clause).

91. See, e.g., *Elk Grove School Dist.*, 542 U.S. at 31–33, 40–42, especially the concurring opinions by Justice O'Connor and Chief Justice Rehnquist, defending use of the words "under God" in the Pledge of Allegiance.

92. See Ronald Dworkin, *Religion without God* (Cambridge, MA: Harvard University Press, 2013), 31–43.

93. See, e.g., *Elk Grove School Dist.*, 542 U.S. 1.

94. Kent Greenawalt, *Religion and the Constitution*, vol. 2, *Establishment and Fairness* (Princeton: Princeton University Press, 2008), 95–102; Martha C. Nussbaum, *Liberty of Con-*

Why is "under God" more religious, especially when it appears as one short blip in a larger patriotic statement, than the blunt, unqualified declaration, staring at us from every dollar bill we handle, that "In God We Trust"? Such perceptions are difficult to explain, no doubt, but perhaps the answer lies in the word "under." Maybe it is a matter of vertical versus horizontal. A God whom we are "under" is necessarily *above* us, and hence by metaphorical implication transcendent, in other words, while a God we "trust" in might be either transcendent or immanent (like a trustworthy brother or sister or friend). Might that be the explanation for Greenawalt's and Nussbaum's puzzling judgments?

In any case, through the haze of arguably incoherent decisions and judgments, two propositions seem tolerably secure. First, *not all* religious expressions by government are forbidden. Second, explicitly Christian expressions are disfavored (unless mixed in with an eclectic congregation of more generic religious language).[95] So it is all right to begin Supreme Court sessions with the invocation "God save the United States and this honorable Court"[96]—the phrase in that context is apparently solemnizing the Court and its proceedings—but it would be unthinkable for the modern Supreme Court to assert that "this is a *Christian* nation" in the way the nineteenth-century Court did.[97] More generally, legislatures are evidently not permitted to pursue goals or advance values distinctively associated with the biblical tradition—traditional marriage, for example[98]—but government *is* free to pursue and advance values perceived by their supporters as having a more immanently "sacred" quality, such as the protection of human life, or human rights, or endangered species.

The effect of these decisions and tacit assumptions, one might argue, is to remove the transcendent or Christian stratum of American civil religion, thereby leaving the immanent or pagan substratum. As we saw in chapter 8, despite its official but arguably superficial triumph over paganism in late antiquity, Christianity did not so much eliminate or replace pagan religi-

---

science: *In Defense of America's Tradition of Religious Equality* (New York: Basic Books, 2009), 308–16.

95. See, e.g., *Allegheny County*, 492 U.S. 573 (invalidating a Christmas crèche in a courthouse while upholding a Jewish menorah); but cf. *Town of Greece*, 572 U.S. ___ (approving city council prayers in which Christian language was mixed with more generic religious language).

96. "The Court and Its Procedures," Supreme Court of the United States, accessed August 19, 2017, https://www.supremecourt.gov/about/procedures.aspx.

97. *Holy Trinity Church*, 143 U.S. at 470 (emphasis added).

98. See above, 274–75.

osity as contain and to some degree reorient it by enveloping it within a sort of overarching transcendent canopy. Once the canopy was removed, pagan religiosity was alive and well, ready and waiting to reassert itself. In their campaign to eliminate the transcendent dimension of American public religiosity, consequently, the courts have in effect pushed our official conceptions of our political community in an immanent or pagan direction.

And yet the decisions have been erratic and controversial, often sharply dividing the justices themselves. Indeed, the "no endorsement" doctrine itself seems unstable, especially since its leading proponent, Justice O'Connor, retired from the Court. More generally, the public debate itself continues as fiercely as ever, as annual battles over "Merry Christmas" and public school holiday programs reflect. Hence the ongoing and intense public struggle over "mere symbols," which seems unlikely to be resolved either by agreement or outright victory by one or the other party anytime soon.

The Struggle over Sexuality

Although conflicts over religious symbols have been frequent and sometimes intense, they pale in their ferocity in comparison to the struggle over a variety of issues connected in various ways with sexuality: contraception, pornography, abortion, homosexuality, same-sex marriage. In these diverse but related conflicts, similar lines of division are discernible. In ancient Rome, Kyle Harper argues, sexuality "came to mark the great divide between Christians and the world."[99] A similar divide seems to have opened up today. Geoffrey Stone observes that "we are in the midst of a constitutional revolution. . . . It has bitterly divided citizens, politicians, and judges. It is a battle that has dominated politics, inflamed religious passions, and challenged Americans to rethink and reexamine their positions on issues they once thought settled. . . . And, best of all, it is about sex."[100]

On one side of the divide, proponents favor a conception of sexual morality that is discernibly aligned with Christian or, more generally, biblical understandings. On the other side, proponents embrace views of sexual morality that in important respects parallel those of pagan Rome; and like the Romans, proponents of this position find the traditional or biblical con-

---

99. Kyle Harper, *From Shame to Sin: The Christian Transformation of Sexual Morality in Late Antiquity* (Cambridge, MA: Harvard University Press, 2013), 85.

100. Geoffrey R. Stone, *Sex and the Constitution* (London: Norton, 2017), xxvii.

ception not only unnaturally and intolerably restrictive, but indeed almost unfathomable. Both sides seek to enshrine their conceptions of sexuality in law; often the legal provisions seem important more for what they symbolize than for their practical or concrete effects.

The Ancient Divide. As we saw in chapter 3, the term "sexual morality" seems almost a misnomer for pagan attitudes toward sexuality: that is because, in the views of pagan Rome, sexuality was not *intrinsically* a matter generating or requiring moral restrictions.[101] It was assumed, rather, that an active sexual agenda was, for men, a necessity; abstinence, or even the confinement of sexual relations to marriage, was unnatural and unhealthy. And pagan religion blessed this permissive understanding. Sexual passion was a manifestation of "the mysterious indwelling presence of the gods"[102]—of Venus, her son Eros (or Cupid), Priapus of the prodigious phallus, Bacchus, and a variety of more peripheral deities. The pagan gods not only inspired sexual drives; they set a divine example through their own frequent carnal consorting, with each other and with the occasional winsome mortal.

In sum, sexual gratification was something to be celebrated and assiduously pursued—by *men*, that is—in either its heterosexual or homosexual variety. Stimulation *to* sexual intercourse (in the form of ubiquitous erotic depictions on household walls and lamps, and in public spaces) and opportunities *for* intercourse (in the form of multitudinous brothels and slaves, in addition, of course, to wives) were pervasive.

Though natural, necessary, desirable, and divinely ordained, however, sexual gratification was subject to *extrinsic* limitations emanating from two other sources or concerns. One was the ethic of manliness. Under this ethic, although homosexual intercourse was permissible and sometimes preferable, to be the passive or receiving partner in such a union was deemed disgraceful and effeminate. In addition, a man should always be the master not only of his household and his slaves but also of himself. So it was shameful to indulge sexual passions beyond the point of self-control.

The other source of limitations on sexual expression, given pervasive fears of population decline, was the demographic demand for reproduction within the patriarchal family. Together with the ethic of manliness, this concern meant that women—respectable women anyway—enjoyed none of the sexual license extended to men. Women were expected to remain chaste

---

101. The point is emphasized in Stone, *Sex and the Constitution*, 4–12.
102. Harper, *From Shame to Sin*, 67.

before marriage, to marry at a young age, and to have relations only with their husbands after marriage.

These sexual norms were reflected in and supported by law. Adultery was legally forbidden (although the prohibition was sometimes violated—and flagrantly violated by emperors). More importantly, law recognized and maintained the institutions—the ubiquitous brothels, the teeming multitudes of slaves—that solved what would otherwise have been an untenable problem of sexual supply.

Christianity, by contrast, firmly rejected these sexual norms in favor of celibacy and marriage, as we saw in chapter 5.[103] Sexual relations were *not* deemed a human necessity—indeed, the celibate life was admired—and were permissible only between spouses. This conception expressed a Christian ideal of purity—of the body as a temple of the Holy Spirit—that pagans found almost incomprehensible. "Christian ideals of sexual exclusivity, including male fidelity were radically discordant with the patterns of life and the expectations of public culture," Harper explains.[104] Conversely, "for Paul the sexual disorder of Roman society was the single most powerful symbol of the world's alienation from God" (94).

As Christianity became the dominant religion of the empire, Christian sexual norms also gradually came to be reflected in law. Prostitution, enthusiastically supported under the earlier emperors, was now legally regulated and discouraged (186–88). Pederasty and homosexual conduct were forbidden (155–56). The shift from pagan to Christian morality amounted to "a revolution" (18). That revolution was hardly limited to sexual morality, to be sure. But in its cultural manifestations, Harper observes, "sex was at the center of it all" (1).

In Rome, in short, the law reflected and reinforced the shift from pagan sexual norms to Christian sexual morality, which in turn was a manifestation of the shift from the immanently religious, pagan world to the Christian world oriented to a transcendent deity.

The Modern Divide. In modern America, a similar process is discernible—except in reverse. Thus, for much of American history, Christian sexual norms prevailed (at least officially, although, as always, actual practice often deviated), and the law reflected these norms. The legal scholar Robert Rodes explains that as late as the 1950s, the law embodied Christian or biblical

103. See above, 121–25.
104. Harper, *From Shame to Sin*, 139. Hereafter, page references from this work will be given in parentheses in the text.

sexual morality. Fornication was still a criminal offense in all but ten states, adultery in all but five, sodomy in all the states.[105] Seduction was both a tort and a crime.[106] The distribution of contraceptives was forbidden by federal law, as well as under the law of most states.[107] Obscenity was prohibited, subject only to faint constitutional protections, and in many states, movies were subject to licensing to screen out objectionable content.[108]

Most of these laws were, to be sure, imperfectly or even rarely enforced. When opponents brought a lawsuit challenging Connecticut's ban on contraception in *Poe v. Ullman*,[109] the case was dismissed because the Court found that in the decades since the statute was enacted in 1879, the state had tried to enforce it only once, and that prosecution had been dismissed on the state's own motion. Moreover, actual behavior often departed significantly, as it long had done, from the official norms. Historians John D'Emilio and Estelle Freedman report that by the 1920s Americans were already moving toward a more liberal view of the functions and limits of sex.[110] Rodes acknowledges these facts but argues that the legal provisions nonetheless expressed and helped to maintain a sort of official or public normative framework: "When Dwight Eisenhower was President, . . . it was well understood that chastity was the prevailing social norm. Whatever their practices, everyone knew what the standard was: married people were to have sex only with their spouses; the unmarried were to abstain."[111]

Survey data support Rodes's observation: in the 1950s fewer than a quarter of Americans approved of premarital sex.[112] Then came the so-called sexual revolution (though it was not exactly the first such revolution, or

105. Robert E. Rodes Jr., *On Law and Chastity* (Durham, NC: Carolina Academic Press, 2006), 9.

106. Rodes, *On Law and Chastity*, 14.

107. Rodes, *On Law and Chastity*, 22.

108. Rodes, *On Law and Chastity*, 20–21. See also Helen M. Alvare, "Religious Freedom versus Sexual Expression: A Guide," *Journal of Law and Religion* 30 (2015): 477: "In the United States, before approximately the 1970s, the state took an interest in maintaining the links between sex, marriage, and children via laws restraining even consensual sexual expression; these included laws banning fornication, cohabitation, and adultery. These laws were enforced quite unevenly, if at all, while at the same time, judges did not hesitate to affirm the legitimacy of the state interests underlying them."

109. Poe v. Ullman, 367 U.S. 497 (1961).

110. John D'Emilio and Estelle B. Freedman, *Intimate Matters: A History of Sexuality in America*, 3rd ed. (Chicago: University of Chicago Press, 2012), 239–42.

111. Rodes, *On Law and Chastity*, 3.

112. D'Emilio and Freedman, *Intimate Matters*, 333.

the last).[113] Cultural, political, and commercial developments converged, D'Emilio and Freedman explain, to produce a "reorganization of sexuality" in America.[114] "The reshaping of sexuality in the 1960s and 1970s was of major proportions. The marketing of sex, new demographic patterns, and the movements of women and homosexuals for equality all fostered a substantial revision in attitudes and behavior. . . . By the end of the 1970s, it was obvious that the [earlier] consensus had dissolved. As Americans married later, postponed childbearing, and divorced more often, and as feminists and gay liberationists questioned heterosexual orthodoxy, nonmarital sexuality became commonplace and open. And all of this took place in a social environment in which erotic imagery was ubiquitous."[115]

Modern sexual norms run parallel in important respects to ancient pagan attitudes and practices—except that these attitudes and practices have been extended to include women as well as men. Now, as then, in the popular morality growing out of the sexual revolution, the term "sexual morality" is something of a misnomer. That is because, according to a common assumption, sex is a normal, healthy human activity that does not *intrinsically* call for moral restrictions. Indeed, sexual intimacy continues to enjoy a kind of priority or even sanctity: it is not merely a particular kind of activity or pleasure that some people happen to enjoy (like gardening, or golf, or playing a musical instrument), but rather is something that is central to a complete human life. In Martha Nussbaum's list of human capabilities that must be recognized and accommodated if people are to live a life that is "truly human" or "fully human," one of the capabilities ("bodily integrity") is explained as including "having opportunities for sexual satisfaction."[116] In Supreme Court decisions, opportunity for sexual fulfillment is explicitly if vaguely tied to "human dignity."[117]

Commenting on "the sacrosanct, nonnegotiable status assigned to contraception and abortion," Mary Eberstadt argues that the new sexual

113. D'Emilio and Freedman speak of "sexual revolutions," in the plural, in describing changes in sexuality over the course of the twentieth century (*Intimate Matters*, 301). Geoffrey Stone enthusiastically chronicles attitudes of sexual libertinism in eighteenth-century America (*Sex and the Constitution*, 80–87).

114. D'Emilio and Freedman, *Intimate Matters*, 327.

115. D'Emilio and Freedman, *Intimate Matters*, 343.

116. Martha Nussbaum, *Women and Human Development: The Capabilities Approach* (Cambridge: Cambridge University Press, 2000), 78.

117. See, e.g., *Obergefell*, 135 S. Ct. at 2596; Planned Parenthood v. Casey, 505 U.S. 833, 851 (1992).

morality is "a new, quasi-religious orthodoxy."[118] As in Rome, it may seem, contemporary society "find[s] in erotic fulfillment nothing short of salvation," as Kyle Harper observes.[119]

Also as in Rome (though to a somewhat lesser extent), both stimulations to and opportunities for sexual expression are pervasive. D'Emilio and Freedman observe that "mid-twentieth-century America witnessed the collapse of most prohibitions on the public portrayal of sexuality."[120] Today, consequently, commercial advertisements routinely display comely, seductively clad women and men who both appeal to and stimulate libidinous inclinations while seeking to entice consumers to buy automobiles, beer, hamburgers, or remedies for erectile dysfunction. Pornography is readily available, now not only in films and magazines but also online; legal attempts to restrict it have fared badly in the courts.[121] The Internet and mobile phone apps are widely used to arrange sexual partners.[122] Historians D'Emilio and Freedman describe "the permeation of sex throughout the culture."[123]

The prevalence of these radically altered norms of sexual morality is reflected in, among other places or media, popular television series. Examples are numerous; as one salient instance, consider the critically acclaimed sitcom *Frasier*, which ran for eleven seasons, from 1993 to 2004. The series featured two culturally refined and obsessively fastidious psychiatrist brothers, Frasier and Niles; their retired police officer father, Martin; Frasier's talk show producer, Roz; and Martin's physical therapist, Daphne.[124] The central character, Frasier, multiply divorced, has over the course of the series numerous short- and longer-term sexual relationships with a variety of women; Niles and Martin have the occasional tryst. The characters often

118. Mary Eberstadt, "The First Church of Secularism and Its Sexual Sacraments," *National Review*, June 15, 2016, http://www.nationalreview.com/article/436602/sexual-revolution-secular-quasi-religion.

119. Harper, *From Shame to Sin*, 21.

120. D'Emilio and Freedman, *Intimate Matters*, 277.

121. See, e.g., Reno v. ACLU, 521 U.S. 844, 885 (1997); Ashcroft v. Free Speech Coalition, 535 U.S. 234, 258 (2002).

122. See, e.g., Nancy Jo Sales, "Tinder and the Dawn of the 'Dating Apocalypse,'" *Vanity Fair*, September 2015, http://www.vanityfair.com/culture/2015/08/tinder-hook-up-culture-end-of-dating.

123. D'Emilio and Freedman, *Intimate Matters*, 329. See also Leigh Ann Wheeler, *How Sex Became a Civil Liberty* (New York: Oxford University Press, 2013), 222 (remarking on the "increasingly sex-saturated public sphere that renders sex anything but private").

124. These characters were played by, respectively, Kelsey Grammar, David Hyde Pierce, John Mahoney, Peri Gilpin, and Jane Leeves.

talk and even agonize over the moral dimensions of these relationships, but the moral reflections have to do with concerns like whether Frasier is being honest with a partner or too shallow in his choice of partners. No one (not even Martin, who is depicted as thoroughly and comically traditional in his attitudes) ever expresses the slightest reservation about the propriety of extramarital sex as a concern in itself. On the contrary, as in ancient Rome, the characters often worry about the deleterious consequences of the absence of such intimacy; thus, Niles and Martin become alarmed when Frasier goes for a protracted period without "being with a woman." Roz, by contrast, is depicted as having sex routinely with almost any man who is willing and minimally attractive; this propensity is a frequent subject of mirthful banter, but not of any sustained moral appraisal or censure.

The fact that traditional sexual morality is so wholly absent from a show in which the characters are portrayed as highly reflective and in some ways morally ultrafastidious is revealing of a dramatic change in prevailing sexual ethics. (In this respect, *Frasier* presents a contrast to a celebrated series like, say, *Seinfeld*, which is similarly oblivious to traditional sexual morality but in which the characters are emphatically *not* portrayed as morally serious.)[125]

Ferdinand Mount summarizes the prevailing mind-set: "Except for a minority of religious fundamentalists, we are reluctant to condemn any specific sexual practice as wrong in itself. . . . Between consenting adults in private, there are almost no limits."[126] This understanding is similar, Mount contends, to the attitudes that prevailed in ancient Greece and Rome. Like the pagan view and unlike the Christian view, in the prevailing modern at-

125. A more recent and in one sense even starker example is the popular and still running drama *Blue Bloods*, about a New York police commissioner, Frank Reagan (played by Tom Selleck), and his family. One son, Danny (played by Donnie Wahlberg), is portrayed as being faithful to his wife, but Frank, another unmarried son (Jamie, played by Will Estes), and divorced daughter Erin (played by Bridget Moynahan) have occasional brief sexual relationships. Although the show is fraught with moral challenges and dilemmas, these occasional sexual interactions are not treated as morally problematic (except insofar as, for example, sexual intimacy with one's police squad partner might create issues in a working relationship). Although sexual relationships are far less common and less prominent as a theme than in *Frasier*, what makes the absence of moral reflection or concern on the subject striking is that the family in *Blue Bloods* is portrayed as deeply Catholic and highly traditional: they meet often for family dinners, always begin the meals with prayers, often explicitly addressing Jesus. And yet there is no evident concern about traditional Christian teachings on sexual morality.

126. Ferdinand Mount, *Full Circle: How the Classical World Came Back to Us* (New York: Simon and Schuster, 2010), 104.

titude "sex is not thought of as sinful in any of its manifestations."[127] Rather, the modern attitude reflects a "Neo-Pagan yearning for a return to the easy, down-to-earth sexual life of the ancient world."[128]

Again as in Rome, however, sexual intimacy, although not intrinsically generative of moral restrictions, is subjected to *extrinsic* limitations arising from independent practical or ethical considerations. Unlike in Rome, these extrinsic sources of restrictions are not the ethic of manliness or the need for population replenishment, but more nearly the opposite of those ancient constraints. Thus, instead of an ethic of masculinity, contemporary culture reflects two more contemporary ethical commitments—to gender equality, and to personal autonomy and hence individual consent. These commitments have combined, in some contexts, to generate severe restrictions on sexual activity—restrictions designed to assure that sexual partners, both male and female, have fully agreed to each act or phase of sexual intimacy.[129] And in place of the ancient social pressure to produce children, modern norms have been structured to promote the *avoidance* of unwanted pregnancies. This concern to limit pregnancy and population growth, together with concerns about the risk of sexually transmitted disease, has sponsored a series of programs and campaigns to facilitate the availability of contraceptives—on which, more in a moment.

Constitutionalizing the Sexual Revolution. Positive law—constitutional law in particular—has played a central role both in expressing and in facilitating this shift from a Christian to a more pagan sexual ethics.[130] As noted, as late as the 1950s, American law expressed traditional Christian or biblical understandings of what was permissible in sexual relations. Beginning in the 1960s, however, the law moved decisively in the opposite direction.

Thus, in 1965, in the case of *Griswold v. Connecticut*, the Supreme Court found in the "emanations" and "penumbras" of various constitutional provisions a right of "privacy" that could extend constitutional protection to the use of contraceptives. Initially, in invalidating Connecticut's anticon-

---

127. Mount, *Full Circle*, 103. In sum, "the twenty-first century is the century of recreational sex, gourmet sex, sex as lifestyle, sex as fulfilling relationship, anything but sex as sacrament" (112).

128. Mount, *Full Circle*, 96.

129. See Kevin Cole, "Sex and the Single Malt Girl: How Voluntary Intoxication Affects Consent," *Montana Law Review* 78, no. 1 (2017): 1–31.

130. For a lengthy and celebratory history of these developments, see Stone, *Sex and the Constitution*.

traceptive law, the Court stressed the sanctity of the marital bedroom.[131] That limiting rationale quickly disappeared, however. In a later decision, spurning the logic and the majestic "sanctity of marriage" rhetoric of the Connecticut case, the justices reasoned that rights belong to individuals; so if a married person had a right to contraceptives, a single person must have the same right.[132]

A year later, in the legendary case of *Roe v. Wade*,[133] the Court construed the Fourteenth Amendment to support a (slightly qualified) right to abortion. *Roe* was heavily criticized, to be sure, including by some "progressive" constitutionalists who in fact liked the substantive outcome but found the legal rationalization untenable,[134] and also by a number of justices. But just over two decades later, some of these robed critics flipped positions and joined to reaffirm the decision, or at least its "essential holding."[135]

Sexual relations between same-sex partners took longer to achieve constitutional recognition. In 1986, the Court declined to strike down a Georgia law prohibiting "sodomy," finding that the centuries-old legal condemnation of such conduct made it impossible to read an implicit prohibition into the Constitution.[136] In 1996, however, the Court creatively construed a Colorado measure denying "special rights" to gays and lesbians so as to render the law vulnerable to invalidation.[137] Then, in *Lawrence v. Texas*,[138] the Court overruled its earlier decision and struck down a Texas sodomy law. Just over a decade later, the Court ruled that states not only could not prohibit homosexual relationships; states could also not deny same-sex couples who desired it the dignifying status of "marriage."[139]

Ratification of the sexual revolution was not limited to constitutional law, however. At about the same time that courts were decreeing that traditional marriage laws limiting marriage to opposite-sex partnerships were

131. Griswold v. Connecticut, 381 U.S. 479, 486 (1965).
132. Eisenstadt v. Baird, 405 U.S. 438 (1972).
133. Roe v. Wade, 410 U.S. 113 (1973).
134. See, e.g., John Hart Ely, "The Wages of Crying Wolf," *Yale Law Journal* 82 (1973): 920. See also Mark Tushnet, *Red, White, and Blue: A Critical Analysis of Constitutional Law* (Lawrence: University Press of Kansas, 2015), 54 ("We might think of Justice Blackmun's opinion in Roe as an innovation . . . —the totally unreasoned judicial opinion").
135. *Casey*, 505 U.S. 833.
136. Bowers v. Hardwick, 478 U.S. 186 (1986).
137. Romer v. Evans, 517 U.S. 620 (1996).
138. Lawrence v. Texas, 539 U.S. 558 (2003).
139. *Obergefell*, 576 U.S. ___. *Obergefell* was strongly foreshadowed in United States v. Windsor, 570 U.S. 744 (2013).

unconstitutional, the Department of Health and Human Services, acting on language in the Affordable Care Act (so-called Obamacare), issued regulations requiring most employers to offer their employees insurance coverage that included contraceptives free of any co-pay. This so-called contraception mandate contained limited exemptions for religious institutions, but it provoked objections from a number of employers who did not qualify for the exemptions and who maintained religious objections either to contraception or to particular contraceptives that they regarded as abortifacients. These objections gave rise to a fierce conflict between supporters of the contraception mandate and proponents of a traditional conception of religious liberty.[140] We will consider that conflict more closely in the next chapter.

The Symbolism of Sexuality. Laws regulating sexual matters can be important for their practical consequences, obviously—prohibitions of abortion may be the clearest case—but they are also important, or perhaps even more important, for what they symbolize. Thus, as noted, laws in the 1950s that appeared calculated to limit sex to marriage went pervasively unenforced. Their direct, formally legal impact on sexual behavior was often *de minimis*. Even so, the laws reflected a community commitment to a Christian or biblical standard or ideal. Insofar as symbols are constitutive of community, as discussed earlier, that symbolic commitment was understandably supported by some and resented by others, even if the laws' practical or coercive impact was negligible.

By the same token, the embrace of the morality of the sexual revolution by modern laws is cherished, or resented, not only (and perhaps not even primarily) for the laws' practical consequences, but rather for their impact in symbolizing the rejection of the older Christian conception of the community in favor of a revised conception—a conception, I have suggested, that might aptly be described as "pagan." This dimension of the laws is perhaps most apparent in the changing legal treatment of contraception.

In fact, most Americans today are not morally opposed to contraception, and hardly any favor legal restrictions. There is no movement to reinstate such restrictions.[141] Even so, contraception is at the expressive or symbolic

140. For a description of these developments and an insightful analysis of their cultural significance, see Paul Horwitz, "Comment: The *Hobby Lobby* Moment," *Harvard Law Review* 128 (2014): 154.

141. See Horwitz, "The *Hobby Lobby* Moment," 172 (asserting that "the acceptability [of contraceptives] is 'as close to cultural consensus as we can get'"). Douglas Laycock observes that "it is unimaginable that any American state would now attempt to ban contraception" and that "the bishops gave up that battle long ago." Douglas Laycock, "Religious Liberty and the Culture Wars," *University of Illinois Law Review* 2014 (2014): 839, 867.

core of the transformation in sexual morality. Thus, what D'Emilio and Freedman call "the contraceptive revolution" is what made possible the separation of sexual intimacy from its traditional connections to procreation and marriage.[142] The new and widespread availability of "the pill" in the 1960s was also closely tied to the new commitment to gender equality: "the pill" made it possible for women to engage in the same sorts of sexual activities previously more available to men without incurring the distinctive risk of pregnancy.[143]

So it is not surprising that the law pertinent to contraception starkly expresses the transformation in public norms. In the 1950s, as noted, the distribution of contraceptives was at least formally prohibited in most states and under federal law. Then, contraception went comparatively swiftly from being (a) legally forbidden to being (b) constitutionally permitted *for married couples*,[144] then (c) constitutionally protected *for adults and presumptively responsible adolescents* whether single or married,[145] and now (d) viewed as something that women—or at least employed women—have a legal right to have supplied free of charge. Indeed, that legal right is increasingly described (including by a majority of Supreme Court justices) not merely as a benefit that government may choose to confer, but as one in which government has a "compelling interest"—an interest that, unless it can be satisfied in some less burdensome way, overrides other long-standing and previously central commitments to things such as freedom of religion.[146]

It would also appear that the law of contraception matters to people—and provokes fierce legal disputes and heated political rhetoric—less because of the practical consequences of the law than because of what it symbolizes. As noted, the old prohibitions on contraception were mostly symbolic; they were rarely if ever enforced. Conversely, most women today could likely obtain contraceptives without legal requirements mandating that employers supply them—by private purchase or from subsidized entities like Planned Parenthood.[147] Indeed, except for the few employers with

142. D'Emilio and Freedman, *Intimate Matters*, 242–55, 338.

143. D'Emilio and Freedman, *Intimate Matters*, 250–51.

144. *Griswold*, 381 U.S. 479.

145. *Eisenstadt*, 405 U.S. 438.

146. This position was embraced by the four dissenting justices in Burwell v. Hobby Lobby Stores, Inc., 573 U.S. ___ , 134 S. Ct. 2751 (2014), and also in Justice Anthony Kennedy's concurring opinion.

147. See Helen Alvaré, "Meanwhile, Outside the Panic Room: Contraception, Hobby Lobby, and Women's Rights," *Public Discourse*, July 10, 2014, http://www.thepublicdiscourse.com/2014/07/13467.

religious objections, it seems likely that most employers would provide such coverage anyway (especially if, as the government has claimed, contraception actually reduces medical costs).[148] In some cases, to be sure, obtaining contraceptives might be a financial burden (although government has long subsidized contraception for poor women,[149] and although most women for whom the burden is significant—for example, unemployed women—would not benefit from the contraception mandate anyway); but then most goods, even essential ones (housing, food, automobiles, . . . cellphones, laptops), are costly and are typically not provided or mandated by government. The recent insistence on public support for contraception is thus understandable in part as a kind of demand that government place its imprimatur on the new sexual morality. And the conspicuous insistence that contraception be provided *by employers*, rather than through a range of other methods that are sometimes proposed, can be seen as an effort to elicit or extract those employers' support for that policy with its underlying morality.

Sex as the Point of Cultural Separation. Neither the morality of the sexual revolution nor the laws and constitutional doctrines that reflect and ratify that morality are embraced by all Americans. D'Emilio and Freedman describe how the new sexual agenda has frequently provoked resistance, as with the so-called Moral Majority and the New Right.[150] Christian scholars and activists among others continue to advocate the position that holds that sex is intrinsically connected to marriage and procreation.[151] Both the "contraception mandate" and the judicial decisions imposing same-sex marriage on all states continue to provoke active opposition.[152]

Sex and the issues associated with it—abortion, contraception, samesex marriage—thus mark the visible boundary separating warring factions in the current culture wars. D'Emilio and Freedman remark on how as the sexual revolution unfolded under the influence of a variety of forces—cultural, political, religious, and economic—differences over sexual morality became the focal point for a whole array of disagreements. "A broad range of social, cultural, and economic concerns all could be channeled into cam-

148. *Hobby Lobby*, 134 S. Ct. at 2763.

149. See Alvaré, "Meanwhile, Outside the Panic Room."

150. D'Emilio and Freedman, *Intimate Matters*, 344–61.

151. See, e.g., Sherif Girgis et al., *What Is Marriage? A Man and a Woman; A Defense* (New York: Encounter Books, 2012).

152. See, e.g., Ryan T. Anderson, *Truth Overruled: The Future of Marriage and Religious Freedom* (Washington, DC: Regnery, 2015).

paigns against sexual expression or for sexual liberation."[153] As a result, as the twentieth century merged into the twenty-first, "Americans witnessed a politics of sexuality more contentious than ever before."[154]

The contentiousness has likely been enhanced by the fact that the changes, both cultural and legal, have occurred with stunning suddenness. D'Emilio and Freedman explain that "the two decades that followed [the 'don't ask, don't tell' policy of the mid-1990s] saw a degree of change unimaginable a mere generation earlier."[155] In a book chronicling the role of the American Civil Liberties Union in securing the constitutionalization of sexual expression and liberty, Leigh Ann Wheeler observes that "as late as 1973, few Americans could conceive of the possibility that the U.S. Constitution might protect sexual rights and provide for sexual citizenship."[156] Geoffrey Stone, former dean of the University of Chicago Law School, agrees; though an enthusiastic proponent of the new jurisprudence of sexuality (and a strident critic of the older, Christian viewpoint), Stone acknowledges that "Supreme Court justices from almost any prior era in American history would be stunned to learn of the role the Supreme Court and our Constitution have come to play in our contemporary disputes . . . over such issues as obscenity, contraception, abortion, sodomy, and same-sex marriage."[157]

Despite occasional wishful proclamations that "the culture wars are over,"[158] there can be no realistic expectation that these fundamental conflicts will disappear anytime soon. D'Emilio and Freedman thus conclude their history of sexuality in America with the confident prediction that "sex will remain a source of both deep personal meaning and heated political controversy."[159]

153. D'Emilio and Freedman, *Intimate Matters*, 361.

154. D'Emilio and Freedman, *Intimate Matters*, 363. See also 387 ("The influence of sexuality on American life has continued to grow. Just as the erotic came to permeate commerce and media earlier in the century, it now has infiltrated national politics as well").

155. D'Emilio and Freedman, *Intimate Matters*, 371. See also Erwin Chemerinsky, "Law Review Symposium Keynote Address," *U.C. Davis Law Review* 48 (2014): 447–48 (explaining that legal recognition of same-sex marriage had come more quickly than he or others had expected).

156. Wheeler, *How Sex Became a Civil Liberty*, 3.

157. Stone, *Sex and the Constitution*, xxvii–xxviii.

158. See, e.g., Mark Tushnet, "Abandoning Defensive Crouch Liberal Constitutionalism," *Balkinization* (blog), May 6, 2016, http://balkin.blogspot.com/2016/05/abandoning-defensive -crouch-liberal.html; Cathleen Kaveny, "Bookending a Culture War," *Commonweal*, April 19, 2016, https://www.commonwealmagazine.org/bookending-culture-war.

159. D'Emilio and Freedman, *Intimate Matters*, 388.

Capturing the Constitution

With respect to public religious symbols and sexuality, we have observed a shift in American law from a legal regime consonant with the long-standing civil religion described by Bellah—a civil religion that was Christian or at least biblical in character—toward a regime more resonant with an immanent religiosity or, as Eliot put it, "modern paganism." A primary instrument in effecting that shift, as we have seen, was the American Constitution, as interpreted and used by the modern Supreme Court. But, naturally enough, causal influences in this transformation have run both ways. If the Constitution has been employed to make public symbols and sexual norms less Christian and more pagan, the deployment of the Constitution for those ends has had the effect of making the Constitution itself a more pagan instrument.

In this instance, however, the change has not been from Christian to pagan, but rather from neutrally agnostic to pagan. That is because, from the outset, the Constitution was not an overtly Christian document. When the instrument was initially being drafted and ratified, there was a faction that wanted to acknowledge Christianity in the nation's fundamental law. But the framers consciously resisted this demand. Thus, unlike its predecessor, the Articles of Confederation, and unlike state constitutions of the time (and since), the Constitution deliberately avoided any meaningful acknowledgment of "Providence," or "the Almighty," or "the Supreme Governor of the Universe."[160]

Some modern scholars infer from the omission of religious or Christian language in the Constitution that the framers intended a constitutional requirement that governments in America be "secular."[161] The inference is a stark non sequitur.[162] The Constitution could have declared that government

160. See, e.g., Kramnick and Moore, *The Godless Constitution*, 27–45. See also Fea, *America Founded as a Christian Nation?*, 150 (asserting that "the Constitution was never meant to be a religious document, nor did its framers set out to use the document to establish a Christian nation").

161. See Kramnick and Moore, *The Godless Constitution*, 27–45. See also Susan Jacoby, *Freethinkers: A History of American Secularism* (New York: Metropolitan Books, 2004), 28 (observing that "without downgrading the importance of either the establishment clause or the constitutional ban on religious tests for officeholders, one can make a strong case that the omission of one word—God—played an even more important role in the construction of a secularist foundation for the new government").

162. See Steven D. Smith, "Our Agnostic Constitution," *NYU Law Review* 83 (2008): 120. See also Fea, *America Founded as a Christian Nation?*, 162 (arguing that "the Constitution

must be secular, as some other nations' constitutions do; it did no such thing. Later, after the Civil War, a movement developed to insert such a "secular government" requirement into the Constitution; the proposal went nowhere. At about the same time, a "Christian nation" amendment was likewise proposed—and rejected. Both at the founding and a century later, Americans opted for a Constitution that took no position on the matter of a Christian or secular government.[163]

Instead, the Constitution provided a legal framework for governance. To be sure, broad constraints on what government could do in matters of religion were imposed.[164] The original Constitution contained a provision forbidding religious tests for federal office. Shortly thereafter, with the adoption of the First Amendment, the national government and later by extension the state governments were forbidden to establish any church or to interfere with the free exercise of religion. The first two of these provisions precluded a return to official Christendom; I will argue in the next chapter that the last of the provisions had a derivatively Christian character. Within those broad parameters, city or state governments or the federal government might develop measures that were consonant with Christianity, with paganism, or with a more positivistic secularism. The Constitution permitted any of these alternatives; it commanded none of them.

This agnosticism served a valuable function. As constituents of what Will Herberg aptly described as "pre-eminently a land of minorities,"[165] almost all Americans would in different times and circumstances likely find themselves out of harmony with positions taken by national, state, or local governments (just as they would find their political party on the losing side of some national or local elections). That condition of alienation could be distressing, even painful. And yet Americans could remind themselves that the positions and political parties that might currently prevail were not ultimately *constitutive* of the political community. Above them in the hierarchy of legal and political authority stood the Constitution—the *agnostic* Consti-

---

does not mention God . . . not because the framers were trying to create a secular nation, but because, as a point of federalism, they believed that religious matters should be left up to the states").

163. See Philip Hamburger, *Separation of Church and State* (Cambridge, MA: Harvard University Press, 2002), 287–334.

164. For an explication of the original meaning and purpose of the First Amendment's religion clauses, see Smith, *The Rise and Decline of American Religious Freedom*.

165. Herberg, *Protestant-Catholic-Jew*, 247.

tution that declined to put its imprimatur on either Christian or secular (or pagan) conceptions of the community.[166]

The value of this more neutral Constitution came to be appreciated in the mid-twentieth century—during what lawyers often call the "*Lochner* era"[167]—as the courts deviated from constitutional neutrality and turned the Constitution into an instrument for supporting laissez-faire public policies against the emerging regulatory state. A principal tool of this commandeering of the Constitution was the idea of "substantive due process"—the idea of importing *substantive* principles or values into a constitutional provision that on its face appeared to be merely a guarantee that government would follow proper legal *procedures*—to employ the Constitution in favor of economic laissez-faire and against the emerging regulatory state. Through this and other interpretive devices (such as construing Article I's commerce power narrowly), the Constitution was sporadically invoked by the Supreme Court to strike down a number of state laws and also of New Deal responses to the Great Depression. As the depression persisted, however, and as Franklin Roosevelt was repeatedly reelected, this resistance effort—and the idea of "substantive due process"—came to be generally discredited.[168]

For a few decades, anyway. But then the campaign against lingering Christian elements in American law—in the public religious symbols and in the laws of sexuality we have been discussing—ran into an obstacle: continuing popular support or at least inertia made it difficult or impossible to eliminate these features merely by using the democratic process. And so proponents of the transformation turned to the Constitution to override the obstinacy or complacency of the electorate.[169]

In the area of religious symbolism, the main device for undoing the older civil religion has been the First Amendment's establishment clause, interpreted in a way that would have surprised earlier generations (and in

---

166. The point is developed in Smith, "Our Agnostic Constitution."

167. So called after the Supreme Court's controversial decision in Lochner v. New York, 198 U.S. 45 (1905).

168. The story of the *Lochner* era is a familiar part of the constitutional narrative learned by all students of law and American history. See, e.g., Bernard Schwartz, *A History of the Supreme Court* (New York: Oxford University Press, 1993), 190–202.

169. Cf. Stone, *Sex and the Constitution*, 383: "Faced with paralysis in the legislative arena, pro-choice advocates began to think seriously about challenging the constitutionality of anti-abortion statutes in the courts. Initially, this seemed a long shot because, in the words of the *New York Times* Supreme Court columnist Linda Greenhouse, the idea of a constitutional right of abortion seemed 'illusory.' But with legislative change effectively blocked, the courts increasingly seemed the best alternative."

a way, ironically, that would actually render earlier landmark religious freedom laws, such as Jefferson's famous Virginia Statute for Religious Liberty, unconstitutional—as violations of religious freedom).[170] But often, in the absence of any substantive provision or language suited to the task, the due process clause once again seemed the most eligible tool. In the area of sexual morality, therefore, the previously discredited idea of "substantive due process" has been rehabilitated and used to invalidate regulations reflecting traditional or Christian sexual norms. Thus, most of the major decisions concerning sexuality described above—the decisions striking down abortion laws, sodomy laws, and traditional marriage laws—have been justified by reading substantive content into the Constitution's seemingly procedural prohibition on depriving people of life, liberty, or property "without due process of law."[171] The due process clause has been supplemented in some instances by a previously almost moribund[172] but newly and aggressively interpreted equal protection clause.[173]

The story of the revival of "substantive due process" and the infusion of new content into other constitutional provisions is perfectly familiar to lawyers; it is a standard part of most first-year constitutional law courses,[174] and is taken for granted by most lawyers and judges. Given that most of this newly imported content was surely not contemplated by previous generations,[175] however, including by the generations that originally drafted and ratified the provisions now being invoked to overthrow traditional and Christian norms, the decisions have been also fiercely criticized, occasionally by critics and scholars who strongly approve the substance of the results reached by the Courts.[176] But the decisions, and the use of the Constitution to undo entrenched traditional measures and norms, have also been energetically defended: indeed, over the past half-century or so, a major enterprise of constitutional theorizing has developed with a cen-

170. For development of the point, see Smith, *Rise and Decline*, 117–20.

171. For a succinct description of the relevant history before the recent same-sex marriage decisions, see Daniel O. Conkle, "Three Theories of Substantive Due Process," *North Carolina Law Review* 85 (2006): 63, 69–76.

172. Justice Holmes famously described the equal protection clause as "the usual last resort of constitutional arguments." Buck v. Bell, 274 U.S. 200, 208 (1927).

173. See, e.g., *Lawrence*, 539 U.S. 558 (O'Connor, J., concurring).

174. See, e.g., Paul Brest et al., *Processes of Constitutional Decisionmaking: Cases and Materials*, 4th ed. (New York: Aspen, 2000), 1131–1360.

175. See above, 294.

176. See, e.g., Ely, "The Wages of Crying Wolf"; Robert Bork, *The Tempting of America: The Political Seduction of America* (New York: Simon and Schuster, 1990).

tral purpose of justifying interpretations of the due process clause and the Constitution generally to support results that admittedly were not intended or contemplated by the Americans who drafted and supported the various provisions.[177]

Whether one finds the theorizing persuasive or merely sophistical, a consequence of this effort is that whatever confidence citizens might once have had that they could govern themselves by deliberating and then carefully formulating and entrenching specific provisions or rights in the Constitution is now largely lost. Enactment of a constitutional provision amounts to approving a text that may be used in the future to accomplish all manner of results, salutary or mischievous, that those who adopted the provision never imagined.

This is a development, obviously, that some celebrate and some deplore. In the celebratory vein, Geoffrey Stone exults that "from 1957 to the present we have seen a profound transformation in American constitutional law," and he enthuses over the "stunning and, indeed, historic shift in our culture and in our law."[178] Conversely, others worry that the courts' commandeering of the Constitution to advance a progressive agenda amounts to the effective demise of democratic government.[179]

What seems clear, though, is that over the past half-century, the Court's establishment clause jurisprudence has had the effect of invalidating public messages and symbols that earlier generations regarded—and that many in the current generation still regard—as entirely acceptable and indeed admirable.[180] And the Court's substantive due process jurisprudence has systematically dismantled the Christian norms of sexual morality and marriage that previously were officially recognized in law, and has moved the law decisively in the direction of a view of sexuality that resonates with the immanent religiosity of both ancient and modern paganism.

In doing so, for better or worse, the Court has transformed the nation's most fundamental law—one that once stood majestically above the

177. This literature is vast. Among leading manifestations, however, are John Hart Ely, *Democracy and Distrust* (Cambridge, MA: Harvard University Press, 1981); Ronald Dworkin, *Law's Empire* (Cambridge, MA: Belknap Press of Harvard University Press, 1986); Bruce Ackerman, *We the People*, vol. 1, *Foundations* (Cambridge, MA: Harvard University Press, 1991); Jack M. Balkin, *Constitutional Redemption* (Cambridge, MA: Harvard University Press, 2011).

178. Stone, *Sex and the Constitution*, 534, 535.

179. See, e.g., *The End of Democracy? The Judicial Usurpation of Politics*, ed. Mitchell S. Muncy and Richard John Neuhaus (Dallas: Spence, 1997).

180. See Smith, *Rise and Decline*, 117–20.

fray of contesting religious and secular conceptions of the community, and hence could serve as an anchor for the allegiance even of citizens who found themselves in the situation of being a political or cultural or religious minority—into a partisan instrument in the struggle between transcendent and immanent conceptions of the city.

CHAPTER 11

Counterrevolution, Part II: Religious Freedom

Pages ago, in the first chapter, we confronted a question in two versions. We first took note of Pliny's question (and Tertullian's), raised almost two millennia ago: Why did the Romans persecute and often execute people just for being Christian—even though (as Tertullian insisted) the Christians sustained and even prayed for the emperors, the legions, and other Roman authorities and institutions?

After surveying the nature of Roman religion and its differences from Christianity, we considered answers to late antiquity's version of the question in chapter 6. The Romans *could have*, and sometimes did, tolerate Christianity. And yet Roman persecution of Christians, it turned out, was not merely gratuitous or malicious. That is because, despite the Christians' sincere protestations of loyalty, in a variety of ways Christianity *was* subversive of the Roman city, or of the kind of political community that the Romans were striving to maintain. Persecution, if not exactly necessary or commendable, was at least an instrumentally and symbolically rational response to that subversive force.

The second, less violent version of the question arises in America today, posed by people like lawyer and scholar Douglas Laycock. Why do proponents of an antidiscrimination agenda bring lawsuits against marriage counselors, wedding photographers, florists, and others who are religiously opposed to same-sex unions, even when the services offered by these professionals are readily available from other providers, and even though no sensible same-sex couple would actually want the services of a provider who is religiously opposed to their union? Generally libertarian in his commitments, Laycock criticizes this litigating zeal as a manifestation of intolerance—an accusation he extends to Christians who support laws regulating sexual conduct they regard as immoral. We considered the issues of sexuality and law in the previous chapter and observed how, by embodying Christian or conversely pagan norms of sexuality, laws are important constitutive symbols expressing and constructing the community along Christian or pagan lines. It is now time to take up the question we started with.

So, why *do* LGBT advocates seek to impose sanctions on religious traditionalists even when these traditionalists' services are neither needed nor desired? Is such litigation a manifestation of intolerance, as Laycock suggests? And even if we stipulate that it is, does this label actually illuminate anything? What is the explanation for this "intolerance," if that is what it is? Why would people take the time and trouble to be affirmatively intolerant in this way?

These questions place us squarely in the middle of one of the major controversies of our time—the controversy over religious freedom. For most of American history, at least since the adoption of the Constitution, religious freedom was a commitment piously embraced (if imperfectly honored) by nearly all citizens, even though the meaning and implications of that commitment were often energetically contested.[1] Today things may appear to be different. Many citizens, activists, and politicians on one side of the cultural and political divide (as well as some critics, like Laycock, who are *not* generally on that side of the divide) perceive activists, politicians, and scholars on the other side of the divide as being indifferent or even hostile to religious freedom. "For the first time in nearly 300 years," Laycock argues, "important forces in American society are questioning the free exercise of religion *in principle*—suggesting that free exercise of religion may be a bad idea, or at least a right to be minimized."[2]

Typically, though, such characterizations are rejected, indignantly.[3] Virtually everyone at least purports to be in favor of religious freedom; few admit to being opposed to it. So, who is right? What exactly is going on in these cultural, legal, and political battles over religious freedom?

The preceding discussions will already have suggested the overall response to be offered in this chapter. The contemporary fight over religious freedom is one battleground—a central one, as it happens—in the larger and

---

1. For a supporting survey, see Steven D. Smith, *The Rise and Decline of American Religious Freedom* (Cambridge, MA: Harvard University Press, 2014).

2. Douglas Laycock, "Sex, Atheism, and the Free Exercise of Religion," *Detroit-Mercy Law Review* 88 (2011): 407.

3. See, e.g., Chris Johnson, "DOJ Touts Anti-LGBT Views, Task Force at 'Religious Freedom' Summit," *Washington Blade*, July 30, 2018, http://www.washingtonblade.com/2018/07/30/sessions-announces-new-task-force-at-anti-lgbt-religious-freedom-summit/.

essentially religious struggle to define and constitute America. The practical reality, of course, as with most such struggles, is that the conflict is confusing and pervasively confused: it is one in which, to enlist again Matthew Arnold's metaphor, "ignorant armies clash by night."[4] So any assessment of the issue will necessarily seek to discern and impose a clarity that is to some extent artificial, as theorizing characteristically does. With that caveat, here is a succinct description.

One side in the struggle favors a conception of religious freedom that is consistent with—and thus symbolically expressive of, and thus to an extent constitutive of—a city or a political community that respects and is open to transcendence. The other side, guided by a different civic vision, seeks to close that opening. In sealing off the city against transcendence, though, this side is not opposed to religion, or even to transcendent religion. Not necessarily, anyway, and not for now. Nor are actors on that side of the divide necessarily opposed to religious freedom. But they work to keep the troublesome, *transcendent* sort of religion out of the public square[5]—outside the inner city walls, so to speak—and thus to maintain a public square whose commitments are confined to the satisfaction of "interests" and to *immanently* sacred values.

They seek, in other words, to repudiate the generically, implicitly Christian city that Americans have inherited—the one the Supreme Court recognized when in 1892 it declared that "we are a Christian nation"[6]—and to reestablish a city with virtues, sensibilities, and a civic character (including an understanding of religious freedom) that could more aptly be described as . . . pagan. And they perceive that transcendent religion within the public square is subversive of such a city in ways analogous to those in which the Romans perceived, correctly, that Christianity was subversive in classical times.

In sum, the contemporary battle over religious freedom is a sort of microcosm of the current and perennial struggle between transcendent and immanent religiosities, and an attempt to roll back the Christian revolution of the fourth century.

---

4. Matthew Arnold, "Dover Beach," Poetry Foundation, accessed July 13, 2017, https://www.poetryfoundation.org/poems/43588/dover-beach.

5. Cf. Stephen Macedo, "Transformative Constitutionalism and the Case of Religion: Defending the Moderate Hegemony of Liberalism," *Political Theory* 26 (1998): 56, 61, 63 (arguing that a liberal state needs to cultivate "wishy-washy religion").

6. Holy Trinity Church v. United States, 143 U.S. 457, 470 (1892).

Religious Freedom, American Style

Political polemics and even academic discussions sometimes address "religious freedom" as if it were some sort of Platonic form with an identifiable and monolithic essence that a person could either approve or oppose. This essentialist, for-it-or-against-it way of thinking may simplify (and polarize, and thereby energize) discussions. But it fails to acknowledge the diverse ways in which governments have tolerated, respected, and sometimes promoted or, conversely, have discouraged, restricted, and even prohibited different forms of "religion."[7]

Although it is artificial to think of religious freedom as a unitary commitment that we either support or oppose, we *can* talk about political arrangements that are more or less conducive to a range of ways of living in accordance with people's diverse understandings of the sacred. And we can discern different general approaches or strategies calculated to enhance or constrict this sort of freedom. In America, as it happens, the dominant overall approach to diversity in religion has traditionally emphasized two central themes or strategies, which we can describe as "nonestablishment" and "accommodation."

The first of these themes is usually associated with the First Amendment's establishment clause ("Congress shall make no law respecting an establishment of religion . . ."); the second is often tied to that same amendment's free exercise clause (". . . or prohibiting the free exercise thereof"). The preceding chapter touched on one aspect of the nonestablishment theme— the constitutional doctrine developed by the Supreme Court that in recent decades has forbidden government to "endorse" religion.[8] By contrast, our primary focus through much of this chapter will be on the second of these themes—the accommodation theme. But we will need to take occasional notice of the first theme as well. In doing so, we will see how a version of nonestablishment may be working together with rising opposition to religious accommodation to bring about a revival or reconstruction of a civic community aptly describable as "pagan."

The Accommodation Strategy. The central idea animating the accommodation strategy is basically this: government should respect people's religious commitments, and should make an affirmative effort to avoid burdening or

7. The point is developed in Steven D. Smith, *Foreordained Failure: The Quest for a Constitutional Principle of Religious Freedom* (New York: Oxford University Press, 1995), 6–8.

8. See above, 268–82.

interfering with those commitments. Put differently: government should affirmatively try to leave space for people to live in accordance with their diverse understandings of the sacred. So if a particular law would require a person or group to violate a sincerely held religious commitment, then a just and humane government will, *if reasonably possible* (because sometimes it will *not* be reasonably possible),[9] find ways to excuse compliance by those people whose religion would be burdened.

Probably the best-known example involves religious pacifism and military service. Quakers have been a discernible presence in American life since colonial days. And Quakers are known to have a sincere religious objection to participating in war. So if there is a practically feasible way to excuse Quakers (and other sincere religious pacifists) from serving in the military, then that is what the government should do. Or at least so an accommodationist understanding of religious freedom would admonish.

Once again, this is not the only stance a government might take toward religion, nor is it even the only approach that might be described as respecting religious freedom.[10] For example, a government might aspire to be simply agnostic or neutral toward religion—neither pro nor con. So the government would leave people free to live in accordance with their various faiths so long as no positive secular public policy is implicated, but it would disclaim any obligation to accommodate religious practices that happen to bump up against some public interest or policy. This sort of agnostic or neutral stance might be described as respecting religious freedom, at least in an attenuated sense, insofar as diverse religious faiths and practices are at least presumptively *permitted*, not targeted for disfavor or persecution. This was, arguably, the sort of approach favored by John Locke and by Roger Williams—usually counted as friendly figures in the development of religious

9. To invoke a commonly used example, see, e.g., Andrew Koppelman, "Secular Purpose," *Virginia Law Review* 88 (2002): 106n68: if a group of devout Aztecs believes it is religiously obligated to cut out the beating hearts of sacrificial victims, application of a state's laws prohibiting homicide would surely burden the exercise of that belief; but, at least in America today, nearly everyone would consider it unreasonable for the government to exempt the Aztecs from the murder laws. The government's interest in preventing murder will outweigh the Aztecs' religious commitment.

10. Governments need not purport to respect religious freedom, of course. Governments might be—and have often been—actively hostile to religion, or at least some religions. Communist governments have often adopted this attitude, for example. So did the Mexican government during the period portrayed in Graham Greene's novel *The Power and the Glory* (New York: Penguin, 1991).

freedom.[11] The accommodationist position goes further, however, treating religion as something valuable that government should affirmatively respect and, if reasonably possible, look for ways to avoid interfering with.[12]

And in fact, accommodation has been the typical American approach to religious diversity. For about three decades in the twentieth century, the constitutional doctrine of the First Amendment's free exercise clause, as expounded by the Supreme Court, explicitly embraced a commitment to religious accommodation. At least as understood by most lawyers and scholars,[13] the doctrine mandated that people whose religion would be burdened by compliance with state or federal law should be exempted unless the government had a "compelling interest" in their compliance that could not be achieved in some less restrictive way. This exemptions doctrine was officially articulated in 1963 in a case called *Sherbert v. Verner*,[14] and the doctrine persisted until it was renounced by the Court in 1990 in *Employment Division v. Smith*,[15] the much-discussed "peyote case."

Given these judicial markers, commentators sometimes suggest that the accommodation strategy prevailed only during a relatively short period of American history.[16] But this characterization greatly understates the historical scope and importance of the accommodation approach. For much of the nation's earlier history, states were the primary locus of governance, and many states built religious accommodation requirements into their state constitutions.[17] Legislators in the early republic also recognized the wisdom and the justice of trying to accommodate religious dissenters;

11. On Locke, see Martha C. Nussbaum, *Liberty of Conscience: In Defense of America's Tradition of Religious Equality* (New York: Basic Books, 2009), 67. On Williams, see Steven D. Smith, "Separation and the Fanatic," *Virginia Law Review* 85 (1999): 230–31.

12. An accommodation strategy can be and has been implemented on a variety of levels. It can be—and *was*, for decades—enshrined in constitutional doctrine. It can also be—and often has been—embodied in statutes, both state and federal. Accommodation can be afforded by institutional policies—of a school district, or a corporation. Often the strategy is implemented on an informal and ad hoc basis: a student asks if she can be excused from class on Friday because of a religious holiday, and the teacher says yes (or no).

13. I have elsewhere offered a slightly different interpretation of what the Court's "free exercise" jurisprudence had called for. See Steven D. Smith, *Getting Over Equality: A Critical Diagnosis of Religious Freedom in America* (New York: New York University Press, 2001), 83–96.

14. Sherbert v. Verner, 374 U.S. 398 (1963).

15. Employment Division v. Smith, 494 U.S. 872 (1990).

16. See, e.g., Ira C. Lupu, "*Hobby Lobby* and the Dubious Enterprise of Religious Exemptions," *Harvard Journal of Law and Gender* 38 (2015): 48–54.

17. See Michael W. McConnell, "The Origins and Historical Understanding of Free Exercise of Religion," *Harvard Law Review* 103 (1990): 1421–29.

they looked for ways to excuse Quakers from various legal requirements such as oaths, removal of hats in court, and military service.[18] In addition, judges supported and practiced religious accommodation; they interpreted constitutional commitments to mean that sincere religious objectors should be excused from complying with laws that would require them to violate their religious obligations. In one early New York case, for example, a judge excused a Catholic priest from revealing information about a crime that he had heard in confessional.[19]

Thus, as Paul Horwitz observes, "accommodation of religion is an aboriginal feature of American pubic law. From the earliest days of the Republic, exemptions from legally imposed burdens on religious belief and practice 'were seen as a natural and legitimate response to the tension between law and religious conviction.'"[20] To be sure, there were all along differences of opinion about whether and when exemptions should be afforded, and about whether exemptions should be granted by legislators or judges. The commitment to accommodation never commanded unanimous support.[21] Even so, the value and the justice of accommodation were widely and repeatedly acknowledged from the outset of the republic.

The major authority apparently contradicting this interpretation is the nineteenth-century case of *Reynolds v. United States*.[22] In this and two follow-up decisions,[23] the Supreme Court rejected the claim of Mormons, or members of the Church of Jesus Christ of Latter-day Saints, who contended that laws prohibiting the practice of plural marriage infringed their freedom of religion by compelling them to violate what Mormons at that time accepted as their religious obligation to enter into polygamous marriages.

18. McConnell, "Origins and Historical Understanding," 1467–72.

19. People v. Phillips, Court of General Sessions, City of New York (June 14, 1813), published in William Sampson, *The Catholic Question in America* (University of Michigan Library, 1813). The decision was privately reported but has been frequently reprinted. See, e.g., Michael W. McConnell et al., *Religion and the Constitution*, 3rd ed. (2011), 139.

20. Paul Horwitz, "The *Hobby Lobby* Moment," *Harvard Law Review* 128 (2014): 167 (partially quoting McConnell, "Origins and Historical Understanding," 1466).

21. See, e.g., Simon's Executors v. Gratz, 2 Pen. & W. 412 (Penn. Sup. Ct. 1831) (rejecting claim for accommodation of Jewish Sabbath).

22. Reynolds v. United States, 98 U.S. 145 (1878). In an interpretation seeking to minimize the value and historic importance of the accommodation, Ira Lupu relies primarily—or rather, solely and entirely—upon *Reynolds* to characterize the pre-1963 constitutional jurisprudence of free exercise. Lupu, "*Hobby Lobby*," 48–49.

23. Davis v. Beason, 133 U.S. 333 (1890); Late Corporation of the Church of Jesus Christ of Latter-Day Saints v. United States, 136 U.S. 1 (1890).

Reynolds, it is conventionally said, interpreted the First Amendment's free exercise clause to protect only religious *beliefs*, not religious *conduct*.[24]

But *Reynolds* is a more complicated decision than the standard description conveys. Indeed, it might be said that there are effectively *two* majority opinions in *Reynolds*. One opinion does contain the "belief/conduct" language that most lawyers and scholars have seized upon.[25] If this were the sole rationale for the decision, however, the Court could and should have ended its analysis at that point. Mormons are free to *believe* that they should practice plural marriage, the Court would have said, but they are not legally free to *act* on that belief. End of discussion.

In fact, however, the Court did not finish up with this conclusion; instead, it went on to argue, at length, that polygamy was a serious evil that could not be countenanced in America's free society.[26] Polygamy undermines the sanctity of marriage, the Court contended, which is vital to American institutions.[27] And polygamy promotes an undemocratic authoritarianism by embracing the oppressive "patriarchal principle."[28] (This argument in *Reynolds* may come as a surprise to those who suppose that nineteenth-century American law and society were thoroughly and unapologetically committed to patriarchy.) These arguments about social harm would seem to be wholly superfluous if the Court was indeed committed to the view that only religious belief, not conduct, is protected by the free exercise clause. But the Court's arguments were nicely congruent with the accommodation/balancing strategy sometimes said to have developed only later in the twentieth century.

Clark Lombardi contends that this second *Reynolds* opinion—the one that insisted that polygamy was an evil so serious that it could not be accommodated—resonated with views commonly expressed by nineteenth-century judges, legislators, and scholarly commentators.[29] Many courts and commentators of the period, Lombardi argues, recognized an obligation

24. See, e.g., Lupu, "*Hobby Lobby*," 48; Daniel O. Conkle, *Religion, Law, and the Constitution*, Concepts and Insights Series (Saint Paul, MN: Foundation Press, 2016), 15–17.

25. *Reynolds*, 98 U.S. at 164.

26. *Reynolds*, 98 U.S. at 164–67.

27. *Reynolds*, 98 U.S. at 165–66.

28. *Reynolds*, 98 U.S. at 166.

29. Clark B. Lombardi, "Nineteenth-Century Free Exercise Jurisprudence and the Challenge of Polygamy: The Relevance of Nineteenth-Century Cases and Commentaries for Contemporary Debates about Free Exercise Exemptions," *Oregon Law Review* 85 (2006): 369, 403–23.

to accommodate religion (though others did not).[30] But proponents of accommodation acknowledged that legal exemption could not be extended to excuse egregious or intolerable evils. One standard example of an intolerable evil (used even before the Mormon religion came on the scene) was polygamy.[31] The *Reynolds* decision fit precisely into this familiar pattern; it listed human sacrifice as an example of an evil so grave that it could not be accommodated,[32] and it argued that polygamy was another such instance. This section of the *Reynolds* opinion thus appears to presuppose a presumptive obligation to accommodate religion.

To be sure, this second theme in *Reynolds* did not erase the first theme—the one suggesting that free exercise protects only belief, not conduct. That interpretation, along with one of the principal arguments that the Court gave for it (namely, that excusing religious conduct would make every citizen "a law unto himself"),[33] was in a sense ahead of its time; we will return to the argument shortly. For now, the important point is that *Reynolds* in no way negates the fact that from the outset of the republic, a commitment to religious accommodation, though not uncontroversial, was a prominent theme—arguably the *central* theme, along with nonestablishment—in the American approach to religious diversity. That theme persisted and was elaborated more explicitly by the Court in the twentieth century.[34]

Then, in 1990, in *Employment Division v. Smith*, the so-called peyote case, the Court disavowed the accommodation doctrine *as a constitutional requirement* in favor of a rule holding that so long as a law is religiously "neutral" and "generally applicable," no accommodation is *constitutionally* required. At the same time, however, the Court explicitly authorized legis-

---

30. Lombardi, "Nineteenth-Century Free Exercise Jurisprudence," 398–403.

31. Lombardi, "Nineteenth-Century Free Exercise Jurisprudence," 432–41.

32. *Reynolds*, 98 U.S. at 166.

33. *Reynolds*, 98 U.S. at 167.

34. Although it is usually reported, as noted, that the Supreme Court did not build the accommodation requirement into constitutional doctrine until 1963 (see, e.g., Lupu, "*Hobby Lobby*," 49), that report is not quite accurate. The Court had explicitly rejected any categorical belief-conduct distinction and had implied a qualified obligation to accommodate religious conduct much earlier in the well-known case of Cantwell v. Connecticut, 310 U.S. 296, 303–4 (1940). Lawyers and scholars are aware of the *Cantwell* statement (see, e.g., Conkle, *Religion, Law, and the Constitution*, 17) but usually fail to regard it as an actual statement of law, perhaps because it was not offered in the formulaic terms that legal "doctrines" later commonly came to take. For a critical and perceptive discussion of this "formulaic" style, see Robert F. Nagel, *Constitutional Cultures: The Mentality and Consequences of Judicial Review* (Berkeley: University of California Press, 1989), 121–55.

latures to mandate religious accommodation as a matter of *statute.*[35] And indeed, legislatures—including Congress and numerous state legislatures—promptly did just that (as in fact they had already long been doing).[36] Congress, for example, adopted a law called the Religious Freedom Restoration Act that essentially reestablished the exemptions doctrine as a statutory matter. That act was adopted with virtually unanimous approval in Congress, and with the support of a range of diverse groups from the ACLU to the National Council of Churches.[37] In signing the statute, President Bill Clinton delivered an eloquent address praising religious freedom as "perhaps the most precious of all American liberties" and urging Americans to "fight to the death to preserve the right of every American to practice whatever convictions he or she has."[38]

Such statutory accommodation requirements continue to be enforced by courts to this day.[39] (Although, for reasons we will consider, they are increasingly embattled, as the vehement response to recent efforts to enact religious accommodation provisions in several states reflects.)

The Transcendent Character of the Accommodation Strategy. But *why* should government recognize any presumptive obligation to try to accommodate religion? As it happens, the accommodation strategy is an approach with a discernibly Christian character. Or, rather, it is an approach oriented toward recognition of a transcendent authority—a recognition that, though hardly limited to Christianity, was part of the legacy that Americans inherited from Christianity. This Christian or transcendently religious character of the accommodation approach is apparent both in the historical antecedents that led up to the approach and in its inherent logic or structure.

First, history. The accommodation approach has its historical roots in distinctive Christian ideas that developed in the West over the centuries since Jesus first proclaimed the Christian gospel to a small band of disciples. This development has been discussed at length elsewhere.[40] What follows is a shamelessly condensed synopsis.

---

35. *Employment Division,* 494 U.S. at 890.

36. See Conkle, *Religion, Law, and the Constitution,* 121–23.

37. Conkle, *Religion, Law, and the Constitution,* 123–24.

38. William J. Clinton, "Remarks on Signing the Religious Freedom Restoration Act of 1993," American Presidency Project, November 16, 1993, http://www.presidency.ucsb.edu/ws/?pid=46124.

39. See, e.g., Burwell v. Hobby Lobby Stores, Inc., 134 S. Ct. 2751, 2763 (2014); Gonzales v. O Centro Espírita Beneficente União do Vegetal, 546 U.S. 418 (2006).

40. For my own, much lengthier but still very summary discussion, see Steven D. Smith, *Rise and Decline,* 17–43.

The New Testament narrates how Jesus, in response to a question about the permissibility of paying taxes, declared that there are *two* authorities that we are obligated to respect: the temporal authority, but also the spiritual authority. "Render unto Caesar the things that are Caesar's," Jesus enjoined, "and unto God the things that are God's."[41] As we saw in chapters 5 and 6, the dualism inherent in this view was elaborated by later Christian thinkers, including by Augustine with his doctrine of the "two cities." The practical and legal implications of this dualism took centuries to develop; indeed, those implications continue to be worked out by Christians in the context of the political challenges of their contingent and ever-changing situations. But the first major political product was a commitment to "freedom of the church" from state control—an idea that began to be asserted by bishops almost immediately after the official recognition of Christianity.

Thus, in the fourth century the emperor Constantius attempted to impose an Arian version of Christianity on the church. Constantius, like his father Constantine, seemingly supposed that the emperor would continue to exercise the control over religion that emperors had always enjoyed. Now, however, orthodox bishops resisted, sometimes incurring the emperor's wrath.[42] In the sixth and seventh centuries, church leaders adopted a similar (and sometimes fatal) resistance to imperial efforts to impose the monophysite and monothelite doctrines on the church.[43] For his opposition to the monothelite doctrine, for example, Maximus the Confessor was tortured and exiled, after being silenced by having his tongue and right hand cut off.[44] It was during this period that Pope Gelasius articulated his often-quoted declaration that "Two there are"—namely, two authorities.[45]

This commitment to freedom of the church, or *libertas ecclesiae*, was developed more systematically and aggressively in the "papal revolution" beginning in the eleventh century.[46] The church's resistance to secular political control produced a torrent of polemics and manifestos and legal and political theories.[47]

---

41. Matt. 22:20–21.

42. See Hugo Rahner, *Church and State in Early Christianity*, trans. Leo Donald Davis, SJ (San Francisco: Ignatius, [1961] 1992), 51–60.

43. Rahner, *Church and State*, 133–224.

44. Rahner, *Church and State*, 235–37.

45. Rahner, *Church and State*, 174.

46. See generally Harold J. Berman, *Law and Revolution: The Formation of the Western Legal Tradition* (Cambridge, MA: Harvard University Press, 1983), 85–113.

47. See Brian Tierney, *The Crisis of Church and State, 1050–1300* (Toronto: University of Toronto Press, 1964).

The struggle also produced its epic battles—the confrontation in the empire between Henry IV and Pope Gregory VII, the clash between Henry II of England and Archbishop Thomas Beckett, the conflict between Henry VIII and the deeply devout former lord chancellor Thomas More. And the struggle produced its villains—including, from the pious perspective, all the aforementioned Henrys—and its sainted martyrs, including both of the aforementioned Thomases.[48]

Then, following the effective takeover of the church by monarchs in England and elsewhere in the sixteenth century, and now more under the direction of Protestant Christians, the "freedom of the church" modulated into the "freedom of conscience"—conscience becoming a sort of "internal church" as the new locus of God's essential interaction with humans.[49] Deference previously given to the *church* as an independent jurisdiction was extended to the individual *conscience*; and indeed, early proponents of the freedom of conscience sometimes defended the commitment in explicitly jurisdictional terms. The government, they argued, had *no jurisdiction* over the conscience, which was Christ's kingdom.[50] This newly vigorous commitment to conscience was energetically expounded by seventeenth-century figures like Roger Williams, William Penn, and John Locke.[51] Later, in the eighteenth century, it was taken up by American founders, including James Madison and Thomas Jefferson.

In this way, the Christian commitment to dual jurisdictions—Caesar and God—wound its meandering way into the American understanding of religious freedom. Madison carefully developed the argument that our

48. For a cogent discussion of the relevance of these medieval precedents to contemporary American law, see Richard W. Garnett, "'The Freedom of the Church': (Towards) an Exposition, Translation, and Defense," *Journal of Contemporary Legal Studies* 21 (2013): 33.

49. See Steven D. Smith, *Rise and Decline*, 36–38.

50. See, e.g., Elisha Williams, *The Essential Rights and Liberties of Protestants: A Seasonable Plea for the Liberty of Conscience, and the Right of Private Judgment, In Matters of Religion, Without any Controul from human Authority* (Boston: S. Kneeland and T. Green, 1744), 12 (italics omitted) (arguing that "if CHRIST be the Lord of Conscience, the sole King in his own Kingdom; then it will follow, that all such as in any Manner or Degree assume the Power of directing and governing the Consciences of Men, are justly chargeable with invading his rightful Dominion; He alone having the Right they claim").

51. See generally Nicholas P. Miller, *The Religious Roots of the First Amendment: Dissenting Protestants and the Separation of Church and State* (New York: Oxford University Press, 2012). With respect to one influential Protestant figure, Isaac Backus, Miller explains: "Backus ultimately rested his defense of full religious liberty on the three points common to Locke, Elisha Williams, and [William] Penn: (1) all spiritual knowledge is personal; (2) there is no ultimate earthly spiritual authority; and (3) therefore, the civil power has no jurisdiction in spiritual matters" (106).

duties to "the Creator" are prior to our duties to society; hence, matters of "religion" are "wholly exempt from [the] cognizance"—or, in other words, the jurisdiction[52]—of state and civil society.[53] Somewhat more loosely and grandly, Jefferson proclaimed that "Almighty God hath created the mind free" from government regulation in matters of religion.[54] Both arguments expressly rest on the premise that there is a higher authority—"the Creator" and "Governor of the Universe" (Madison) or "Almighty God" (Jefferson)— on whose jurisdiction earthly governments should not intrude. The classic American statements were thus remote progeny of Jesus's "Render unto God [and thus, by implication, *not* to Caesar] the things that are God's."

But the Christian character of the American approach is not merely genealogical; it is also logical or structural. Once again, the basic idea of religious accommodation, as it has been understood and practiced in America, is a modern expression or instantiation of the same kind of political dualism evident in the "two cities" doctrine of Christian thinkers like Augustine, or in Jesus's teaching that we have obligations to a temporal authority—Caesar, or the state—but also to a higher and transcendent authority, or God. As discussed, the recognition of that higher authority was precisely the basis of the commitment to religious freedom as articulated by Madison, Jefferson, and others. Even if Madison and Jefferson had never heard of Jesus or Christianity, in other words, or even if they had consciously rejected Christianity—as it can be argued that they (or at least Jefferson) *did*[55]—we could still say that their approach to religious freedom reflected the same dualist logic and the same deference to the transcendent that had been central to Christian thinking.

Not surprisingly, the American version of the dualist theme had its distinctive character. In the Middle Ages, for example, the higher authority or God was represented by the church—by *the* church, in the singular—which was viewed as an independent jurisdiction, or a sort of embassy of the heav-

52. Cf. Vincent Blasi, "School Vouchers and Religious Liberty: Seven Questions from Madison's *Memorial and Remonstrance*," *Cornell Law Review* 87 (2002): 783, 789 (observing that the term "cognizance" as used by Madison could not have meant "knowledge" or "awareness" but must rather be understood to mean "responsibility" or "jurisdiction").

53. James Madison, "Memorial and Remonstrance against Religious Assessments [Virginia] 1785," in *Church and State in the Modern Age: A Documentary History*, ed. J. F. Maclear (New York: Oxford University Press, 1995), 59.

54. Virginia Act for Religious Freedom, in Maclear, *Church and State in the Modern Age*, 63, 64.

55. See Joseph J. Ellis, *American Sphinx: The Character of Thomas Jefferson* (New York: Vintage Books, 1996), 309-10.

enly kingdom, that the state was obligated to respect. If a priest was accused of committing a theft or a rape, the state could not simply apprehend the culprit and apply its law; it was required to turn the offending cleric over to the church, to be tried in an ecclesiastical court[56]—just as today an offending foreign diplomat might be turned over to the nation that he or she represents. Later, as conscience came to assume the role of the church as the locus of communion between God and human beings, deference was extended to the conscience. In England, nonetheless, and in some American states, this sort of claim of conscience would still be asserted against the backdrop of *the* church—of the officially recognized and established church, which itself propounded some orthodoxy or official version of the higher truth.

As American constitutional understandings developed in the late eighteenth and early nineteenth centuries, by contrast, no such institution and no such orthodoxy were recognized. (This was, of course, the other major American theme—the nonestablishment theme.) The acknowledgment here was of the *reality* of transcendence (or, in a more modest and agnostic version, of the *possible* reality of transcendence).[57] It was deliberately *not* a recognition either of any particular institution deemed to represent that transcendence or of any official or "orthodox" version of the transcendent truth. In that important sense, the American position—unlike, say, the British position—was *not* specifically or exclusively Christian. Influenced by the Christian legacy, though, the American position recognized the jurisdiction of the transcendent, or of "religion," over which civil society and government had no "cognizance," as Madison put it.

The consequence of this acknowledgment of transcendence in conjunction with the rejection of an established religion or orthodoxy was that within wide bounds it was left to individuals (and to associations or churches with which individuals might freely choose to affiliate) to judge what the transcendent truth and its corollary obligations might be. The government's obligation was merely to refrain from interfering with—or, put positively, to *accommodate*—matters within that jurisdiction over which the state had no authority, or no "cognizance."

In sum, both in its historical roots and in its inherent structure or logic, the characteristic American commitment to religious accommodation had, and has, a Christian or transcendently religious character. It is based on

56. See Robert E. Rodes Jr., *Ecclesiastical Administration in Medieval England* (Notre Dame: University of Notre Dame Press, 1977), 56–59.

57. See below, 338–39.

an acknowledgment of a transcendent reality, or at least of the possibility of such a reality.[58] In that sense, the accommodationist approach to religious freedom not only grows out of a Christian history and conception, it also betokens a community, or a city, constructed and constituted not on Christianity per se but on a conception of transcendence that was a legacy of the Christian tradition. Much in the way that public symbols like those discussed in the preceding chapter, and also laws regulating sexuality, operate as symbols that construct and express the kind of community that we are, the accommodationist approach to religious freedom is more than just a strategy for dealing with religious diversity. It is a symbol—a *constitutive* symbol, a *transcendently religious* constitutive symbol—of the kind of community America is. This is a community, as Lincoln and now the Pledge of Allegiance put it, that is "one nation *under God.*"

The Turn from Transcendence

Which is precisely the underlying problem, at least for citizens who reject a Christian or transcendently religious conception of American community.[59] Thus, it should hardly be surprising that as transcendent religiosity has come to be challenged and to a significant extent displaced by some combination of positivistic secularism and a more immanent religiosity, the historic commitment to religious freedom, at least in its familiar American version favoring religious accommodation, has come to be increasingly embattled.[60] It is challenged by a different conception of religious freedom resonating with a different conception of community—one that rejects the "*two* cities" position (with its acceptance of transcendence) in favor of *the* city. Of the fully and exclusively sovereign city,[61] we might say—a city that, much like

---

58. For a forceful argument to this conclusion, on both theoretical and historical grounds similar to those presented here, see Michael Stokes Paulsen, "The Priority of God: A Theory of Religious Liberty," *Pepperdine Law Review* 39 (2013): 1159.

59. For a forceful statement of this objection, see Jean L. Cohen, "Freedom of Religion, Inc.: Whose Sovereignty?" *Netherlands Journal of Legal Philosophy* 44 (2015): 169.

60. For similar reasons, it should be unsurprising that in advocating a version of immanent religion, as we saw in chapter 9, Ronald Dworkin also argues *against* religious accommodation or special legal treatment of "religion." See Ronald Dworkin, *Religion without God* (Cambridge, MA: Harvard University Press, 2013), 105–49.

61. See generally Cohen, "Freedom of Religion, Inc."; see also Cécile Laborde, *Liberalism's Religion* (Cambridge, MA: Harvard University Press, 2017).

the ancient pagan city, can recognize and celebrate immanent sanctities but is unwilling as a public matter to recognize or defer to any higher or supposedly transcendent authority.

Against Accommodation. Religious accommodation, as noted, has never been uncontroversial, but over the last decade or so it has been subjected to more vigorous and sustained opposition than in the past. Not only is religious accommodation not constitutionally required, critics argue; it is also profoundly objectionable and constitutionally problematic.[62] At present, the outcome of this conflict is very much in the balance.

The opposition to religious accommodation has become conspicuous and pervasive; for now, one illustrative instance may be sufficient. In the spring of 2015, Indiana enacted a law mandating presumptive accommodation of people whose religion was burdened by state laws unless the state had a "compelling interest" in requiring their compliance. And, as they say, all hell broke loose. The law was virtually word-for-word identical to statutes adopted some years earlier in approximately twenty other states and also to the federal Religious Freedom Restoration Act that, as described above, was enacted in 1993 with virtually unanimous congressional support and with the effusive praise of President Bill Clinton. But in the twenty-plus years since that momentary feel-good effusion of national consensus, the political climate had changed, drastically. This time around, Indiana's religious freedom law had its supporters, to be sure, but it was vehemently denounced by a veritable legion of politicians, pundits, government officials, scholars, CEOs, late night talk show hosts, athletic directors, and major corporations. Boycotts were threatened. Governors and mayors announced that public officials would not be reimbursed for travel to do business in the Hoosier state. And Indiana promptly issued its "mea culpa" and amended the offending law into ineffectuality.[63]

The deluge of denunciation was remarkable for its ferocious, almost frantic, quality, so foreign to the cool pragmatism that supposedly distinguishes Americans, especially those of a "secular" disposition. The campaign

---

62. See, e.g., Marvin Lim and Louise Melling, "Inconvenience or Indignity? Religious Exemptions to Public Accommodations Laws," *Journal of Law and Policy* 22 (2014): 705; Louise Melling, "Religious Refusals to Public Accommodations: Four Reasons to Say No," *Harvard Journal of Law and Gender* 38 (2015): 177.

63. For brief summaries of the episode, see Steven D. Smith, "The Tortuous Course of Religious Freedom," *Notre Dame Law Review* 91 (2016): 1553, 1561–65; Patrick J. Deneen, "The Power Elite," *First Things*, June 2015, http://www.firstthings.com/article/2015/06/the-power -elite.

was notable as well for its apparent mendacity: the law provoked, as Douglas Laycock observes, "a massive, and massively false, propaganda campaign from the opponents."[64] Although the Indiana law was routinely castigated as granting an open license to discriminate against gays—or was simply described as Indiana's "antigay" law—defenders pointed out that the law provided no such license and that none of the dire consequences confidently predicted for the Indiana law had occurred with the federal law or with the substantially similar laws in other states.[65] In fact, these laws had *not* been interpreted to license discrimination against gays, and very few claimants had even tried to use them in this way.[66]

But this sort of sober appeal to facts appeared to have no impact at all on the critics. It was hard to avoid the conclusion that their campaign was only secondarily about remedying real, concrete deprivations likely to be suffered by real people. Its primary purpose was different, larger, more evangelical, and it was being pursued with an evangelical zeal. The campaign was about affirming righteousness and stamping out wickedness, and the Indiana law provided a convenient symbol or focal point; the law was more important for what it symbolized—or for what, construed with an advocate's ample license, it could be *made to symbolize*—than for its actual legal and practical effects.

This motivation was strikingly manifest in the massive public reaction to a reported statement by the owner of a pizza shop, Memories Pizza, who said that his religious convictions would preclude him from catering a same-sex wedding reception. One can imagine a calmer world in which the reaction to such a statement would be "What's the big deal?" As it happened, this particular pizza shop had reportedly not catered weddings anyway. Nor are pizza providers in short supply; television commercials for aggressively competitive pizza vendors seem almost as ubiquitous as commercials for auto-

64. See Douglas Laycock, "The Campaign against Religious Liberty," in *The Rise of Corporate Religious Liberty*, ed. Micah Schwartzman et al. (New York: Oxford University Press, 2016), 231, 248 ("The public debate over the Indiana RFRA presented mostly falsehood from both sides"). For further discussion of the mendacious quality of the debate, see Steven D. Smith, "Tortuous Course," 1563–65.

65. See Laycock, "Campaign against Religious Liberty," 249–50. See also an interview of Douglas Laycock: "Why Law Professor Douglas Laycock Supports Same-Sex Marriage and Indiana's Religious Freedom Law," *Religion and Politics*, April 1, 2015, http://religionandpolitics .org/2015/04/01/why-law-professor-douglas-laycock-supports-same-sex-marriage-and-indi anas-religious-freedom-law.

66. Such mendacity has become a recurring spectacle. Much the same display occurred in another episode leading (just last week, as of the time I write) to the veto of a similar law in Georgia.

mobiles, beer, or remedies for erectile dysfunction. And yet in the overheated context of the Indiana controversy, the pizza owner's statement provoked a torrent of outrage and protest, forcing the business to close temporarily—but also an outpouring of support, as sympathizers raised over $800,000 for the beleaguered business.[67] Evidently, the disagreement was not about access to pizza. It was about a conflict between justice and injustice, between good and evil—as (differently) understood by the opposing partisans.

The conflict generated by the Indiana law has been replayed again and again since then—with generally similar results—in other states that have attempted to enact religious accommodation requirements. Similar conflicts have arisen around applications of the federal Religious Freedom Restoration Act, as in the much-discussed *Hobby Lobby* and *Little Sisters of the Poor* cases.[68] As all these conflicts reflect, the idea that government ought if reasonably possible to accommodate people's religious commitments, which as recently as 1993 appeared to enjoy almost universal support, is now deeply contested and fiercely resisted—at least when the substantive policy at stake involves contraceptives or nondiscrimination. (When the substantive issue is further removed from "culture war" controversies—involving, for example, the desire of a Muslim prisoner to wear a short beard—accommodation can still command an almost effortless consensus.)[69]

The Constitutional Arguments. In the popular debate, as the Indiana experience indicates, the opposition to particular religious accommodations may be expressed in aggressively critical characterizations (or mischaracterizations) of the legal provisions that the critics oppose. In the courts and academic journals,[70] by contrast, the opposition has typically been framed in terms of variations on two partly overlapping[71] objections, which we can call the "nonestablishment" objection and the "equality" objection. The first of these objections, drawing on modern establishment clause doctrine that

67. See David McCabe, "Indiana's Memories Pizza Reopens after Gay Rights Furor," *Hill*, April 10, 2015, http://thehill.com/blogs/blog-briefing-room/news/238415-indiana-pizza-parlor-embroiled-in-religious-freedom-law-reopens.

68. *Hobby Lobby*, 573 U.S. ___, 134 S. Ct. 2751; Zubik v. Burwell, 578 U.S. ___, 136 S. Ct. 1557 (2016).

69. Holt v. Hobbs, 574 U.S. ___, 135 S. Ct. 853 (2015).

70. For an extended discussion and criticism of the arguments and a systematic defense of religious accommodation, see Kathleen A. Brady, *The Distinctiveness of Religion in American Law: Rethinking Religion Clause Jurisprudence* (New York: Cambridge University Press, 2015).

71. Ronald Dworkin's more recent objection sounds in both the establishment and equality rationales. See Dworkin, *Religion without God*, 114–16.

forbids government to act in ways that have "a principal or primary effect of *advancing* religion,"[72] contends that accommodating religious believers, or exempting them from burdensome laws, has the impermissible effect of advancing religion. The second objection argues that the religious accommodation violates the fundamental American commitment to the equality of citizens by treating religious dissenters more favorably than nonreligious dissenters.

Whether one finds these arguments persuasive seems to depend mostly on whether one antecedently favors the conclusion to which they lead. Neither argument is at all compelling; conversely, either is sufficiently plausible to justify rejection of accommodation of religion if that is the conclusion one wants to arrive at. Thus, with respect to the nonestablishment objection, it is surely possible as a matter of semantics to describe accommodation as a way of "advancing" religion. And yet the claim that the establishment clause forbids this sort of accommodation—or, if you like, of "advancing"—is far from compelling, and quite alien to the American tradition, as discussed above. Thus, recent scholarship persuasively shows that modern establishment doctrine goes well beyond anything contemplated for the clause by its enactors, who likely thought of themselves as simply keeping the national government out of the domain of religion.[73] And even if we accept modern doctrine forbidding government to "advance" religion, the courts for decades distinguished between "advancing" and "accommodating" religion; the latter, courts maintained, was not forbidden and indeed was up to a point constitutionally commanded. To be sure, an accommodation might go too far, in which case it *could* impermissibly advance religion.[74] But accommodation per se was not unconstitutional; indeed, it was to be encouraged.[75]

72. See, e.g., Lemon v. Kurtzman, 403 U.S. 602, 612–13 (1971).

73. See Steven D. Smith, *Rise and Decline*, 48–66. In this vein, at the conclusion of a recent study, Donald Drakeman explains that "It is important to appreciate that [the establishment clause] was not the statement of a principle of secularism, separation, disestablishment, or anything else. It was the answer to a very specific question: Would the new national government countenance a move by the larger Protestant denominations to join together and form a national church? The answer was no. . . . At the time it was adopted, the establishment clause addressed one simple noncontroversial issue, and the list of those who supported it demonstrates that it cannot reasonably be seen as encompassing a philosophy about church and state." Donald L. Drakeman, *Church, State, and Original Intent* (New York: Cambridge University Press, 2010), 330.

74. See Estate of Thornton v. Caldor, 472 U.S. 703 (1985).

75. See, e.g., Corporation of the Presiding Bishop v. Amos, 483 U.S. 327 (1987). Cf. Richard W. Garnett, "Accommodation, Establishment, and Freedom of Religion," *Vanderbilt Law*

The equality argument, likewise, can seem persuasive and even compelling if you start off agreeing with its implicit premise and with the conclusion
it seeks to support; if you are not antecedently so predisposed, the argument
will seem blatantly question begging. The most famous kind of accommodation—an exemption from military conscription for religious pacifists—can
serve to illustrate the objection, its rhetorical force, and its question-begging
character. Suppose the government exempts Jacob, a Quaker, from serving
in Vietnam because he has a religious objection to war. Meanwhile, Peter,
who has a carefully considered moral but not religious objection to war, is
required to serve (and, possibly, die). Doesn't this preferential treatment of
Jacob over Peter treat the two men unequally, or "discriminate" against Peter
(as Ronald Dworkin puts it)?[76] More generally, doesn't the differential treatment of religious and nonreligious conscientious objectors violate American
commitments to treating citizens equally?

Upon a little reflection, however, the initial rhetorical force of the
straightforward "equality" objection dissipates. Equality means that "*like
cases* should be treated alike"; it obviously cannot mean that all citizens
must be treated *in the same way*.[77] In fact, virtually *every* law inevitably

Review En Banc 67 (2014): 39, 41 (arguing that "it often makes sense and is the right thing to
do—it is not only 'permissible' but also 'praiseworthy'—to accommodate religious believers
through exemptions from otherwise generally applicable laws, including laws that the majority
regards as well-meaning and wise"). In recent years, several scholars have attempted to distinguish this earlier acceptance of accommodation by arguing that although accommodation
per se is not unconstitutional, accommodation becomes unconstitutional if it imposes harms
on third parties. See, e.g., Frederick M. Gedicks and Rebecca Van Tassell, "RFRA Exemptions
from the Contraception Mandate: An Unconstitutional Accommodation of Religion," *Harvard
Civil Rights–Civil Liberties Law Review* 49 (2014): 343. This argument has at best a tenuous
grounding in the case law, and it is embarrassed by the fact that in the best-known and settled
instance of religious accommodation—namely, exemption of religious pacifists from military
service—the harm to third parties seems both real and severe: for every Quaker exempted
from serving in Vietnam, someone else will presumably have to serve (and perhaps die) in
his place. Proponents of the third-party-harm position sometimes attempt to distinguish the
military case by arguing that accommodation is unconstitutional only when a burden falls on
identifiable third parties, but the relevance of this qualification is far from obvious. If we know
that third parties are being burdened or harmed, what difference should it make whether we
can identify precisely who those third parties are? For a cogent critique of the third-party-harm
argument, see Marc O. DeGirolami, "Free Exercise by Moonlight," *San Diego Law Review* 53
(2016): 105, 131–44.

76. Dworkin, *Religion without God*, 125–26.

77. The issue has been extensively discussed in legal literature. The classic treatment is
Peter Westen, "The Empty Idea of Equality," *Harvard Law Review* 95 (1982): 537. For application

and necessarily treats people differently—or, if you want to put it that way, "discriminates." Virtually every law, that is, defines a class of people (e.g., people who are over age eighteen, people who suffer from a disability, people who earn more than or less than a certain income, etc.) to define a status, impose a penalty, or confer a benefit; those within the legally defined class gain the benefit or incur the burden, while those not in the defined class do not. That is how laws work and achieve their purposes—by distinguishing (or "discriminating") among classes of people and treating them differently. The question, always, is whether there is sufficient justification for a classification drawn by the law. Equality means, and can only mean, that the law must not classify people for different treatment *for no good reason*, or without adequate justification. Or, as lawyers say, laws must not treat *"similarly situated"* people differently.[78]

With respect to religious accommodation, therefore, the crucial question is whether there is any good justification for treating people with a *religious* objection to complying with a law differently from people with a sincere but *nonreligious* objection. Maybe there is, maybe there isn't: the question is surely debatable. The fact that the First Amendment explicitly singles out religion as a special legal category suggests that differential treatment does *not* in itself violate constitutional equality requirements. In any case, the straightforward argument that exempting religious believers violates equality *because* it treats them differently, or because it "discriminates," is merely a conclusory form of begging the essential question.

Still, what *is* the answer to that question? (Because "The Constitution—or the statute—says so; we don't know why" is not a very satisfying or powerful response.) People's conflicting answers to the question will naturally reflect their underlying conception of what kind of community we live in, or aspire to live in.

---

of the point to current controversies, see Richard W. Garnett, "Religious Accommodations and—and among—Civil Rights: Separation, Toleration, and Accommodation," in *Institutionalizing Rights and Religion: Competing Supremacies*, ed. Leora Batnitzky and Hanoch Dagan (Cambridge: Cambridge University Press, 2017), 42–56. See also Steven D. Smith, "Equality, Religion, and Nihilism," in *Research Handbook on Law and Religion*, ed. Rex Ahdar (Northampton, MA: Edward Elgar Publishing, 2018).

78. People may, of course, be "similarly situated" for some purposes but not for others. Thus, a law forbidding blind people to *vote* would violate equality, because for purposes of voting blind people and sighted people are similarly situated. But a law forbidding blind people to *drive* would not violate equality, because with respect to driving there is an adequate justification for distinguishing between people who are blind and people who are not.

Thus, in a political community that recognizes the reality or at least the possibility of a transcendent authority, it will seem that someone who thinks *God forbids* him or her to do something is differently situated from someone who has some other, sincere but *nonreligious* reason for not wanting to do something. Similarly, a government that defies what a transcendent authority is thought to command would be in a different and more unsatisfactory position than a government that merely declines to recognize some other sort of potentially meritorious objection.[79]

And in fact, as we have seen, Jefferson's and Madison's arguments for religious freedom were explicitly grounded in the recognition of such a higher authority, thus implicitly reflecting the transcendent assumption in their conception of the American political community. A similar conception of the community as under or subject to a higher authority has been reiterated repeatedly through the course of American history. The Declaration of Independence invoked the authority of "Nature, and nature's God." In his revered Gettysburg Address, Lincoln contended that this is a nation "under God" (although, in faintly Orwellian fashion, contemporary progressives have sometimes tried to excise the phrase).[80] "We are a religious people whose institutions presuppose a Supreme Being," declared Justice William O. Douglas for the Supreme Court as recently as 1952.[81] "In God we trust," proclaims the national motto, printed on all our dollar bills. Over and over and over again, the nation's acknowledgment of a higher authority has been expressed.

So long as this conception was widely accepted, the equality objection to religious accommodation carried little force, including in the courts; reasonable accommodation of religion was not only permissible but constitutionally mandated (although, as noted, it could go too far and thereby amount to an "establishment" of religion). Conversely, as that older conception of the community as grounded in an acknowledgment of transcendent authority

79. See, e.g., Michael W. McConnell, "Accommodation of Religion," *Supreme Court Review* 1985 (1986): 1, 15–24.

80. See Robert P. George, *Conscience and Its Enemies: Confronting the Dogmas of Liberal Secularism* (Wilmington, DE: Intercollegiate Studies Institute, 2013), 147–52. George explains how in a version of the Gettysburg Address printed for distribution by the progressive American Constitution Society, the society used an earlier draft of the talk that did not contain the words "under God," even though historians agree that the language was included in Lincoln's actual address. "These groups know exactly what they are doing," George asserts, "and, to achieve the result they want, they are willing to violate scholarly consensus, common sense, and the memorization of generations of schoolchildren" (151–52).

81. Zorach v. Clauson, 343 U.S. 306, 312 (1952).

has come to seem increasingly problematic, there has seemed to be little reason to distinguish or favor objections grounded in an appeal to such an authority; and the equality argument has accordingly come to seem more compelling. Hence the recent, vigorous opposition to religious accommodation, as evidenced in Indiana and other situations.

A Law unto Himself? The altered conception of community away from the transcendent conception is reflected in a curious comment tossed out by the Court in *Reynolds*, the polygamy case, and taken up more earnestly over a century later in *Employment Division v. Smith*, the peyote case that repudiated the idea of constitutionally mandatory religious accommodation. In *Reynolds*, the Court remarked that it would be unacceptable to exempt religious conduct from a law burdening such conduct because to do so would make the religious objector "a law unto himself."[82] The comment may be understandable in a context in which the Court had rarely declared federal laws unconstitutional and was unfamiliar with the idea of "balancing" or "weighing" interests to declare partial exemptions from enacted laws.[83] By 1990, however, over a century later, when *Smith* was decided, that idea had become commonplace. Nonetheless, in rejecting the idea of mandatory religious accommodation, the Court excavated the language from *Reynolds* and declared that mandatory accommodation would effectively and unacceptably make every man "a law unto himself."[84] Indeed, the majority opinion repeated the claim three times.[85]

On its face, this claim—namely, that religious accommodation renders the accommodated religious believer "a law unto himself"—seems patently and indeed doubly spurious. From the believer's standpoint, the Court's claim gets the situation exactly backward. After all, the believer is asserting precisely that he is *not* a law unto himself, but rather is bound by a higher law or obligation—something like the law of God—that is independent both of government and of his own preferences. If instead we look at the matter from the Court's perspective, or the government's, the claim again seems mistaken. If the Court were to recognize and grant the exemption, in other words, the believer would be excused *not* because he is a "law unto himself" but, on the contrary, because the Court itself chose to craft or interpret the

---

82. *Reynolds*, 98 U.S. at 167.

83. See T. Alexander Aleinikoff, "Constitutional Law in the Age of Balancing," *Yale Law Journal* 96 (1987): 943, 948–52. The *Reynolds* Court's all-or-nothing approach to the legal validity of a statute is apparent at *Reynolds*, 98 U.S. at 166–67.

84. *Employment Division*, 494 U.S. at 885.

85. *Employment Division*, 494 U.S. at 879, 885, 890.

community's own law—in these cases, the free exercise clause of the First Amendment—to authorize the exemption.

From either the believer's or the government's perspective, in short, a "law unto himself" is precisely what the conscientious objector is *not*. He is, rather, subject at least to the law of the land (which the Court retains the authority to construe and apply) and, in his own eyes, to the law of God as well.

More generally, both legislatures and courts routinely create exceptions or exemptions to laws, without any apparent concern about rendering people who come within the exceptions "laws unto themselves." A legislature creates an exception to a minimum wage law, or to an antidiscrimination law, for small employers with fewer than some specified number of employees.[86] Or the legislature enacts a homicide statute but creates an exception for self-defense.[87] Or the Supreme Court interprets the Constitution to forbid particular kinds of official conduct—unwarranted detentions, perhaps, or entrapments by police that induce suspects to commit crimes—but also creates an exception of "qualified immunity" shielding from liability some officials who violate the constitutional standards.[88] Critics are unlikely to attack these exceptions on the ground that they make people covered by the exceptions "laws unto themselves." And if that criticism were raised, the answer would be obvious: "No, the characterization is simply and flatly wrong. The exceptions themselves are as much 'law' as the general rules are, and people within the exceptions are as much subject to the law as people *not* within the exceptions."[89]

The same response should be available, it would seem, if the law, adopted by "we the people" or by Congress and interpreted by the courts, autho-

---

86. See, e.g., Fair Labor Standards Act, 29 U.S.C. § 213 (providing exemptions for minimum wage requirements of section 206); Title VII of the Civil Rights Act, 42 U.S.C. § 2000(e) (defining an "employer" as "a person engaged in an industry affecting commerce who has fifteen or more employees").

87. See, e.g., Cal. Penal Code § 198.5 (allowing for use of deadly force in the home if there is a "reasonable fear of imminent peril or great bodily injury"); Ariz. Rev. Stat. Ann. § 13–411 (justifying the use of deadly force in preventing crime); see also "Self Defense and 'Stand Your Ground,'" National Conference of State Legislatures, March 9, 2017, http://www.ncsl.org/research/civil-and-criminal-justice/self-defense-and-stand-your-ground.aspx (citing as many as twenty-four states with codified self-defense exemptions).

88. See Harlow v. Fitzgerald, 457 U.S. 800 (1982).

89. Every law has a finite scope; it applies to some class of people but not to people outside the class. An exception is simply a way of defining the scope of the law. It no more makes anyone a "law unto himself" than the fact that a law applies only to a defined class makes everyone outside that class a "law unto himself."

rizes an exemption for religious believers whose religion is burdened by a particular legal requirement or prohibition.[90] Religious objectors would be exempted *under that law*. No one would be "a law unto himself."

Why, then, would both the *Reynolds* Court and the *Smith* Court express a profound concern about making a religious believer a "law unto himself"? Looking more closely at the question, though, we may discern a (somewhat strained and scholastic) sense in which the Courts' characterization can seem almost correct.

After all, the religious objector *is* asserting that he is subject to a higher law not made by the government. And he is asking the court to recognize and defer to that higher law—not in general, to be sure, and not for the government itself (the religious pacifist, for example, is *not* saying that the government is legally forbidden to wage war), but at least to the extent of excusing his own compliance with the government's law in deference to that higher law. Perhaps most importantly, the objector is asking the court and the government to defer to the higher law *as interpreted and understood by him* (the objector).

In a very loose sense, acceptance of this sort of claim might be described as rendering the dissenting religious believer a "law unto himself." But whether or not that description is apt, the important point is that this kind of claim for an exemption *is* significantly different from other sorts of requests for exemptions. When a legislature chooses to create an exception for small businesses, or for people who kill in self-defense, the legislature is acting on the basis of this-worldly interests or values that *it* (the legislature) can assess, and it is creating an exception whose scope and content *it* fully defines. The legislature is not deferring to some higher authority or transcendent jurisdiction; much less is it deferring with the understanding that individual objectors, rather than the government, will get to determine what that higher authority or transcendent jurisdiction demands.

---

90. Opponents of religious accommodation often argue that there is no good justification for giving "special treatment" to religion. See, e.g., Brian Leiter, *Why Tolerate Religion?* (Princeton: Princeton University Press, 2013); Micah Schwartzman, "What If Religion Is Not Special?" *University of Chicago Law Review* 79 (2012): 1351; Gemma Cornelissen, "Belief-Based Exemptions: Are Religious Beliefs Special?" *Ratio Juris* 25 (2012): 85; Christopher L. Eisgruber and Lawrence G. Sager, *Religious Freedom and the Constitution* (Cambridge, MA: Harvard University Press, 2007); Anthony Ellis, "What Is Special about Religion?" *Law and Philosophy* 25 (2006): 219; James W. Nickel, "Who Needs Freedom of Religion?" *Colorado Law Review* 76 (2005): 941. But in fact, it is their position that singles out religion for special treatment by making it an impermissible basis of legal accommodation.

So the claim for religious accommodation *is* distinctive. Still, is there anything especially problematic about this distinctive sort of claim? Not under the traditional American approach to religion. That approach, as we have seen, resonates with a conception in which the political community *does* conceive of itself as subject to a transcendent authority—as "one nation under God." And, as we have seen, the logical implication of that conception together with the decision to forgo any established church or official religious orthodoxy is that the determination of what the transcendent authority demands will be left to individuals. This is precisely the logic of Jefferson's invocation of "Almighty God" who "made the mind free" and not subject to earthly authorities, and of Madison's careful demonstration that every person's first obligation (over which the state and civil society have no "cognizance") is to God—an obligation, Madison stressed, that must be measured by the person's own judgment.[91]

Indeed, as we have seen, the basic conception of the community as under or subject to a higher authority (from which the rest of the accommodation logic follows at least naturally, if not quite ineluctably) has been reiterated repeatedly through the course of American history. Conversely, as that conception of the community comes to be displaced by a secular conception—"secular" in the immanent and positivistic senses—the acknowledgment of such a higher authority will come to seem offensive, unacceptable, almost incomprehensible. Deference to a higher power will now seem an impermissible relinquishment of the community's complete sovereignty.[92]

In the exercise of that sovereignty, to be sure, a tolerant and humane community will feel free to "accommodate"—to soften the harsh force of its laws by granting exceptions or indulgences or dispensations or variances— on all sorts of grounds. It may exempt people from otherwise applicable laws on grounds of physical impairments, or economic hardship, or medical necessity, or on any number of other grounds. But a plea for accommodation based on the claim that the community itself is subject to a higher authority? *That* sort of plea will stand out as distinctive, and distinctively

---

91. See James Madison, "Memorial and Remonstrance against Religious Assessments [Virginia] 1785," in *Church and State in the Modern Age: A Documentary History*, ed. J. F. Maclear (New York: Oxford University Press, 1995), and above, 312–13.

92. For a spirited presentation of this view, see Cohen, "Freedom of Religion, Inc." In a similar vein, Laborde, *Liberalism's Religion*; B. Jessie Hill, "Kingdom without End? The Inevitable Expansion of Religious Sovereignty Claims," *Lewis and Clark Law Review* 20 (2017); Richard Schragger and Micah Schwartzman, "Against Religious Institutionalism," *Virginia Law Review* 99 (2013): 917, 939–45.

objectionable. The community may choose to accommodate people, but it is the community—the sovereign community—that will choose to extend or not extend such accommodation. It will not accommodate in deference to some supposed higher authority.

Unless it is taken as simply false or nonsensical, the Supreme Court's objection to making a religious believer "a law unto himself" is best understood as a confused expression of that conception—of a conception of community that declines to acknowledge any higher authority.[93] This shift in conceptions also helps to account for the increasing opposition to religious accommodation. In *Smith*, to be sure, the Court raised the "law unto himself" concern as an objection only to *constitutionally mandated* religious accommodation; the Court explicitly authorized legislative accommodation. But the logic (or illogic) of the "law unto himself" objection is not confinable to constitutional interpretation. Understood as a garbled expression of opposition to public deference to any higher or transcendent authority, the point should carry equal force in the legislative realm, and indeed in any aspect of the civic sphere. Hence, opponents of statutes (like the Indiana law) that would prescribe presumptive religious accommodation are simply taking the Court's "law unto himself" concern to its logical conclusion.

And yet the opposition, once again, is not to accommodation per se. It is opposition to *religious* accommodation specifically—opposition to accommodation based on the distinctive claim that the state is subject to a higher or transcendent power. Like an ancient Roman *paterfamilias* who aspires to be fair-minded and kindly but who brooks no challenge to his ultimate authority within the household, the sovereign secular community may strive to be just and humane, and it may (and does) accordingly grant

---

93. To be sure, there was something curious about the contexts in which the Supreme Court expressed this concern. As a general matter, the nineteenth-century Supreme Court seemingly had no strong reservation about acknowledging a higher authority. This was after all essentially the same Court that struck down an Illinois law authorizing women to practice law on the ground that "the law of the Creator" had ordained that women should fulfill the role of wives and mothers. Bradwell v. Illinois, 83 U.S. 130, 141 (1873). And the same Court would later declare that "we are a Christian nation." *Holy Trinity Church*, 143 U.S. at 470. The "law unto itself" remark in *Reynolds* is perhaps best explained as an overwrought expression of the abhorrence felt by many nineteenth-century Americans toward Mormonism and Mormon polygamy. Justice Scalia's expression of the "law unto himself" worry in *Smith* likewise seems curious, given Scalia's open and unapologetic religiosity; but then a good deal in Scalia's *Smith* opinion seems odd, and difficult to defend. See Michael W. McConnell, "Free Exercise Revisionism and the Smith Decision," *University of Chicago Law Review* 57 (1990): 1109.

indulgences and dispensations—accommodations—of various kinds. But it will bristle at claims for accommodation that deny the ultimacy of its authority.

Transvaluation of Values: The Curious Career of "Freedom of Conscience"

That statement, however, requires qualification, or at least clarification. A political community that refuses to recognize any higher or transcendent authority *might* still honor even transcendently religious claims asserted by individuals—*not* out of deference to a higher authority, but out of solicitude for the individuals who assert them. Thus, even the more aggressive contemporary critics of special accommodation of *religion* are typically respectful of *conscience*. And they may allow that religious claimants for exemption might often be able to bring themselves within the category of freedom of conscience.[94]

The subordination of religion to conscience reflects a striking overall reversal—or "transvaluation of values," so to speak—that is further indicative of a transformative shift in prevailing conceptions of the political community away from a transcendent and toward a more immanent conception. We can appreciate this transformation by considering three phases in the career of freedom of conscience. (This division into three phases simplifies a messier and more complicated history, obviously, but it is useful for expository purposes.)

Trading Places: "Religion" and "Conscience." In the earliest phase, conscience is inherently religious, and freedom of conscience simply *means* "that government must ensure a free response by the individual called distinctively by the Divine within,"[95] as Marie Failinger observes. So "freedom

---

94. See Micah Schwartzman, "Religion as a Legal Proxy," *San Diego Law Review* 51 (2014): 1085; Leiter, *Why Tolerate Religion?*, 64 ("If matters of religious conscience deserves [*sic*] toleration . . . then they do so because they involve matters of *conscience*, not matters of *religion*"). Although Leiter argues that accommodation of conscience can be justified and that accommodation of religion cannot be justified, however, he is ultimately skeptical about the accommodation of conscience as well. Leiter, 17, 63–67, 94–100. For a description and criticism of Leiter's position, see Mark L. Rienzi, "The Case for Religious Exemptions—Whether Religion Is Special or Not," *Harvard Law Review* 127 (2014): 1395.

95. Marie A. Failinger, "Wondering after Babel: Power, Freedom, and Ideology in U.S. Supreme Court Interpretations of the Religion Clause," in *Law and Religion*, ed. Rex J. Ahdar (Aldershot, UK: Ashgate, 2000), 94.

of *religion*" and "freedom of *conscience*" are essentially synonymous and interchangeable ideas.[96]

In phase two, the concepts become severable; and insofar as they are distinguished, it is freedom of *religion*—not freedom of conscience—that the law seeks to protect. And on the pertinent premises, this assignment of priority to religion over conscience is entirely logical. The rationale for accommodating religion, once again, as articulated by figures like Madison and Jefferson, is based on deference to an acknowledged transcendent authority. "Render unto Caesar the things that are Caesar's, and unto God the things that are God's." So if a person asks to be excused from complying with Caesar's law but does not base the request on any appeal to God, or to a higher authority, then the rationale for exemption simply does not apply. In this vein, Michael McConnell argues that the framers of the First Amendment consciously distinguished between freedom of religion and freedom of conscience, and they chose to protect only the former.[97] As a historical matter, McConnell's interpretation is debatable,[98] but if the framers did what McConnell thinks they did, they would have been acting in wholly logical fashion.

Even on these assumptions, though, "conscience" might seem close enough to religion that it still might receive legal protection through loose analogy and as a matter of legislative or judicial grace. Such a process is apparent in the much-discussed *Seeger*[99] and *Welsh*[100] draft exemption cases from the Vietnam War period. As enacted by Congress, the provision exempting "conscientious objectors" from military service had been explicitly crafted in theistic and transcendent terms.[101] The Supreme Court nonetheless managed to extend the exemption to objectors who were morally serious but who were by their own account not theists; the Court achieved this

96. See Nathan Chapman, "Disentangling Conscience and Religion," *University of Illinois Law Review* 2013 (2013): 1457, 1464–71; Michael J. White, "The First Amendment's Religion Clauses: 'Freedom of Conscience' versus Institutional Accommodation," *San Diego Law Review* 47 (2010): 1075, 1075–76, 1081.

97. McConnell, "Origins and Historical Understanding," 1488–1500.

98. See Chapman, "Disentangling Conscience and Religion."

99. United States v. Seeger, 380 U.S. 163 (1965).

100. Arising from any human relation, but Welsh v. United States, 398 U.S. 333 (1970).

101. In the first case, *Seeger*, the federal exemption applied to persons who were opposed to war on the basis of "religious training and belief," and it defined such training and belief as "an individual's belief in a relation to a Supreme Being involving duties superior to those arising from any human relation, but [not including] essentially political, sociological, or philosophical views or a merely personal moral code." *Seeger*, 380 U.S. at 165.

extension by construing the statutory exemption to cover not only theistic convictions but also other convictions that had a "parallel [position]"[102] in the lives of nontheistic objectors like Daniel Seeger and Elliott Welsh.

The decisions in *Seeger* and *Welsh* also reflect the subtle transition from stage two, in which *religion* is distinguished from and privileged over *conscience*, to a third stage in which *conscience* comes to be privileged over *religion*. On the face of the conscription law and of the Court's opinions, it was still "religion"—theistic, transcendent religion—that was the primary object of the law's solicitude; mere "conscience" not grounded in traditional and transcendent religion received protection by extension and analogy, so to speak. In a sense, "conscience" piggybacked onto its more pious sibling: theistic "religion." And yet in treating the two as close kin, so to speak, or in treating nontheistic conscience as essentially equivalent to or "parallel" with more theistic commitments, the Court tacitly demonstrated that in its view, what mattered was not an individual's actual or perceived obligation to a higher or transcendent authority—because in that respect theistic religion and nontheistic conscience were *not* similar—but rather the depth or subjective importance of a conviction in the individual's life. It was only on such an assumption that theistic convictions and nontheistic "conscience" would be relevantly "parallel."[103]

Officially and formally, in short, transcendent religion was still the primary value and conscience was the dependent partner. But *in substance*, it was conscience that the Court respected and deferred to.

In a third phase, this reversal of what is primary and what is subordinate becomes open and explicit. The reversal is conspicuous in the position of those today who oppose *religious* accommodation but endorse freedom of *conscience*.[104] In this view, conscience is the primary value, and the legitimate object of the law's respect and protection; religion is the dependent partner. The former relations are reversed. In *Seeger* and *Welsh*, or at least in the explicit law of those cases, "conscience" could claim protection only by casting itself as "religious," or as having a "parallel position" to religion. Now, in this final phase, it is religion that can receive protection only by casting itself as conscience. And insofar as government or the courts grant protection to religion, they do so not in deference to any higher authority, but rather because religion has a sort of "parallel position" to that of con-

102. *Seeger*, 380 U.S. at 166.
103. See Eisgruber and Sager, *Religious Freedom*, 114.
104. See above, 328.

science in the lives of religious believers. Now it is "religion" that must plead for the piggyback ride.

In fact, this essentially upside-down understanding unites many scholars and advocates today who appear to disagree (and who may *think* they disagree) about the obligation or permissibility of religious accommodation. Thus, contemporary scholarly debates in this field tend to center on whether there is justification for "special treatment" of "religion."[105] On one side, as discussed above, scholars who oppose religious accommodation say no—there is no adequate justification for giving special treatment to religion—but they may still be friendly to freedom of conscience. And they allow that religious claims might sometimes be recognized and respected—by placing themselves under the heading of "conscience." On the other side, scholars who explicitly favor religious accommodation argue that there *is* adequate justification (such as the constitutional text itself) for giving special protection to "religion."[106] At the same time, however, these ostensible supporters of religious accommodation may condition their support on the assumption that "religion" will be construed very broadly to encompass just about any nontheistic but existentially earnest belief or value that could be described as "conscience."[107] Moreover, in justifying protection for "religion," they rarely rely on the kinds of transcendent religious justifications that led Madison, Jefferson, and others to favor religious freedom in the first place; indeed, they may suppose that such justifications would be inadmissible in today's pluralistic and "secular" civic society.[108] Instead, they typically rely on more purely humanistic rationales, such as the importance of religion in the lives of believers, or the association of religion with personal autonomy or personal integrity.[109] They rely, in other words, on the same kinds of rationales

105. See above, 325n90.

106. See, e.g., Douglas Laycock, *Religious Liberty*, vol. 1, *Overviews and History* (Grand Rapids: Eerdmans, 2010): 58–61; Kent Greenawalt, *Religion and the Constitution*, vol. 1, *Free Exercise and Fairness* (Princeton: Princeton University Press, 2006), 3–9.

107. See Laycock, *Religious Liberty*, 69–80; see also Kent Greenawalt, "Religious Toleration and Claims of Conscience," *Journal of Contemporary Legal Issues* 21 (2013): 449, 461 (concluding after careful discussion that "for individuals, but not organizations, . . . most exemptions granted for moral conscience should be extended to nonreligious claimants").

108. See, e.g., Laycock, *Religious Liberty*, 58; Kent Greenawalt, *Religion and the Constitution*, vol. 2, *Establishment and Fairness* (Princeton: Princeton University Press, 2008), 57, 195, 492–93, 523–24.

109. See, e.g., Greenawalt, *Religion and the Constitution*, 1:3 (arguing that "people should be free to adopt religious beliefs and engage in religious practices because that is one vital aspect of personal autonomy"); Alan Brownstein, "Protecting the Religious Liberty of Religious

that contemporary thinkers are likely to give for respecting "conscience." The labeling differs—and provokes apparent disagreement—but at bottom the positions are substantively very similar.

Conscience and the Immanent Sacred. All of which points directly to two residual questions that have been lurking around our discussion all along. First, what exactly *is* this "conscience" to which government should be respectful? If conscience is no longer understood in theistic terms as a response to obligations imposed by a transcendent authority, then what is it?[110] And, second, why should "conscience" (whatever it is) be entitled to claim special respect and protection from the law, now that the law's erstwhile favorite, "religion," has lost that claim? The answers to those questions are indicative of the shift in conceptions of the community that we have experienced.

With respect to the definition of "conscience," usage obviously varies. But the best answer, arguably, is that "conscience" refers to individuals' judgments about and commitments to what they perceive as inviolable or "sacred"—if not to the "sacred" in a transcendent sense, then to the immanently "sacred." And the position favoring "freedom of conscience," or accommodation of conscience, suggests a conception of the political community in which the community remains sensitive to and respectful of at least *that kind* of sanctity. The continuing respect given to conscience even by opponents of "religious" accommodation thus suggests that the move away from a city that acknowledges a transcendent higher power has not been (as it might have been, at least in principle) to a city that is purely "secular" in a positivistic sense. The shift, rather, has been to a community that remains respectful of the immanently sacred.

To be sure, a standard account of conscience today would probably not be presented in precisely these terms. Instead, conscience is typically defined and understood in terms of sincere "moral" convictions or commitments.[111] But this label—"moral"—while not necessarily wrong, is unilluminating[112]

Institutions," *Journal of Contemporary Legal Issues* 21 (2013): 201, 206 (arguing that "the most persuasive justifications for protecting the religious liberty of individuals are grounded in a commitment to personal autonomy and human dignity").

110. See Andrew Koppelman, *Defending American Religious Neutrality* (Cambridge, MA: Harvard University Press, 2013), 136–41 (distinguishing among four distinct conceptions of conscience).

111. See, e.g., Greenawalt, "Religious Toleration," 452–53 (observing that "in most contexts, asserting that something is a matter of 'conscience' implies a strong moral conviction").

112. With respect to greatly divergent conceptions of what "morality" even refers to,

and probably overbroad for conveying the typical meaning of "conscience." Thus, utilitarianism is standardly classified as a "moral" position, but the young pacifist who declares, "I'm a utilitarian, and on my calculations, war almost always reduces the net amount of human happiness," will probably not be viewed as asserting an objection of "conscience" in the necessary sense. Even the young Kantian who explains, "I've thought about it, and I can't come up with a maxim for serving in the army that I can will to be a universal law," will likely not seem to be quite what we think of as a "conscientious" objector. Conscience, rather, typically connotes something like a reflective judgment in favor of some value or commitment that the person deems to be inviolable, or sacred.

And indeed, this was precisely the nature of the celebrated nonreligious (or not conventionally religious) "conscientious objectors" in the Vietnam War period. Elliott Welsh described his objection to war in these terms: "I believe that human life is *valuable in and of itself*; in its living; therefore, I will not injure or kill another human being. This belief (and the corresponding 'duty' to abstain from violence toward another person) is *not 'superior to those arising from any human relation.'* On the contrary: it is essential to every human relation."[113]

Welsh was thus clear that in his view, human life had a sacred or inviolable quality. He was equally clear that this inviolable or sacred quality was immanent in life; it was *not* derived from any outside or transcendent source. And it was this sort of conscience—namely, one that was respectful of such immanent sacredness—that the Supreme Court found so compelling, and that more contemporary commentators find attractive.

In advocating the importance of conscience while rejecting the deference to a higher or transcendent "religious" authority, the critics of "religious" accommodation demonstrate their commitment to a community that, while declining to acknowledge any transcendent authority, is nonetheless open to and respectful of immanently sacred values. To a community, or a city, that is pagan (in Varro's philosophical sense).

---

philosopher Michael Smith has observed that "if one thing becomes clear by reading what philosophers writing in meta-ethics today have to say, it is surely that enormous gulfs exist between them, gulfs so wide that we must wonder whether they are talking about a common subject matter." Michael Smith, *The Moral Problem* (Malden, MA: Blackwell, 1994), 3.

113. *Welsh*, 398 U.S. at 343 (emphasis added).

God outside the Gates

The development we have been considering—namely, the development away from the accommodation of (transcendent) religion and toward a commitment to conscience, now understood in immanent terms—is not an isolated development. That development, rather, is best understood as one aspect of a broader movement away from a conception of the political community influenced by Christianity—or, more generally, by a transcendent religiosity—to a conception of the community closed to such transcendence but open to a more immanent religiosity. As with the movement from freedom of religion to freedom of conscience, this more general development can be divided into three phases—three phases in the city's closing off of itself to transcendence. (Although, again, the phases are artificial and for purposes of exposition. In reality the changes overlap, and all are still to some extent in progress and subject to contestation.)

In the first phase, commitments and values deriving from transcendent religion, formerly deemed respectable and legitimate in public discourse, come to be excluded *from the city's own political decision making*. In America, this change is discernible both in political thought and in constitutional law. In political philosophy, a central conversation in recent decades has debated and refined the idea of "public reason," an idea associated with but hardly limited to John Rawls.[114] Although the idea has been elaborated in a variety of versions, and although Rawls himself continually modified and qualified his position in various ways, the central contention is that in a diverse political community, important political decisions should not be based on "sectarian" considerations or on "comprehensive doctrines" that not all citizens share.[115] And "religion"—or at least "religion" in the traditional sense—would seem to be the most conspicuous member of this class of "comprehensive doctrines" that are now deemed inadmissible in important public decision making; indeed, an express purpose of Rawls's theorizing was to find a way of overcoming the differences that had resulted

114. John Rawls, *Political Liberalism* (New York: Columbia University Press, 1996). For alternative elaborations, see, e.g., Kevin Vallier, *Liberal Politics and Public Faith: Beyond Separation* (New York: Routledge, 2014); Gerald Gaus, *The Order of Public Reason: A Theory of Freedom and Morality in a Diverse and Bounded World* (New York: Cambridge University Press, 2011); Stephen Macedo, "Liberalism and Public Justification," in *Liberal Virtues: Citizenship, Virtue, and Community in Liberal Constitutionalism* (New York: Clarendon, 1990), 39–75.

115. See Rawls, *Political Liberalism*, 212–47. The point is further developed in the following chapter.

with the breakup of Christendom and the consequent development of religious pluralism.[116]

This restriction on religious reasons, however, is not understood to exclude reliance on what we have here described as immanently religious values. Thus, the proponents of public reason do not seem to contemplate excluding arguments asserting that human beings, or human rights, have a sacred or inviolable quality. None of Ronald Dworkin's invocations of the "sacred" in his approaches to abortion and euthanasia would be out of bounds;[117] indeed, Dworkin and Rawls later collaborated, along with several other prominent thinkers, to write a "philosophers' brief" in the Supreme Court's assisted suicide cases.[118] But the requirements of public reason *would* exclude, as sectarian, any decisive reliance[119] on the more "comprehensive doctrines" of transcendent religious faiths.

Within academic discussions, to be sure, the "public reason" proposal has been controversial. The proposal has its prominent and powerful advocates, but it has also been subjected to what some will regard as devastating objections by critics like David Enoch and Christopher Eberle.[120] In the less rarefied and reflective context of actual political decision-making under the supervision of constitutional law, however, something like a public reason requirement—or, at least, an exclusion of "sectarian" or transcendently religious justifications of laws—has come to have a "taken for granted" quality.[121] Constitutional scholars take it as axiomatic that public decisions cannot be based on religious or theological claims.[122] Citizens and even politicians may,

116. Rawls, *Political Liberalism*, xxiv–xxviii.

117. Dworkin's invocation of the "sacred" was discussed in chapter 9.

118. Reprinted as Ronald Dworkin et al., "Assisted Suicide: The Philosophers' Brief," *New York Review of Books*, March 27, 1997, http://www.nybooks.com/articles/1237.

119. In what he called "the proviso," Rawls eventually qualified his restriction to permit the expression of "comprehensive doctrines" so long as "in due course public reasons . . . are presented sufficient to support whatever the comprehensive doctrines are introduced to support." Rawls, *Political Liberalism*, 152. That sort of religion could be invoked in debate on important public issues, in other words, so long as it did not ultimately make a difference to the outcomes.

120. See, e.g., David Enoch, "The Disorder of Public Reason," *Ethics* 124 (October 2013): 141; Christopher Eberle, *Religious Conviction in Liberal Politics* (Cambridge: Cambridge University Press, 2002).

121. For an example of this sort of less examined reliance on a supposed secularism constraint by a respected legal scholar, see Edward Rubin, "Assisted Suicide, Morality, and Law: Why Prohibiting Assisted Suicide Violates the Establishment Clause," *Vanderbilt Law Review* 63 (2010): 763.

122. See, e.g., Douglas Laycock, "Equal Access and Moments of Silence: The Equal Status of Religious Speech by Private Speakers," *Northwestern University Law Review* 81 (1986): 1, 7

to be sure, invoke religion or quote the Bible in general public discussions; freedom of speech protects such expressions. But legislators and, even more so, lawyers understand that when a law is challenged in court, they cannot rely on conventionally "religious" reasons to provide justifications; to do so would be fatal to their cause.

The recent same-sex marriage decisions represent a stark manifestation of this condition. Laws limiting marriage to opposite-sex couples were of course challenged in many states, and eventually in the Supreme Court, as violations of the Fourteenth Amendment's due process and equal protection clauses. As interpreted by the courts, those clauses mean that a state must have at least a "rational basis" for laws it adopts. In attempting to supply such a basis, lawyers defending traditional marriage laws emphatically did not invoke the Bible, or the law of God, or anything of that sort. Instead, they argued basically that traditional marriage is good for children, for the institution of marriage, and hence for society. And in striking the laws down, the courts often suggested that whatever the lawyers might have argued, religion was in fact the real reason for the laws.[123] Since religion could not

---

(asserting that "the establishment clause absolutely disables the government from taking a position for or against religion. . . . The government must have no opinion because it is not the government's role to have an opinion"). Michael Perry elaborates on the theme: "No matter how much some persons might prefer one or more religions, government may not take any action based on the view that the preferred religion or religions are, as religion, better along one or another dimension of value than one or more other religions or than no religion at all. So, for example, government may not take any action based on the view that Christianity, or Roman Catholicism, or the Fifth Street Baptist Church, is, as a religion or church, closer to the truth than one or more other religions or churches or than no religion at all—or, if not necessarily closer to the truth, at least a more authentic reflection of the religious history and culture of the American people. . . . Similarly, no matter how much some persons might prefer one or more religious practices, government may not take any action based on the view that the preferred practice or practices are, as religions practice . . . , better—truer, or more efficacious spiritually, for example, or more authentically American—than one or more other religious or nonreligious practices or than no religious practice at all." Michael J. Perry, *Religion in Politics: Constitutional and Moral Perspectives* (New York: Oxford University Press, 1997), 15. For a critical examination of this widely held assumption, see Richard J. Garnett, "A Hands-Off Approach to Religious Doctrine: What Are We Talking About?" *Notre Dame Law Review* 84 (2009): 837.

123. See, e.g., Varnum v. Brien, 763 N.W.2d 862, 904 (Iowa 2009) ("The County's silence reflects, we believe, its understanding [that religious sentiment] cannot, under our Iowa Constitution, be used to justify a ban on same-sex marriage"); United States v. Windsor, 133 S. Ct. 2675, 2693–94 (2013) (describing DOMA as expressing a moral conviction that comports with "traditional [especially Judeo-Christian] morality").

provide a legitimate basis for law (or so the judges assumed), it followed that the traditional marriage laws were unconstitutional.

In excluding such "religious" considerations, both the lower courts and the Supreme Court have rarely if ever offered any serious analysis of the issue; instead, they have dismissed the "religious" considerations summarily and in an "as everybody knows" tone. Asked to supply a constitutional ground, however, the courts and most lawyers would likely refer to the requirement in establishment clause doctrine that governments act only for "secular" purposes.[124] Or they might invoke the legendary "wall of separation between church and state" from Thomas Jefferson's letter to the Danbury Baptist Association.[125] Critics of these and similar decisions accordingly react, often, by decrying the "secularism" requirement or the "wall of separation."[126]

As a historical matter, in fact, both sides are on shaky ground; both the invocations and the critical reactions are misplaced. It is true that the closing off of political decision making to the transcendent has occurred under the cover of an understanding that government must be "secular." In itself, though, that understanding is perfectly unobjectionable; political thinkers from Augustine to Aquinas to Madison could all have cheerfully agreed that government, in contrast to the church, is supposed to be "secular." Indeed, the insistence that government must be limited to the "secular" might almost be said to be a Christian invention, and even a Christian dogma;[127] no such restriction would have been recognized—or, probably, even understood—in ancient Rome. And, although not explicitly used in the Constitution, the

124. See *Lemon*, 403 U.S. at 612–13.

125. For an incisive discussion of the letter, see Daniel L. Dreisbach, *Thomas Jefferson and the Wall of Separation between Church and State* (New York: New York University Press, 2002), 66.

126. See, e.g., David Barton, *Original Intent: The Courts, the Constitution, and Religion* (Aledo, TX: WallBuilder Press, 1997); John Eidsmoe, *Christianity and the Constitution: The Faith of Our Founding Fathers* (Brentwood, TN: Wolgemuth and Hyatt, 1987), 242–45, 406–11. More stridently, then-representative Katherine Harris declared that church-state separation is a "lie we have been told" to exclude religious believers from public life. Jim Stratton, "Rep. Harris Condemns Separation of Church, State," *Orlando Sentinel*, August 26, 2006, A9.

127. Charles Taylor, "Modes of Secularism," in *Secularism and Its Critics*, ed. Rajeev Bhargava (New York: Oxford University Press, 1998), 31. See also Bernard Lewis, *What Went Wrong? Western Impact and Middle Eastern Response* (New York: Oxford University Press, 2002), 96 ("Secularism in the modern political meaning . . . is, in a profound sense, Christian. Its origins may be traced in the teachings of Christ, confirmed by the experience of the first Christians; its later development was shaped and, in a sense, imposed by the subsequent history of Christendom"). For further discussion, see Steven D. Smith, *The Disenchantment of Secular Discourse* (Cambridge, MA: Harvard University Press, 2010), 112–15.

phrase "wall of separation between *church* and state," if read literally (as it hardly ever is, especially by the modern advocates who most often invoke it),[128] could be taken as an apt metaphor for the political dualism that has characterized Christian thinking from Jesus through Augustine through Luther and Calvin (with their doctrine of the "two kingdoms")[129] and on to the less overtly Christian Madison and Jefferson.

The decisive change, rather, has come not with the idea that government should be "secular," but instead with the subtle and perhaps almost unconscious transformation of that term to exclude what in chapter 9 we called the Christian or transcendent secular, leaving only the positivistic and pagan conceptions of the secular. It is under those conceptions that the contemporary "secular" city is conceived.

This conclusion, though—namely, that transcendent religious considerations cannot be permitted to influence the city's own political decision making—would in itself still leave open the possibility of legal and political deference to *individuals' judgments* about the transcendent *with respect to their own lives*. "Although we *as a city* do not act on transcendent reasons or commitments," a community's authorities might explain, "we recognize that some of our citizens do believe in and act on such reasons. And we try to make room for, and thus to avoid interfering in, that sort of religiosity."

This position would be compatible with complete civic agnosticism with respect to transcendent religion. Judge and professor Michael McConnell has occasionally proposed a version of such civic agnosticism.[130] The liberal state, McConnell argues, is obligated to be religiously neutral, and is accordingly barred from asserting either that theistic religion is true or that it is false. Some citizens hold to theistic beliefs; the liberal state cannot affirm that these citizens are right, but neither can it say that they are wrong. So the state in effect acknowledges that they *might* be right. And if they *are* right—if, that is, God commands them to do or not to do particular things (like go to war,

---

128. "Separationist" commentators or scholars manage to slip from "church" to "religion" almost effortlessly without even noticing the crucial substantive change. See, e.g., T. Jeremy Gunn, "The Separation of Church and State versus Religion in the Public Square: The Contested History of the Establishment Clause," in *No Establishment of Religion*, ed. T. Jeremy Gunn and John Witte Jr. (New York: Oxford University Press, 2012), 15, 18 (advocating an interpretation that "favors the 'separation of church and state' (or more properly *religion* and the state)") (emphasis in original).

129. See John Witte Jr., *Law and Protestantism: The Legal Teachings of the Lutheran Reformation* (Cambridge: Cambridge University Press, 2002), 87–117.

130. See, e.g., McConnell, "Accommodation of Religion," 15–24.

or assist in celebrating a same-sex marriage)—the state would not want to compel them to disobey God (and in doing so to put itself in opposition to God). Hence, the state—the agnostically neutral state—should accommodate these citizens' religious commitments if it can.

Insofar as they argue that religious accommodation is not merely not mandatory but impermissible, however, opponents of accommodation would forbid the state to recognize the possibility of transcendence even in that indirect and agnostic sense. That, of course, is the conclusion argued for, sometimes in qualified form,[131] by proponents of the nonestablishment and equality objections discussed earlier in the chapter. Their position thus reflects a second phase in the closing off of the city to transcendence. In this second phase (which is still in progress, and contested), the city not only declines to acknowledge or act on transcendent reasons in *its own decision-making*; it declines to afford respect to such reasons *as embraced by individual citizens*.

Successfully consummated, the first and second phases would leave the city thoroughly insulated against transcendence. In another sense, though, it might still be said that the city is not *hostile* to transcendence, exactly. Some of its citizens still believe in transcendence, and the city does not prosecute or punish them for doing so—as it *could* do, and as some governments *have* done. On the contrary, citizens are still left free to believe in and act on transcendent religion—to profess, pray, worship, congregate, even proselytize—so long as these activities do not enter into public decision-making and do not conflict with any public interest or policy or law. The city might thus even sincerely proclaim that it respects "religious freedom." Religion is free to flourish in *the private sphere*—outside the city walls, so to speak.

There is precedent for such a position. In ancient Rome, Christians often lived and practiced, and were largely left free to live and practice, outside the walls of the city. That is where the Christian catacombs were located, for example, where Christians often buried their dead. And in the confessional states of early modern Europe, dissenting religious communities were sometimes permitted to meet and worship outside the city walls.[132] This was religious freedom—of a tenuous sort, to be sure. It was far from full inclusion. But the faithful could live out their faith, as long as they were willing to pay the price of staying out of the public sphere. It was a steep price; still, religion has often fared worse.

---

131. See above, 320n75.

132. See Benjamin J. Kaplan, *Divided by Faith: Religious Conflict and the Practice of Toleration in Early Modern Europe* (Cambridge, MA: Belknap Press of Harvard University Press, 2007), 144–56.

As noted, the successful completion of phases one and two would leave the contemporary devotees of transcendent religion in a similar position. Considering the alternatives, many might be satisfied with—even thankful for—this sort of free space "outside the walls" in which to practice their faith.[133] But then a third phase may set it. In this phase the city swells and the walls are moved outward, so that the space for the free practice of transcendent religion becomes ever more cramped.

Such a process is discernible in America in recent decades, as the public sphere has expanded, leaving less room for the private. Although various factors have contributed to this expansion, probably the most important factor for these purposes has been the enactment and expansion of ambitious antidiscrimination laws, in a variety of forms, on the national, state, and local levels. Such laws differ in their content, obviously, but many or most of them apply to institutions of various sorts, including nearly all businesses of any significant size, and many or most of them prohibit discrimination on grounds of race, religion, sex, often sexual orientation. Antidiscrimination laws have the effect of annexing the marketplace, once mostly thought of as part of the *private* sphere, into the *public* domain, at least for many important purposes. Or perhaps more accurately, the marketplace has long been thought to have both public and private dimensions; antidiscrimination laws have the effect of significantly expanding the public component of that domain.[134] And the result is that people whose religious views conflict with public policies are still free to practice their religion in private. But the "private" no longer includes the domain of business, or economic activity.

These are, of course, the laws that directly provoked the question that we noticed at the outset of this chapter. A wedding photographer, say, is religiously opposed to same-sex marriage. Probably she has no objection to providing services to gay individuals—it would never occur to her to decline to do a portrait of someone because he or she is gay—but the photographer *does* object to using her creative and artistic talents to assist in celebrating a union that she believes to be contrary to the Bible, or to God's will. Her

---

133. See, e.g., Rod Dreher, *The Benedict Option: A Strategy for Christians in a Post-Christian Nation* (New York: Penguin, 2017).

134. See Richard A. Epstein, "Public Accommodations under the Civil Rights Act of 1964: Why Freedom of Association Counts as a Human Right," *Stanford Law Review* 66 (2014): 1241, 1261–77. For a contrary interpretation, see Andrew Koppelman, with Tobias Barrington Wolff, *A Right to Discriminate? How the Case of Boy Scouts of America v. James Dale Warped the Law of Free Association* (New Haven: Yale University Press, 2009), 5–17.

refusal to do so, however, may bring her into conflict with a state antidiscrimination law, and the prospect of potentially devastating sanctions.

Such conflicts have multiplied, and have gained increasing public attention, in recent years.[135] At least a large part of the elite public seems unsympathetic to the wedding photographer's plight—hence the critical outcry against the Indiana law that primarily sought to protect people in the photographer's position—and the standard response to her plea is by now comfortably (or perhaps wearisomely) familiar. The photographer is perfectly free to practice her religion, the argument goes; no one is trying to stop her from doing that. She just cannot practice her religion while working as a wedding photographer. And if she finds that constraint unacceptable, then she needs to relinquish her profession and practice her religion somewhere else—in private.[136]

If the photographer is a traditional Christian, of course, it is probably not only the business of wedding photographer that will no longer be open to her. Public annexation of the marketplace under nondiscrimination and other public norms not qualified by religious accommodation may mean that she will also be inhibited from being a marriage counselor,[137] a doctor in general practice,[138] perhaps a pharmacist,[139] a baker,[140]

135. See Warren Richey, "How the Push for Gay Rights Is Reshaping Religious Liberty in America," *Christian Science Monitor*, July 11, 2016, http://www.csmonitor.com/USA/Justice/2016/0711/How-the-push-for-gay-rights-is-reshaping-religious-liberty-in-America.

136. See, e.g., Warren Richey, "A Push to Help Gay Couples Find Wedding Joy—without Rejection," *Christian Science Monitor*, July 17, 2016, http://www.csmonitor.com/USA/Justice/2016/0717/A-push-to-help-gay-couples-find-wedding-joy-without-rejection ("But many advocates for the lesbian, gay, bisexual, and transgender [LGBT] community take a firmer line. They insist that if conservative religious business owners can't serve every customer equally they should find new work").

137. See, e.g., Ward v. Polite, 667 F.3d 727 (6th Cir. 2012).

138. North Coast Women's Care Medical Group, Inc. v. San Diego City Superior Court, 44 Cal. 4th 1145, 1156, 189 P.3d 959, 967 (2008) ("The First Amendment's right to the free exercise of religion does not exempt defendant physicians here from conforming their conduct to the Act's antidiscrimination requirements even if compliance poses an incidental conflict with defendants' religious beliefs").

139. Stormans, Inc. v. Wiesman, 794 F.3d 1064 (9th Cir. 2015) *cert. denied*, 136 S. Ct. 2433 (2016) (state regulations requiring pharmacies to dispense lawfully prescribed drugs, including emergency contraceptives, did not violate the free exercise clause of substantive due process).

140. Craig v. Masterpiece Cakeshop, Inc., 2015 COA 115, 370 P.3d 272, *cert. granted sub nom.* Masterpiece Cakeshop, Ltd. v. Colorado Civil Rights Commission, 137 S. Ct. 2290 (pending before the Supreme Court to be heard in its 2017 term) ("Masterpiece violated Colorado's public accommodations law by refusing to create a wedding cake for Craig's and Mullins' same-sex wedding celebration").

or a florist.[141] Teaching may be problematic; at least she may be required to keep some of her Christian convictions to herself.[142] The same may be true if she wants to be a judge.[143] Exactly what conflicts she may face will depend, of course, on the specifics of her faith, on her particular talents and career prospects, on the jobs that happen to be available, and on the particulars of the antidiscrimination and other laws where she happens to reside. In the abstract, it can still be said that she is free to practice her faith in the private sphere—outside the city walls. But the city walls have expanded significantly, and the private sphere has shrunk accordingly.

Once again, this development brings to mind features of the ancient struggle between Christians and pagan authorities. As we saw in chapter 6, "as a prerequisite to engaging in any commercial transaction [Christians] had to give specific divine honours to the Caesars. Without doing so they would not have been able to secure provisions for their daily needs, as all goods could only be bought or sold through the authorized markets in a first-century city."[144] Subjects had to be certified for economic activity: "then, and only then, could they sell or purchase essential commodities."[145] A similar logic is being applied, it seems, to pharmacists, doctors, marriage

141. State v. Arlene's Flowers, Inc., 187 Wash. 2d 804, 389 P.3d 543 (2017) (finding that refusal to provide wedding floral services to a same-sex couple constitutes sexual orientation discrimination and thus violates Washington State's bar on discrimination in public accommodations). See also Warren Richey, "A Florist Caught between Faith and Financial Ruin," *Christian Science Monitor*, July 12, 2016, http://www.csmonitor.com/USA/Justice/2016/0712/A-florist-caught-between-faith-and-financial-ruin.

142. Roberts v. Madigan, 921 F.2d 1047, 1050 (10th Cir. 1990) (upholding the authority of a public school principal to order a teacher to remove the Bible from his desk and other religious posters hanging in the classroom). See also Freshwater v. Mt. Vernon City School District Board of Education, 2013-Ohio-5000, ¶ 97, 137 Ohio St. 3d 469, 1 N.E.3d 335 (finding that an eighth-grade science teacher "is fully entitled to an ardent faith in Jesus Christ and to interpret Biblical passages according to his faith," but he cannot inject his religious beliefs into the classroom and "ignore direct, lawful edicts of his superiors while in the workplace").

143. In re Neely, 2017 WY 25, 390 P.3d 728, 753 (Wyo. 2017) (the Wyoming Supreme Court censured a judge for refusing to preside over same-sex marriages, holding "Judge Neely shall either perform no marriage ceremonies or she shall perform marriage ceremonies regardless of the couple's sexual orientation"). See also Glassroth v. Moore, 335 F.3d 1282 (11th Cir. 2003) (placement of a Ten Commandments monument in the Alabama State Judicial Building violated the establishment clause, resulting in Chief Justice Roy S. Moore's removal from office for judicial misconduct).

144. Bruce W. Winter, *Divine Honours for the Caesars: The First Christians' Responses* (Grand Rapids: Eerdmans, 2015), 286.

145. Winter, *Divine Honours*, 286.

counselors, wedding photographers, florists, bakers, and others who are told: accept requirements that put you in violation of your religion or else get out of your business or profession.

The Question Continued

At the outset of the chapter, it was promised that we would address a question posed in chapter 1: Why would proponents of same-sex marriage, or of laws forbidding discrimination on the basis of sex or sexual orientation, bring lawsuits against, say, counselors who oppose same-sex marriage when those professionals' services are readily available elsewhere and when no sensible same-sex couple would actually want to be counseled by someone who is religiously opposed to their union?

Our discussion has answered that question only halfway. We have considered reasons why proponents of the antidiscrimination policy would oppose a constitutional or legal doctrine *requiring accommodation* of the religious counselor, wedding photographer, pharmacist, or doctor. Such a doctrine, reflective of a Christian or transcendent religiosity, is incongruous in the city now reconceived in secular and immanently religious terms.

Still, even if the objecting professionals or providers are not legally entitled to an exemption, it does not follow that the laws must be aggressively applied against them. Why do at least some proponents of the antidiscrimination policies strongly favor this sort of aggressive application? We will revisit that question in the next chapter.

CHAPTER 12

Coming Home?
The Imminent Immanent City

In the previous two chapters, we have observed how the so-called culture wars—specifically the conflicts over public symbols, over the legally recognized norms of sexuality, over the Constitution, and over religious freedom—can be understood as a sustained effort to reengage the fourth-century struggle and to reverse the religious revolution by which Christianity supplied the dominant regulative ideal in the Western world. The culture wars amount to a counterrevolution, or a campaign to retake the city, so to speak, for immanent religiosity—for "modern paganism," as T. S. Eliot put it.

Whether and in what form that campaign will succeed remain uncertain. Occasionally a critic or combatant will pronounce the conflict over, with the immanent or "progressive" side triumphant. In this spirit, Harvard law professor Mark Tushnet recently declared victory for the progressive party. *"The culture wars are over; they lost, we won."*[1]

Tushnet's declaration of victory seemed ungracious but not implausible; at the time, the momentum seemed all on the side of immanent progressivism. Probably it still does. The reelection of Barack Obama (and perhaps even more so his "evolution" on issues like marriage), the judicial crushing of opposition to same-sex marriage, the filling of the judiciary with Democratic appointees—all portended further victories for the devotees of immanence, further defeats for the party of tradition and transcendence. Still, it is worth remembering that just over a decade ago, after the reelection of George W. Bush, observers were sometimes rendering the opposite verdict (usually in

1. Mark Tushnet, "Abandoning Defensive Crouch Liberal Constitutionalism," *Balkinization* (blog), May 6, 2016, http://balkin.blogspot.com/2016/05/abandoning-defensive-crouch-liberal.html.

despairing tones).[2] And just what the unexpected electoral victory of the mercurial Donald Trump may presage in these matters is at this point anyone's guess. Lacking a Tiresias or an Isaiah to call upon, we would be wise to forgo confident predictions.

Still, let us suppose that Tushnet is right, that the recent trajectory holds, and that modern paganism manages to grow in strength and to consolidate its hold on the city. Would this development be one to celebrate or to lament?

In chapter 8 we surveyed two closely related themes that have characterized the Western historical and political imagination—first, a persistent, gnawing regret for the loss of (and a yearning to recover) the freedom and the "shining beauty and grace"[3] of the classical pagan city, and, second, a smoldering resentment of the Christianity that subjugated that city. Restoration of the pagan city might seem to achieve the fulfillment of that entrenched yearning, the assuagement of that long-standing resentment. Like long-tried royal Odysseus, enlightened governance would after many hardships and ordeals have at long last returned home and triumphed over its foes.

Indeed, it may seem that the fully realized modern pagan city would in fact be a vast improvement over the ancient one. The Enlightenment historian Edward Gibbon was able to imagine second-century Rome as a "golden age," as we saw in chapter 3, and as the most enviable period in the history of humanity—but only by studiously neglecting to notice or dwell on the vast slave populations, the ubiquitous brothels staffed by desperate and downtrodden women, the lethal savagery of the gladiatorial games, the widespread practice of infanticide, and the dismal tenement housing afflicted by fire and filth and disease. In our own times, by contrast, the pagan city would be one that has renounced slavery, has declared an equality of men and women, and has condemned (though not actually eliminated, alas) not only physical violence but also harassment, bullying, and microaggressions.

---

2. Writers of an apocalyptic bent foretold an imminent "theocracy." See, e.g., Kevin Phillips, *American Theocracy: The Peril and Politics of Radical Religion, Oil, and Borrowed Money in the 21st Century* (New York: Penguin, 2006). Ronald Dworkin reported that "many Americans are horrified"—it is not wholly clear whether Dworkin counted himself among the company of the horror-stricken—"by the prospect of a new dark age imposed by militant superstition; they fear a black, know-nothing night of ignorance in which America becomes an intellectually backward and stagnant theocracy." Ronald Dworkin, *Is Democracy Possible Here? Principles for a New Political Debate* (Princeton: Princeton University Press, 2006), 79.

3. Robin Lane Fox, *The Classical World: An Epic History from Homer to Hadrian* (New York: Basic Books, 2006), 50.

Moreover, spectacular advances in economic productivity, technology, and medicine afford modern citizens a level of flourishing unimaginable to their distant predecessors.

And yet we also saw, in the first chapter, that T. S. Eliot (whose thesis has guided us through this book) took just the opposite view. Eliot favored a city based on a renewed Christian vision, but he recognized that most of his audience would find that vision *prima facie* unenticing, or worse. People would come around to the Christian view, Eliot thought, only after contemplating—seriously contemplating—what the alternative of "modern paganism" would actually entail.[4] The suggestion may seem improbable; on the contrary, as we have just been reflecting, modern paganism may seem distinctly alluring. Still, we have stuck with Eliot this far, and we may as well finish by considering his suggestion—by reflecting on what a city framed by modern paganism would entail, and by pondering whether that is in reality the sort of city we would want to adopt as home.

Longing for Home

Writing in the mid-twentieth century, the novelist and physician Walker Percy remarked on "Western man's sense of homelessness and loss of community." Percy discerned in contemporary man a "sense of homelessness in the midst of the very world which he, more than the men of any other time, has made over for his own happiness."[5] Surely not everyone feels this sense of homelessness, or feels it with equal intensity. Or perhaps the condition has become so familiar that many hardly notice it anymore, or hardly manage to conceive of any different condition; people who have never known a home may not feel its lack. And yet, some such implicit or submerged sense of homelessness or alienation arguably underlies the recurrent communitarian aspirations of modern progressivism—on which more in a moment.

This condition of homelessness, or this yearning for community, might plausibly be diagnosed as the product of two of the three main existential orientations we have considered in this book: the Christian or transcendent orientation, and the orientation of positivistic secularism. Conversely, the third orientation we have considered—the orientation of immanent reli-

---

4. See above, 9.

5. Walker Percy, "The Coming Crisis in Psychology," in *Signposts in a Strange Land: Essays*, ed. Patrick Samway (New York: Farrar, Straus and Giroux, 1991), 251, 252.

giosity or "modern paganism"—might seem to supply the remedy for this sense of homelessness.

Thus, as we saw in chapter 5, by making "eternal life" the transcendent goal and God the transcendent authority, Christianity left human beings as "resident aliens," no longer fully at home in the world.[6] The "disenchantment" of the world described by Max Weber[7] and associated with modern secularism may seem to have completed this process of alienation, leaving human beings isolated strangers stranded in a purposeless world. As we saw in chapter 9, this bereft condition has been evocatively described and lamented (or reveled in?) by thinkers like Bertrand Russell, who urged that in a meaningless world we must proceed "on the firm foundation of unyielding despair."[8]

But as we also saw in chapter 9, the revival of immanent religiosity bids to offer a remedy for this condition, reassuring us that sacredness, sublimity, and meaning are real after all—all the more real and accessible because they are no longer sloughed off onto an unattainable transcendent source or deferred to some future state. Rather, these qualities are intrinsic to *this* world, and to *this* city. We need not look to some other sphere for meaning and comfort; we can realize these values here and now. The immanent religiosity of modern paganism promises to consecrate this world, this life, and this city in a way that has not been possible since the Christian revolution.

In short, the revival of immanent religion and the restoration of the pagan city amount to an invitation to come home—to come back to the home that was lost with the Christian revolution. It is a compelling, almost irresistible invitation. But is the invitation genuine? Or is it bidding us to indulge in a kind of fantasy?

Yearning for Community. The pagan city of antiquity enjoyed a fraternal solidarity that the city has not exhibited since the emergence of Christianity. Or at least so modern admirers of antiquity have supposed. To describe the ancient city as unified and fraternal may seem a hopelessly naive idealization, to be sure. Do we have any reason to suppose that the vast hosts of slaves—Spartacus and his brethren—or lower-class plebeians, or subordinated women, felt any civic solidarity with the rich and aristocratic males

---

6. See above, 115–16.

7. See, e.g., *From Max Weber: Essays in Sociology*, ed. and trans. H. H. Gerth and C. Wright Mills (New York: Oxford University Press, 1946), 155 ("The fate of our times is characterized by rationalization and intellectualization and, above all, by the 'disenchantment of the world'").

8. Bertrand Russell, "A Free Man's Worship," in *Why I Am Not a Christian* (New York: Simon and Schuster, 1957), 104, 107.

whose lives of opulence they supported? Still, the ancient city was unified at least in the sense that its citizens and subjects could be counted on to give whatever civic allegiance they felt to *the city*, unqualified by loyalties to some other, foreign or transcendent sovereign. Moreover, among themselves the various pagan or polytheistic cults enjoyed a kind of unity of mutual acceptance and respect.

As we saw in earlier chapters, this solidarity was lost with the ascendancy of Christianity. Or at least Christianity *aspired* to subvert the monolithic solidarity of the pagan city. Now the citizens' allegiance was, or was supposed to be, divided. They were loyal to the city, yes, but their higher and stronger commitment was to the heavenly city, or the city of God. Moreover, far from respecting and cordially embracing the diversity of religious beliefs and practices, Christians condemned pagan cults (and also unorthodox Christian sects) as damnable error and heresy.

Both political philosophy and constitutional jurisprudence over the last few decades have exhibited a desire to overcome the divisions introduced by Christianity and to recover, in modern form, the civic solidarity of antiquity. Rather than attempt any general survey, let us notice this aspiration in two important progressive thinkers. The first is the most influential political philosopher of recent times; the second is a well-known and respected legal scholar.

By reputation, the political philosopher John Rawls was a secular and individualistic thinker who attempted to screen religious beliefs out of political deliberations and who was criticized for giving insufficient weight to humans' communal character.[9] But both labels—secular and individualistic—underestimate the complexity of Rawls's thought. Joshua Cohen and Thomas Nagel report that "those who have studied Rawls' work, and even more, those who knew him personally, are aware of a deeply religious temperament that informed his life and writings."[10] At one point, Rawls had seriously considered entering a seminary to study for the Episcopal priesthood.[11] His religious and communal inclinations were exhibited in his senior thesis, written as a precocious Princeton undergraduate, entitled "A Brief Inquiry into the Meaning of Sin and Faith: An Interpretation Based

9. The criticism of Rawls from a communitarian direction is manifest in Michael Sandel, *Liberalism and the Limits of Justice*, 2nd ed. (New York: Cambridge University Press, 1998).

10. Joshua Cohen and Thomas Nagel, "Introduction to John Rawls," in John Rawls, *A Brief Inquiry into the Meaning of Sin and Faith*, ed. Thomas Nagel (Cambridge, MA: Harvard University Press, 2009), 1, 5.

11. Cohen and Nagel, "Introduction to John Rawls," 1.

on the Concept of Community."[12] The thesis adopted as a "fundamental presupposition" the idea that "there is a being whom Christians call God and who has revealed Himself in Jesus Christ."[13] "Man is dependent on God," the young Rawls affirmed, "and . . . everything is a gift of God."[14] This theistic presupposition had communal implications: "the universe is a *community* of Creator and created." And this communal dimension needed emphasis, Rawls thought: "the flavor of the times seems to point to a revival of 'communal' thinking after centuries of individualism."[15] Robert Adams remarks that "clearly there is nothing that Rawls commends more highly in the thesis than community."[16]

As it happened, Rawls entered the military, not the priesthood, and (as he explained in a later personal statement)[17] his Christian faith dissipated in the carnage and terror of World War II. But his commitment to community persisted, and the religious dimension of his thought persisted as well, albeit in a transformed and more subtle form. The fundamental goal of Rawls's theorizing, as is true of liberal political philosophy generally, was to figure out how, in a pluralistic world, citizens of different views and values could live together peacefully and in accordance with their various conceptions of the good life.[18] Rawls, however, was conspicuously unwilling to rest content with arrangements or compromises that might work pragmatically but would amount to a mere "modus vivendi."[19] His ambition, rather, was to articulate the basis for a more genuinely united community—a community bound together not merely by negotiated mutual self-interest but by commonly shared principles of justice, and by a public discourse in which all could participate on equal and respectful terms.[20]

But how to achieve this unity in the face of de facto differences in the citizens' fundamental moral and religious views and commitments? The ancient city was able to maintain the kind of unity Rawls sought because the

12. John Rawls, "A Brief Inquiry," in Rawls, *A Brief Inquiry*, 105 (written in 1942).

13. Rawls, "A Brief Inquiry," 111; Cohen and Nagel, "Introduction to John Rawls," 6.

14. Rawls, "A Brief Inquiry," 242.

15. Rawls, "A Brief Inquiry," 108 (emphasis added).

16. Robert Merrihew Adams, "The Theological Ethics of the Young Rawls and Its Background," in Nagel, *A Brief Inquiry*, 24, 68.

17. John Rawls, "On My Religion," in Rawls, *A Brief Inquiry*, 259.

18. John Rawls, *Political Liberalism* (New York: Columbia University Press, 1996); John Rawls, *A Theory of Justice* (Cambridge, MA: Belknap Press of Harvard University Press, 1971).

19. Rawls, *Political Liberalism*, xxxix–xl.

20. On the influence of an ideal of respect in Rawls's theorizing, see Paul Weithman, *Why Political Liberalism? On John Rawls's Political Turn* (New York: Oxford University Press, 2010).

various pagan or polytheistic cults were already inclined to take a relaxed attitude toward truth, as historians have emphasized,[21] and to cheerfully suppose that their superficially diverse deities were probably just the same set of gods going under different names, or at least were members of a common pantheon. So, bracketing the vexing cases of Judaism and Christianity, religious fraternity came naturally, so to speak; the "overlapping consensus"[22] that Rawls sought was a cultural fact, not a philosophical artifice or a legal prescription.

In the modern Christian or post-Christian world, by contrast, that kind of natural unity is no longer available. So how is the genuine community to be achieved? And how is the disruptive force of Truth (about which humans can never seem to agree) to be tamed?

Rawls's answer (and that of other like-minded liberal theorists) was, basically, to distance the political community from divisive Truth by constructing a civic sphere from which transcendent religion and other potentially disruptive "comprehensive doctrines" would be excluded. Citizens might retain their religious or philosophical convictions for private purposes, but upon entering the civic sphere they would put aside these rival "comprehensive doctrines" and would deliberate with mutual respect under the canopy of a shared "public reason."[23] In this way, the unity and community that came naturally to the ancient pagan city would be reconstructed artificially, so to speak—by constructing walls around a core civic sphere and keeping Christianity and other strong faiths and philosophies outside those walls.

21. See above, 83–85, 108.

22. Rawls, *Political Liberalism*, 133–72.

23. This at least was the ideal, although the practical realities of modern pluralism forced Rawls to compromise by introducing various qualifications, such as the "wide view" of public reason, as he called it, and the "proviso." Originally, Rawls debated whether political liberalism supported the "exclusive view" of public reason, which would categorically exclude invocation of comprehensive doctrines, or the "inclusive view," which would "[allow] citizens, *in certain situations*, to present what they regard as the basis of political values rooted in their comprehensive doctrine, *provided they do this in ways that strengthen the ideal of public reason itself*" (Rawls, *Political Liberalism*, 247 [emphasis added]). He concluded that the proper view could vary with historical and social circumstances (247–54), while acknowledging (in what critics may take as a wry understatement) that "much more would have to be said to make this suggestion at all convincing" (251). Later, Rawls explicitly revised this position to adopt what he called the "wide view" elaborated by "the proviso," which held that "[comprehensive] doctrines may be introduced in public reason at any time, provided that in due course public reasons, given by a reasonable political conception, are presented sufficient to support whatever the comprehensive doctrines are introduced to support" (li–lii).

Although screening out the doctrines associated with a transcendent faith like Christianity, however, "public reason" would not preclude appeal to immanent values of the kind favored by Ronald Dworkin and supported by his "religion without God."[24]

In a similar spirit, legal scholar Robin West has exhibited a yearning for community from her earliest scholarship in the 1980s. In an article called "Jurisprudence and Gender," West advocated a feminist jurisprudence centered on the claim that in contrast to men and the masculine, which are characterized by separateness, individualism, and competitiveness, women and the feminine are constituted by "connectedness"—a relational orientation grounded in the experiences of sexual penetration, pregnancy, menstruation, and breast feeding.[25] This orientation to connectedness meant that the feminist project put special value and emphasis on community—an emphasis, West said, that is desperately needed in the world today.[26] Later, in a *Harvard Law Review* article, West looked to the Czech author and political leader Václav Havel for a vision of a "liberal, tolerant, diverse community" that might guide American constitutional law.[27]

Recently, West has again promoted the communitarian ideal in opposition to Supreme Court decisions upholding particular rights—to church autonomy, to religious exemptions, to gun ownership, to parental rights to direct the upbringing of children—that, as West views the matter, permit citizens to "exit" from "our civil society" and its norms.[28] These rights, West contends, "splinter our communities. They divide us up every which way. . . . They move us, inexorably, . . . from an aspirational ideal of *e pluribus unum*, to that of *e pluribus pluribus.*"[29]

The ideal, and the yearning for community, are the more powerfully and poignantly apparent because West presents her position in terms of an ostensible description of American community that, measured against the actual

24. See above, 335.

25. Robin L. West, "Jurisprudence and Gender," *University of Chicago Law Review* 55 (1988): 1.

26. West, "Jurisprudence and Gender," 64–66.

27. Robin L. West, "Taking Freedom Seriously," *Harvard Law Review* 104 (1990): 43, 60.

28. Robin West, "Freedom of the Church and Our Endangered Civil Rights: Exiting the Social Contract," in *The Rise of Corporate Religious Liberty*, ed. Micah Schwartzman et al. (New York: Oxford University Press, 2016), 399; Robin West, "A Tale of Two Rights," *Boston University Law Review* 94 (2014): 893.

29. West, "Freedom," 412. See also West, "Tale of Two Rights," 911 ("The new generation of exit rights . . . have the potential to unravel civil society, depending on the extent to which they are embraced").

conditions of contemporary life, partakes more of fantasy than of reality. Thus, at a time of increasing (and increasingly acrimonious) polarization,[30] West talks over and over of a community united by "shared" values and commitments.[31] (If these commitments are indeed "shared," one wonders, why are so many thousands or millions of citizens seeking to "exit" from them? And why does West need to implore that their "exit" be blocked?) West describes a community grounded in an ostensible "social contract," but, unlike some social contract theorists, she makes no effort to explain how citizens have or could be deemed to have (constructively?) consented to that contract; nor does she attempt to expound the terms of the contract. Communities are, to be sure, "imagined," as we saw in chapter 10, but in this instance the imagining seems to reside entirely in the wishful thinking of West and a few like-minded theorists.[32]

But however distant it may be from contemporary realities, West's community presents an alluring vision—one consonant with the image of the ancient community (with its "mild spirit of antiquity")[33] that inspired thinkers like Gibbon. "Our civic society," West says, is "less insulting, less hurtful, more inclusive, more fully participatory, more generous, and fairer" than alternatives.[34] It promises "a world of equal opportunity and full participation that is free of racism and sexism and their related effects."[35] It is "a national community of broad based participation and civic equality."[36] Who would not want to live in such a community—if it existed?

Can Modern Paganism Support Community? But does modern paganism contain the resources needed to support the kind of rich community envisioned by thinkers like Rawls and West?

Here the differences between ancient and modern paganism become pertinent. Ancient paganism, as we saw in chapter 3, was predominantly public and communal in nature. It was manifest in spectacular temples and noisy processions, in public sacrifices and auguries. And all citizens were

---

30. See, e.g., "Political Polarization in the American Public," Pew Research Center, June 12, 2014, http://www.people-press.org/2014/06/12/political-polarization-in-the-american-public.

31. E.g., West, "Freedom," 407, 409, 410, 412, 416.

32. In a similar vein, see Jean L. Cohen, "Freedom of Religion, Inc.: Whose Sovereignty?" *Netherlands Journal of Legal Philosophy* 44 (2015).

33. Edward Gibbon, *The History of the Decline and Fall of the Roman Empire*, 2 vols. (London: Penguin, [1776] 1995), 1:57.

34. West, "Freedom," 400.

35. West, "Freedom," 401.

36. West, "Freedom," 404.

expected to participate in rendering sacrifices and libations to the gods, including the divinized Caesars; indeed, the pervasiveness of these ceremonies—in the forum, in the games, in the marketplace—made it nearly impossible to avoid participation.

Modern paganism, by contrast, lacks these communal elements. As we saw in chapter 9, modern paganism, as reflected in Ronald Dworkin's "religion without God,"[37] is more a sort of philosophical sanctification of experiences, judgments, and commitments that individuals are free to have or not to have. It is mostly of the type that Marcus Varro classified as *philosophical* religiosity, as opposed to the *mythical* and *civic* forms, and it is thus predominantly personal in character.[38]

Vestiges of the old "civil religion" remain, to be sure—presidential inaugurations, Fourth of July gatherings (with fireworks and parades), Constitution Day programs. But the American civil religion was Christian or biblical in character, as we saw in chapter 10. Modern paganism (and the "progressivism" under which it travels) is accordingly more suspicious than supportive of civil religion.[39] Consequently, both in its occurrence and in its aftermath, a presidential inauguration today is more likely to be divisive than unifying. In short, present paganism, unlike its venerable predecessor, seems more conducive to a "bowling alone" type of religiosity than to a communal one.

What about the language or discourse of political community? As we have noticed, philosophizing like that of John Rawls is animated by the aspiration to sustain a "public reason" that all citizens can join in on equal and respectful terms—a discourse cleansed of the strife and offensiveness associated with more "sectarian" voices. It aims to achieve this laudable goal by screening out potentially divisive "comprehensive doctrines" (like Christianity) from public decision-making.

So, how has this project fared? It is frequently observed that public discourse today seems both more shallow and more bitterly contentious than in times past.[40] And, upon reflection, these disappointing results should not be surprising; if notions of "public reason" cannot be held solely responsi-

37. Ronald Dworkin, *Religion without God* (Cambridge, MA: Harvard University Press, 2013).

38. See above, 88.

39. See, e.g., Frederick Mark Gedicks and Roger Hendrix, "Uncivil Religion," *West Virginia Law Review* 110 (2007): 275.

40. See, e.g., Susan Jacoby, *The Age of American Unreason* (New York: Random House, 2008); Dworkin, *Is Democracy Possible Here?*, 4.

ble for this condition, they have likely contributed to it.[41] After all, people whose deepest convictions (embodied in their "comprehensive doctrines") have been declared inadmissible in public discourse will understandably feel excluded from public deliberations, and alienated from the city governed by such deliberations. In addition, as basic beliefs and commitments are screened out of public decision making, there is less and less discursive and rhetorical material to work with as people attempt to reason together and to persuade each other.[42] Sometimes purely utilitarian or pragmatic desiderata will govern, and people will be able to argue about those—about whether free trade or protectionism will better stimulate the economy, for instance. But with regard to the most basic human concerns (concerning life and death, for example, or sexuality, or marriage), what are people supposed to say when their fundamental principles have been ruled out of bounds in the debate?

It can happen—indeed, it increasingly *does* happen—that the main or only rhetorical resources that remain will appeal to the one thing that everyone can still agree on—namely, that it is bad or wrong to act from hatred, bigotry, or a mere desire to harm. Consequently, public debate on all manner of fundamental issues increasingly degenerates into clashing accusations of hatred or bigotry, delivered with a cultivated righteous indignation. In this respect, both the United States Supreme Court and the United States Civil Rights Commission have recently set a depressing example.[43] And thus the aspiration to construct a community grounded in and guided by an elevated and respectful public discourse from which divergent and divisive "comprehensive doctrines" have been excluded leads instead to a shrill and shallow cacophony in which opposing parties can do little other than accuse each other of being racists, sexists, homophobes, and bigots.[44]

41. For further argument on this point, see Steven D. Smith, *The Disenchantment of Secular Discourse* (Cambridge, MA: Harvard University Press, 2010).

42. See Steven D. Smith, "Recovering (from) Enlightenment?" *San Diego Law Review* 41 (2004): 1263, 1297–1306.

43. See United States v. Windsor, 570 U.S. 744, 133 S. Ct. 2675 (2013). For a manifestation by the US Commission on Civil Rights, see the commission's ironically titled "Peaceful Coexistence: Reconciling Nondiscrimination Principles with Civil Liberties," U.S. Commission on Civil Rights, September 2016, http://www.usccr.gov/pubs/Peaceful-Coexistence-09–07-16. PDF.

44. For discussion, see Steven D. Smith, "Against Civil Rights Simplism" (San Diego Legal Studies Paper No. 17–294); Steven D. Smith, "The Jurisprudence of Denigration," *U.C. Davis Law Review* 48 (2014): 675–701.

Community and Tradition. More generally, one need not be a disciple of Edmund Burke to understand that genuine human communities are not decreed into existence either by philosophical prescription or by governmental fiat; they are a product of people living together, over time, under traditions and customs that are shared or at least acquiesced in. The paganism that animated and consecrated the ancient city was communal and traditional in just this sense: it reflected patterns of living and thinking that had evolved over centuries. Conversely, Christianity was at that time the new, defiant, critical upstart. So perhaps the most central and powerful pagan indictment of Christianity (eloquently expressed, for example, in Symmachus's poignant plea for retention of the Altar of Victory)[45] was that the new religion was subverting the customs on which the Roman city was founded. ("Allow us, we beseech you, as old men to leave to posterity what we received as boys. The love of custom is great.")[46]

Today these relations are flipped. Now it is Christianity that has provided the dominant ideal for centuries, and has served to orient and inform ways of life that by now possess the character of tradition. Conversely, modern paganism has had to assert itself *in opposition to* received customs and traditions, now associated with Christianity, and hence has of necessity been critical and adversarial in character, not traditional. Thus, a central characteristic of the "modern paganism" that Peter Gay discerned and celebrated in the Enlightenment was its antitraditionalism and its relentlessly, aggressively critical quality.[47]

Modern paganism can hardly be blamed, exactly, for opposing and undermining tradition; under the circumstances, what else could it do? Still, this critical, antitraditional, acidic posture subverts rather than sustains the social material with which actual communities are built and maintained.

Sometimes proponents of the modern de-Christianized city at least implicitly understand the importance of tradition, and attempt to connect their more immanent and progressive vision to the transcendently oriented traditions that have undergirded the nation, at least until recently. But such efforts can end up underscoring the gaping disjunction between the contemporary immanent vision and the received tradition. In this spirit, John Rawls attempted to explain how his prescription of a public discourse purged of

45. See above, 175–76.
46. Symmachus, *Relation* 3, para. 5, reproduced at https://people.ucalgary.ca/~vandersp /Courses/texts/sym-amb/symrel3f.html (introduction by J. Vanderspoel).
47. Peter Gay, *The Enlightenment: An Interpretation; The Rise of Modern Paganism* (New York: Norton, 1966), 127–203.

transcendent religion could nonetheless make allowance for Lincoln's majestic Second Inaugural Address ("With malice toward none, with charity for all . . ."), perhaps the most profound and revered statement ever made by an American official or politician. This was no easy task because, as noted, Rawls's "public reason" attempts to screen out theological appeals, while Lincoln's speech was pervasively theological in character. Indeed, the speech was, as one historian observed, a "theological classic, containing within its twenty-five sentences fourteen references to God, many scriptural allusions, and four direct quotations from the Bible."[48]

Rawls aptly described the speech as offering a "prophetic (Old Testament) interpretation of the Civil War as God's punishment for the sin of slavery." He nonetheless suggested two reasons why the speech might escape censorship under his theology-averse "public reason." But Rawls's first suggestion—that the speech had "no implications bearing on constitutional essentials or matters of basic justice"—seems almost comically implausible. Slavery wasn't a matter of basic justice? The reconstitution of the republic after secession and civil war wasn't concerned with "constitutional essentials"? Rawls's second suggestion—that Lincoln's basic message "could surely be supported firmly by the values of public reason"[49]—seems almost astonishingly tone-deaf. To be sure, a president more attuned to Rawls's prescription *could* give a talk saying something like the following: "My fellow citizens, slavery was a bad business and a violation of equal respect, but there's no use pointing fingers now: we need to let bygones be bygones and get on with life." But this bland, theologically sanitized speech would not even come close to approximating the power and insight of Lincoln's actual address.

In the end, Rawls's effort to explain why his own civic vision would not exclude the most powerful interpretation of the American experience ever given by a political leader merely reveals the chasm between the contemporary progressive conception of the political community and the political traditions that in fact have constituted that community.

In sum, modern paganism may yearn for community, but it has been forced to take an adversarial stance toward the actual substance of the community against which it has had to assert itself. Aspiring to reestablish the solidarity of the ancient city, modern paganism has in fact been subversive of

---

48. Elton Trueblood, *Abraham Lincoln: Theologian of American Anguish* (New York: HarperCollins, 1973), 135–36.

49. Rawls, *Political Liberalism*, 254.

the community or communities that actually exist. Hence the oft-observed growing polarization in American society.

Modern Paganism and the Problem of Tolerance

Central to the possibility of community under conditions of pluralism is the practice of tolerance. The ancient Roman city was able to maintain solidarity in diversity because of, as Gibbon affectionately (and wishfully) put it, its "universal spirit of toleration."[50] To be sure, as we saw in chapter 6, Roman authorities did not explicitly endorse the idea of "tolerance." Theirs was "not tolerance born of principle,"[51] as J. A. North has observed; it consisted rather of indifference to most of the religious diversity that flourished in the empire together with an ability to absorb or annex most religious cults and practices into the pagan framework.[52] When a religion resisted absorption, as Christianity and Judaism did, Roman authorities could be brutally and unapologetically repressive. Nonetheless, whether we describe its attitude as "tolerance" or as indifference/assimilation, ancient paganism did manage to embrace a vast variety of different cults and deities.

Advancing beyond their ancient predecessors, modern progressive proponents of community tend to talk explicitly and favorably about toleration; indeed, tolerance is central to their self-understanding. Thus, we have already noticed Robin West's advocacy of a "liberal, tolerant, diverse community." Conversely, to the progressive mind, intolerance or bigotry seems to be the cardinal sin (as it was not to the Romans).

Their more open and explicit endorsement of the principle might suggest that modern progressives would be even more tolerant than their pagan forebears were. Paradoxically, and sadly, this turns out to be a situation in which open endorsement of a virtue in fact works to undermine that virtue.

Intolerance of the Intolerant. How so? Well, if tolerance is a virtue, then intolerance is a vice. And so the more emphatically I insist on tolerance, the more censorious I am likely to be toward the vice of intolerance wherever I perceive it (or think I perceive it). The observation leads to a familiar question, or conundrum: How should a tolerant person, or a tolerant society, treat people who are intolerant?

---

50. Gibbon, *History of the Decline*, 1:56.
51. J. A. North, *Roman Religion* (New York: Cambridge University Press, 2000), 63.
52. See above, 155–56.

Probably there is no logically compelled answer to this question. One possibility is that even the intolerant should be tolerated. In this vein, Justice Holmes countered the argument that Marxists were undeserving of the freedom of speech their philosophy rejected with the observation that "if, in the long run, the beliefs expressed in proletarian dictatorship are destined to be accepted by the dominant forces of the community, the only meaning of free speech is that they should be given their chance and have their way."[53] But Holmes's sobering interpretation was not the *only* possible meaning of free speech. Others have argued that those who oppose free speech forfeit their right to it.[54] More generally, the very notion of toleration implies that although much that is disagreeable should be put up with, there may be practices or ideas that are *intolerable*, or beyond the scope of what should be tolerated. And on either logical or prudential grounds, one might conclude that one thing even a tolerant society surely must not tolerate is . . . intolerance.[55]

In this way, the enthusiastic endorsement of tolerance can provide a powerful rationale for excluding, marginalizing, or sanctioning people or institutions whose views are deemed intolerant. The notion of "intolerance" is in turn so elastic that it can be used to cover virtually anyone whose views or commitments imply rejection of beliefs or ways of life to which others adhere. You believe my way of life is immoral? You're being intolerant.

Another paradox lurks here, to be sure. Isn't the condemnation of beliefs or practices deemed intolerant itself a rejection of beliefs or practices to which others adhere? Pressed, this interpretation risks dissolving "toleration" into the proposition that "we should put up with all manner of diverse beliefs and practices—except for those that fundamentally disagree with our own."[56] But in practice, it seems, this paradox can easily be overlooked by those who proudly self-identify as proponents of tolerance. And hence, ironically, a commitment to tolerance can supply a justification for the massive margin-

---

53. Gitlow v. New York, 268 U.S. 652, 673 (1925).

54. See Robert Bork, "Neutral Principles and Some First Amendment Problems," *Indiana Law Journal* 47 (1971): 1, 31; Carl A. Auerbach, "The Communist Control Act of 1954: A Proposed Legal-Political Theory of Free Speech," *University of Chicago Law Review* 23 (1956): 173, 188–89.

55. For more detailed consideration of these questions, see Steven D. Smith, "Toleration and Liberal Commitments," in *Toleration and Its Limits*, ed. Melissa S. Williams and Jeremy Waldron (New York: New York University Press, 2008).

56. This irony is zestfully developed and exposed in Stanley Fish, "Mission Impossible: Setting the Just Bounds between Church and State," *Columbia Law Review* 97 (1997): 2255.

alization or sanctioning of people whose beliefs or practices disagree with those of "tolerant" elites.

As I write, this logic of intolerant tolerance is at work in epidemic proportions. As noted already, the logic informs large swaths of public discourse, as advocates accuse and seek to marginalize their adversaries for ostensible bigotry or intolerance. The logic enters into law as well. Tolerance is invoked by high-minded judges, without any apparent sense of irony, as a justification for imposing heavy sanctions on the photographer or florist or baker who is religiously opposed to servicing and celebrating a same-sex wedding.[57] An otherwise exemplary fire chief is dismissed from his job for self-publishing a Sunday school manual containing a section teaching traditional biblical sexual morality, which is deemed intolerant.[58] Legislators advocate cutting off state funding for religious universities that do not accept the prevailing "tolerant" orthodoxy supporting same-sex marriage.[59] Instances proliferate.

In an important sense, this policy of intolerant tolerance parallels the approach of ancient Rome to religious diversity. As we saw in chapter 6, Roman authorities could accept all manner of religious cults and deities, so long as the adherents were willing to sacrifice to the deified Caesars and to have their deities enrolled in the pantheon along with the other gods. To the Romans, this appeared to be a reasonable, reciprocal, "live and let live" approach: we'll accept your god if you'll accept ours. To monotheistic Christians and Jews, by contrast, the proposition came across very differently: we'll accept your religion if you'll in effect renounce it in favor of the kind of polytheistic religion we favor. In a similar way, contemporary progressive tolerance is happy to respect any number of different religious views—so long, that is,

57. Elane Photography, LLC v. Willock, 2013-NMSC-040, 309 P.3d 53 (ruling that the application of accommodations laws to wedding photographer Elane Huguenin did not violate the first amendment). Judge Bosson concurred: "the Huguenins have to channel their conduct, not their beliefs, so as to leave space for other Americans who believe something different. That compromise is part of the glue that holds us together as a nation, the tolerance that lubricates the varied moving parts of us as a people" (at ¶ 92 [Bosson, J., concurring]).

58. In 2014, Kelvin Cochran, Atlanta City's fire chief, was fired for publishing an "anti-gay" book on biblical and sexual morality for his Bible study group. Abby Ohlheiser, "Atlanta Fire Chief Suspended after Distributing His Religious Book to Employees," *Washington Post*, November 26, 2014, https://www.washingtonpost.com/news/post-nation/wp/2014/11/26/atlanta-fire-chief-suspended-after-distributing-his-religious-book-to-employees.

59. The California legislature, for example, proposed to limit religious exemptions from the discrimination provisions in California's Equity in Higher Education Act. Alan Noble, "Keeping Faith without Hurting LGBT Students," *Atlantic*, August 15, 2016, https://www.theatlantic.com/politics/archive/2016/08/christian-colleges-lgbt/495815.

as they do not actually proclaim their own truth and hence, expressly or by implication, the error of contrary views.

But if modern progressive paganism runs parallel to the Roman approach to religious diversity, the potential repressiveness today is significantly greater in at least two respects than it was in antiquity. First, ancient paganism mostly prescribed outward behaviors—sacrifices to the gods, for example—but cared little for what a person thought or felt.[60] Christianity, by contrast, was deeply interested in what was in a person's mind and heart; lustful desires were condemned along with actual adultery, and hateful feelings and words were deplored in the same way that actual violence was.[61] This is a feature of Christianity that modern paganism seems to have incorporated wholeheartedly; it is severely censorious not just of antisocial *actions* but also of what it perceives as racist or sexist or homophobic *attitudes* or expressions. Remember Memories Pizza.[62]

Second, the class of people and institutions deemed "intolerant," and hence intolerable, is likely much larger today than it was in the Roman era. For the most part, the Romans managed to reach a *modus vivendi* accommodating the Jews (although, as noted, there were occasional horrific exceptions).[63] The primary conflict was with Christians, who represented a novel religion with relatively few adherents, even into the fourth century. Today, by contrast, it is public paganism that is the newly emerging force, in opposition to adherents of Christianity or traditional religion who have in one degree or another constituted a sizable portion of the population. Hence the scope of conflict and potential repression is much larger than it was in antiquity.

Laycock's Question Revisited. Which brings us back to one of our initial questions—the one to which we gave only half an answer in the preceding chapter. Why do the proponents of a familiar antidiscrimination agenda insist on suing marriage counselors who object on religious grounds to counseling same-sex couples and wedding photographers and florists who object to serving same-sex weddings—even when these professionals' goods and services are available elsewhere, and even when no same-sex couple would actually want to receive counseling or service from such persons? Douglas Laycock and others say that the activists are attempting not so much to

60. See above, 108.

61. Matt. 5:27–28.

62. See above, 317–18.

63. See Martin Goodman, *Rome and Jerusalem: The Clash of Ancient Civilizations* (New York: Vintage Books, 2008), 366–487.

gain a needed remedy as to drive these traditionally religious people out of business.[64] Perhaps, but why?

While advocates describe the possibility of material harm in some circumstances, in other contexts they are sometimes explicit in explaining that the suits are not about the denials of services per se.[65] There are, after all, plenty of other photographers, florists, and bakers. And in any case, the damages for this type of marketplace injury would usually be *de minimus*— perhaps for the time and expense of calling up another photographer, florist, or baker.[66] The injury, rather, comes from the message implicit or perhaps explicit in the denial of services; the injury is the affront to the "dignity" of the same-sex would-be customers or clients.[67] As Douglas NeJaime and Reva Siegel argue, refusals of service "address third parties as sinners in ways that can stigmatize and demean." For example, a pharmacist who objects to filling a prescription for contraceptives conveys a message that "he deems [the use of contraceptives] 'wrong' or 'a sin.'"[68]

This logic is understandable, and plausible; it is also ominous. Once the distinction is made between the denial of services per se and the message sent, it would seem to follow that the actual denial of services is merely incidental: the message would inflict similar injury even if conveyed in some other (perhaps more explicit) way. And indeed, this corollary is entirely plausible. To be sure, a refusal to serve someone may be an especially vivid or painful form of delivering the message. Or maybe not: in some instances, providers have attempted to be delicate and respectful in expressing their

64. See, e.g., Douglas Laycock and Thomas C. Berg, "Protecting Same-Sex Marriage and Religious Liberty," *Virginia Law Review in Brief* 99 (2013): 1, 9.

65. See Douglas NeJaime and Reva B. Siegel, "Conscience Wars: Complicity-Based Conscience Claims in Religion and Politics," *Yale Law Journal* 124 (2015): 2516, 2566–78.

66. In the much-publicized Arlene's Flowers case, for example, the gay couple forced to find an alternate florist claimed $7.91 in monetary damages for this expense. See Warren Richey, "A Florist Caught between Faith and Financial Ruin," *Christian Science Monitor*, July 12, 2016, http://www.csmonitor.com/USA/Justice/2016/0712/A-florist-caught-between-faith -and-financial-ruin.

67. See, e.g., Louise Melling, "Religious Refusals to Public Accommodation: Four Reasons to Say No," *Harvard Journal of Law and Gender* 38 (2015): 177, 189–91; Marvin Lim and Louise Melling, "Inconvenience or Indignity? Religious Exemptions to Public Accommodations Laws," *Journal of Law and Policy* 22 (2014): 705. Cf. Helen M. Alvare, "Religious Freedom versus Sexual Expression: A Guide," *Journal of Law and Religion* 30 (2015): 475, 476 ("On the part of a person who identifies as LGBT, another's refusal to recognize a state-recognized marriage is often interpreted as a rejection of his or her entire person, and an affront to dignity, equality, and social responsibility").

68. NeJaime and Siegel, "Conscience Wars," 2576.

religious reservations,[69] whereas some nonprovider expressions can be extremely caustic and confrontational. Think of the Westboro Baptists,[70] for example.

In any case, the same logic that says the offended customer suffers an injury to his or her "dignity" when a professional declines services on religious grounds—because of the implicit message that the customer's conduct is "wrong" or "a sin"—would suggest that the speaker who advocates a "comprehensive doctrine" condemning (as "wrong" or "a sin") homosexual conduct or same-sex marriage inflicts the same type of injury to personal dignity. Ultimately, in fact, it is not merely the overt expression of the offending view that inflicts injury, but rather the fact that someone holds the offending view and is known to hold it.[71] In the Proposition 8 case, federal judge Vaughn Walker said as much: he issued a "finding of fact" asserting that "religious *beliefs* that gay and lesbian relationships are sinful or inferior to heterosexual relationships harm gays and lesbians."[72]

The judge did not actually rule that lawsuits or prosecutions should be permitted against churches or individuals merely for holding these harmful beliefs. Nor does it seem likely that such suits or prosecutions will be authorized in the foreseeable future. Judge Walker's "finding of fact" nonetheless reflects a fundamental tension in the modern pagan city and a fundamental obstacle to the realization of its vision of community. As we saw in chapter 6, one understandable reason that pagans might resent Christians was that Christianity imposed, morally if not legally, severe restrictions on people's freedom—their sexual freedom, their freedom to live according to whatever values or goals they might prefer. Even insofar as Christianity did not legally restrict conduct, its moral condemnation could be perceived as a kind of assault on the dignity and moral worth of people who chose to reject Christian standards. The same is true today.

Is true *a fortiori*, in fact. At least through the end of the third century, after all, Christianity was a marginal and politically impotent faith, condemned by the authorities and rejected or ignored by the vast majority of Roman subjects. So the injury inflicted on pagans by Christian moral censure

---

69. See Richey, "A Florist Caught between Faith and Financial Ruin."

70. See Snyder v. Phelps, 562 U.S. 443 (2011).

71. Larry Alexander develops a similar argument with care regarding the dignitary harm inflicted by "hate speech." See Larry Alexander, "Banning Hate Speech and the Sticks and Stones Defense," *Constitutional Commentary* 13 (1996): 71, 76–78.

72. Perry v. Schwarzenegger, 704 F. Supp. 2d 921, 985 (N.D. Cal. 2010) (factual finding #77) (emphasis added).

was arguably *de minimis*. Today the situation is utterly different. Christianity has provided the regulative ideal for centuries (even if that ideal has never actually been realized, even approximately). Christianity has been in a sense the dominant regime against which non-Christian dissenters like Gibbon and Hume and Voltaire and Mill have had to assert their independence. Its sexual norms were embodied in law, as we saw in chapter 10, into the 1950s, even into the 1970s.[73] Its strictures are thus more real and forceful, less easy to ignore, and arguably more injurious to dignity than they were in late antiquity. And this makes the active or open presence of Christian ideals in the public space more troublesome and threatening than those ideals might have been in the first, second, and third centuries.

So it is understandable why activists and litigants would want to drive overtly Christian employers and professionals out of the public square and the public marketplace. Their goods and services may or may not be needed, but their message is a standing affront to dignity, and their presence is an irritant and an insult to the kind of community to which modern progressive pagans aspire.

More generally, as in the ancient city, citizens with commitments to strong versions of Christianity or other truth-oriented faiths are today a foreign and divisive element in the city of "modern paganism." Now, as then, devout Christians do not accept the city's terms of cooperation—terms that require citizens to check their religious beliefs at the door before entering the civic sphere. Their commitment to particularistic or "sectarian" versions of the Truth, and their attempts to bring such Truth into the public square, threaten and disrupt the "overlapping consensus" and the mutually respectful deliberation and communion that Rawls and like-minded citizens seek to achieve.

Little wonder that the proponents of the Rawlsian liberal community would ostracize these views, and the citizens who insist on maintaining them, from the civic sphere and consider them "unreasonable."[74] Unreasonable in the same sense that Christians were viewed as uncivil and unreasonable in the Roman Empire.[75] And little wonder that Robin West and other progressives would force such citizens to accept the "shared" public norms as a condition of participating in the public sphere, including the economic marketplace.

Toleration or War? It is not that the de-Christianized city *could not* put up

73. See above, 284–86.
74. Rawls, *Political Liberalism*, 61.
75. See above, 152.

with such views and such citizens. During the decades and centuries in which Christianity still dominated the civic understanding, at least as a sort of residual regulative ideal, dissenters like John Stuart Mill expounded attractive visions of a more "open" society[76] committed to a more principled and expansive tolerance than what prevailed in ancient Rome. In the tolerant modern city, people of fundamentally different convictions could gather together, forcefully advocate and debate their competing and incompatible "comprehensive doctrines," and then decide democratically what course the community would take. This more classically "liberal" vision contemplates a robust community of confident, tough-minded citizens who do not bracket their commitments to truth, who understand that other citizens have different and sometimes incompatible views, and who are prepared to encounter and respond to strong condemnations of their own views and ways of life (sometimes, if that is where the argument leads, by modifying those views and ways of life). Public discourse in such a community would be, as the Supreme Court once explained, "uninhibited, robust, and wide-open."[77] Self-confident, thick-skinned citizens would accept, perhaps even appreciate, what Andrew Koppelman only partly sardonically describes as "the joys of mutual contempt."[78] Surely there are still citizens and theorists who cling to that more "liberal" vision of "a confident pluralism," as John Inazu describes it in a recent book.[79]

Moreover, at least some of the reasons that animated the ancient pagan city's episodic but forceful suppression of Christianity do not seem to apply today. The devotees of "modern paganism," for example, typically would not assert that there are deities who will be angered, and who will accordingly smite the city or fail to answer its auguries, because of the community's toleration of the blasphemies or sacrileges committed by Christians.

So it is imaginable that Christianity, along with other strong and transcendent religiosities, *could* be tolerated and accommodated even in a pagan community—in a classically *liberal* (as opposed to immanently *progressive*) pagan community.

76. John Stuart Mill, *On Liberty*, ed. Alburey Castell (New York: F. S. Crofts & Co., Inc. [1859] 1947); Karl Popper, *The Open Society and Its Enemies* (Princeton: Princeton University Press, [1945] 1994).

77. New York Times Co. v. Sullivan, 376 U.S. 254, 270 (1964).

78. Andrew Koppelman, "The Joys of Mutual Contempt," in William N. Eskridge Jr. and Robin Fretwell Wilson, eds., *Religious Freedom, LGBT Rights, and the Prospects for Common Ground* (New York: Cambridge University Press, 2018).

79. John D. Inazu, *Confident Pluralism: Surviving and Thriving through Deep Difference* (Chicago: University of Chicago Press, 2016).

Still, a triumphalist paganism may see no reason to extend such accommodation to citizens whose views and values reject and disrupt the immanent religiosity on which the pagan city is built. Recall Harvard professor Mark Tushnet's declaration, noted earlier in the chapter: "*They lost, we won.*" Tushnet goes on to advocate a "hard-line" approach to the defeated religionists. "You lost, live with it."[80]

Tushnet's recommendation raises a prudential question: Could a "hard-line" approach succeed in realizing the genuine community to which the pagan city aspires? At present our politics are polarized and our public discourse is shrill, shallow, and nasty, as observers on all sides of the cultural divisions often complain. But perhaps that is because the cultural conflict is still active. Civility never flourishes during wartime. But if the party of immanence were to prevail, decisively, and then were to consolidate its control through "hard-line" measures as contemplated by Tushnet and others, perhaps a genuine, peaceful, respectful community could be achieved after all.

Maybe. That is no doubt the progressive aspiration. But here an observation of the historian Edward Gibbon may be pertinent. As noted in chapter 7, some historians have surmised that if the fourth-century pagan emperor Julian had reigned for a longer period, paganism might have been reestablished and Christianity gradually eliminated.[81] Gibbon disagreed. By the mid-fourth century, Christians still may not have represented a majority of Roman citizens; even so, "if we seriously reflect on the strength and spirit of the church, we shall be convinced, that before the emperor could have extinguished the religion of Christ, he must have involved his country in the horrors of a civil war."[82] As we saw in the previous chapter, proposals today are not for "extinguish[ing] the religion of Christ," exactly, but rather for excluding it from an ever-expanding public sphere—one now construed to include the economic marketplace—and relegating its committed practitioners to a shrinking domain outside the city walls. But a similar prudential question is presented. And a similar if somewhat scaled-down prediction seems plausible.

Plausible—not certain. As we saw in chapter 9, surveys showing that a large majority of Americans are still Christian are for these purposes largely

80. "For liberals, the question now is how to deal with the losers in the culture wars. That's mostly a question of tactics. My own judgment is that taking a hard line ('You lost, live with it') is better than trying to accommodate the losers." Tushnet, "Abandoning Defensive Crouch Liberal Constitutionalism."

81. See above, 171.

82. Gibbon, *History of the Decline*, 1:908.

unreliable. Many people who mark the box for "Christian" (or "Methodist," or "Catholic") may be profoundly uncommitted to or altogether ignorant of their ostensible faith. The ranks of self-professing Christians are likely pervaded by people who are realistically more pagan than Christian.[83] And there is no way to take an accurate head count.

Even so, it seems likely that there are still enough genuine and committed Christians to make the "hard-line" imposition of a pagan society difficult. Moreover, unlike the Christians of late antiquity, who could hardly have supposed that *they* had built the empire (which, after all, had largely assumed its shape and boundaries before their religion even came onto the scene), modern Christians can assert with some plausibility that they and their Christian forebears were responsible for the construction of the civilization that is now being wrested from them. Christians, to be sure, are taught to be submissive and to "turn the other cheek." But that injunction is subject to interpretation, and in any case, with this as with other precepts, Christians have often fallen short of their announced ideals. It would be understandable if they did not passively acquiesce as modern paganism seizes the city that they and their ancestors have constructed and attempts to relocate them to the shrinking space outside the city walls.

Predictions are precarious, and it is possible that a "hard-line" refusal to accommodate traditional Christianity—with respect to marriage, sexuality, employment, education, commercial activity, and other matters—could succeed in more or less peacefully repressing the nonconforming constituencies. "You lost, live with it," as Professor Tushnet says.[84] But it seems at least as likely that the uncompromising approach will merely raise to a new level of intensity the culture wars that over the last several decades have flourished mostly in unedifying but nonviolent forms.

And so in the end, alas, it may be that the shimmering pagan city, like the Christian one, is simply not to be realized in this world—or at least not by the application of law and force.

---

83. A recent series of surveys by the American Culture and Faith Institute concluded that only about 10 percent of Americans maintain a biblical worldview for purposes of making practical decisions. Among younger Americans—the so-called millennials—the percentage was much lower. See "Groundbreaking ACFI Survey Reveals How Many Adults Have a Biblical Worldview," American Culture and Faith Institute, accessed August 29, 2017, https://www.culturefaith.com/groundbreaking-survey-by-acfi-reveals-how-many-american-adults-have-a-biblical-worldview.

84. Tushnet, "Abandoning Defensive Crouch Liberal Constitutionalism."

Modern Paganism and Human Fulfillment

As we have seen, in its aspiration to create community, the modern progressive project has sought to separate the city, or at least the civic sphere, from claims about Truth—claims that came with the Christian revolution and are likely to be divisive. We have thus far been considering whether that strategy is likely to succeed in constructing genuine community, and we have seen that the prospects are doubtful. But now let us set doubts aside and ask a different question. Suppose the modern pagan city could be established and maintained. Would that city allow us to come home again at last, after centuries of wandering in the wake of the fourth-century Christian revolution? Would it dispel the sense of "homelessness" that Walker Percy discerned in the modern world? More generally, how efficacious would a triumphant modern paganism be in providing people with spiritual fulfillment—in providing the kinds of goods that (as we discussed in chapter 2) many people seek and that religion has typically sought to supply?

In considering these questions, we will not attempt to arrive at any final judgments about Truth—about the truth of paganism (in its diverse forms), or Christianity (in its diverse forms), or any other religion. Rather, as in chapter 7, we will attempt to survey the strengths and weaknesses of modern paganism relative to these truth- and spirituality-oriented desiderata.

Minimalism and Believability. One relevant feature of modern paganism of the philosophical sort—a feature that may be either a strength or a weakness—is that, unlike many other religions, it does not seem to demand much of its adherents, either creedally or behaviorally. Think of Ronald Dworkin's "religion without God," which we discussed in chapter 9. An adherent of Dworkin's religion will affirm that life has "objective" meaning and that there is in the world "objective" beauty or sublimity. Nothing more is required, really. The religion does not instruct adherents on what and where meaning and beauty are, on how these "objective" qualities have come to exist, on what if anything they demand of anyone. Susan Wolf, as we saw in chapter 2, argues that philosophers have no very good account of what it even means for value to be "objective"; Dworkin's religion does not remedy that deficiency.

In short, by contrast both to ancient mythical paganism (which at least implicitly asked its devotees to believe, in some sense, in a host of divine beings) and to Christianity (which affirms a series of refined creeds and doctrines), Dworkin's "religion without God" asks for very little. To be counted as a congregant, it is seemingly enough to affirm, "I think that my life is *really* (and not merely subjectively) valuable, and that the world and the sunset and the Grand Canyon are *really* (and not merely subjectively) sublime."

With respect to believability, this minimalist stance is in one sense a strength. Most people today—certainly people with higher educations—would find it impossible to believe in anthropomorphized deities like Zeus, Apollo, and Athena (just as many educated people in late antiquity found it impossible to believe in these deities in any literal way). Many of the same people, whether or not they have devoted any study to the issue, are likewise convinced that science or historical criticism or something else has rendered the claims of the Bible or the Christian creeds unbelievable as well. We noted the philosopher Luc Ferry's observation that "neither the ancient model nor the Christian model remain credible for anyone of a critical and informed disposition."[85]

Correct or not, Ferry surely describes the mind-set of many educated people in our times. At the same time, not many people are willing to relinquish the idea that there are things that are "sacred" or "sacrosanct" or "inviolable"—the human person, perhaps, or maybe the natural environment, or a species of animal or plant. Modern paganism allows people to affirm this sort of minimal, immanent sacredness without signing on to the more ambitious, complex, and (for many) incredible claims of either full-bodied paganism or the transcendent religions. Recall, from chapter 9, Barbara Ehrenreich's explanation that by contrast to the transcendent God of Christianity and Judaism, whom she rejected, "amoral gods, polytheistic gods, animal gods—these were all fine with me, if only because they seemed to make no promises and demand no belief."[86]

If modern paganism's creedal minimalism is a strength, however, that quality may also be a weakness: modern paganism may be vulnerable in much the same way that ancient philosophical paganism was vulnerable. Ancient philosophical paganism attempted to shore up a polytheism that was becoming increasingly implausible (at least for the more educated) by interpreting the gods as symbolic representations of a more unitary and encompassing divine reality. But as we saw in chapter 7, the position rendered itself vulnerable to Christian critics like Augustine, who contended that if the divine Reality was actually unitary, it would be more sensible to

85. Luc Ferry, *A Brief History of Thought: A Philosophical Guide to Living*, trans. Theo Cuffe (New York: HarperCollins, 2011), 97.

86. Barbara Ehrenreich, *Living with a Wild God: A Nonbeliever's Search for the Truth about Everything* (New York: Twelve, 2014), 213.

acknowledge and worship that single Reality than to persist in pretending to honor a vast and unruly host of merely metaphorical deities. Thus, as R. T. Wallis observes, "In seeking to establish traditional worship on a philosophical basis the [later pagan philosophers] ironically ensured the triumph of Christianity."[87]

Put differently, whether or not they were ultimately true, both full-bodied polytheism and articulated Christianity at least had a sort of integrity. Philosophical paganism, by contrast, was neither one thing nor the other; it attempted to occupy a sort of no-man's-land in between these positions. But that middle position turned out, arguably, to be less defensible and attractive than either of the leading alternatives. Hence, philosophers today still study and debate Plato and Aristotle on their merits; they take an interest in Plotinus and Porphyry mostly as a matter of antiquarian interest. As a historical proposition, the philosophical paganism of Plotinus and Porphyry turned out to be important mostly because it could be a sort of stepping-stone to Christianity (as it was for Augustine).

In an analogous way, the modern philosophical paganism reflected in Dworkin's "religion without God" attempts to occupy a sort of middle position between the "disenchanted" world of scientific naturalism and the full-blooded transcendent religions of Christianity and Judaism. Unlike naturalism, Dworkin's religion wants to affirm that "objective" value, "objective" beauty, sublimity, and the sacred exist; unlike biblical faith, this religion wants to disavow any reference to or reliance on a transcendent source, like God, for such qualities. But without such a reference, it is wholly unclear what these affirmations mean or why we should accept them.

True, as Dworkin observes, most of us have the experience of encountering things that seem valuable or beautiful. And we experience these things and their qualities of value or beauty as real. Naturalistic science offers reductionist accounts of such experiences as subjective projections. By contrast, transcendent religion attempts to account for such experiences by reference to a transcendent source. Each kind of account has its logic, its own sort of integrity. The naturalist will think that the reductionist accounts are sufficient and securely grounded in empirical observation, and that the transcendent accounts reflect a kind of "wish fulfillment" or intellectual immaturity.[88] Conversely, a traditional religious perspective may perceive that reductionist and naturalistic accounts are insufficient (because they fail to credit or ade-

87. R. T. Wallis, *Neoplatonism*, 2nd ed. (Indianapolis: Hackett, 1995), 130–37, here 137.
88. See above, 30.

quately account for the fullness of such experiences) and that an expanded ontology that includes at least one transcendent reality—God—offers a more adequate account of our experience. The debate has been flourishing for centuries; it will likely not abate any time soon.

The "religion without God" of modern paganism, by contrast, agrees that the reductionist and naturalist accounts are inadequate—hence Dworkin's sharp criticisms of Richard Dawkins—but it is unwilling to expand its ontological inventory[89] to include anything supernatural or transcendent. Rather, while rejecting the naturalist's reductionist normative judgments, it attempts to stay within the naturalist's more immanent ontology. But within the naturalist ontology, it is wholly unclear why we need to posit "objective" values, "objective" beauty, or immanent sacredness. Reductionist and subjective accounts will seem to give us all we need, to explain all that we observe. Indeed, it is unclear what it even means to posit such "objective" entities or qualities, or what "objectivity" consists of; it seems to be a foreign or alien element within the naturalistic framework.

Upon reflection, the "religion without God" of modern paganism (at least as manifest in its Dworkinian version) may thus come to resemble a kind of self-referential pulpit pounding, or an exclamation mark added to first-person judgments. "This Rembrandt painting isn't just beautiful *to me*; it really *is* beautiful, dammit, and if you don't think so you're just wrong!" Such claims have neither the tough ontological frugality of the naturalistic position nor the expansive sublimity of the theistic vision. They seem understandable mostly as a sort of unstable halfway house or way station for people in transition, either from scientific naturalism to transcendent religion or vice versa.

Minimalism and Spiritual Efficacy. If its minimalism is a strength but also a weakness of modern paganism with respect to believability, the same is true with respect to spiritual efficacy. Humans are both social and embodied beings; both the immanent religions of ancient paganism and the transcendent religions of Christianity and Judaism have accordingly sought to address people's religious nature through performances, spectacles, sacrifices, or liturgies that bring people together and engage them through their bodily senses—sight, hearing, smell, even touch and taste. Humans are also intellectual beings, so religions ancient and modern have provided material for the mind—whether in narrative form (as in the elaborate pagan myths

---

89. On the concept of an "ontological inventory," see Steven D. Smith, *Law's Quandary* (Cambridge, MA: Harvard University Press, 2004), 8–21.

and also in the Hebrew and Christian Scriptures) or in more dialectical (as in the Jewish Talmud) or propositional form (as in the Christian creeds, theologies, *summas*). Such narratives, discussions, and propositions speak to questions like the origin and purpose of life, the meaning of evil, the significance of death.

Humans are also active and embodied beings, living in the world; so religions both ancient and modern have provided their adherents with precepts and commandments—with things to *do*, ways to *live*. These have included the rituals and libations and sacrifices of ancient paganism and Judaism and the moral instructions and liturgies of Judaism and Christianity.

By contrast, modern philosophical paganism (at least of the Dworkinian variety) offers none of these things. It sponsors no ceremonies, prescribes no rituals. It does not attempt to explain why the world exists, why we suffer, or whether there is anything for us after death. In this respect, once again, modern paganism is minimalist in comparison either to its ancient predecessor or to its more modern transcendent competitors. One wonders whether modern paganism is simply too intellectually, morally, and ceremonially or liturgically thin to provide what religions are supposed to provide.

But then, perhaps this critical judgment is unfair, overlooking the obvious. True, the "religion without God" may not offer ceremonies, rituals, even moral codes *separable from the rest of life* and identifiable as pagan religious ceremonies or codes. But then, that is arguably the whole point of immanent religion—namely, to discern and declare the existence of the sacred *within the world*, and within life. In this sense, it might be said that modern paganism does engage the senses and prescribe ways to act and live. It engages the senses in . . . musical concerts, or plays, or athletic contests—or walks on the beach or in the woods. It allows us to ponder the big questions of existence and life and death in whatever ways we are already inclined to ponder them. And it authorizes us to receive instruction in how to act and how to live through whatever media and means we already receive such instruction—school, home, movies, podcasts, philosophy books.

The whole point, once again, is to close the gap between the sacred and the world as we actually dwell in it. To consecrate life as we already know and live it. To allow us to feel once again at home in the world—not left distracted and dissatisfied by an illusion of an outside and unreachable transcendence. To the lost soul who yearns for home, modern immanent religiosity says, "But you already are at home; you only need to look around yourself, more attentively, and to give up your distracting and futile search for some other home somewhere else."

Transcendent religion, in short, seeks to lift our gaze toward an ideal that lies beyond our present mundane existence—to show us that there is a higher reality, if we will only be humble and attentive enough to see it. Immanent religion, by contrast, seeks to consecrate our present existence, or to show us that our present existence is already consecrated—if we only have eyes to see it (and if we can resist the allure of transcendent religion, which teaches us that the sacred is somewhere else, not here).

So, which of these perspectives is more alluring? More illuminating? More intellectually and spiritually satisfying?

Is the World Sufficient unto Itself?

The questions take us back to alternatives that we considered in earlier chapters. One way of posing the question is in terms of goods. From the Christian perspective, as we saw in chapter 5, thinkers like Augustine have contended that the world provides an array of goods—friendship, pleasure, sexual gratification, professional recognition, aesthetic experience—and these *are* genuine goods. But they are also transitory, in two senses. In time, they grow stale and unsatisfying. And they end with death—our own death, or the deaths of friends and loved ones. These goods are thus not stable ends-in-themselves, but rather glimpses of and pointers to a higher good—eternal life, or the life of and with God. Take away that transcendent reference, and this world—and this earthly city—lose their purpose and become, as Augustine said, a kind of "death-in-life, or life-in-death."[90]

Was Augustine right? Or are the goods of this world sufficient, or at least as good as it gets, and thus the only goods we should concern ourselves with?

Another way to put the question is in terms of meaning. In chapter 2 we considered the view of Viktor Frankl, Susan Wolf, Rabbi Jonathan Sacks, Leo Tolstoy, and others, that human beings are meaning-seeking creatures. We are not content with "flourishing"—in the sense of satisfying our "interests"—or even with living by a code of morality; rather, we want and need to see our lives as having some sort of "meaning." And in seeking to ascertain the sense of that elusive notion, we considered the proposal of the philosopher John Wisdom that we might understand the idea of "meaning" by analogy to a play. We can see part of a play, perhaps, and wonder how it

---

90. Augustine, *The Confessions of St. Augustine*, ed. and trans. Albert Cook Outler, rev. ed. (New York: Dover, 2002), 1.7, p. 4.

fits within the whole play. Or we can see the whole play and wonder what it "means." What is the character or point of the narrative? Is it a tragedy, a comedy, an exhibition of the absurd, or something else? In the former case, we are wondering about the larger play that would complete and thus give sense to the fragment we saw. In the latter case, we are wondering about "the order in the drama of Time."[91]

Following Wisdom's suggestion, we might present our current question in this way: each of us directly observes only an infinitesimally small slice of the human affairs of our own time—namely, the ones we are personally involved in—but we can indirectly learn about some of the affairs of other human beings (still only a tiny fraction, probably) both in our own times and at earlier stages in human history. And with respect to these various human doings, we can ask: Does all this human activity, our own and that of others—all this living and striving and dying—have some sort of meaning? As Viktor Frankl asked as he clung to life as a prisoner in the Nazi death camps: "Has all this suffering, this dying around us, a meaning?"[92] Does human existence fit into some sort of overarching plot or narrative? And if so, is that narrative one that plays out and makes sense *within this world*? Or do the human doings of this world seem more like an act or fragment of a larger narrative that will be fulfilled and redeemed in some other dimension of existence, and without which our mundane doings are ultimately lacking in narrative sense—"sound and fury signifying nothing"?

These questions generate a variety of answers, obviously. But, rounding off, the answers might be sorted into four logical categories. It might be that neither individual lives nor human activity and history as a whole have meaning in the narrative sense. Or, second, it might be that human history as a whole has no meaning, but individual lives do. Conversely, and third, history as a whole might possess some kind of narrative sense, but individual lives might not. Finally, it might be that both individual lives and human activity as a whole have some sort of narrative meaning.

Perhaps the safest and most familiar answer today, at least in elite circles, is the first one: there is neither any overall meaning in human history nor any "objective" meaning in individual lives. "The more the universe seems comprehensible," physicist Steven Weinberg declares, "the more it also seems

---

91. John Wisdom, "The Meanings of the Questions of Life," in *The Meaning of Life*, ed. E. D. Klemke, 2nd ed. (New York: Oxford University Press, 1999), 257, 258–59.

92. Viktor E. Frankl, *Man's Search for Ultimate Meaning* (Cambridge, MA: Perseus Publishing, 2000), 183.

pointless."[93] Individuals, likewise, are born; they live; they experience plea-sure and pain, happiness and disappointment. And then they die. They may if they like try to think of their lives under the form of some sort of story—a story of which they themselves are the putative authors. But from a detached perspective, there is no overall "meaning" or story in their existence. It is what it is, as the saying goes—no less, but emphatically no more. To Tolstoy's question—"is there any meaning in my life that will not be annihilated by the inevitability of death that awaits me?"[94]—the most plausible answer is "No. There isn't." As Bertrand Russell declared, "No fire, no heroism, no intensity of thought and feeling, can preserve an individual life beyond the grave. . . . The whole temple of man's achievement must inevitably be buried beneath the debris of a universe in ruins."[95]

As we saw in chapter 9, this is the view most congruent with scientific naturalism, taken not as a framework for research but rather as a worldview. Modern paganism, by contrast, appears to favor the second answer. An indi-vidual's life has meaning, Ronald Dworkin insists—indeed, "objective" and not merely "subjective" meaning—but it does not seem to follow that there is any overall meaning in human history. None that Dworkin managed to articulate, at least. The "religion without God" seems calculated not to supply any such overall meaning, but rather to offer the consolation that although there may be no overall point to it all, our individual lives can still have "objective" meaning (whatever that is).

Measured against Wisdom's suggested narrative or theatrical analogy, though, the contention that individual lives have meaning *within the frame of this world* seems wildly implausible, at least as any sort of general prop-osition. To be sure, some people's lives may add up to a satisfying narrative pattern. They live through and savor the stages of life—youth, adulthood, old age.[96] They posit and achieve worthwhile goals, perhaps, enjoy many of the pleasures and achievements they set out to enjoy, or raise healthy and productive children who will remember them and carry on their legacy. Good for them—for the "favourites of fortune," as Gibbon put it.[97]

93. Steven Weinberg, *The First Three Minutes: A Modern View of the Origin of the Universe* (New York: Basic Books, 1977), 154.

94. Leo Tolstoy, "A Confession," in *A Confession and Other Religious Writings*, trans. Jane Kentish (London: Penguin, 1987), 34–35.

95. Russell, "A Free Man's Worship," 104, 107.

96. See Ronald Dworkin, *Life's Dominion: An Argument about Abortion, Euthanasia, and Individual Freedom* (New York: Vintage Books, 1993), 88–89.

97. Gibbon, *History of the Decline*, 1:80.

But then, many other people's lives are deformed by deprivation or truncated by tragedy. They meander aimlessly through life, never even figuring out what they want from it. Or they have aspirations but fail miserably to achieve them. Maybe they inflict immense and gratuitous harm on themselves and others, and perhaps die prematurely (sometimes at their own hand) while their aspirations and potential remain unrealized. If a novelist or playwright abused, tortured, or killed off her characters in these arbitrary and senseless ways, we would rebel: that is not how a coherent story is supposed to go. But, all too often, that is how actual human lives *do* unfold.

The French philosopher Luc Ferry attempts valiantly and reflectively to develop some notion of meaning and value within this life[98]—"transcendence within immanence," as he calls it[99]—but he admits that the fact of death poses a serious obstacle to this enterprise. Of the various possible responses to the inevitability of death, Ferry says, "I find the Christian proposition infinitely more tempting—except for the fact that I do not believe it."[100]

The skeptical or resigned response to these morose observations, of course, would be that human lives simply do not have, and do not need to have, meaning of the kind Wisdom describes and Ferry seeks. That again was the answer of Bertrand Russell and countless others. But if human lives *do* have meaning in the sense of a satisfying or fulfilling narrative, it is surely not realized here. Even the "favorites of fortune," as Gibbon put it, die after a relatively brief span; even if their legacy somehow lives on, they are not around to appreciate the fact. For individual people, it seems, this world is not sufficient unto itself. Hence Gibbon's own melancholy in his more advanced years.[101]

Another possibility is that individual lives lack meaning in the narrative sense but human history as a whole *is* meaningful. Marx offered one version of this answer.[102] Hegel offered a different version.[103] History in its vast sweep is like a grand master's chess game that will culminate in some splendid victory—the classless society, perhaps, or the final triumph of reason; individual human beings are merely the pawns who are pushed about, sometimes advanced, and often sacrificed in the pursuit of that grand

---

98. Ferry, *Brief History of Thought*, 232–64.

99. Ferry, *Brief History of Thought*, 236.

100. Ferry, *Brief History of Thought*, 263.

101. See above, 187.

102. See Karl Löwith, *Meaning in History: The Theological Implications of the Philosophy of History* (Chicago: University of Chicago Press, 1949), 33–51.

103. See Löwith, *Meaning in History*, 52–59.

culmination. Or, as Hegel put it, history is "the slaughter-bench at which the happiness of peoples, the wisdom of States, and the virtue of individuals have been victimised"—but all as part of an overarching agenda in which reason will ultimately be realized in the world.[104]

So, should we individuals—we pawns on the chessboard, or sacrificial victims at the slaughter-bench of history—find consolation in the reflection that our own lives, while meaningless in themselves and perhaps miserable, are the ingredients for a larger and triumphalist historical story? Some people have evidently found that thought comforting—all those who willingly sacrificed themselves for the Marxist dream, for example. But should they?

Unlike the preceding answers, Christianity teaches that there *is* an overall meaning, and also that individual lives have their own meanings or meaningful narratives—meanings that fit into and fulfill the overall narrative or meaning. This is a teaching, though, that may require a leap of faith. And the teaching seems utterly implausible if we limit our framework to this world and this life. *This world* is not sufficient unto itself: taken merely on its own terms, it does not add up to any discernible or satisfying narrative. And so Christianity expands the scope, and looks to a transcendent frame and goal. As G. K. Chesterton's fictional priest-detective Father Brown put it, "We are here on the wrong side of the tapestry. . . . The things that happen here do not seem to mean anything; they mean something somewhere else."[105]

In this respect, the theologian E. L. Mascall argued that "the modern absurdists [like Sartre and Camus] are fully right in maintaining that the world does not make sense of itself."[106] Mascall quoted Wittgenstein: "The sense of the world must lie outside the world. . . . All that happens and is the case is accidental. What makes it non-accidental cannot lie within the world, since if it did it would itself be accidental. It must lie outside the world."[107] And Mascall summarized the alternatives: "So we are presented with this choice. We may, if we so decide, make the best of a world which is in the last resort a senseless and hostile desert, in which we must either bury our heads in the sands or make, each for himself, our little private oases. Or we may look for

104. Quoted in Löwith, *Meaning in History*, 53.

105. G. K. Chesterton, "The Sins of Prince Saradine," in *The Complete Father Brown Mysteries* (Los Angeles: Enhanced Media Publishing, 2016), 97.

106. E. L. Mascall, *The Christian Universe* (London: Darton, Longman and Todd, 1966), 42.

107. Mascall, *The Christian Universe*, 39 (quoting Ludwig Wittgenstein, *Tractatus Logico-Philosophicus*, 6.41).

the world's meaning in some order of reality outside and beyond it, which can do for the world what the world cannot do for itself."[108]

The Pagan City and The Christian City

Our discussion in this book would suggest a slight revision of Mascall's description of the alternatives. Mascall supposed, as so many have, that the live alternative to Christianity or transcendent religion today is something like the "disenchanted" scientific naturalist worldview that resonated with the resigned or heroic (or mock-heroic) declarations of people like Bertrand Russell and Walter Stace, and that we considered in chapter 9. But as we have seen, that sort of "disenchanted" worldview, though it may in some sense be the official orthodoxy of domains like contemporary academia, probably has a comparatively small constituency. Nearly everyone believes and asserts that *something* is sacred and inviolable. And so in the political domain, the leading potentially viable alternatives, once again, seem to be the city centered on the immanent religiosity of "modern paganism" or the city that continues to accept Christianity, or transcendent religion, or at least the possibility of transcendence, as a regulative ideal.

Although we cannot know exactly what the pagan city would look like, we have tried in this chapter to assess the strengths and weaknesses of such a prospect. The pagan city would be one that accepts and respects immanent sanctities but is self-consciously closed off against transcendence. The city might not actually prohibit belief in transcendence. But such belief is a foreign and offensive element within the ethos of pagan civility; the city would accordingly try to marginalize transcendence and its devotees—to relocate them outside the (ever-expanding) walls that define the civic or public sphere. Forceful measures might be needed to achieve such closure and marginalization.

In this chapter we have questioned whether this sort of civic paganism is a viable basis for community under current circumstances and, even if it is, whether the community that it contemplates is the sort of city we really want to live in. Would the pagan city allow us to be free and at home again in the world, after so many centuries of alienation? Or would it entail a new and more repressive authoritarianism? And would it impoverish and degrade our communal and individual existence, reducing that existence to

---

108. Mascall, *The Christian Universe*, 45.

the mundane pursuit of fugitive and ultimately futile goods and pleasures in a world understood to have no ultimate point or purpose, and relegating those with a different and more transcendent vision to a life of civic pariahs subsisting outside the city walls? Eliot suggested that something like the latter scenario was more likely.

Many will take a different view. And they might ask: What, after all, is the alternative—the "Christian" alternative that Eliot preferred? This book is almost at its conclusion, and we have said little about that alternative. But that is because, as with the pagan city, we cannot know exactly what the Christian city would look like; but in another sense the Christian city, unlike the pagan one, is one we have known and inhabited already, for centuries.

So we know that Christianity has proven to be compatible with—and at the same time in tension with—a whole variety of political and cultural regimes. Christianity has persisted under monarchies, oligarchies, and democracies; in poverty or prosperity; in societies that were technologically backward or technologically advanced. The common feature has been that Christian societies have embraced as an aspiration and critical standard a transcendent ideal ("Thy kingdom come; thy will be done, on earth as it is in heaven") that they have known in advance would not be realized in this world. That transcendent ideal has been—and would surely continue to be—the source sometimes of intolerance (toward those who do reject the ideal), of criticism (of the society for its ubiquitous and inevitable failures to realize the ideal), and of progress (as society attempts to respond to criticism and to move closer to the ideal). Hence inquisitions and persecutions—and also campaigns for the abolition of slavery, discrimination, and poverty, and in favor of religious freedom. And hence also a sort of perpetual restlessness, because in the Christian earthly city the citizens are never, and are not supposed to be, fully at home. The human heart, as Augustine said, will be restless until it rests in its eternal abode.[109]

Unlike in some past instantiations, a central feature of any contemporary Christian society under conditions of modern pluralism is that it is unlikely to sponsor any official account of what transcendence is and requires—any official orthodoxy. The modern Christian society would be open to transcendence, and it would attempt to accommodate its citizens in their efforts to live in accordance with their understandings of transcendence. It would not declare or prescribe what the transcendent Truth is.

109. Augustine, *Confessions* 1.1, p. 3.

In this openness, and in this ongoing struggle to grasp and approach a transcendent ideal that cannot be officially articulated and that is not realizable in this world, the city would of necessity call upon the political skills and virtues, the creative efforts, the moral aspirations and imagination, the empathy, and the willingness to sacrifice of its citizens. Which seems to be what Eliot contemplated—and this seems a fitting conclusion to our investigation of his thesis—when he observed that "the only hopeful course for a society which would thrive and continue its creative activity in the arts of civilisation, is to become Christian. That prospect involves, at least, discipline, inconvenience and discomfort: but here as hereafter the alternative to hell is purgatory."[110]

Purgatory, of course, is a transitional place or condition. As is human life—for pagans and Christians alike. This world is a fugitive state. Unlike the gods, and for better or worse, we mortals have here no abiding city.

110. T. S. Eliot, "The Idea of a Christian Society," in *Christianity and Culture* (New York: Harcourt/Harvest, 1948), 18–19.

Index

TITLES PUBLISHED IN
EMORY UNIVERSITY STUDIES IN LAW AND RELIGION

Harold J. Berman, *Faith and Order: The Reconciliation of Law and Religion* (1993)

Stephen J. Graybill, *Rediscovering the Natural Law in Reformed Theological Ethics* (2006)

Johannes Heckel, *Lex Charitatis: A Juristic Disquisition on Law in the Theology of Martin Luther* (2010)

Timothy P. Jackson, *The Best Love of the Child: Being Loved and Being Taught to Love as the First Human Right* (2011)

Timothy P. Jackson, *Political Agape: Christian Love and Liberal Democracy* (2015)

Paul Grimley Kuntz, *The Ten Commandments in History: Mosaic Paradigms for a Well-Ordered Society* (2004)

Douglas Laycock, *Religious Liberty*, Volume 1: *Overviews and History* (2010)

Douglas Laycock, *Religious Liberty*, Volume 2: *The Free Exercise Clause* (2011)

W. Bradford Littlejohn, *The Peril and Promise of Christian Liberty: Richard Hooker, the Puritans, and Protestant Political Theology* (2017)

Ira C. Lupu and Robert W. Tuttle, *Secular Government, Religious People* (2014)

Martin E. Marty, *Building Cultures of Trust* (2010)

R. Jonathan Moore, *Suing for America's Soul: John Whitehead, The Rutherford Institute, and Conservative Christians in Court* (2007)

Joan Lockwood O'Donovan, *Theology of Law and Authority in the English Reformation* (1991)

Jean Porter, *Ministers of the Law: A Natural Law Theory of Legal Authority* (2011)

Charles J. Reid Jr., *Power over the Body, Equality in the Family: Rights and Domestic Relations in Medieval Canon Law* (2004)

Noel B. Reynolds and W. Cole Durham Jr., eds., *Religious Liberty in Western Thought* (1996)

A. G. Roeber, *Hopes for Better Spouses: Protestant Marriage and Church Renewal in Early Modern Europe, India, and North America* (2013)

James W. Skillen and Rockne M. McCarthy, eds., *Political Order and the Plural Structure of Society* (1991)

Steven D. Smith, *Pagans and Christians in the City: Culture Wars from the Tiber to the Potomac* (2018)

Brian Tierney, *The Idea of Natural Rights: Studies on Natural Rights, Natural Law, and Church Law, 1150–1625* (1997)

Glenn Tinder, *The Fabric of Hope: An Essay* (1999)

Glenn Tinder, *Liberty: Rethinking an Imperiled Ideal* (2007)

Johan D. Van Der Vyver and John Witte Jr., *Religious Human Rights in Global Perspective: Legal Perspectives* (1996)

Johan D. Van Der Vyver and John Witte Jr., *Religious Human Rights in Global Perspective: Religious Perspectives* (1996)

David VanDrunen, *Divine Covenants and Moral Order: A Biblical Theology of Natural Law* (2014)

David VanDrunen, *Natural Law and the Two Kingdoms: A Study in the Development of Reformed Social Thought* (2009)

David A. Weir, *Early New England: A Covenanted Society* (2005)

John Witte Jr., *God's Joust, God's Justice: Law and Religion in the Western Tradition* (2006)

Nicholas Wolterstorff, *Justice in Love* (2011)